OPERATION CHAOS

Matthew Sweet is a writer and broadcaster with a doctorate in Wilkie Collins. He presents *Night Waves* and *Free Thinking* on BBC Radio 3 and *The Philosopher's Arms* and *The Film Programme* on BBC Radio 4. He is the author of *Inventing the Victorians* and *Shepperton Babylon: The Lost Worlds of British Cinema* – which he adapted as a film for BBC Four.

MATTHEW SWEET

OPERATION CHAOS

The Vietnam Deserters Who Fought the CIA,
the Brainwashers, and Each Other

PICADOR

First published 2018 by Henry Holt, 175 Fifth Avenue,
New York, New York 10010

First published in the UK 2018 by Picador
an imprint of Pan Macmillan
20 New Wharf Road, London N1 9RR
Associated companies throughout the world
www.panmacmillan.com

ISBN 978-1-4472-9476-4

1 3 5 7 9 8 6 4 2

A CIP catalogue record for this book is available from the British Library.

Printed and bound by CPI Group (UK) Ltd, Croydon, CR0 4YY

Visit www.picador.com to read more about all our books
and to buy them. You will also find features, author interviews and
news of any author events, and you can sign up for e-newsletters
so that you're always first to hear about our new releases.

For David Sweet

CONTENTS

WHO'S WHO IN *OPERATION CHAOS*

This is a strange story and a populous one. Some of its protagonists lost their grip on their own identity. Some of them are not what they seem. This guide will help you decide who you're dealing with.

THE DESERTERS

BILL JONES
Former seminarian. Deserted from his army base in Germany in 1968 and became the leader of the American Deserters Committee in Stockholm. Now believes that the Queen of England secretly rules the world. Look out for him at White House press briefings.

CLIFF GADDY
Schoolboy prodigy from Danville, Virginia. Athlete. Cellist. Good teeth. Deserted from the Army Security Agency base at Fort Devens. World-renowned expert on the mind of Vladimir Putin.

WARREN HAMERMAN
Draft dodger. Poet. Beret wearer. Left Baltimore for Paris, where he joined the French Union of American Deserters and Draft Resisters. Fled to Stockholm in the summer of 1968.

JIM MCGOURTY
A pseudonym. Clerk in the Marine Corps. Deserted to Sweden from Camp Pendleton in 1968. Returned to the States on a false passport. Arrested after his involvement in a campaign to destroy the Communist Party USA with martial arts.

GEORGE CARRANO
A hustler. A mystery. Escaped the draft on an obscure technicality. Son of an army colonel. Later worked for the New York transit system.

CHUCK ONAN
Born on a military base in Germany. Grew up in the Chicago projects. Joined the U.S. Marines, deserted to Sweden via Iceland. Now a fan of medicinal marijuana and the alt-right.

MARK SHAPIRO
Army corporal from Minnesota. Deserted from Vietnam in 1968, traveling from Japan in the hold of a Russian trawler with five other deserters, namely . . .

EDWIN ARNETT
Army specialist. Member of the "Moron Corps." Claimed to have witnessed atrocities, and said so on Russian television. The first Vietnam deserter to be court-martialed in America.

PHILIP CALLICOAT
Cook's helper on the USS *Reeves*. Volatile. Untrustworthy. Informed on his fellow deserters. Former member of the Singing Callicoats, a Pentecostal variety act.

KENNETH GRIGGS
Also known as Kim Jin-Su. Korean war orphan adopted by a couple from Boise, Idaho.

JOE KMETZ
New York GI. Spent too much time in isolation and lost his knack for the English language.

TERRY WHITMORE
Decorated marine from Memphis, Mississippi. Deserted via Tokyo and Moscow with Mark Shapiro. A deserter with a movie career.

RAY JONES III
Army private from Pontiac, Michigan. The first deserter to seek asylum in Sweden, arriving with his wife and son in 1967. Ballet coach. Sharp dresser.

THE INTREPID FOUR
The Beatles of Vietnam desertion. A quartet of serving sailors smuggled from Tokyo to Moscow by Japanese anti-war activists. They landed in Stockholm at the very end of 1967. Their names were John Barilla, Michael Lindner, Rick Bailey, and Craig Anderson. But in this story, the most important is . . .

CRAIG ANDERSON
Californian. Now known as the author Will Hart. His big idea: the CIA has a base on the moon.

ROB ARGENTO
Deserter from Miami Beach, Florida. Arrived in Sweden on the day the American Deserters Committee was born.

JOHN ASHLEY
Son of a Pentagon official. Gifted writer. One of many drug users among the deserters.

WALTER MARSHALL
Also known, briefly, as Jesus Zeus Lorenzo Mungi. Reform school runaway.

JAMES DOTSON
Texas deserter used as bait to trap a suspected CIA agent.

FRED PAVESE
Dope-smoking former artilleryman from New York State. Guitar player. Porn performer.

THOMAS TAYLOR
Painter. Hawaiian exile. Would file the author of this book in the section below.

THE SPIES

RICHARD OBER
The chief of Operation Chaos, the CIA's campaign against the deserters, the New Left, and the Black Panthers. Other spies thought him paranoid and secretive.

HARRY ROSITZKE
Freewheeling, ungovernable, crossword-loving, Brooklyn-born intelligence officer. Attached to Operation Chaos in its early days.

PETUNIA AND MHYIELD
Code names for Operation Chaos assets who spied on the deserters.

GUNNAR EKBERG
A Swedish James Bond. Handy with a harpoon. Excellent liar, competent burglar.

FRANK RAFALKO
The man at the Black Panther desk of Operation Chaos. The only officer on the project who has spoken publicly about his experiences.

THE REBELS AND REVOLUTIONARIES

MICHAEL VALE
The éminence grise of the American Deserters Committee (though some preferred to think of him as its Rasputin). Interested in travel, Trotsky, and Soviet psychiatry. Suspected of being a CIA infiltrator.

BO BURLINGHAM
Also known as Arlo Jacobs. Weatherman. Student radical. Organizer of a deserters' group in Paris. Also suspected of being a CIA infiltrator.

THOMAS LEE HAYES
Episcopalian minister. Padre to the deserters.

LYNDON LAROUCHE

Also known as Lyn Marcus or Hermyle Golthier Jr. Quaker. Management consultant to the shoe industry. Cult leader. World's greatest economist. Founder of the National Caucus of Labor Committees.

CAROL WHITE

Also known as Carol Larrabee. Math teacher. Socialist. Bird-watcher. Partner of Lyndon LaRouche before her marriage to . . .

CHRIS WHITE

British student socialist. Unwilling lead in the Manchurian Candidate Scare of 1973–74.

BILL ENGDAHL

Mild-mannered conspiracy theorist. Walks with crutches. Now a pundit on Russia Today.

MICHELE LLOYD

Daughter of a military family. Persuaded her husband to desert to Sweden. First wife of the man we know as Jim McGourty.

CHRISTINA NELSON

New York congressional candidate. Second wife of the man we know as Jim McGourty.

MAX WATTS

Also known as Max Cook or Thomas Schwaetzer. Adventurer. Trotskyist. Organized safe houses for deserters in Paris.

CLANCY SIGAL

Novelist, activist, Hollywood agent. Stationmaster of the London safe house.

KAREN FABEC

Hippie chick from Pittsburgh. Free-spirited, good singing voice. Narrowly avoided spending her twenties in a Moroccan jail.

NANCY AND EDWARD SPANNAUS

Married students studying at the Columbia School of Social Work. LaRouchian loyalists.

KERSTIN TEGIN

Psychology student from Uppsala, Sweden. Leader of the European Workers Party. Taught at the Catholic University of America until 2017.

VICTOR GUNNARSSON

Right-wing extremist. Fantasist. Lothario. Pool player. Suspected assassin.

THE HOSTS

BERTIL SVAHNSTRÖM

Former foreign correspondent. Old-school peace campaigner. Vice chair of the Swedish Committee for Vietnam. Awarded the Lenin Peace Prize in 1970. Despised by Michael Vale and Bill Jones.

ÅKE SANDIN

Peace activist who gave deserters the use of his spare bedroom. Tried to stop Edwin Arnett giving himself up at the U.S. Embassy in Stockholm.

SVEN KEMPE

Textile importer and philanthropist. Donated a farm to Michael Vale and the American Deserters Committee.

HANS GÖRAN FRANCK

Tall, soft-spoken lawyer to the deserters. Head of the Swedish section of Amnesty International. Cousin of . . .

MIRJAM ISRAEL

Child psychologist and advice columnist. Friend of Michael Vale. Once married to . . .

JOACHIM ISRAEL

Sociologist. Refugee from Nazi Germany. Landlord to Mark Shapiro. Accused of being involved in a secret plot to brainwash the population of Sweden with the help of the CIA and . . .

OLOF PALME

Leader of the Swedish Social Democratic Party. Prime minister of Sweden, 1969–76, 1982–86. Assassinated in February 1986. The crime remains unsolved.

OPERATION CHAOS

DEEP SNOW

ONE FEBRUARY MORNING, shortly before I became part of the queen's secret plot to start World War III, I knocked on the door of a retired Catholic schoolteacher in the wealthiest county in the United States. His home—large, elevated, comfortable—rose from the snow-covered ground of Loudoun County, Virginia, a region populated by civil servants, senators, and spies. The cold heart of America.

There was no answer. I kicked the snow from my boots, watched my taxi disappear down the dirt road, peered through the window, and met the gaze of a plaster saint perched on the sideboard. Jim McGourty had sounded nervous on the phone, and I feared he'd changed his mind about our interview. It had taken weeks of negotiation through a third party and came with a condition attached: that I would refer to him only by his nom de guerre. The man inside this house was not the real Jim McGourty. The real one had been dead before his second birthday. But in 1970, the first facts of his little life were resurrected, inscribed in a new passport, and used to bring an American fugitive back to his homeland. Back from exile, to take control of the United States. And then the world. And then the planet Mars.

Like many of the people enmeshed in the events of this book, Jim had no obvious reason to talk to me, and many to keep silent—not least the presence of those civil servants, senators, and spies. I wouldn't have blamed him for getting cold feet. Many of his former comrades had ignored my letters and emails. Some, when I reached them by phone, appeared to suffer sudden attacks of amnesia—or insisted that they were a different person with the same name.

Others made it clear that my request for an interview was about as welcome as an envelope of compromising photographs. "I do not wish to be defined by my past," read one whiplash reply from an American author who, in a former life, was smuggled from Tokyo to Moscow with the help of the KGB. (The story of his court-martial and his UFO encounters must be told instead by those who knew him.)

"I would be reluctant to participate in this project on any basis," wrote an American academic dismayed to be reminded of the time when he fought the same fight as Jim McGourty. (No firsthand account from him, then, of the nights he and his friends kept a woman imprisoned in her Manhattan apartment, playing Beethoven in an attempt to reprogram her brain.) Another witness, whose name I gleaned from a CIA surveillance report, agreed to have a drink with me in order to offer his discouragement. "I had dinner with some of the other guys last night and we agreed that none of us should speak to you," said the former high school principal, when we met under the eye of the clock at Stockholm Central Station. "Keep my name out of it." He was so agitated that he spilled his Diet Coke all over the café table.

It was Christina, Jim's wife, who heard me knocking and invited me in from the snow. A tall, immaculate woman in her sixties. "I know the English have tea at three," she said. And there it was, laid out on the table in the music room at the back of the house. Finger sandwiches, crudités, slices of fruitcake. Beside it, in the corner armchair, was her husband, a soft-spoken man in the plaid shirt and slacks that are the uniform of retired Americans the world over. He had a folder of notes laid out on his knee. Dates, names, the details in proper order, as if he were preparing to teach a class on his own past. I asked him why he wanted to tell his story. He furrowed his brow. Perhaps, he reasoned, it would be a way of explaining himself to his estranged son, the offspring of his first marriage. Maybe the boy would read it and better understand his father's motives—the road he took at the end of the 1960s from protest against an unjust war to participation in something darker and more outlandish.

Certainly there was much to understand. Half a century later, some of it was still unclear to Jim. "I didn't intend to do anything against the government," he said, tears swimming in his eyes, "but then Bobby Kennedy was shot. Martin Luther King was shot. And I didn't feel the sense of security that I had before."

That anxiety brought him to the decision that forms the common link among most of the people in this story. It was the choice upon which an American generation was skewered: whether to accept a kind invitation from the government to fight in the Vietnam War or to decline that offer and accept the consequences. Many men refused and suffered little. But Jim was part of a group that trod a more difficult path. Men who were already in uniform. Men who deserted from the military and went into exile in Sweden, the only non-Communist country in Europe that offered asylum to those who refused to fight.

Jim could recount his steps toward that choice. He could remember the sinking feeling of knowing that he was to be sent from his desk job into action on the front line. He could give a good and comprehensible account of his arrival in Stockholm, the life he led among the thousand-strong community of deserters and draft resisters who'd made the same decision; how he'd become a prominent member of the American Deserters Committee, a group of radical exiles who sowed so much discord that many Swedes suspected they were a CIA front. Other details, though, were less sharply focused. How had he become a revolutionary, living underground in 1970s America? What about the business with the nunchakus? Or his prison sentence? Or the phalanx of Cuban frogmen lurking in the Hudson River, waiting for the order to kill? What about the men from Operation Chaos?

Jim McGourty was right to be confused. His life remains part of a story that began fifty years ago but has never quite ended, thanks to the unhealed wounds of Vietnam, the secret strategies of the American and Swedish intelligence services, and the influence of a cult run by one of the weirdest personalities in American political history—a management consultant from New Hampshire who, even today, at the age of ninety-four, wants you to know that Britain started the Vietnam War, that the

Beatles were created as an instrument of psychological warfare, and that he is the only man in the world who can save you, me, Jim, Christina, and everyone from the genocidal ambitions of Her Majesty Queen Elizabeth II.

"So," said Christina, with the directness of someone who has spent a career as a professional copy editor. "How are you going to structure this? What are you going to begin with?"

"Maybe," I said, "with the brainwashing part. The moment when everything went nuts."

IT HAPPENED IN the Marc Ballroom, a shabby venue on the west side of Union Square in Manhattan, on January 3, 1974. In those days, New York was a city sliding toward bankruptcy. Thanks to the oil crisis, it was also brutally cold. Gas stations across America were closed for business. Speed limits were brought down to reduce fuel consumption. Thermostats were dialed down, store windows darkened early. Inside the ballroom, they were already shivering.

The events of that night would be beyond reconstruction, had Christina not been present, taking notes—and had the political organization to which she and Jim belonged not had a mania for converting its proceedings into print. Despite its achingly dull name, the National Caucus of Labor Committees had no qualms about publishing sensational accounts of its own crises. They were spelled out in press releases and telegrams to the White House. They were spun from mimeograph machines and sold on the streets in ten-cent installments, then typeset for the pages of its newspaper, *New Solidarity*. The atmosphere in the Marc Ballroom was panicky and febrile. Many in the crowd were NCLC delegates enduring their fourth consecutive sleepless night. The rest were journalists, activists, and members of the public who had been summoned by flyers that promised to blow the whistle on the greatest conspiracy of modern times—"the takeover by the CIA of the United States of America."

At eight p.m., the head of the NCLC swept into the room—a sharp-eyed, tweedy, balding figure a good two decades older than the students and twentysomethings who formed his audience. They called him Lyn

Marcus—an alias he'd been using since 1949. In recent months, however, he had begun referring to himself as *Der Abscheulicher*, the Abominable One—a name that nobody had called him when he was giving marketing advice to the footwear industry. As he went to the lectern, Marcus hushed the applause.

"Don't get freaked out by anything," he said, "but I don't want to create conditions which are not healthy for one or two individuals in the group here. I'm going to give you the worst part of the thing as well as the best so that there's no question in your mind that I've given the whole scoop. We are now in the second phase of a psy-war game designed by the CIA, that is, a psychological warfare game conducted on a scale of four continents." Everybody, quite naturally, freaked out.

The Central Intelligence Agency—the state body tasked with gathering, processing, and analyzing national security information from around the world—had, he explained, turned some of their most trusted colleagues into killers. It had drugged them, imprisoned them, reconditioned their minds, erased their memories of the experience, and returned them to their friends as unknowing vehicles of a murderous conspiracy. The principal victims, Marcus explained, were now confined in a number of apartments across Manhattan, where their programming had been broken and the details of the plot had come tumbling out. One had spoken of "Operation Chaos and Confusion." Another had been reduced to babbling in computer code—the language in which his instructions had been implanted. "This isn't speculation," Marcus insisted. "No guessing. This is hard fact. We *know* it."

The theater of operations had many scenes: a submarine lurking in New York Harbor; a hotel near Gatwick Airport at which the guests were spies; a classroom in a North London school where the only pupils present were not real but photographs.

The big opening number of the conspiracy, however, had been performed at a secret facility near Stockholm. Here, Marcus explained, brainwash candidates had been put under hypnosis, subjected to electric shocks, forced to eat their own excrement and endure sexual humiliation, and tortured until they whined like puppies. Once they had been reduced to mental pulp, the programming began. A literal kind of programming, following the rules of the computer age. Numbers linked to functions. Infinite loops of coded instructions, drilled into the subject by repetition, violence, the application of electrodes to bare skin. Finally, cyanide pills had been secreted inside their bodies, in order to eliminate the killers once they had fulfilled their programs. "We have the scoop," declared Marcus, "on one of the nastiest, most vicious CIA operations—the brainwashing institutes of Sweden. It's a great place to go for a vacation. But don't eat anything, don't drink anything. You may not come back a man, or a woman."

As he neared the end of his speech, Marcus looked around the room. There might, he suggested, be sleeper agents among the audience. Manchurian Candidates, conditioned to kill. Questions from the floor, therefore, would be taken in written form, to prevent the accidental utterance of a trigger word that would activate the program and bring bloodshed to the ballroom. "It is a crisis situation," he said. "We are in class war. No significant shooting has started here yet. Shooting will occur. People will be killed. People will suffer brainwashing."

"Perfectly sane people were saying that they had been brainwashed," recalled Christina. "It just kept getting weirder and weirder." As, in the course of the following three years, it would for me.

THIS IS A book of impossible things, and how a group of men came to live their lives by them because they did not want to die in Vietnam. It is about how it felt to be faced with the great moral decision of the age, and the terrible consequences that came from calling it right. It is about how being paranoid doesn't mean they're not out to get you.

It contains imagined conspiracies and real ones. Some of the people you will meet are telling the truth. Some of them are liars. I belong in the former category, but I'll understand if you have your suspicions. A few of my interviewees certainly did. "The same CIA operatives have been working for years," raged one Stockholm deserter, in an email from Hawaii. "I am not sure about YOU."

That uncertainty, and how to live with it, also became a subject of the story. I was getting to know a band of comrades who had made a stand against an unjust conflict and came to believe, almost immediately, that enemy infiltrators were operating among them. Nearly fifty years later, documents released by the intelligence archives of America and Sweden suggested that this suspicion was well founded. But the names of the informants had been redacted from the files. As they entered their seventies, the deserters faced the possibility that life for them was an espionage whodunit from which someone had torn the last page—the one that revealed which of their friends had sold them out to the spooks. Except that the story was too strange for any spy novel. As time went on, I realized that I had joined something much weirder than a fifty-year-old mole hunt. Moles are unsensational creatures. They snuffle about. They dig tunnels. They make molehills. I was on the trail of fantastic beasts.

In their teens and twenties, the figures at the heart of this story were American boys who felt the eye of war upon them and went to Sweden to escape its gaze. They joined the American Deserters Committee, a noisy and radical political organization that proved a thorn in the side of the Swedish political establishment. Then, tired of marching through Stockholm under earnest slogans about U.S. imperialism, they became revolutionaries and dreamed of taking over America and Europe, as the Bolsheviks had taken power in Russia. But the National Caucus of Labor Committees was not the Bolsheviks. It was an apocalyptic cult that believed in the satanic nature of the Queen of England, the prime minister of Sweden, and the Beatles and used violence, harassment, and financial fraud to achieve its goals. Goals that its successor organization is still working to accomplish.

THIS IS NOT the book I intended to write. At first I planned a grand historical survey of the act of desertion from the Second World War to the present day. I went down to St. Paul's Cathedral in London, where deserters from Iraq and Afghanistan were among the protestors living under the nylon tents of the Occupy camp. I read about the handful of American and British men who crossed the lines into North Korea and, because they were among the only white inhabitants of a closed state, were cast as the villains in *Nameless Heroes*, Pyongyang's answer to the James Bond films. (YouTube will satisfy the curious.) I visited the retired British gangster "Mad" Frankie Fraser, whose desertion and housebreaking during the Second World War had put him in Wormwood Scrubs prison alongside the stage and screen star Ivor Novello. ("As Ivor passed down the landing," he recalled, "all the prisoners came to their cell doors and sang 'We'll Gather Lilacs.'")

But the Vietnam deserters who went to Stockholm began to push these other figures from my mind. Partly because their very existence, once front-page news all over the world, was so little remembered beyond Sweden, and only hazily there. Partly because death was beginning to silence them and lock away their stories. Mainly, though, because I had a growing sense that I was exploring events that were mysterious even to those who had actually experienced them—and that those mysteries were now exerting their power over me.

As I talked to the survivors of the American Deserters Committee, I heard them puzzle over incidents that remained undiscussed with friends, with children, with the spouse sleeping in the next room. I heard them voice doubts about the gaps in their memories, express bewilderment at the actions of the people they had once been. I became fascinated, too, by what they wanted from me—renewed contact with long-lost comrades; the opportunity to kick against press reports about their conduct; the means to settle an old score; some help to discover, fifty years on, who had been loyal and truthful, and who had secretly betrayed them. And in some cases, it was much simpler. All they wanted was a bit of company, and a free lunch to make the food stamps stretch a bit further.

The pursuit of their stories took me to a cannabis refinery in Eugene, Oregon, and a maximum-security prison in Taylorsville, North Carolina. I met my subjects in parking lots and cafés; waited in hotel lobbies in Sweden and the States to keep appointments with former intelligence officers. I made a nuisance of myself at a prestigious Washington think tank and attended a cult meeting in the basement of a New York hotel. The story worked its way into my bones. I began dreaming of confrontations with the men who seemed to be the villains of the piece. I found myself awake at three a.m., reliving conversations with interviewees; getting up while my family slept to read emails that had arrived in the night, bearing more theories, names, scraps of information, scans of declassified documents. I entered the paranoid zone in which some of my subjects had spent a lifetime. A place it would be possible to wander for-ever, opening doors that led to more doors, and yet more beyond those.

One day in April 2016, a friend, no older than I, suffered a near-fatal heart attack. The news appeared on my Facebook feed as I walked to the Tube from my office at the BBC. As I tapped something optimistic into the comments thread, I had that thought that often strikes middle-aged men whose working lives are slightly more exhausting than they ought to be. What would happen if I fell dead in the street? After the usual images—my wife alone, my children fatherless, my coffin disap-pearing to the laid-back Laurie Johnson jazz theme that ended every episode of *The Avengers*—another idea presented itself. If I were to die without finishing this book, then someone out there would undoubtedly set up a Web page claiming that I'd been bumped off, by either the CIA, the Swedish secret services, or the bizarre political group that had once counted many of my interviewees as its members—and would, by the time my research was concluded, come to regard me as an enemy infil-trator. And that was when I knew I'd been swallowed by my own story.

Swallowed, but not brainwashed.

1 / THE HIGH ROAD

A JAPANESE FISHING boat, moving north to Soviet waters. Six Americans in the forward hold below the captain's cabin. Trying to stay warm. Trying to keep their nerve. Trying not to vomit too loudly. One is too drunk to feel seasick. He's up on his feet, swigging from a bottle of sake, peering into the moonless night, swearing he can see dolphins in the water and helicopters in the sky. The others don't bother to look. But when the beam of a searchlight streams through the crack in the door, all six scramble to the porthole, jostling to catch sight of the ship that has come down from the ice floes to meet them.

"It's them, man," says one. "The Russians are coming. We gonna be free now, baby."

Most of us would find it hard to pinpoint the single act that determined the course of our lives. Mark Shapiro can reenact his with the cutlery. When we spent the day together in San Diego, he collected me in a cream-colored vintage Volvo wagon, which was where most of our interview took place—stationary in the hotel parking lot or riding around the streets, where other drivers expressed their admiration for the age of his vehicle by beeping their horns and keeping a wary distance. But we did stop for lunch. And using the implements with which he was about to eat pasta, Mark illustrated the moment during the small hours of April 23, 1968, when he crossed from one life to another.

His knife and fork became two ships on the churning waves of the Sea of Japan. One was the fishing vessel that brought him and his five companions from a little harbor at the northeast tip of Hokkaido island. The other was the Soviet coast guard craft that edged alongside, and that, slammed by the relentless sea, appeared like a cliff soaring and sinking before them.

Between the two vessels was a six-foot span of furious air, through which Mark and his comrades were ordered to jump. Time was limited. The coast guards had boarded the fishing boat and were inspecting the captain's paperwork and checking the hold for contraband, the bureaucratic pretext for maneuvering so close. The Soviets had dragged a mattress to the cutter's deck of their ship and were holding it up like a firefighters' life net. One by one, displaying varying degrees of bravado and terror, the Americans slithered across the fishing boat's deck and around a funnel to reach an area unprotected by railings and open to the sea. One by one they jumped. Into the arms of a gang of Russian sailors, and into history.

IT TOOK THREE years to persuade Mark Shapiro to meet me. His first email was a blunt rejection. "I do not wish," he wrote, "to be contacted again on the matter." But the deserter grapevine brought him news of my inquiries and he changed his mind. Intimations of mortality also had something to do with it. Mark's health was fragile. He had heart trouble, and he slept with an oxygen cylinder by his bed. A tumor, he said, was growing in his skull. (He traced his finger over the place where it lay buried.) He knew that his time was limited and wanted to answer a question that was gnawing away at him. He wanted to expose the mole within the American Deserters Committee. His suspect was not among the five who traveled with him from Japan. The man upon whom Mark's suspicions turned—the man he'd been trying to catch out for years—had arrived in Sweden months before him, and he was one of the founders of the ADC. I said I would do my best.

I knew the bones of Mark's story from the accounts of his peers. On his tour of duty with the army in Vietnam, he'd found it hard to stomach talk of "gooks" and "slant-eyed bastards." Then, out on patrol one day, the soldier beside him was felled by a Viet Cong bullet. A murderous wake-up call for twenty-two-year-old Corporal Shapiro, with an unblemished service record and good prospects for promotion as a military cryptographer.

I was ready to take down more details, but Mark seemed incapable of fleshing out his narrative. Instead, he told me a story about his recent visit to a hypnotherapist.

"I told him that there was something in my past that I wanted to remember," he said. "And I didn't tell him any more than that. The guy was a little skeptical. He asked for the money in advance." The next thing Mark remembers is having his cash pressed back into his hand, and the therapist, visibly perturbed, assuring him that some stones were best left unturned. "So," Mark told me, with a shrug, "I have nothing to say about Vietnam. It's a form of amnesia." I accepted the explanation. I was already used to thinking of my interviewees as jigsaws with missing pieces.

Mark's decision to desert was not so lost to him. It was a textbook example of the act. In the first days of 1968, he read a newspaper article about four men who had successfully escaped the war. They had been on leave in Japan but were now poised to begin new lives in neutral Sweden. Their names were Craig Anderson, Rick Bailey, John Barilla, and Michael Lindner, but the press nicknamed them "the Intrepid Four," after the U.S. aircraft carrier that had sailed without them from Yokosuka, the Japanese home of the Seventh Fleet. Another expression was also used to describe them. *Defectors.* Used in recognition of what many saw as an act of treachery.

On their journey from east to west, the Intrepid Four had passed through the Soviet Union and accepted several weeks of Russian hospitality. Maybe more than hospitality. They had shared their anti-war sentiments with the international press, attended celebrations for the fiftieth anniversary of the Russian Revolution, shaken hands with members of the Politburo, and flown from Leningrad to Stockholm with a $1,000 stipend from the Kremlin in their pockets. But they looked pretty happy in the photographs, waving and smiling on the tarmac at

Stockholm Arlanda Airport, with their neat new haircuts and sharp new suits. And nobody was asking them to kill anyone in an increasingly unpopular war. Mark decided to follow their example and booked himself some R & R in Tokyo.

The news reports offered another helpful detail. The Intrepid Four did not make their journey unaided. They had been smuggled into Russia by an outfit called Beheiren, a group of activists who were fast becoming the focus of the Japanese anti-war movement. Beheiren had organized a rally in Tokyo at which Joan Baez had performed. It had taken out full-page ads in the *Washington Post* declaring that 82 percent of the Japanese population was opposed to the Vietnam War. It had sent its members to U.S. naval bases with leaflets encouraging sailors to desert, intending to make a provocative gesture—and had been rather surprised to find the offer being taken up. All over Japan, doctors, teachers, shopkeepers, and Buddhist monks began preparing hiding places and airing the spare bedding.

Beheiren, however, was a loose-knit organization, and when Mark arrived in Tokyo, determined to make contact, nobody seemed to know its address. "So," he explained, "I got into a cab and just said, 'Beheiren.'" The driver thought for a moment and made for Tokyo University and the office of Oda Makoto, a Harvard-educated novelist and academic who was the group's most visible spokesperson—the man who had gone before the cameras to announce the disappearance of the Intrepid Four. Makoto made some calls, and his associates sprang instantly into action.

By the end of the day Mark had checked out of his hotel and was installed in a Beheiren safe house. He soon discovered that he wasn't the only deserter being sheltered by the group. Five others were also in hiding, kept in circulation among the homes of sympathizers across Japan until the time was right to make the journey to Russia. "When I eventually met the others it was a shock," Mark said. "We had nothing in common, and it was immediately clear that two of them were nutcases."

His first American companion fit squarely into the category. Philip Callicoat was a nineteen-year-old sailor whose swaggering manner was at odds with his lowly status as a cook's helper on board the USS *Reeves*. Perhaps the attitude was a gift from his background: his father was a

Pentecostal minister who press-ganged his enormous brood of children into service as the Singing Callicoats—a gospel act best known for having saved Ed Sullivan from humiliation by breaking into an unscheduled second number when a chimp act went badly wrong during a live TV show. Phil Callicoat had turned up at the Soviet Embassy seeking advice on how to defect, but his motives had less to do with politics and more to do with having drunk the last of his $120 savings in an all-night Tokyo jazz bar. Navy discipline did not suit him, and he had recently been confined to his ship for twenty-eight days for vandalism. He and Mark were brought together on a train from Osaka to Tokyo, then put up for the night in the apartment of a visiting French academic. Mark sensed that Phil was going to be trouble, and he was right.

The fugitives were taken to Tokyo International Airport, where three more deserters made a party of five. The noisiest was Joe Kmetz, a bullish New Yorker whose opposition to the war, he said, had earned him a month in a dark isolation cell on a diet of bread, water, and lettuce heads. The oldest of the group, twenty-eight-year-old Edwin Arnett, was a skinny, stooping Californian who chewed his fingernails and spoke in slow, somnolent tones. He was not a clever man. His educational progress had halted after the eighth grade, after which he'd trundled gurneys in a New York hospital and spent two years in the merchant marine. The army had expressed no interest in him until 1967, when a Defense Department initiative called "Project 100,000"—cruelly nicknamed the "Moron Corps"—admitted a huge swathe of low-achieving men. The other deserters called him "Pappy"—partly in honor of his age, partly to distance themselves from his oddness.

The sanest of the gang, it seemed clear to Mark, was its only African American: Corporal Terry Marvel Whitmore, a marine infantryman from Memphis, Mississippi, who had been wounded in action in Vietnam and received a Christmas bedside visit from President Lyndon B. Johnson, who saluted his bravery and pinned a Purple Heart to the pillow. When Whitmore learned he was also to receive the honor of being returned to the front as soon as he was upright, he discharged himself from the military hospital at Yokohama and lay low with a Japanese girlfriend, pretending to anyone who asked that he was a student from East Africa— and hoping not to encounter any actual East Africans.

Their Beheiren guide, a Mrs. Fujikowa, encouraged the deserters to behave discreetly on their trip. Easier said than done. As they boarded the plane, Mark got into an argument with the flight attendant about the size of his suitcase. When they landed at their destination, Nemuro airport on the island of Hokkaido, Phil Callicoat struck up a loud conversation with a local bar owner whose establishment offered more than just cocktails.

Before they could get into any serious trouble, the deserters were steered toward a pair of waiting cars and driven for four hours to a remote spot on the coast, where a gaggle of Beheiren sympathizers were huddled around a radio unit, exchanging messages with a Soviet ship—which informed them that the handover would have to wait until the following night. The plan postponed, the Americans were taken to a nearby fishing village, where the captain of their escape vessel was waiting at his home to greet them. He poured out the sake and told his nervous guests not to worry. He had been a kamikaze pilot in the Second World War, and he had come back.

The following night, the captain supplied the deserters with a change of clothes calculated to increase their chances of passing as Japanese fishermen during the short walk from his house to the floodlit harbor. Terry Whitmore wrapped himself in a blanket to conceal his conspicuous blackness. Fortified with more alcohol, the deserters went out into the freezing night and climbed aboard their host's fishing boat. They were told to stay belowdecks and keep quiet: most of the crew were unaware of their existence. As the vessel began chugging from the harbor, a sixth man stumbled into the hold: army private Kenneth Griggs, born in Seoul but adopted as a baby by a white couple from Boise, Idaho. Griggs—who introduced himself under his Korean name, Kim Jin-Su—had spent the better part of a year hiding out in the Cuban Embassy in Tokyo, and he seemed to have made good use of the free literature. His reasons for desertion were expressed as an intense critique of U.S. imperialism. He had a position to maintain: he had already said his piece in a four-minute film, shot by Beheiren and screened for journalists in a Tokyo restaurant.

When the Russian coast guard pulled alongside, Kim was the first to jump, leaping with reckless enthusiasm into Soviet-administered space. Joe Kmetz, his fears numbed by alcohol, went just as eagerly. Callicoat followed, sliding across the deck and launching himself with a Tarzan yodel. Mark went next. Hesitated. Watched the rust-marked hull of the Russian ship surge up and down before his eyes. "Jump, you dumb cunt!" shouted Kmetz, unsympathetically. Arms flailing, Mark made it, his suitcase tossed after him by the Japanese skipper.

Edwin Arnett, though, was in a worse state, paralyzed by the sight of the rising, falling ship. Whitmore muscled past him, hurled himself across the divide, and was caught by two burly Russian sailors before he hit the deck. Left behind, Arnett seemed unable to compute the physics of the situation. Instead of jumping as the Russian ship fell, he jumped as it rose, colliding with the railing and leaving himself dangling over the sea by one leg. Whitmore and one of the Russians dragged him back to safety.

THE SOVIET SHIP was old. The plumbing hissed and thudded. The deserters registered the signs in Cyrillic and knew that they had passed from one political sphere to the next. But the Russians made them comfortable, allocating the deserters quarters beside the officers and giving them as much vodka as they could hold. For their whole time in the Soviet Union, it seemed to Mark, they were carried on a small river of colorless alcohol. "I guess," he reflected, "they thought it would increase the amount of careless talk."

There were toasts at dinner. To each other. To the interpreter, an incongruously flamboyant man with a cigarette holder. To the captain, who ended the meal by challenging his guests to a drinking game. Only Callicoat accepted, pushing a hunk of black bread inside his mouth and taking a huge slug of some unidentified spirit. He was soon carried back to his bunk.

For four days and nights the deserters knocked back vodka, dined on salmon, looked through the portholes, and watched the thickening ice. The interpreter took the opportunity to steer each man away from the group for a thorough discussion of his background and history. On April 25 the ship neared the coast of Sakhalin island, where a patrol boat brought the passengers ashore. Officials confiscated their passports and identity papers. A doctor examined Arnett's injured leg and shrugged.

Then, for four dizzying, vodka-sluiced, bouquet-filled, flashbulb-illuminated weeks, Mark Shapiro and his comrades went on a publicity tour of the USSR: Vladivostok, Moscow, Tbilisi, Gorki, Leningrad, with a short break in the Black Sea resort of Batumi. They accepted flowers from little girls. They saw circus shows. They browsed at the GUM department store. They visited Lenin's tomb. ("Who's Lenin?" asked Terry Whitmore.) They saw more circus shows. All under the supervision of a small staff of well-mannered KGB officers and neckless security men in Al Capone fedoras. Some of the security men, they learned, had also kept an eye on the Intrepid Four. One had been taught a single phrase of English, which he repeated over and over again: *American cinema— I love you.*

In Leningrad the deserters were installed in the Hotel Astoria, where Mark shared a room with Terry Whitmore. "Terry could hear this whining noise," Mark recalled. "He was convinced that the Russians were bugging the room. So he turned everything over, looking for a hidden microphone. But it was only the sound of the elevator. Just being in Russia made us all nervous."

Their edginess caused conflict: Kim and Callicoat got into a fistfight, apparently over Kim's plan to acquire and burn an American flag. On the rare occasions they were allowed to wander about on their own, the deserters assumed they were being followed. Assumed, too, that they were being informed on by the local women who were so eager to come up to their rooms—not least because they seemed so fascinated by the intricacies of the U.S. Navy. The minders never objected to these one-night stands, as long as they took place in the hotel. Conversely, when Whitmore and Kmetz broke bounds and spent the night with two women in an apartment, the security guys were not pleased and accused them of going out on a spying mission for the CIA. It wasn't, it seems, a very relaxing evening: the women expected payment and though the Americans obliged, they were soon interrupted by a jealous husband, who upended the dining table in anger and then, rather more weirdly, began to show a gentle curiosity in the texture of Terry Whitmore's hair.

The grand propaganda coup of the trip happened on May 3. The broadcast of *We Cannot Be Silent*, a half-hour television program in which the six deserters were interviewed about their experiences in

Vietnam. Joe Kmetz, hiding under his shades, said the war was a sickness. Terry Whitmore compared the conflict in Indochina to the U.S. Civil War. Phil Callicoat read out a protest poem of his own composition. Kim Jin-Su played the ideologue, suggesting that a nuclear strike on the States might be the only way to defeat "stormtroopers and criminals who are carrying out Washington's policy of annihilating the Vietnamese as a race and proud people." He delivered his message down the barrel of the camera. "For those of you on the battlefields," he said, "I would advise you to follow me and hundreds of others, and just remember that it may take guts to go, but it takes balls to say no."

I asked Mark about his contribution to the film. "I said as little as I could," he replied. "It was Pappy Arnett who did most of the talking."

Arnett couldn't shut up. In his droning monotone, he gave testimony that shocked and baffled the world. He said that he'd been trained at a special intelligence school at Fort Meade, Maryland, where he had learned forty ways of torturing a suspect. He said that he'd been assigned to a chemical warfare unit, and arrived on the coast of Vietnam aboard a ship loaded with gas that could cause hemorrhages, paralysis, and blindness. He spoke of saltwater poured in the wounds of prisoners, of GIs making necklaces with the ears of dead North Vietnamese. He said that his commanding officer had "treated the sweeps we made through peasant villages as a turkey shoot"; described how the same officer had executed a Puerto Rican serviceman who refused to join the hunting party and then recorded the dead man as a victim of the Viet Cong; and reported that on another occasion, a superior had disemboweled a baby and thrown the tiny corpse back into its mother's arms. The interviewer, Yuri Fokin of the Soviet television service, was silent. The camera operator began to weep. The other deserters were horrified. They might have been more horrified had they known the truth: that Edwin C. Arnett had been an army cook on board a floating maintenance shop moored in Cam Ranh Bay. The only violence he had witnessed in Indochina had been inflicted upon potatoes.

VIETNAM WAS THE place the bodies were buried or flown back from, the place where the bombs fell and the air burned. But the Vietnam conflict raged far beyond the borders of a former French colony on the South China Sea. It was an undeclared world war, fought between the representatives of two opposing ideologies to spare them the agony of adding Moscow, Peking, and Washington to a list that had begun with Hiroshima and Nagasaki.

Nothing about it was clean or uncomplicated. In 1954, the Geneva Accords split Vietnam into two zones, the Communist north, administered from Hanoi by the revolutionary leader Ho Chi Minh, and the non-Communist south, ruled from Saigon by a succession of Western-backed leaders, who were advised—and sometimes hired and fired—by the hidden hand of the Central Intelligence Agency.

From 1960, the National Liberation Front, a Communist insurgency also known as the Viet Cong, added its firepower to the argument. Away from the bullets, the war's foreign stakeholders invested their millions. China and the Soviet Union supplied expertise, money, and guns. The United States matched that commitment and, from 1965, sent roughly 2.7 million ground troops into the territory. Most found a place in the war's decade-long ritual—boredom and terror in the battle zone, rest and recuperation in Tokyo, funerals and homecomings back in the States. But thousands of GIs rejected their roles and became deserters. The act carried the penalty of imprisonment and hard labor—and the possibility of becoming an unwitting combatant in the propaganda war.

As Mark Shapiro's little platoon went in a vodka haze on their guided tours around Russia, Yuri Andropov, the head of the KGB and future leader of the USSR, must surely have permitted himself a smile of satisfaction, if not a high-kicking rendition of "Kalinka" on top of his mahogany desk. He and his colleagues had been expecting the deserters' arrival since the first week of March. It had been their idea to use a Japanese fishing boat to transport the men. (The Intrepid Four had been put aboard a Soviet passenger steamer, which had caused some diplomatic awkwardness.) They had planned their itinerary, scheduled their media appearances, authorized the Novosti Press Agency to offer them a book deal. To obscure the KGB's involvement, they had appointed a state-backed peace group, the Soviet Afro-Asian Solidarity Committee, as official sponsor of the trip. The Central Committee of the Communist Party had even discussed some of the deserters individually, causing phonetic Russian renderings of their names to be added to the Politburo minutes: *Knet, Arnet, Kollikot.*

During the first week of May 1968 those names chuntered from telex machines all over the world. America's journalists went hunting for more details. A former Singing Callicoat responded to the sudden reappearance of her brother Phil: "I thought he was dead or we would have heard from him by now," she said. "If it's true, we disown him," said Joe Kmetz's stepbrother. But Arnett's tales dominated the headlines, in all their wound-salting, village-burning, baby-killing horror.

Before the tour came to an end, Yuri Andropov paid the deserters a visit. Mark remembered his polite manners and exceptional English, the feeling of being inspected. Had the deserters been used? Of course they had. But the process was more complex than exploitation. "They showed us the country," said Mark, "in the hope that it would make us more supportive of Russia in later years. In my case it worked. I sometimes wonder whether I wasn't a little brainwashed on that trip." He wasn't talking Benzedrine injections and a psychedelic light show, but something subtler. Something that ensured that he never developed an enthusiasm for capitalism and, during his years of exile in Sweden, was always happy to pop into the Soviet Embassy for a chat. Something that put him at odds with America for the rest of his days.

THE SOVIETS DID not grant every wish of the deserters but hinted that they might help realize their future plans. Each man was given a pencil and a piece of paper and asked to describe his ideal post-military life. Whitmore and Kmetz looked at a map and plumped for a future in Finland. Kim dreamed of a new life in North Korea. But the six knew that Sweden would be their first port of call, and they were given the name of a helpful contact in Stockholm: Bertil Svahnström, a veteran foreign correspondent and vice chair of the Swedish Committee for Vietnam, an alliance of liberals and Social Democrats opposed to the war in Indochina.

They were also given a friendly warning. "They told us," said Mark, "to keep our distance from a man named Michael Vale and an organization called the American Deserters Committee." Vale, said their KGB guide, would try to contact them and gain their confidence.

On May 24, 1968, a fleet of limousines arrived at the Hotel Astoria to drive the deserters to the Leningrad airport, where they each received $300 in cash from the Soviet Afro-Asian Solidarity Committee and bear hugs and kisses from their minders.

After an hour staring at the legs of the Swedish cabin crew, the deserters touched down at Stockholm Arlanda Airport to a repeat of the reception that had greeted the Intrepid Four six months before. On that occasion, the waiting photographers had borrowed the iconography of a visiting rock band. Stepping from the plane in identical black suits, John, Craig, Mike, and Rick were framed as the Fab Four of Vietnam War desertion. The Soviets must have seen this, too, and counted it a mistake. The new band of six arrived unscrubbed, unsmartened: authentic members of the counterculture. The Rolling Stones to the Intrepid Four's Beatles. In the shots from that day, Kim pouts from behind a pair of shades. Mark, in a Red Army fur hat, has a foot perched on his battered suitcase. Whitmore is dragging on a cigarette. Callicoat smiles wryly. Joe Kmetz, a chubby wise guy with a guitar dangling from his right hand, squares off with the camera like a nightclub bouncer. Edwin Arnett hovers at the back, eyes downcast, pale, serious. And, as it would turn out, doomed.

As the Russians had predicted, Bertil Svahnström was the first person to welcome the deserters to Sweden—a friendly, patrician figure happy to be acting as envoy for liberal opposition to the Vietnam War, and to be a conduit for messages from Moscow. But there was little opportunity for private conversation. Reporters and photographers had already swarmed into the arrivals lounge. A press conference was coalescing around the deserters. Reporters fired off questions. Were the men Communists? Had they been influenced by their Russian hosts? Terry Whitmore said the questions were stupid. Joe Kmetz got to his feet and declared that nobody would say a word until the representatives of U.S. press agencies had left the room. "We'll talk with everybody but Americans," he insisted. He didn't trust them. They wrote bullshit and they were probably working for the CIA. The hacks from Associated Press and United Press International had little choice but to withdraw. Svahnström looked quietly pleased at that.

Once the questions had been exhausted, the deserters were whisked into detention by a phalanx of Swedish policemen so courteous that they carried their bags to the waiting cars. Svahnström followed behind in his Volvo. They were taken to a police station in Märsta, a northern suburb of Stockholm—a holding pen for asylum seekers to this day. Here, the men were searched, questioned, given Coke and hot dogs, and permitted to relax in front of the television. They watched a program in which the African American singer Lou Rawls received a rapturous reception from the studio audience. ("At least Sweden ain't Mississippi," thought Whitmore.) Although they were told not to smoke in the cells, Joe Kmetz managed to light one of his Russian cigarettes by heating a piece of metal in a plug socket.

Before lights-out, Svahnström came to speak to them. The deserters, he said, would soon be released and issued with permits to remain in Sweden. He could help them negotiate the complexities of the local benefits system, find accommodation and a job. But he also repeated the warning of their Soviet hosts. Recently, Svahnström explained, a group had been established to help fugitive GIs in Sweden. Its representatives would soon be paying them a visit. But the men from the American Deserters Committee, he said, were not to be trusted. They were ideological extremists who would attempt to make the newcomers follow their hard political line.

As the men considered Svahnström's warning, one of the American news agencies banished from the Arlanda Airport press conference was exacting its revenge. On May 26, UPI sent out a story by Virgil Kret, a correspondent in Tokyo, that was calculated to humiliate the man who had bawled its reporter out of the arrivals lounge.

Kret claimed to have interviewed Joe Kmetz in February, just before Beheiren took the fugitive marine under its wing. The encounter, he said, had taken place in a bar in Tokyo, where Kmetz, drunk and disconsolate, confessed that he'd been hiding for the past sixteen months in the room of a one-eyed Japanese woman ten years his senior, drinking Suntory whisky and cursing his fate.

"He found it difficult to speak, and when he did he spoke English like a Japanese bar girl," wrote Kret. "He pronounced 'wife' as 'wifu,' 'house' as 'housu,' 'Vietnam' as 'Vietnamu.' " Kret advised him to get a lawyer and turn himself in. "Never happen!" exclaimed Kmetz. "Never happen! They'll put me in the monkey housu until I'm an old man!" After this, Kret reported, a member of Beheiren came to collect Kmetz from the bar and take him to a safe house. He was, said the reporter, "the most unhappy and desperate person that I have ever known."

Was this story true? Was Virgil Kret for real? Apparently so. But the nature of his reality offered a warning about what awaited some of the deserters further down the line. I found his old stories for UPI and the *Los Angeles Times* and a mention of his presence at a California charity dinner attended by Mr. and Mrs. Zeppo Marx. But an article from an underground newspaper revealed that Kret had been expelled from Japan in 1969, accused of involvement in revolutionary politics. It also noted that in 1975, a source had warned Kret of an imminent assassination attempt on President Gerald Ford. Unfortunately, the source transpired to be God, who issued the tip, Kret claimed, in the form of a "time poem."

The trail ended with a long-neglected blog called *The Obituary of the World*, in which Kret explained that he had received telepathic warning of God's declaration of war against the Earth, and that the Almighty had already supplied the codes that would enable him to launch nuclear revenge upon those who had wounded him most grievously. The Buffalo Bills football team would be among the first to perish. Nothing new had been posted on the site since 2008. Since when, I couldn't help noticing, the Bills have consistently failed to reach the NFL playoffs.

WHEN THE REPRESENTATIVES of the American Deserters Committee turned up at the police station, Mark and his comrades were ready to be suspicious. But the men who came to speak with them didn't seem to be the dangerous figures described by Bertil Svahnström and the KGB. Their manner was friendly and reasonable. They explained that the Swedish welfare system would provide a modest income and that a network of sympathetic Swedes would be only too happy to offer them temporary accommodation. For many of Stockholm's activist elite— left-leaning actors, journalists, and academics—a deserter in the spare bedroom had become that season's most fashionable accessory.

Bill Jones, the chairman of the ADC, was a twenty-one-year-old former seminarian from St. Louis, Missouri, who'd deserted from Germany during his training as an army medic. Earnestness seemed his defining quality. Bill explained that he had hoped to meet the deserters in Leningrad, but Svahnström and the Swedish Committee for Vietnam had declined to pay for the ticket.

Bill's colleague Michael Vale was older and more self-assured. A short, stocky man with a crinkly smile and unironed clothes, Vale was not a deserter but a professional translator from Cincinnati, Ohio, with an address book full of Swedish intellectuals and an apartment in Stockholm where everyone was welcome. Unlike the patrician figure of Svahnström, Vale talked the language of rebellion and revolt. In that moment, it was not clear how profound a revolution he had in mind. Nor was it possible to know that joining the American Deserters Committee would send some of its members to a prison they would never escape.

2 / THE COMMITTEE

IN OLDER WARS, the refusal to fight led only to the criminal underworld, a defector's battalion, or a final cigarette in a cold field at dawn. When the Intrepid Four arrived at Arlanda Airport in December 1967, they rewrote that story. Their journey transformed desertion from an individual act of conscience or cowardice to a political step that GIs could take together: one that offered the possibility of a new life in a prosperous, liberal, neutral European country. Nobody planned this. Nobody organized it. It was as spontaneous as a love affair. The Intrepid Four walked from a café in Tokyo and asked for help from a young man with a plausibly countercultural haircut. He took them to Fūgetsudō, a smoky dive in the Shinjuku district where students came to drink bad coffee and talk about Mao. From this, a movement grew.

It may have been inevitable. The Vietnam War was unpopular. Fighting-on-the-streets unpopular. Tear-gas unpopular. Uniformed men could not be insulated from this bad news, no matter how far they were from home. Dissent in America meant dissent on American bases, in American ships, in American barracks. To the gathering dismay of their officers, men learned how to say no. It scarcely mattered whether their objections were conscientious or self-interested: whether they wanted to strike a blow for peace or sidestep military discipline. The exit signs had been illuminated. On the other side, a new generation of political radicals was ready to give support to anyone who passed through—hoping, perhaps, that the deserters might be recruited for a new kind of war. The war against war.

Discreetly, carefully, these tiny groups of activists approached the buzz-cut, hare-eyed young men they spotted loitering in cafés and at railway stations and offered board, lodging, help with paperwork. They secured funds from film stars and intellectuals, from church groups and charities. Clandestine assistance came from enemy governments and shady guys involved with armed struggles in the Third World. Through hand-delivered letters and quiet meetings in flats and farmhouses, they began working with one another, moving deserters over borders, from refuge to refuge. They sometimes worked against one another, too—impelled by the natural forces of left-wing factionalism, or by the mischief of hostile infiltrators. Nobody could be sure about that. But together they laid the tracks of an international underground railroad, built to shuttle dissenting men away from the napalm and razor wire to sanctuary.

Its ghostly infrastructure spanned the globe. Short routes carried deserters and draft dodgers over the American border into Canada. Beheiren managed the transpacific, trans-Siberian branch, on which the Intrepid Four had been shunted westward from Tokyo to Stockholm. Deserters opened up their own lines from bases in Germany, driving or hitchhiking north through Denmark and taking the ferry from Helsingør to Sweden. Some flew from Canada via Reykjavík. Anti-war activists too old for the draft became stationmasters of safe houses in Paris, London, Amsterdam, and Berlin. Underground publishers produced pamphlets to guide men through the system: Baedeckers of desertion that listed the phone numbers and addresses of friendly lawyers and welfare groups. Anyone considering migrating to Sweden was directed to the officers of the American Deserters Committee—the organization about which Bertil Svahnström had issued his gloomy warning.

The first time I heard its name, I thought the ADC sounded rather innocuous. I imagined a room of sober young men passing resolutions against the military-industrial complex. Now I think of it as a phenomenon of a different order. Something through which we might read the times, like the psychedelic bus trip undertaken by Ken Kesey and the

Merry Pranksters; or the Stanford Prison Experiment, inside which the psychologist Philip Zimbardo barricaded a group of impressionable boys and watched them sink into barbarism.

To describe the experiences of all those whose lives were touched by the committee would require more than a book. It would require an immense illuminated map of the world, and an army of uniformed croupiers pushing stacks of color-coded tokens in the direction of Sweden. Some tokens would represent deserters and draft resisters. Others would stand for men who looked like deserters or draft resisters but mysteriously fit neither category.

The ADC was always at the center of the argument—with the Swedish government, with the Swedish anti-war movement, with the counterculture, with America, with itself. It could not be conciliatory. It could not form amicable alliances. It had a knack for turning friends into enemies and biting hands that fed. Like many groups on the radical Left, its real talent was for reducing itself to increasingly smaller, purer fractions, until, eventually, it boiled away entirely. I heard it described as a revolutionary brotherhood, a goon squad, and an intelligence service front led by agents provocateurs.

"Whether they were CIA or KGB or just crazy, they were bad news," said one boy who declined to join the choir. But even he was fascinated by them. As I traveled Sweden and the States, listening to the stories of its former members, it became clear that half a century later they were still computing the experience—whether they looked back on it with nostalgia or anxiety, or were determined not to look back on it at all. Several alumni of the ADC would have preferred not to be mentioned in these pages and told me so. But they were the men at the heart of the story, and as they decided not to fight the Viet Cong, I decided not to fight the story.

WILLIAM CUTHBERT JONES, the chairman of the ADC, was an early arrival in Stockholm. A good-looking Catholic boy from St. Louis, with a slight frame, soulful brown eyes, and a strong line in radical hep talk. "They call you a man," he rapped, "and they treat you like an animal. They feed you their line and you think it's the truth. Remember in basic training: double time, chow line, right face, left face? They wanted you disciplined like a well-running machine, easy to control, easy to handle. Uncle Sam needs you—to stop the bullets, to smother the grenades, to make the world safe for Coca-Cola."

Right from the start, Bill Jones was the public face of the American Deserters Committee. He led its marches, spoke on its behalf from soap-boxes and conference lecterns, wrote editorials for its newspaper, and gave its official interviews to the press—until he decided that those reporters who weren't intelligence agents were probably going to stitch him up anyway and decided to remain silent. He would go silent for me, too, once he realized that I knew the story of the brainwashing institutes of Sweden, and the stranger story of what happened after. But at first things went swimmingly. We had lunch. We got on so well that he broke his diet and had a piece of pecan pie.

Our venue was the Old Ebbitt Grill, a Washington institution snug beside the White House: padded booths, brass railings, pink-tinged bou-doir paintings, like some recently democratized gentlemen's club. He chose it because it was convenient for his work as Washington bureau chief of a glossy magazine called *Executive Intelligence Review*. His email warned that he didn't look like the boy in the pictures anymore, and that I should watch out for someone in a Red Army fur hat. ("Without the star," he added, unnecessarily.) I knew him straight away, despite the extra weight and the loss of his fuzzy Che beard. People don't change that much. Except politically.

Although Bill described himself as "very working-class," this was a matter more of feeling than fact. The family tree was luxuriant and deep-rooted. His father was a real estate broker who dealt in upscale apart-ment blocks in downtown St. Louis. The first William Cuthbert Jones was a distinguished criminal lawyer who had earned the rank of major in the Civil War and, with something preying on his mind, made a deathbed conversion to Catholicism. Rome's influence extended to Bill's generation: a sister and two of his uncles entered religious life, and Bill was educated by Benedictine monks. "The martyrs were my heroes," he said. "This is how I saw my life."

Being a martyr for God was one thing. Being a martyr for President Lyndon B. Johnson was another. One night in 1966, at Christian Brothers

College High School, Bill decided to do something about it. "I tore up my draft card and put it in the mail. My friends thought I was totally nuts. I thought I'd make a difference. Have an effect." He shook his head sardonically. "And then I got scared. I went down to the mailbox and waited for the postman to get this damn letter back. Which I did."

Having silenced his own protest, he enlisted in the army and began training as a medic. First he drove a truck between military hospitals in Germany. Later he took electrocardiograms of wounded soldiers and watched the flickering needles describe the consequences of punctured lungs, shattered bones, buried bullets: a thousand more reasons not to go to Vietnam. But it was the Intrepid Four who pointed the way to Sweden. When Bill saw them on the cover of a magazine, he began plotting a journey north. ("Like Yogi Berra says," reflected Bill, "when you come to a fork in the road . . .")

Another medic in his unit had the same impulse and acted first, selling his car and hitchhiking to Denmark. Bill intended to join him, but didn't like what he found when he arrived. "He was something in the Copenhagen club scene," he recalled. "I met some of his friends, and it seemed somewhat seedy."

So he kept moving north to Stockholm, arriving on a snowy afternoon in late January 1968 and making his way to the main railway station, where he asked a passerby how to get in touch with one of the Swedish anti-war groups. "It's Saturday," he was told. "They'll all be out marching." They were. Processing through the street under banners demanding an end to American aggression in Indochina. Bill joined the march, explained who he was, and found himself treated as the hero of the hour. And in that moment he was reconciled to a life in exile. Destiny was calling. "If you think you're doing something that's going to have an effect upon history," he said, "that's a very powerful force."

There were, Bill said, several former seminarians in the ADC. They made good revolutionaries. Looking back over his old speeches, it was easy to see how well the rhetoric of sin and redemption mixed with the sixties' language of struggle and revolution. The present system, Bill argued, was corrupt and stagnant. A new one was required. The wretched of the earth—exploited laborers, Third World guerrillas, Vietnam deserters—would create it with violence.

"And is not," he asked, "this violent indignation of alienated people one of the highest forms of love? The love of human brotherhood which refuses to abandon one's fellow man to the scourge of hell on earth?" Bill's medical background provided more enriching imagery. "It is comparable to a competent surgeon who must excise a malignant organ in order to save a life," he argued.

> And those concerned with man's spirituality must participate in the operation or be seen for what they are—"hypocrites, whited sepulchers, and the people will vomit them out of their mouths." We the American Deserters Committee of Sweden have seen clearly our duty faced with the situation of the world today. As members of the U.S. Army we were the prime instruments of these same forces of repression and reaction, and we have excised ourselves from this malignant body. We saw our function and refused to carry it out. We answered a higher call of the people of the world who were crying for help from their brutal oppressors.

If Bill had made this speech in London, he would have risked deportation. If he had made it in Paris, he would have been kissing goodbye to his next fourteen-day *carte de séjours*. In Stockholm, however, it was fine. In Stockholm, he could make the speech while receiving a free bus pass and $20 weekly welfare payments, attending state-funded language classes, and enjoying the protection of humanitarian asylum—a new diplomatic category created for the benefit of the deserters by a political class that wanted to signal its opposition to the Vietnam War.

But the ADC was in no mood for gratitude. Its members were revolutionaries, and revolutionaries never said please or thank you. "Some people were typically liberal and didn't want you to go too far," Bill told me. "We had a lot of fights about that. But there was a feeling that we had been lied to for years, and now we had to try something else."

IN THE 1960S and '70s, Sweden was another word for utopia—particularly in countries afflicted by industrial decline and rising unemployment. The Swedish model, as it was called, with no hint of double entendre, appeared to have delivered the Swedes from anxiety. They had the highest living standards in Europe. They had big cars and tasteful modernist furniture. Their welfare state was a miracle of generosity: this was a country without visible deprivation.

Poised between the two power blocs of the Cold War, Sweden also had political neutrality and moral independence: how many other states would have permitted Bertrand Russell and Jean-Paul Sartre, two foreign intellectuals, to convene a private tribunal to investigate American war crimes in Vietnam? But that's what happened—witnesses were called, napalm burns examined, testimonies taken from the bombers and the bombed, and in May 1967 a jury of writers, thinkers, and activists announced that they had found the United States of America guilty of genocide against the Vietnamese people. The horrific details were tele-graphed around the world.

The Swedes also seemed to enjoy impressive social and sexual liberty. Theirs was the country that exported all those blue movies, all those blond masseuses and au pairs. It was a place where sex education was enshrined in the school curriculum and condoms were dispensed from vending machines on the street. American commentators looked on this from afar with a mixture of envy and horror. *Time* magazine set the tone as early as 1955, with a notorious article entitled "Sin and Sweden," which depicted the country as a topsy-turvy zone "where sociology has become a religion itself, and birth control, abortion and promiscuity—especially among the young—are recognized as inalienable rights." Jaws dropped across America, also a little drool.

For the U.S. press, Swedish sociology was a gift that kept on giving. Its pioneering collection of data on the habits and experiences of its citizens was a rich source of inspiration for American journalists research-ing their stock shock-horror pieces on Swedish sex. In February 1966, for instance, *U.S. News & World Report* published a report on the increase of sexually transmitted diseases in the Swedish population. "Ten percent of the infected boys," it claimed, "had had relations with 200 dif-ferent girls." Easy to imagine which part of that statistic burned most fiercely in the mind of the male reader.

What sold newspapers also sold films. The Italian director Luigi Scattini had an international hit with *Sweden: Heaven and Hell*, which depicted the Swedes as lesbian clubbers, married swingers, and space-hopping nudists. (It also premiered Piero Umiliani's song "Mah Nà Mah Nà," years before the Muppets made it their own.) Sweden's own film culture produced *I Am Curious (Yellow)*, the art movie that combined explicit sex scenes with footage of the education minister Olof Palme, sitting in his little back garden in Stockholm and talking about "our dream of a classless, egalitarian society."

OLOF PALME DID not make an explicit invitation to the deserters, but he did plump up the cushions and put on some seductive mood music. At first, these were quiet moves: behind-the-scenes conversations with colleagues that smoothed the fugitives' progress into Swedish airspace.

Then, on the night of February 21, 1968, something noisier: Palme leading a five-thousand-strong march on the U.S. Embassy in Stockholm, with Nguyen Tho Chan, the North Vietnamese ambassador to Moscow, at his side; Palme addressed the crowd with a flaming torch in one hand and inflammatory speech in the other. "The goal of democracy," he told them, "can never be reached by means of oppression. One cannot save a village by wiping it out, putting the fields on fire, destroying the houses, captivating the people or killing them." A continent of people, he argued, thought the same. "The truth is that the overwhelming majority of people in Europe dissociate themselves from this war, want to have an end put to the sufferings, want to give the people of Vietnam the right to decide over their own future. This democratic opinion does not experience the war of the United States in Vietnam as a support for democracy, but as a threat against the democratic ideas, not only in Vietnam but also throughout the world."

Palme was a rising star in the Social Democratic Party, but those words made him brightly visible everywhere. In December 1967, an unofficial anti-war demonstration in Stockholm had ended with police batons drawing blood outside the U.S. Embassy. Palme's walk with Nguyen Tho Chan implied a change of policy.

He was denounced in the U.S. press, his audience dismissed as a "leftist mob." America's ambassador to Sweden, William Heath, a beady-eyed Texan whose preferred epithet for anti-war protestors was "rattlesnakes," withdrew to Washington beneath a barrage of hate mail and rotten eggs. American sabers rattled. The U.S. State Department threatened to halt the export of Redeye missiles to Sweden. The International Longshoremen's Association warned that Swedish goods might be denied entry to American ports. The NBC anchorman Frank McGee suggested that this was the end of Swedish neutrality. And as relations between the two governments cooled, American dissidents registered a rise in temperature and followed its spring warmth north.

BILL JONES LED the American Deserters Committee. Michael Vale was its guru. But it was Hans Göran Franck, a lawyer and the head of the Swedish branch of Amnesty International, who conjured the ADC into being. Franck had been one of the organizers of the Russell Tribunal and, though he knew Bertil Svahnström and the respectable liberals of the Swedish Committee for Vietnam, he was closer to more radical forces on the left—the Front for National Liberation (FNL), young student activists who were for militancy, Mao, and swift victory for North Vietnam. Franck's office processed the bulk of the deserters' asylum claims, and did so tirelessly and for free. Other forms of practical assistance came from volunteers, many of whom were members of Amnesty International: teachers, doctors, and academics who opened up their spare rooms and summer houses, laid extra places at the dinner table.

They were not the only ones providing this help. Only a month after the arrival of the Intrepid Four, more than forty different grassroots groups were doing their bit. Franck reasoned that if the deserters formed their own organization, they might take on some of this work themselves. Old hands would assist new arrivals, advising them how to fill out the forms, negotiate interviews with the police and the social bureau. Together, they might also develop a unified voice, allowing them to make their own representations to the authorities—and to rebut the claims of their enemies.

At the end of January 1968, General Lewis F. Shull, former Pentagon intelligence man and the judge advocate of the U.S. Army in Europe, told the press that the Stockholm deserters were apolitical dropouts. "They are bums," he said, "not the highest type of soldier." If the deserters formed their own political organization, then charges like this would be harder to make. All Franck needed was someone to coordinate it for him.

He had already met his candidate six months previously, and in unusual circumstances. On May Day 1967, the first day of the Russell Tribunal, Franck had been out on the streets of Stockholm to show his opposition to American imperialism. The lawyer got caught up in a scuffle. He watched a group of policemen drag a demonstrator down a concrete stairwell into a parking lot and set upon him with their nightsticks. "You don't have to beat him raw!" Franck shouted. Before he could intervene, the man was loaded into a van and driven away.

Later that day, Franck received a phone call from his cousin Mirjam. Mirjam Israel was a prominent child psychologist who, in the clinic and from her advice column in the daily newspaper *Aftonbladet*, advocated the distinctly Swedish permissiveness that made most Americans want to jump on a chair and scream. She had recently separated from her husband, Joachim, a sociology professor and her coauthor on the landmark study *There Are No Naughty Children*, which discouraged the young from blind obedience to their parents. (Another outrageous Swedish idea.) In Joachim's absence, Mirjam had taken an American visitor under her wing. He was a sharply intelligent professional translator in his early thirties, Ohio-born, Caltech-educated, much traveled, and now sitting in a police cell, bruised and in need of legal representation. When Franck turned up at the police station, he was surprised to see a familiar face. The man who had been beaten in the parking lot. Michael Vale.

Vale claimed a scientific journal as his main employer. The fees must have been generous, as he seemed to have plenty of time on his hands, much of which he spent enthusing about Trotsky, or hanging out with the teenage Maoists of the Swedish anti-war movement. The May Day incident gave him a taste for action. When a large but unofficial Vietnam demonstration erupted across Stockholm on December 20, 1967, Vale turned his flat into a communications nerve center. His apartment had two telephone lines. One was used to receive incoming reports on police movements from activists calling in from phone booths across the city; the other was used to feed that intelligence back to demonstrators on the street. "We issued orders from there," one former teenage rebel told me. "Where to reassemble to keep the demonstration together after the police had shattered it. It was like a field battle." Michael Vale secured its victory.

THE AMERICAN DESERTERS Committee held its first meeting at the premises of Verdandi, a Swedish temperance society, on the afternoon of Sunday, February 11, 1968. The space was packed with people, though there were, perhaps, only fifteen Americans in the room; activists, hangers-on, and Social Democrat grandees made up the rest. The star attractions were the Intrepid Four, who, six weeks after landing in Sweden, had already acquired luxurious sideburns and Scandinavian girlfriends. Beside them moved a figure with just as strong a claim on history: Ray Jones III, a twenty-one-year-old private from Pontiac, Michigan, officially the first Vietnam deserter to seek asylum in Sweden. He and his German wife, Gabriele, had arrived from Germany via Copenhagen in January 1967 and had been quietly granted leave to stay by the Swedish Aliens Commission. After ten months of unemployment Jones had secured work teaching classes in jazz ballet, but having a regular job did not reduce his appetite for giving a hard political line to reporters who asked about his case. "Vietnamese people," he declared, "are being treated by Americans like the Negroes in America." For African American soldiers like him, Jones argued, desertion was "a matter of self-preservation."

Other strong characters were also making their presence felt. Men who had found their way to Sweden without making much-publicized tours of the Soviet Union. George Carrano was the son of an army colonel from Blauvelt, New York, who quickly emerged as the strategist and amanuensis of the American Deserters Committee. Fast-talking, hyperactive, with a fondness for gangster slang, George was a former merchant marine who had avoided military service on a technicality that nobody could quite understand. He had not put in a claim for humanitarian asylum but instead held a visa that allowed him to work in Sweden as a journalist—secured, he said, through connections made while studying at Columbia University. It was an odd story, but suspicion had yet to infect the body of deserter culture: he had his own apartment, his own typewriter, and an enthusiasm for the radical left. He had helped Michael Vale to draft the ADC's Statement of Principles and secured a letter of support from Bertrand Russell, the secular saint of the anti-war movement.

Robert Argento, a twenty-three-year-old deserter from Miami Beach, Florida, watched all this, wide-eyed. For him, it had already been an eventful Sunday. That morning he had stepped off the night train clutching a piece of paper slipped into his hand by a friend at the Club Voltaire in Frankfurt: the address of a student anti-war group that might help him claim asylum. When he turned up at their offices with his knapsack, suitcase, and guitar, nobody looked up. They were too busy preparing for a demonstration, writing banners and cranking out flyers from the mimeograph machine. When Rob announced himself as a deserter, the room stopped.

"Suddenly it was like one of those *Twilight Zone* episodes where everyone is frozen in their places," he told me. "It seemed like time stood still." Only for a moment, though. The next few hours were a blur of activity. Smiles broke out; coffee and pastries appeared. Good-looking young Maoists vied for Rob's attention, then whisked him off to an anti-war rally beside the ice rink in Kungsträdgården park. Rob listened to the speeches, declined the offer to give one of his own, and was then driven to the offices of Verdandi, where Hans Göran Franck shook him by the hand, welcomed him in a soft, mumbling voice, and invited him to join the meeting.

Michael Vale chaired. "He gave a rather disheveled impression," remembered Rob, "but was, at the same time, a man of authority and purpose with some sort of pent-up anger. At that time none of us knew who he was, except that he adeptly took over the meeting. We each assumed, individually, that the others knew him and that his assuming the leadership was through some sort of previous consensus." Looking back, Rob recalled the meeting as a series of fait accompli. Michael Vale taking charge; the committee called into existence; the skinny, elfin figure of Bill Jones, enthroned as spokesman. "Who were these guys?" he wondered. "All this time later, I'm still not sure."

IN THE STORY of the Vietnam deserters and war resisters who sought refuge in Sweden, no single figure looms larger than Michael Vale. He was not a big man. Not physically imposing. He seemed to wear the same clothes every day, and the cold Swedish weather gave him a permanent snuffle. When reporters turned up at the office of the American Deserters Committee, Vale declined to give interviews. When cameras clicked, he found ways to avoid their gaze. But he exerted a powerful influence upon those around him. He did it with twinkling charm and well-timed bursts of anger. He did it with an unforced interest in the opinions of young people and a strong grasp of their psychology. Some deserters to whom I spoke suspected there was a sexual element in his attachment to them, though if that was the case he never tried to steal a kiss. They respected him. Even the ones who didn't like him. An inner core of members developed such loyalty to him that it aroused comment. "I don't know what Michael did to them," one witness told me, "but he had power over them." That power earned him a nickname. The Gray Eminence—a title he rejected, though not perhaps too firmly.

Once the ADC was formed, Michael Vale's apartment became the hub of deserter life. A set of rooms where everyone was welcome, if they could bear the fog of cigarette smoke and the revolutionary disregard for cleanliness. Open one door and you might see Bill Jones sitting on the bed, a clattering typewriter on his knee, or George Carrano, arranging for deserters to give interviews to the press. (If the journalist was not sufficiently radical, a fee was levied.) Open another and you might discover a pair of copulating Swedish Maoists, or one of the drug-addled deserters to whom Vale gave space if they were trying to wean themselves from their habit. There was always somewhere to sleep, if you didn't mind the bathtub, or sheets waxy with dirt. And there was always something to read, if you liked Marx, Émile Durkheim, or Isaac Deutscher's three-volume life of Trotsky.

So much about Vale seemed questionable. He was not a deserter but the guardian of the deserters. He was not an anti-war campaigner but saw the war as an engine of revolutionary change. He devoted most of his time to political activity, and yet he was never short of cash. He told people that *Chemical Abstracts* paid his bills, but the ground between politics and psychology seemed to be his real enthusiasm. Michael Vale despised liberalism, individualism, the hippie counterculture. He wanted ADC members to peel away their attachment to these things in order to discover their true revolutionary selves. "Political dry-cleaning" was the term he favored. "Ego-stripping" was the one that would acquire currency in the group that surrounded him.

MIND GAMES WERE popular among radical groups of the period. If you followed the ideas of Wilhelm Reich, you could purge yourself of fascistic impulses by confessing your moral errors and having more orgasms. If you were a Maoist, you could achieve ideological purity by submitting to the brutal assessments of your peers. Michael Vale's methods involved the intense examination of his subject's class and family background, their political motivations, their dreams and fantasies. Those who had endured the treatment did not always want to discuss the experience. "It was personal and it doesn't belong in anybody's publication," said one old associate I met, staring angrily into the middle distance as I attempted to probe further.

A full and dramatic description was provided by the man with whom we began this story, Jim McGourty, the California marine with the false passport. "Ego-stripping," he explained, "meant to take people and tell them that they were really nothing. That they were pretentious and spoiled. Not cadre material. Not working-class. And on and on. To strip away the positive structure that person represented in terms of their mind, ego, and spirit. It was done one-on-one by Michael Vale, to people he wanted to get under his control."

I asked what Vale did and was struck by the raw, present-tense nature of Jim's reply. "He degrades you. Tells you that you're worth nothing. Unless you do what he says. When all the defenses are down, he imposes." It sounded like classic psychological manipulation: a long session of criticism and self-criticism, confession and humiliation, leading the subject to a state of submissive gratitude. Jim saw it as a form of brainwashing. There was a time, he said, when he and others at the core of their group would have done anything that Michael Vale asked.

Looking for clues to the view of the human mind that emerged in that crowded, smoky flat in central Stockholm, I ordered copies of all the translations for which Michael Vale had been credited during 1968 and 1969. Most were articles for the journal *Soviet Psychology*. Their emphasis was on research into the conditioned reflex—a phenomenon first recorded in 1902 by the Russian physiologist Ivan Pavlov, when he noticed that his dogs salivated at the sound of the dinner bell, even if no dinner was provided. The translations showed that by the 1960s researchers had upgraded from dogs to apes and monkeys. One experiment Michael rendered into English involved an attempt to induce neurosis in laboratory apes by passing an electric current through the milk they were given to drink. Another observed the effects of "conflict situations" on captive baboons and langurs. The scientists disrupted their sleeping and feeding routines, kept them physically restrained, then released them into an outdoor enclosure and observed the change in their behavior.

Michael had also toiled on a much longer work. *Forensic Psychiatry*, a textbook edited by Dr. Georgi Morozov, director of the Serbsky Central Scientific Research Institute of General and Forensic Psychiatry in Moscow. This book, with its lurid green psychedelic cover, was a landmark in the literature. But its significance was more political than medical. By early 1969, the Serbsky had begun to acquire a reputation as a psychiatric gulag, a place where doctors examined dissidents, diagnosed them with schizophrenia, and kept them docile with psychotropic drugs. Michael's translation gave English readers one of the earliest accounts of the methods used by Soviet doctors to manage rebellious minds.

IN 1973, LUCINDA Franks, a twenty-seven-year-old Pulitzer Prize–winning journalist, went to Sweden and interviewed deserters who had passed through Michael Vale's orbit: her book *Waiting Out a War* depicted men who were still smarting from the experience. "You've got to admire him, though," said one. "He's like a Rasputin and he's got technique. He browbeats new guys for the first few days and lets up and they end up loving him because it feels good when you stop banging your head against the wall." A comrade agreed. "Yeah, you've got to admire him . . . like you admire the work of a butcher."

Following the same trail four decades later, I found the quotes had barely changed. One old acquaintance bristled at the mention of Vale's name. He was, she told me, "a nasty piece of work . . . a monster."

Another suggested that he might have been a creature of the U.S. Army Security Agency, employed to spy on the deserters.

Margareta Hedman, a Swedish Maoist who hung around Mike's apartment and married Bill Jones just after her eighteenth birthday, had a different suggestion for me: "We assumed he was KGB." On the phone from a beachside apartment in Hawaii, a deserter named Thomas Taylor told me that his life in Stockholm had come unraveled after he spotted Vale in the lavatory at Verdandi, receiving a bag of cash from a representative of North Vietnam. "I thought that was treasonous," said Taylor. "Accepting money from the fucking enemy. Michael is lucky he's alive. My friend Paul wanted to kill him, but I talked him out of it." Another veteran told me: "I don't know exactly what Michael Vale was up to, but I do know that he was like the guy in the jungle in *Apocalypse Now*."

The most vivid account of Mike Vale's activities came from Clancy Sigal, a novelist and critic who, in the late 1960s, ran a safe house for deserters lying low in London. Sigal had been an army observer at the Nuremberg trials, where his plan to assassinate Hermann Göring failed when his service revolver was confiscated on the way to the trial. (Once inside, the *Reichsmarschall* bested him in a staring competition across the courtroom.) Working in Hollywood after the war—on pictures such as *Bride of the Gorilla*—he was blacklisted for distributing anti-McCarthy literature. The FBI tapped his phones, heard him refer to himself and his friends as Iranoff, Buljanoff, and Kopalski, and took them to be Russian spies, rather than three men making a joke about Greta Garbo's Soviet sidekicks in *Ninotchka*. This misunderstanding propelled Sigal toward London, where by 1968 he was receiving deserters in a flat above the Royal Asiatic Society on Queen Anne Street, and sometimes helping them move on to Paris and Stockholm.

"Nobody knew where Mike Vale came from," he told me at his kitchen table in West Hollywood. "Nobody. I'd run into his type before and always run a mile." What was his type? I wondered. "Conspiratorial," said Sigal. "He breathed conspiracy. Now, when you get guys who are already paranoid, all you have to do is send out that vibe and, right away, you will draw people into your circle. A lot of the guys in Sweden went through the Mike Vale training program. They scared the shit out of me. Much to Mike's delight."

Sigal showed me an extract from his diary for January 1969. "Movement protocol," it read, "demands I kiss the ring of the local Pope, 'Mike Vail' (perhaps his real name), the Stockholm stationmaster."

> A small, intense American in his angry forties, he insists on meeting in a gloomy Kungsgatan café whose only other customers at nearby tables appear to be his praetorian guard of young Americans in parkas and sulky expressions. Vail inhabits a world of festering paranoia and factional intrigue. Exile politics, always overheated, boils over in Sweden where there is so little else to do in long winter months. Toward the end of my visit, Vail and some of his boys entice me to a basement apartment in the Gröndal district and refuse to release me until I repent of my petty bourgeois crimes.

It wasn't the worst experience he had in Stockholm. Another group of deserters, he said, had interrogated him in a second-floor office. "They threatened to kill me unless I confessed to being a CIA spy," he recalled. "One of them pulled out a gun. So I climbed out of a window and jumped into a snowdrift."

WHAT HAD HAPPENED to Michael Vale? Where had he gone? I contacted dozens of deserters, but none seemed to know. The book stacks of the British Library held some evidence. A long trail of translations, leading from his Swedish period to the first decade of the present century. Pristine, unfingermarked copies of *Recent Trends in Soviet Psycholinguistics* and *The Genesis of the Stalinist Social Order*. His name listed on the editorial board of *Critique*, a journal of socialist economic theory published by Glasgow University. (Ralph Miliband, the father of a future British Labour Party leader, was involved in the early days.) I emailed its editor, who replied that he would try to discover whether Vale wished to be contacted. Months passed without an answer. Then I found an address for an American academic who had shared a conference platform with Vale in 2009, where he was described as an "independent scholar." She said she would forward my message. Vale himself replied within the hour.

His email was sent from Ukraine. A country which was then in turmoil, its president overthrown, tires burning in front of the parliament building, Russian tanks rattling over the border. It was not a place to visit without good reason, and being a spy seemed as good a reason as any. Vale suggested that we meet in London in the autumn. Three weeks later, however, he emailed again to say that he was already in town. I suggested lunch at my workplace, the BBC, but the idea didn't appeal to him. Instead, he proposed meeting in a park in North London.

"Islington Green. Last bench on the right. I'll be carrying something red."

3 / THE TRANSLATOR

WHEN I ARRIVED, the bench had two occupants. One with a greasy blue anorak and street-drinker's tan; one with a crumpled linen jacket spread over his knees like a seaside blanket. My eye moved from one to the other. "I guess you got the right guy," said the man with the linen jacket, lifting up his something red—one of those calculator-like gadgets for checking your account when far from the bank.

He looked down-at-heel, depleted. His face, as cracked as late-period Walter Matthau's, was shaved carelessly. If Michael Vale was in the pay of a government intelligence agency, then he needed to ask for a raise.

I tried to get some sense of his recent movements. He'd spent many years, he said, in France—so many that he now preferred to use the French version of his Christian name. He owned an apartment in Paris, but that was leased to a pair of Kazakh sisters, both astronomers, whose rent helped to fund his travels. Where had he been? Anywhere but America. There was no way he could go back there. Vietnam was now the place he felt most at home. The people were so friendly. Tactile. He had a theory that their sexuality was subtly different from that of Europeans. He'd coined a word for it: *integumental*. "Meaning that the skin—the integument—is a very sensuous organ."

His plans for a summer on the Black Sea coast, he explained, had been cut short. The weather was fine, but the trigger-happy nationalist militias patrolling the roads had not encouraged him to prolong his visit. (Like a Russian patriot, he spoke of "the Ukraine," subtly erasing its quarter century of independence.) Looking for a safer option, he'd driven to Bucharest and booked himself into a hostel, where his passport and wallet had been stolen by a plausibly charming American. Hotels, he said, were beyond his means, but he preferred it that way. The kids who stayed in cheap dormitories were better conversationalists. "They stop me from becoming fossilized," he said.

I took him to a restaurant at the top of the green. He looked at the menu as if he'd never seen one before. The place was noisy. So noisy that the waitress, noticing my voice recorder and notepad, moved us to a quieter table. Over fish pie and a bottle of house white, Michael Vale told me the story of his life. He was born on August 17, 1935, into a world of domestic mysteries. One of these was pretty easy for him to crack and concerned his strong physical resemblance to the head of the Garfield Uniform Company of Cincinnati, where his mother made up the bills in the mail-order office. The other concerned Richard Alvin Hug, the cigar store clerk who received undeserved top billing on Michael's birth certificate. Michael remembers glimpsing him only once, a figure on a brisk visit to his mother's sickbed. ("That was your father," said a helpful aunt.)

Mike's surname was an inheritance from his stepfather, a lawyer named Emil Vale. Emil, too, had lost his original name, on the advice of a judge who told him that Isador Velemirov sounded too Serbian for the Cincinnati circuit. In more painful circumstances, he had also lost his left arm—sheared off in a bus accident. (His buddy in the seat in front suffered the same bloody forfeit.) Michael had no fond memories of Emil. His jaw clicked when he chewed. His favorite movie was *Chetniks! The Fighting Guerillas*, a gung ho World War II action film about Yugoslavia's nationalist partisans. He once confined Mike to his bedroom for two and a half days, in a failed attempt to get the boy to call him "Daddy." The head of the Garfield Uniform Company didn't like Emil, either, and warned Mike's mother against the marriage. Eleanor Hug, however, was thirty-four years old and lumbered with the sadly inappropriate name of a husband with whom she had never lived. She made the pragmatic choice. As did her son. After agreeing to address Emil as "Pop," Mike never spoke another word to him again.

At fifteen, Mike said, he ran away from home and went on the road, selling magazine subscriptions door-to-door. It was, he said "a semi-hobo existence." He told impressionable farmers that both his parents were dead and he was raising money to go to college. He sometimes slept under railway bridges. He was slammed briefly against the body of a police car when a Pennsylvania housewife called the FBI after mistaking him for the Lipstick Killer, a serial murderer who had dismembered a six-year-old girl and scattered her remains through the Chicago sewer system.

When Mike tired of this species of hustling, he returned to Cincinnati and reenrolled in high school. Not the relatively prestigious one he had abandoned—alma mater of Rosemary Clooney and Doris Day—but a place where his classmates, most two years his junior, were the children of farmers and employees at the Procter & Gamble factory. He thrived there. "In those days," he said, "the system gave you second chances."

It also recognized talent. In 1954, Mike enrolled at Caltech, where he attended lectures by the physicist Richard Feynman. But the life did not suit him. He quit after a single term and began a bumpy four-college ride through an education system with limited sympathy for his preferred passions: by day, hermit-like occupation of the library among the shelves of Russian and German literature; by night, wandering around campus with a flask of gin and tonic, arguing about Kant and Hegel. Ohio State was the place he finally acquired his degree—by paying a fellow student to go through Reserve Officers' Training Corps in his place.

Michael might have studied further—the University of Chicago, he said, made him an offer—but in the summer of 1961 he went back on the road, fixing the pattern he follows to this day. Wandering the world, absorbing new languages, supporting himself with translation and teaching assignments, getting into long conversations with strangers.

Why, I asked, had he gone to Sweden? "For love," he said. But it soon became clear that he meant the opposite. Love was what he wanted to escape. In the summer of 1962 he fell into a relationship with a sculptor from Copenhagen. They met by accident on a hillside near Florence. Mike's car had broken down; she was sitting at a café table, saw him trudging by, took pity. Like all the girlfriends he would tell me about, she was a young mother with a husband somewhere in the background, out of focus.

The affair was intense. She introduced him to Scandinavian literature. They imagined themselves as the doomed couple in the New Wave film *Hiroshima Mon Amour*. The sculptor wanted to leave her husband, but Mike had no desire to settle down. He was, he said, in the grip of an existential crisis. "The basic philosophical question for me was: if human problems were caused by Man, then could Man solve them? Because if not, if there was simply some fault in human nature that was impossible to remedy, then the only way out was mysticism." It was a very Left Bank, Gauloises-smoking, turtleneck-sweater-wearing kind of crisis, but no less overwhelming for that. Which is why, to preserve his lover's marriage and his own solitary lifestyle, Mike crossed the Öresund strait to Sweden, then entered the radical intellectual circle that would appoint him guru to the deserters.

THROUGH A SERIES of chances he couldn't quite reconstruct, Mike found refuge in the household of Mirjam Israel, cousin of the Swedish lawyer Hans Göran Franck. (There was, insisted Mike, no romantic relationship between him and his new mentor.) One thing he recalled very clearly: it was a child of the household who triggered his political awakening— Dan Israel, Mirjam's twelve-year-old son. He and his schoolmates were passionately opposed to the war in Vietnam and already considered themselves Maoists. "These kids were amazing," said Mike. "They could summon up a demonstration overnight." They clamored around the visiting American and bombarded him with questions about Marx, the class struggle, and the aims of the North Vietnamese—none of which he could answer.

Intoxicated by their enthusiasm and embarrassed by his ignorance, Mike immersed himself in the literature of the Left. He read Marx for the first time. ("Holy shit!" he thought. "This guy can solve our problems.") He read Mao. ("A deviation.") He read Isaac Deutscher's three-volume biography of Leon Trotsky, the man who helped to lead the Bolshevik revolution—and, thanks to Stalin and an assassin's ice ax, its most celebrated martyr. And here the Michael Vale story required a dramatic organ chord and a flash of lightning. Deutscher's *Trotsky*—particularly the first volume, *The Prophet Armed*—was the book that illuminated the landscape and revealed to him his place within it. It was the story of an intellectual who became a revolutionary leader at the age of eighteen, who traveled the world, learning languages, writing for the radical press, and dealing with the chicanery of agents provocateurs. It seemed to speak directly to him, to offer him a blueprint for living.

"The abstract, humanitarian, moralist view of history is barren," Trotsky asserted. "But this chaotic mass of material acquisitions, of habits, of customs, and prejudices, which we call civilization, had hypnotized us all, giving us the false impression that we have already achieved the main thing. Now comes the war and shows us that we have not even crawled out on our bellies from the barbarous period of our history." For Trotsky it was the First World War; for Vale, it was Vietnam. When Hans Göran Franck offered him the job of overseeing the welfare of the American deserters arriving in the wake of the Intrepid Four, Mike was armed and ready.

"It was a fluke," he insisted. "I just happened to have done my homework. But it quite quickly became more than a managerial position. I was struck by the grandness of the task. It wasn't just about individual men who had come to Sweden for a variety of reasons, some of them pretty comical. These men were existential subjects. And I was responsible for them, because politically speaking, they were in a limbo. On the edge of the abyss."

HERE, BETWEEN THE main course and the pudding, we had arrived in Rasputin territory. It was time to discuss the story told by everyone who had ever written about him. How he'd become a guru to an army of troubled young men, teenagers and twentysomethings, far from home. How he had dismantled them, psychologically, in order to fit them for the new revolutionary age. Jim McGourty had called it brainwashing. Lucinda Franks had written about butchery. How, I wondered, would Michael describe it?

I showed him the passages from Franks's book. He smiled as he read it. "Yeah, I did that," he said. "But that wasn't the intent. I would harangue them for not wanting to be involved in politics. I would say: *you're in politics now whether you like it or not.* If you harangue forcefully, people come around." It was, he explained, a critical moment in history. "If it was true that the system had reached its end point, and there was going to be chaos, we had to be prepared for that. It's like you do with kids. You don't try to shield them from the realities around them. It was not a very nice or pleasant thing to do. But what else could I say to them? *You're safe, you're in Sweden, you're all right*? I couldn't tell them that because it wasn't true."

I thought Michael would be unwilling to discuss the subject of ego-stripping, but I was quite wrong. He was happy to share the history, theory, and practice. "I was obsessed," he said, "with trying to work out why we have the values we have." He had read Freud. He had read Wilhelm Reich. He wanted to use their therapeutic techniques to help the young men in his care. "It was a very serious and legitimate attempt to bring two theories together," he said. "If you're a social revolutionary you must do what you can within the domain over which you have power."

Michael did not require a closed room and a lamp shone in the eyes. He used intense, sustained questioning, either one-to-one or within a group. He was not afraid to interrogate any aspect of a subject's personality, politics, or emotional history. He was not afraid to shout. If they wept or broke down, that was a healthy part of the process. Those who did not rebel against him bound themselves to him. Sometimes, he said, he was embarrassed by their acts of submission. One man, he recalled, sought to please him by learning German, giving up pipe smoking, and spending his savings having one of Michael's favorite books expensively rebound.

Middle-class deserters required the most work. They had to be cured of their attachment to liberal concepts and values. ("Oh God," Michael exclaimed. "I can't even move my mouth to say these words. Self-realization! Individual creativity!") They had to learn that their objections to the Vietnam War were not moral, as they believed, but aesthetic. War offended them not because it was wrong, but because it was ugly. "They didn't like that message," he said. "But they all listened. Even the ones who didn't like me."

Most of all, the deserters had to relinquish their egotism and abandon their sense of themselves as heroic individuals taking a stand. "There was one guy who came over," said Michael, his mouth twisting in disgust. "A psychologist. A *liberal*. He brought his kids over. And he was so concerned about the war. He came in to me one day and he told me about a dream that he'd had. He'd dreamt that he was in a tank, driving down Pennsylvania Avenue from the Capitol Building. And he reaches the White House and it explodes. And he wanted me to interpret it. I was embarrassed for him! *What ego!*"

What, I asked, were the psychological consequences of this treatment? "Human beings have certain principles that we don't know about until we overstep them," he told me. "You can violate them, but once you do, you cease, even at the organic level, to be yourself. It exposes so many contradictions that you cease functioning as a human being." Did he drive people over the edge? "Getting angry with people and raising your voice, that's just normal," he said. "But in Sweden, it's not done." He started talking about the women who allied themselves to the deserters. "Those girls, those little girls. I would make them cry!" he hooted. "There was this one. She was such an animal. Such a frail little thing. I made her cry so many times!" He was speechless with laughter.

It sounded sadistic. It sounded damaging. It sounded like a Pavlovian experiment designed to produce tears rather than saliva. But Michael insisted that ego-stripping was an essentially harmless process. It could not produce psychological trauma, he argued, because the idea of psychological trauma itself was a myth.

To illustrate his argument, he told me about a thought experiment he once conducted upon himself, using a memory from his childhood in Cincinnati. When he was eight, he said, his grandmother went to a bingo game and left him playing in the street. Another boy, three or four years his senior, proposed that they go out to meet some girls.

"We didn't find any, of course," he recalled. "So he took me to a public toilet and tried to hump me from the back. He was totally ineffectual. It didn't last more than a couple of minutes. And I have that very stark memory, right? I could convert that into a real trauma. So I started thinking about it." He imagined a choir of people telling him that this older boy was bad and cruel. "And I can find myself in my mind, doing that.

Making it into a real event in my life. That's what the trauma merchants do." Similar figures in Sweden, he suggested, encouraged the belief that his work with the deserters amounted to a form of moral and psychological torture. "It left me open to charges."

What charges? I asked.

Mike Vale scanned the restaurant theatrically and replied in a stage whisper: "C . . . I . . . A!"

WE MET MANY times over the next three years. In the British Library. In coffee bars around London. In Paris, when he decided to sell his flat and move permanently to Vietnam. I never turned down one of his invitations. His charisma, I suppose, had begun to exert its effect over me.

Once he summoned me to Edinburgh, where he was registered with an NHS doctor. (Mike Vale must be one of the few International Men of Mystery with a hearing aid paid for by the British taxpayer.) On that occasion, we spent the day together. We had a long brunch at an American-style diner on Trongate, walked down the Royal Mile, and took refuge from the cold in a café, where he ordered soup and a sandwich. (Somehow he always managed to get two meals out of me.) I then accompanied him to the doors of the hospital. I asked him where he was headed next. As usual, it was some international hot spot. "To the Turkish-Syrian border," he said. "It looks very interesting down there."

Certain rituals developed. He would encourage me to track down figures from his past, often men whom he thought he might have treated too roughly. If they condemned him, like Jim, he shrugged. If they praised him, he would express satisfaction and joke about his "psychovoodoo skills."

Between these exchanges, Mike would maintain long periods of silence. Just at the point I'd convinced myself he'd been killed while poking his nose in some skirmish halfway across the world, an email would appear in my in-box: "Just a quick note to let you know I haven't died yet. Although, like any good lefty I do a bit of dying every day when I read the news."

We often talked about politics. Michael would usually take the pro-Kremlin line. He doubted that Russia was responsible for the crash of

Malaysia Airlines Flight 17. He asked why the BBC was not investigating a building in Ukraine that looked like a chocolate factory on the outside but was probably a Mossad listening post. Did I know that Petro Poroshenko, the president of Ukraine and a vocal opponent of Putin, had made his fortune in the confectionery business and was really a Jew named Valtsman? "It all fits," he said.

THERE ARE SOME people in life who become an object of speculation to all who know them. Michael Vale is one of them. If two of his acquaintances happen to meet, he is never far from the conversation. "Michael Vale," said Rob Argento, the deserter from Miami Beach, "was dedicated to an idea, single-minded, a manipulator who didn't really care for the consequences for any one individual because the end goal was so significant. And he had a way of attracting people who needed a leader. Or a father figure."

Perhaps Michael's own fatherless childhood helped him to understand what was required. Lost boys seemed most drawn to him, and their company amused him. "There was a guy called Hyatt," he told me, "who left his base in Germany because he was behind in the payments on his Ford Mustang. He only ended up in Sweden because he took a wrong turn on the road to Belgium. I tried to coach him for his interview with the Swedish police. I told him to say that he was opposed to the war in Vietnam. But the kid just looked at me and said, 'Where's Vietnam?' "

I heard many stories about the lost boys of the ADC. Walter Marshall, a reform school runaway who had joined and deserted from the army under a name borrowed from a stolen passport. (The name was unhelpfully exotic: his deception was revealed when the real Jesus Zeus Lorenzo Mungi was killed in action.) Billy Staton from Wichita, Kansas, hooked on speed, who spent an entire winter disassembling and assembling a clock. (He was jailed in 1970 for dealing LSD.) John Ashley, the son of a senior civilian official at the Pentagon, who tried to use a suicide attempt to avoid a Vietnam posting. (The army psychiatrist told him this was a logical response to his situation and declined to recommend a discharge.) A gifted writer who supplied a witty memoir of his desertion to the *Washington Post*, Ashley incinerated his talent with amphetamines. I'd hoped to track him down for this book. One deserter told me he'd seen Ashley drinking on the street. Others that he changed his name and died under it. The trail led to a homeless hostel in Stockholm and no further.

Another force drew members of the American Deserters Committee tightly together, one that would also eventually split them apart. The fear that there were spies working among them to break up their movement, to persuade, cajole, or blackmail them into returning. Almost all of my interviewees had a story about being followed. Michael Vale could describe the man who watched him take breakfast each morning at the all-you-can-eat buffet in Stockholm's Central Station. A draft resister from Seattle told me of the time two American eavesdroppers were found hiding in a cupboard in the office of the ADC. Bill Jones, the chief spokesman of the ADC, talked of anonymous threatening letters; the harassment of families back home in the States; calls made to deserters by strangers who asked to meet in out-of-the-way places.

The most insidious threat was that of infiltration. "If someone had a disagreement with somebody, they would accuse them of being a cop or an agent," said one old comrade of Michael Vale. "That, unfortunately, was absolutely part of the culture."

THE FIRST REAL blow came on March 12, 1968, when ADC members opened their newspapers to see a familiar face in an unexpected context. Ray Jones, ballet teacher and Sweden's first American deserter, was interviewed by reporters in the arrivals lounge of Frankfurt Airport. A pair of military policemen and the U.S. Army's regional provost marshal had met him at the steps of the plane and allowed him to speak to the press before being driven off to the stockade at Nuremberg—the very facility from which he had deserted. Jones stated that he was not a Communist. He said that he loved America and did not want to run from its problems. The Swedes had used him as a political pawn, and, moreover, they were not as liberal-minded as their reputation suggested. "The Swedes have a natural prejudice against black people," he said, "and know nothing about Negroes." How long did he think he would spend in prison? "I figure ten years," he said.

The photographs showed Jones staring grimly into the middle distance. In the foreground of one picture, his wife, Gabriele, looks apprehensively toward the camera, perhaps because the photographer has swooped in close to get a shot of the object lying between her and her husband—a bassinet containing their three-month-old son, Ray Jones IV.

Two days later, a man and a woman appeared in Stockholm to claim responsibility for wooing Jones back from exile. The man was William R. Russell, a corpulent, middle-aged American journalist from Mississippi, editor of a privately run newspaper for soldiers called *Army Times*. The woman was his twenty-five-year-old deputy Patton Lindsley Hunter. "I am here," Russell announced, in a rowdy press conference at the Strand Hotel, "to get in contact with the Americans who have left their military service and set up residence here. I cannot see why these boys should have to live outside their homeland for the rest of their lives."

Russell accused the Swedish government of exploiting the American exiles for its own political advantage. He alleged that some of the deserters were criminals on the run, and that others were agents provocateurs stirring up anti-American sentiment on behalf of some foreign power. He knew, he said, that many genuine deserters wanted to return home, but he did not know how. To those men, he offered a deal. He would be leaving Sweden on Sunday night. Anyone who wished to join him would be guaranteed a free flight out of Stockholm and lenient treatment from the military authorities. Those who waited, those who had to be brought in, could expect much rougher handling. Hans Göran Franck, he said, did not understand American law. "All these men are still enlisted, and belong to the army or the navy, and they will remain so for as long as they live."

The Swedish press was no happier to hear this than Michael Vale and Bill Jones. Reports in the next day's papers compared Russell to the protagonist of *The Quiet American*, Graham Greene's novel about an undercover CIA man in Vietnam. They also expressed puzzlement about who had sponsored his mission. "Despite our concerted attempts," wrote one journalist, "it was impossible to grasp on whose behalf he was speaking; for himself, for his publication, for his country, or for the army." The photographers were no more sympathetic: they took shots that depicted Russell as a startled amphibian in pencil tie. Not a man with whom you might elope on a night flight to Frankfurt.

The ADC struck swiftly back with its own press conference the next day. Russell's offer, it said, was a publicity stunt intended for an audience back home in the States, who might conclude that deserters who did not accept his generous terms were Communist sympathizers or Soviet agents. With impressive confidence, the committee accused Russell of being part of a CIA operation against them, which meant that the deserters must be near the top of the White House agenda and should expect the full force of the agency's firepower. It was a story of harassment, coercion, conspiracy—and Bill Jones could not resist a melodramatic flourish: "This is a clear indication that the U.S. government intends to abduct people who are seeking political asylum." Russell and Hunter were present to hear the statements. When they were spotted in the audience, they were asked to leave. One of the deserters pursued them down the street and asked Hunter out to dinner. She declined.

"We were sure that Russell and that girl weren't really journalists," said Michael Vale, as we sat drinking coffee at a café under the arches of St. Pancras station. "They were intelligence agents who'd come to Sweden to make a big propaganda ploy to get the deserters to go back."

"So what did you do?" I asked.

"The idea was a natural," he said. "It just flowed from the situation. We set a trap for them. And used a deserter as bait."

4 / THE JERUM AFFAIR

THE JERUM DORMITORY rises eight stories above Gärdet, a modernist garden suburb of Stockholm where lawns and footpaths connect concrete apartment blocks, and the odd fat brown rabbit lollops across the grass. The building, an accommodation block built for students of Stockholm University, has undergone some cosmetic changes since the 1960s. White plastic panels now clad its concrete skin. The basement has been transformed, incongruously, into a car dealership. But the student bicycles remain, rowed below the big plastic letters that spell out the name of the block, and memorialize what became the event old deserters still know as the "Jerum Affair."

It began at breakfast time on Sunday, March 17, 1968, when William Russell received a phone call from a mysterious man named John Armfield. (Actually a mysterious man named Michael Vale.) Armfield said he was a Fulbright scholar staying at a student hostel in Stockholm and had news of an African American deserter staying in the Jerum building who wanted to leave Sweden but lacked the documents to get through customs. Russell assured Armfield that if the deserter came to the U.S. Embassy, then the consul, Merl Arp, could authorize the necessary paperwork. Armfield said that wouldn't be possible. The man was too ner-

vous. The embassy would have to come to him. Russell agreed to the proposal. He summoned Patton Hunter from her hotel room. He called the
embassy and got Merl Arp out of bed. And with a typewriter and a sheaf
of blank forms, the three took a taxi out to Gärdet to receive their prize.

The ADC's own account of the affair, preserved in the personal
archive of Hans Göran Franck, contains what purports to be a transcript
of the call between Russell and Vale. Russell is allocated lines that might
have suited Robert Mitchum in *Cape Fear*. He talks about putting troublesome deserters in straitjackets, or kidnapping them, or subduing them
with the weaponized charms of Patton Lindsley Hunter. "Patton can take
care of him," he says. "She'll bring a lot of joy to him."

"Who is the girl?" asks Vale.

"Oh, she's another agent," replies Russell.

Vale asks why any deserter would trust an agent.

"Because he's a nigger," says Russell.

Vale asks him to repeat the word.

"Ah didn't say nigger," reads the transcript. "Ah said *negro*."

When I asked Michael Vale about these events, I received a spontaneous dramatic performance. Michael reenacted his version of the phone
conversation with Russell, holding an invisible receiver to his ear and
adopting the accent of a fastidious Mississippi gentleman. *You have a
boy for us? We sure would appreciate that. That would be mighty fine.*
The tone was appropriately stagey. The whole affair was a piece of theater. Jimmy Dotson of Ballinger, Texas, who had recently deserted from
his garrison in northern Italy, was cast as the young African American
deserter who, like Ray Jones, had grown disenchanted with Swedish
society and longed to return home. George Carrano, the fast-talking
New York draft dodger with the puzzling visa status, was also a part of
the sting. His girlfriend was awarded the role of Dotson's Scandinavian
sweetheart. A photographer and reporter from *Tidsignal*, a left-wing student newspaper, were directed to hover in the wings, awaiting their cue.
Down below, Vale and Carrano watched Russell, Hunter, and Arp ascend
the stairs, then indulged in a bit of comic business with the taxi driver. "I
did the stupidest thing," Michael told me. "I should have taken their bags
out and looked through them. Carrano suggested it, but I said it was

against the rules of the game." Instead, they sent the car away. It was probably a prudent decision. Photographing a U.S. diplomat was one thing. Stealing his luggage would have been espionage.

PATTON LINDSLEY HUNTER retired from journalism long ago and is now an artist who paints and teaches in the Tampa Bay region of Florida. She was rather surprised to be contacted about a strange incident in a Swedish dormitory five decades ago, but she had admirable recall of the details. She described William Russell as secretive and self-centered. She knew he had a strained relationship with his family back home in the States, and she recalled his purchase of an armful of out-of-season Christmas gifts, for dutiful dispatch later in the year. She remembered the buildup to the trip: Russell looking pleased with himself and making excited calls from the *Army Times* office in Frankfurt. She remembered flying back from Sweden with Ray and Gabriele Jones, Russell trying to hide his disappointment when only a handful of journalists turned up to meet them at Frankfurt Airport. She also remembered that when she and Russell came back to Stockholm to fish for more deserters, Merl Arp was not an enthusiastic participant in the plan. "Even though I was right in the middle of it, I didn't really know what was going on," she said. "But I guess Bill chose to take me to Sweden out of all his reporters because I was young and single, and these were young boys he was trying to attract."

As her name suggests, Patton Hunter is from a military family. A well-connected one: in 1968, her uncle was the head of Army Intelligence in Heidelberg. ("He took me aside and warned me that I was mixing with some dangerous people," she recalled.) However, despite this background—and the pro-war editorial line of *Army Times*—she had a strong personal sympathy for the deserters' cause. Secretly, Hunter said, she admired their political stand, their articulate speeches, even the intelligence they had shown in setting the trap at the dormitory. "It was a smart thing to do," she said, "because Bill bit hard on that bait."

When Hunter, her boss, and the diplomat arrived at the correct room in the Jerum dormitory, they found it occupied by two Swedish women, one of whom introduced herself as the girlfriend of the deserter who wished to return. Moments later James Dotson appeared. They sat down to discuss how to proceed. Russell said he was pushing the authorities to begin the trial of Ray Jones as briskly as possible—so that the other deserters would feel assured about the promise of light treatment. "Light?" Dotson asked. "What do you think is a light sentence?" Russell estimated four months or less. Merl Arp unpacked his portable typewriter and began taking down Dotson's details. The papers were soon ready to sign.

"Then," said Hunter, "there was a commotion and three or four guys ran in and started taking pictures of us. Bill said: *Smile, Pat, just smile, they won't hurt you!* I remember that I tried to stand in front of the guy who was signing the papers so they couldn't get a good shot of him. I did that out of pure instinct." Russell asked the intruders what they wanted. "You can read about it in tomorrow's paper," they declared. The camera clicked, bodies jostled, Hunter, Russell, and Arp went skittering back down to the ground floor, and the ADC and its allies had their story. The American consul and two supposedly independent journalists caught in a student bedroom, attempting to cajole a deserter into going home. Jim Dotson saved from the same fate as Ray Jones. A CIA plot foiled.

The Soviet daily *Izvestia* spoke of a "stormy operation" carried out in neutral Sweden by the U.S. intelligence services. *Tidsignal* had thunder of its own: "There is evidence for close collaboration between the U.S. Embassy in Stockholm and the secret U.S. agents who are working on the ground in Sweden. They are a threat to political refugees who have been granted asylum in our country. The government should take action against these agents for the security of these refugees." The ADC handed out a press release bearing the names of seven embassy employees they believed were CIA officers. One deserter proposed that the ADC should petition Merl Arp for office space and a phone line at the U.S. Embassy, saving him the expense of tapping their phones and keeping them under surveillance. "See how we love our country?" he said. "We even save the taxpayer money."

Was Russell working for the CIA or some other American intelligence service? "I thought that was laughable at the time," said Patton Hunter. "Bill was such a goofy person. Back then I got the feeling he was doing it because it was a really big story and he wanted to cover it. He wanted the glory." It was, perhaps, an understandable desire.

William Russell was a man with a great future behind him. At the end of the 1930s he had been working as consular clerk at the U.S. Embassy in Berlin, processing visas for the thousands attempting to leave the country. His well-received account of these years, *Berlin Embassy*, published in 1941, argued that the majority of Germans were not fanatical Nazis, but politically apathetic—and warned that America might succumb to the same darkness. During the forties he maintained an impressive double career. He spent four years attached to U.S. military intelligence in London, working on battle strategy and liaising with his opposite numbers in the exiled governments of Poland, Norway, Belgium, and Czechoslovakia. At the same time, he produced a steady output of fiction and plays that seem strong evidence against the ADC's portrait of him as a drawling southern racist.

His novel *Robert Cain* is about a white Mississippi planter who fails to save his mixed-race friend from a lynching. His play *Cellar* depicts a gang of thieves who leave their only African American member to die of a bullet wound. (George Orwell read it, tagged him as a writer worth watching.) Once hostilities had ceased, Russell took an apartment in Greenwich Village and enrolled at the Professional Writers Clinic of New York University, where Saul Bellow was his tutor. The result was *The Wind Is Rising*, a novel so critical of American racism that its publisher felt compelled to expurgate the U.S. edition.

By the late 1950s, however, Russell's lights were not quite so bright. He worked two years as a deck yeoman in the merchant marine, crossing and recrossing the Atlantic on board the USS *General A. W. Greely*. In 1955, he moved to Frankfurt and found a job as the office manager of a car showroom. By 1957 he was churning out pieces for Army Times Publications and living the uncertain life of a freelance reporter. His personal life also acquired a complexity that would not have endeared him to the Central Intelligence Agency. He began a relationship with a German man, who fathered a child for them to adopt. But Russell's lover ran off with its mother, leaving the journalist holding the baby—a situation that seemed to suit everyone concerned. "He was," said Hunter, "a good father to that child."

Russell's paternal instincts, however, did not extend to Ray Jones, the deserter he delivered from Stockholm. As the reporter played his part in the Jerum Affair, Ray Jones was cracking up in a cell in Nuremberg. On his first day in the stockade he charged at an armed guard, hoping, it seems, to earn a fatal bullet. A couple of days later he attempted to slash his wrists with a razor blade. Soon, however, some good news came. Despite his fifteen months in Sweden, Jones was not to be charged with desertion. Instead, he would be court-martialed for going absent without official leave, which carried a much milder punishment.

On April 3, 1968, ten officers of the Fourth Armored Division heard the details of his case. Jones had traveled with forged papers from Italy to Denmark to Sweden, and he had come to Frankfurt with William Russell to prove that he was not a political extremist. "I think communism is wrong," he attested, "and not the answer for the black people."

Jones's defense counsel asked the court to consider the political impact of their judgment: too harsh a penalty, and no more men would be coming back from Sweden. The argument stuck. Jones was handed a bad conduct discharge and four months' hard labor. He managed a weak smile as sentence was passed. Gabriele Jones ran to the barrier that separated spectators from the court. The military police looked the other way to allow the couple an embrace before Jones was taken back to the stockade.

In Stockholm, the deserters computed the news. One, twenty-four-year-old Parker Smith, from Glen Ridge, New Jersey, put his thoughts on paper and sent them to Hans Göran Franck: "Ray will now be free, after he completes his four months of hard labor, to take his white wife and his bad conduct discharge back to the freedom and opportunity of the black ghetto."

That, more or less, was what Jones did. After four months of rock breaking in the stockade in Germany, he returned to Michigan but was no happier there, failing to find work and complaining of harassment by the FBI. He and his family flew back to Stockholm in May 1969, where Jones made an application for Swedish citizenship. The bureaucratic process ensured that he left another account on the record—a darker and more paranoid picture of his dealings with the American authorities.

In Ray Jones's deposition to the Swedish Aliens Commission, he claimed that the decision to return was forced upon him by the bullying and threats. General Lewis Shull, Jones claimed, had called him at home to warn that the Swedes might easily be persuaded to revoke Jones's asylum status, which would force him to relocate to a Communist country. "I was then warned by Mr. Russell that if a word of this was repeated I or my wife and child would end up dead by forces which he did not represent. And that these forces would not hesitate to do so if they thought I was trying to be a hero revolutionary." Once he had agreed to come quietly, said Jones, Russell used the flight to Frankfurt to coach him in the anti-Swedish sentiments he made to journalists at the airport. Jones also claimed that Russell had offered him a $10,000 advance for a book in which Jones would denounce communism and declare his support for the Vietnam War.

As HAPPENED SO often in the history of the deserters, every door seemed to lead to another. Jones's deposition contained a paragraph that added another mysterious figure to the story. "One of the first days of March I was contacted by Richard Gibson, an American journalist, who expressed to me the fact that I was in danger and received no protection from the Swedish people and police. He threatened me that I could be killed by the American intelligence [services] for playing political games with them. I was frightened by this. . . . He expressed that he knew of similar situations where people playing politics were harassed or killed."

Who was Richard Gibson? For once, the archive was bounteous. Richard Thomas Gibson—born Los Angeles, 1931—was the first African American reporter on the CBS staff and the acting executive secretary of the Fair Play for Cuba Committee. He was also a man who seemed to have lived his whole life in the shadow of other people's doubts. His declassified FBI and CIA files were easily available online, and they told a peculiar story.

Here, in cables and cuttings, was an account of his dismissal from *Révolution Africaine*, a Marxist magazine funded by the Chinese government, whose editor believed him to be an agent sent "to penetrate the ranks of the international revolutionary movement." Here was an FBI report from August 1961, speculating how Richard Gibson's affinity for prostitutes might be used to disrupt his political activism. Here was a letter typed by Gibson the following summer, offering the CIA his cooperation in exchange for "expenses." (It was signed "A Friend," and invited a discreet reply.) Here was paperwork demonstrating that, a few months later, Gibson had made similar overtures to the FBI, which sent a pair of special agents to meet with him and pump him for background data on Cuba.

Files of this kind are not customarily released until after the death of the subject. One source suggested that Gibson had succumbed to cancer in Belgium in the early 1980s. I was surprised, therefore, to see his name in the London phone book. And more surprised when he agreed to meet me.

I FOUND RICHARD Gibson in an agreeably shabby flat two floors above Little Venice, where the Regent's Canal flows toward the gardens of London Zoo. A neatly dressed octogenarian with a Peter Lorre giggle, he had forgotten our appointment but invited me up all the same; he put coffee on the stove, gave me the tour. He showed me brittle editions of his old books, the bed given to him by John Kerry's great-aunt Clara, the space on his shelves that once housed his personal archive, now administered by George Washington University. A retired air force colonel, he explained, had brokered the deal but was now failing to return his emails. To demonstrate, he wheeled over to the computer and invited me to inspect his in-box, which was stacked with pornographic spam. "I have a cousin in the CIA," he twittered as he clicked through the files, "and she's always saying to me—remember, there's such a thing as freedom of information. You don't know what things they're going to pull out about you."

We sat at the kitchen table, beside which was a huge sack of rice, the property of his lodger. Richard poured coffee, and I spread copies of Ray Jones's documents in front of him. At first he ignored them, preferring to rehearse some of his favorite stories. A jaunt in Mozambique with Robert Mugabe. The day he took Fidel Castro to the Hotel Theresa in Harlem for a meeting with Malcolm X. His trip to the Cuban frog farm owned by William Morgan, the *"yanqui comandante"* who helped bring

Castro to power and was later executed for plotting against him. Other anecdotes, numerous and wistful, laid their scene in brothels from Santiago to Copenhagen.

Prostitution was a leitmotif of our conversation: the streets of Richard's memory were thronged with call girls. Gradually, however, we inched closer to Stockholm, and the trips he made in 1967 and 1968 to report on the proceedings and aftermath of the Russell Tribunal. His employer, in this instance, was *Tuesday*, a black interest supplement slipped into newspapers across America and, it turned out, secretly funded by the CIA through a front organization, the Congress for Cultural Freedom. The spooks, it seems, settled Richard Gibson's bill for his trips to Sweden.

Sex, he suggested, was what had attracted the deserters to radical politics. Trotskyists, he said, "always had girls who would lie down for you. That is true. I remember one very attractive young lady. I certainly took advantage of her. Or she took advantage of me . . ." He loosed another giggle.

Richard picked up Ray Jones's deposition and read it aloud. He seemed unhappy to see his name in the first paragraph. The story, he said, was all wrong. He had not contacted the deserter, still less threatened him. Instead, Jones and his German girlfriend had turned up outside his hotel and asked for help. "So I gave my advice. I said to him if he didn't want to go to the States maybe he should go to China."

Richard had contacts at the Chinese Embassy in Cairo and experience of using this route out of trouble—the previous year he had helped Robert F. Williams, an activist and the author of *Negroes with Guns*, to leave Cuba and acquire asylum in Peking. The two men remained in touch by letter. Williams, said Richard, was having an interesting time in China, where he lived a comfortable life, had regular meetings with Chairman Mao, and made revolutionary broadcasts to African American soldiers serving in Vietnam. Perhaps Jones could join him there? But Jones didn't fancy a new life in Red China. Perhaps Sweden was far enough from home. Perhaps he feared entrapment.

With this, Richard's recollections ran dry. He asked me—not for the first time—whether Ray Jones was alive or dead. The question seemed to be gnawing at him. I couldn't supply him with an answer.

Richard sent me on my way with a friendly warning. In 1985, he recalled, he'd successfully sued an author who'd accused him of being a CIA agent. It produced a nice little check from his British publisher. There might have been more, had he decided to pursue it. I took the hint, but he need not have worried. A few days after my visit I read the CIA file in which the agency expressed its feelings about my interviewee. Gibson, the agency decided, was not good informant material, but "a weasel-like character, evasive, opportunistic, with very little or no moral fiber at all."

A full two years later, I discovered the fate of Ray Jones III. He had been expelled from Sweden in 1979 and was alive, if not well, in his hometown of Pontiac, Michigan. His wife, Gabriele, had taken her own life in 1986. The information was supplied by Ray Jones IV, the baby in the bassinet, who wanted to impress a point on me. You don't need to be in combat to suffer the traumas of war.

THE JERUM AFFAIR was a famous victory for the ADC, but it also produced a subtle poison. It demonstrated that the deserters' anxieties about agents, surveillance, and infiltration were not entirely irrational. It proved that paranoia had its uses. But it made the limits of those uses much harder to perceive. Now everyone was a potential spy. Journalists who wanted to report deserter stories. Liberal Swedes who offered the spare bedroom to a fugitive in need. The Swedish Committee for Vietnam and its vice chairman, Bertil Svahnström, above all. For Mike Vale and Bill Jones, Svahnström became a dragon to be slain. Fifty years on, the mention of his name caused both of them to wince. "That awful man!" Mike exclaimed. Bill's old speeches revealed his position: "A prominent Swedish figure," one said, "tried to infiltrate our organization and made offers of financial assistance if we would become politically silent." His words bent the meaning of infiltration beyond recognition, but his listeners were the young student Maoists who prayed for the victory of the Vietnamese National Liberation Front over America—and they liked what they heard.

"Bill Jones was the type of guy who would say 'damned fascist swines' and that kind of rhetoric," said Mats Widgren, a former spokesperson for these radical groups who sat beside Bill at many press conferences in early 1968. "But we were very happy to hear his accusations against Svahnström. We were embracing that ultra-leftist thinking even though we sometimes thought that he went too far." Bill poured scorn on the Swedish Committee for Vietnam and attacked Svahnström's campaigns for peace in Indochina. Peace implied compromise, settlement, a recognition of American influence in the region. The ADC favored complete victory for the forces of Ho Chi Minh. "We have chosen a side in the struggle and abide by the choice," said Bill, "and lest we be accused by bigoted minds of cowardice, let them know that we shall continue to act, and that our enemies will continue until they silence us with their guns." Talk like this was thrillingly un-Swedish.

COLD WAR BETWEEN the ADC and the Swedish Committee for Vietnam. Hot rhetoric from Bill Jones. Mutterings about spies and infiltrators. This was the background noise in May 1968 as Beheiren's second batch of smuggled exiles sat in their Stockholm police cells, waiting for their paperwork to be completed. Mark Shapiro, Terry Whitmore, and the four other men who'd made that terrifying jump from a Japanese fishing boat to a Soviet trawler had no knowledge of the fevered conversations going on beyond the room. They did not know that their arrival had been anticipated for weeks and had scant sense that they had become glittering trophies for whichever faction they decided to favor.

Their luster was a product of their combat experience. Bill Jones was a hospital technician. Mike Vale and George Carrano weren't even deserters. But the six coming from Leningrad had seen action, and this made them assets of tremendous value.

Military officials had always insisted that the kind of men who deserted were the "rotten few" who would be unlikely to be trusted with active duty. "We'd rather not take a chance on foul-ball soldiers under battle conditions," said an army spokesman in January 1968. "It wouldn't be fair to GIs whose lives are at stake." But a month before those remarks were made, Terry Whitmore had been on patrol near Con Thien, just a thousand yards below the demilitarized zone that separated North from South Vietnam. His platoon stumbled into the crosshairs of an enemy company three times its strength. Men were cut down around him. As the bullets flew, Whitmore pulled his wounded commanding officer to safety, then did the same for a second soldier. But the bomb crater in which he'd taken refuge came under mortar attack, leaving a hundred pieces of hot shrapnel fizzing in his flesh. For these actions, Whitmore had earned his Purple Heart. If he joined the ADC, then the arguments about "foul-ball soldiers" would be much harder to make.

After two days of custody, Mark and his comrades were allowed to walk free. Five went to the ADC offices in a large, scruffy Volkswagen bus with Mike Vale at the wheel. Kim Jin-Su, who had already decided that any life in a Communist society was preferable to being part of a left-wing group in a capitalist one, took a more radical path. Looking for clues to what became of him, I found a Japanese TV documentary in which a former Beheiren activist went to the States with the same question on his mind. The filmmakers visited Mr. and Mrs. Philip Griggs, the white couple who had adopted Kim after his parents were killed in the Korean War. In the living room of a modest bungalow, Philip Griggs wept as he watched old footage of his lost boy denouncing the imperial ambitions of the United States. "He was wrong," said Mr. Griggs. "My gut feeling says that he was one scared GI who found a way out." The old man had his own denunciation to make—of Beheiren and the Soviets, for using his boy as a political pawn.

Kim's old friend Mark Shapiro, who had traveled with him in the hold of a Russian trawler, knew the next part of the story. As we barreled through the San Diego traffic, he told me what he knew. "He went to North Korea," Mark said. "He's still there. I believe he's a major in the army." Mark spoke wistfully of his lost comrade. He was trying to contact him, but the process was complicated. "It's like doing a crossword puzzle in a dark room," he said.

The others in his party did not travel so far. Having boarded the ADC bus, most found berths with anti-war activists among Hans Göran Franck's circle. Mark was billeted in the spare bedroom of the sociologist Joachim Israel—a lively household in which Soviet diplomats were sometimes to be found sleeping off their hangovers on the settee. Phil Callicoat lodged with an *Aftonbladet* journalist and her psychologist husband in an apartment in central Stockholm. Joe Kmetz was taken in by a couple of pacifists in the Södermalm district, who turned out to be swingers of the sort depicted in *Sweden: Heaven and Hell*. Terry Whitmore slept in a makeshift bed in the kitchen of Jay Wright, a New Orleans deserter who, he discovered, had also come to Sweden via Moscow, but with rather less ballyhoo. The pair became fast friends. A furious Bertil Svahnström accused the ADC of kidnapping the men, but he need not have worried. Kmetz and Arnett soon drifted away from the group. Phil Callicoat moved in with a Swedish girlfriend and then went to the coastal town of Oxelösund to find work on the docks. (He managed a week before he was laid off.) Only Mark Shapiro and Terry Whitmore remained faithful to the ADC project.

In May 1968, that project was gathering momentum. Volunteers were needed to give speeches on campuses and at anti-war rallies and to talk to journalists asking for interviews. (Student publications got the deserters for free; American papers were charged a hefty administration fee.) Copy was required to fill the pages of the *Second Front*, a newspaper distributed to potential deserters on bases in West Germany and printed for the ADC by an anti-war press in Paris.

New arrivals wrote up the story of their desertion and exhorted readers to acquire one of their own. The tone was friendly and foul-mouthed. "The man with the guts is the one who tells Uncle Sam to fuck himself," declared Don McDonough, a deserter from Boston who, like Bill, had been educated in a Catholic seminary. "The more shit you will take, the better the officers like it," argued former petty officer Ray Krzeminski, late of the aircraft carrier USS *Wasp*. "The more you suffer, the more those sadistic bastards enjoy it." The paper also carried poetry, graphic pictures of U.S. soldiers posing with the severed heads of National Liberation Front fighters, and travel tips for fugitives coming north to Sweden. (Legal entry with a passport was preferable to more exuberant strategies, such as screaming up in a stolen jeep or arriving by hijacked plane.) A sister publication, the *Second Front Review*, featured longer, less demotic pieces, and was eventually published in both English and Swedish.

Not all their propaganda was printed. It also came in the form of radio programs. Vincent Strollo, a mechanic's son from Philadelphia who deserted from a military hospital near Landstuhl, told me how these came about: "At one point very early on I was so disgusted with the war that I said, 'Well, I can go to North Vietnam and fight for the North Vietnamese.' So we went for a meeting at their mission in Stockholm." This generous offer was declined, but the officials proposed another idea. "So myself and a number of other people made tapes, with a lot of music, encouraging men to desert."

These programs—many featuring a jive-talking Terry Whitmore—were recorded on a reel-to-reel tape deck at the ADC offices, hand-delivered to the North Vietnamese mission, and sent on to Hanoi, where they were played on *Second Front Radio*, along with demoralizing sentimental music and the admonishing voice of a female announcer nicknamed Hanoi Hannah. By 1970, the mix included Steppenwolf's "Draft Resister," Bob Dylan's "I Threw It All Away," a Mandarin version of "The Internationale," and sardonic patter that was the unconscious house style of propaganda stations throughout the twentieth century: "Hello, all you happy defenders of freedom out there in Viet Cong land. This is *Second Front Radio* prepared by the American Deserters Committee here in Stockholm, Sweden, and broadcast to all you schmucks and peons in Southeast Asia over Liberation Radio, South Vietnam. The National Liberation Front urges you to form local cease-fires with the local Viet Cong units. You form your own peace talks. Only you can end this war. Demand to be sent home immediately. Kidnap an airplane, go home anyhow!"

THE DESERTERS PUT on a special performance for Independence Day 1968. Its leading man was Chuck Onan, a marine from the Chicago projects—an eighteen-year-old boy with long curly hair and a short temper, who had arrived in Sweden in February and had become one of Michael Vale's most loyal lieutenants. Its unwitting host was Ambassador William Womack Heath, newly returned from Washington and protected by a pair of armed security men.

Heath decided to coax some warmth back into Swedish-American relations with a Fourth of July garden party on the embassy lawn. Hundreds of guests, a mixture of U.S. tourists and diplomatic families, turned up. Hot dogs and bottles of Coca-Cola were handed out. A band played "The Star-Spangled Banner."

But just as Heath was about to begin his speech, twenty deserters—among them Chuck Onan, Bill Jones, and Mark Shapiro—leapt over a rope barrier and sat cross-legged under the flagpole. George Carrano, standing on the sidelines, started up a chorus of "U.S. out of Vietnam!" A knot of outraged guests tore the wooden stakes from the grass and steamed into the cordoned area to confront the protestors. One hundred fifty Swedish police officers followed. Chuck Onan shinnied up the flagpole. A security guard dragged him down, got him in a headlock until he lost consciousness, and threw him into the back of a paddy wagon with six of his comrades. George Carrano was too slow and felt the hand of the law on his shoulder. The rest of the ADC contingent melted into the crowd.

As the police van screeched off, Gunnar Helén, the governor of the county of Kronoberg and heir to the leadership of the liberal Folkpartiet, stood on the lawn and gave a speech about how Swedes were too sensible to listen to the sloganeering of the New Left.

That night, his words acquired a measure of irony. A hundred-strong crowd from the ADC and the radical student groups stood outside the police station and chanted their demand for the release of Bill, Mark, Chuck, and their fellow prisoners. "And inside," Mark Shapiro told me, "all the Swedish prisoners started banging their tin cups against the wall and shouting, 'We don't want the Americans in here!'" The duty officer, fed up with the noise and unable to locate the correct paperwork, unlocked the cell doors and propelled Bill, Mark, Chuck, and the others back out on the street, much to the delight of the demonstrators.

Mark Shapiro looked back on that day with pride. So much that on July 4, 2007, he went back to Stockholm, put on his best suit, and attempted to gate-crash the Independence Day garden party at the U.S. ambassador's residence. "Sir, what are you here for?" asked the security guard. "I'm here to protest peacefully," replied Mark. The old deserter enjoyed telling me the story. Half a century on, his radical credentials were still intact. "You could almost see the smoke coming out of his ears," he said.

We began chatting about the people who had accompanied him to the cells on that afternoon in 1968. "Who are you talking to next?" he asked. I told him that I was about to fly to Eugene, Oregon, to see his old comrade Chuck Onan. The look on Mark's face was pretty unambiguous. He thought this was a terrible idea. All the same, I got on the plane.

5 / PETUNIA

MARK SHAPIRO WAS not the only person to warn me off a meeting with Chuck Onan. Chuck, I was told, had a complicated relationship with the truth. But Michael Vale encouraged me to get in touch, curious to know what kind of impact he'd made on the life of his former follower. "I am not so sure," Michael said, "whether it might not be likened to that of a wrecking ball." He asked me to send Chuck a book on his behalf. *The Birds*—a novel by the Norwegian author Tarjei Vesaas. I read it before I mailed it. The protagonist is a naïve man named Matthew, who comes to an unfortunate end in an icy Scandinavian lake.

Chuck's welcome, however, couldn't have been warmer. I'd booked myself into a nearby motel, but he insisted that I stay in the spare room of his home, a bungalow beside a gravel pit on the industrial edge of Eugene, Oregon. Sitting in his kitchen, with his agreeably scruffy terrier, Ninja, asleep under the table, Chuck told me his story. He had, he said, once worked as a management consultant. A course in Ayurvedic medicine, however, had so convinced him of the health benefits of the cannabis plant that he took advantage of Oregon's liberal drug laws and set up a business cultivating and refining medical marijuana. He sold cannabis oil capsules, cannabis watermelon drops, cannabis sour worms.

His commitment to the drug was an article of faith. Chuck, I learned, was the founding pastor of Canna Church Rocks, a group that assigned a sacramental role to the spliff. Marijuana, he asserted, brought spiritual as well as medical benefits. It allowed him access to a higher astral plane. Recently, while in a trance, he had seen a vision of his long-estranged brother, bathed in an aura that indicated his spirit had departed the earth. Tears filled his eyes as he described the experience. Then he pulled back his long steel-gray hair to reveal a scar: marijuana, he said, mixed with black pepper and pink Himalayan sea salt, had cured his stage-four melanoma. I became lost in his explanation of the cancer-killing properties of cannabinoids.

Despite this enthusiasm, Chuck's business seemed in trouble. His website pictured thriving greenery, but the propagation bays in his garden were empty; the fence used to screen the crop from the street was in a state of disrepair; the car parked outside his house was clearly going nowhere. The dry yield of an older crop, stored in airtight jars on a kitchen shelf, seemed to be his main source of income. Staying with him showed me something of the precarious nature of American life. When we left the house, either to go for burgers at a nearby strip mall or to walk Ninja by the river, we passed a small encampment of homeless men. Faces deformed by poverty and alcohol. It was a picture out of Steinbeck. They sat in folding chairs beneath the trees, waiting for America to be somewhere else. And each time we passed, Chuck gave them a respectful nod.

The 2016 U.S. election was only a few months away. Chuck was voting for Donald Trump. Chuck wanted that wall on the Mexican border, and he scorned those who said it couldn't be built. Chuck believed that a Muslim invasion of America was taking place and that rape was the enemy's weapon of choice. He'd been thrown off Facebook for saying so, but that only increased his sense of being in the right. Feminism, too, was a dangerous and unjust force. Chuck played me videos of his favorite alt-right commentators explaining why. I told him I couldn't concur. But it was easy to see why he was angry. What had America ever done for him?

CHUCK ONAN HAD a specific reason for giving me an interview. He wanted to defend the reputation of Michael Vale. Before my arrival, they had spoken together on the phone. It was their first contact since the early seventies. "In Vietnam," he said, "Michael should be a hero." We discussed the charges against his old mentor. The CIA rumors. The accusations of psychological manipulation. I described Jim McGourty's account of one-to-one ego-stripping. Chuck dismissed it. I showed him my copy of Lucinda Franks's book. Chuck's brow furrowed as he read out those rough quotes about Rasputin and butchery. "It doesn't make sense," he muttered. "Michael Vale was a real revolutionary. 'Ideas are the most important thing,' he'd say. 'The revolution will take care of itself.' He read a lot. He worked a lot. He wasn't our buddy. We didn't drink together. But he helped us. To me he seemed selfless. He wanted to change the world. We were prepared for the shit to hit the fan, and when it did, we were going to go back to America like Lenin went back to Moscow."

Chuck reminisced about their first meeting in the office of the lawyer Hans Göran Franck. It was February 1968, a couple of weeks after the arrival of Bill Jones, three months before the landfall of Mark Shapiro and his comrades.

"We'll take care of this boy," said Michael.

"I'm not a boy," replied Chuck, gruffly. "I'm a man."

But he was eighteen years old, and happy to be taken care of. Paternal figures were in short supply in Chuck's life. His father, Thomas Onan, loved war more than he loved his family—loved it so much that after spending the early 1940s scudding over the Pacific in a patrol torpedo boat, he enlisted in the air force, which is why Chuck was born on an air base in Wiesbaden, Germany, in August 1949. The family did not remain intact. When a substantial sum of money went missing from the base, Technical Sergeant Thomas Onan's gambling habit was found to be the cause. In February 1954, he received a dishonorable discharge from the air force.

He also discharged himself from his marriage. Rosemary Onan moved her children to Chicago, where the family rented an apartment in a high-rise block from which many of the internal walls had been removed in order to allow gang members swift passage from apartment to apartment. They were the only white residents, which made Mrs. Onan's pale little boy an object of intense curiosity: the other kids were always asking him to hold his breath and make his face go red.

Life was tough. After school Chuck shined shoes and gave the money to his mother, who used it to buy the ingredients to bake her own bread. Enlisting in the U.S. Marines was a ticket out of deprivation. But it took him to a place that was worse.

During my visit to Oregon, I sat down with Chuck to watch a 2005 Swedish television documentary that followed Terry Whitmore on a return visit to the battlefields of Vietnam. Chuck translated effortlessly and made the odd affectionately disparaging remark about his old comrade's clumsy command of Swedish. Whitmore, looking frail and bug-eyed from years of drinking, spoke of being ordered to go into a village and kill everyone there—men, women, children. The film showed him meeting survivors from that day, people who claimed to have seen the bodies piling up.

Chuck wept as he watched. He was reminded, he said, of the brutalities of his own military training, for which he and his fellow marines had run through a mocked-up Vietnamese village, throwing grenades into hidey-holes. Those exercises felt like an extension of his Chicago childhood. "I could beat the shit out of the other boys," he said. "The most aggressive is always the winner. People don't do that naturally. But a childhood like mine trained me that way. Thousands of others, too. Boys who believed all that stuff about the evils of Communism and weren't afraid to shoot."

Chuck feared he had become one of those boys. He was eloquent about this moment, and had posted a short account of it online, describing how, when he deserted from his base in February 1968, he had abandoned most of his possessions but felt compelled to bring his standard-issue M14 rifle. He recalled breaking the gun down, wrapping the pieces in duct tape, and taking them as hand luggage on board Flight 32 from JFK to Sweden. "I am not indoctrinated," he muttered, as he placed it under his seat. "I am not wed to my weapon." As we talked, he supplied an unexpected parallel scene: when Vietnam came around, said Chuck, Thomas Onan, too old to serve, went there all the same, opening a bar in Saigon where he supplied younger men with beer, cigarettes, and prostitutes.

After boot camp and the Chicago projects, Stockholm seemed like paradise to Chuck. He spoke of it as a sunlit world from which he had been banished. (He could not acquire a new passport, he said, until he had paid off his debts.) Back in 1968, he flourished in the language classes and lucked out in the difficult business of finding accommodation, sharing a spacious apartment with an Italian American deserter named John Picciano, which, by coincidence, had just been vacated by Ambassador Heath. (They also inherited his dog.) It sounded unlikely, but Chuck opened up Google Maps and found the building with ease.

Chuck's relationship with the American Deserters Committee was conducted on his own terms. Sometimes he joined in, sometimes not. His background made him useful to the group. Mike Vale and Bill Jones saw the ADC as a cell of proletarian deserter revolutionaries but found it hard to live up to the image. The core members were impeccably middle class. George Carrano was the son of an army colonel; Bill Jones's family were a mixture of lawyers and nuns; John Ashley's mother collected antiques and owned a Siamese cat named Sylvia. Chuck was authentically working class. Which is why he became the star of the ADC's summer tour of Europe.

THE WORLD FESTIVAL of Youth and Students was a ten-day jamboree for socialist college boys and girls from all over the globe. In previous years, it had been held in Helsinki, Vienna, and Moscow, where most of the delegates had smiled for the camera and cheered in all the right places. Sofia was the host city for 1968, and in the year of the barricades the Bulgarian authorities had a small taste of student revolution. They confiscated Little Red Books. They took away placards bearing the image of Alexander Dubček, the reformist leader of Czechoslovakia. They kept a wary eye on the German student leader Karl Dietrich Wolff as he led an unofficial demonstration outside the U.S. Embassy. (Once he started disrupting the carefully choreographed political debates, they dragged him from the stage and smashed his glasses.)

The Swedish Aliens Commission warned the deserters against traveling to Bulgaria. They were free to leave the country, but they might not necessarily be granted permission to return—news that was reported with pleasure by the American press. Mark Shapiro was in a particularly vulnerable position. Most of the ADC delegates held valid American passports. Mark had only the temporary permit that Sweden granted to recent immigrants. But he began the journey all the same, taking the ferry to Helsinki, where George Carrano, the chief fixer of the ADC, proposed a somewhat risky solution.

Carrano advised Mark to go to the U.S. Embassy and apply for a fresh passport like a tourist in a spot of bother. The two men went together and soon found themselves in the middle of a diplomatic farce. An embassy official gave them some forms to complete and told them to wait while he fetched a colleague. Suspecting that they were about to be put in handcuffs, Mark yanked open the office window and jumped out. George followed a moment later. Both men threw themselves over a scrub hedge and scrambled into a taxi. "Floor it, driver!" yelled Carrano, and the car screeched off.

A few days later the ADC representatives arrived in Sofia. A Soviet production company, the Central Documentary Film Studios, committed the evidence to celluloid. *A Time to Live* opens with images of rosy-cheeked Bulgarian children hunkered down on the pavement, chalking a suspiciously accomplished picture of a Vietnamese mother breast-feeding her baby. We then cut to an immense montage of the world's anti-imperialist youth, marching through the streets of Sofia and looking optimistically into a headwind. (All except the U.S. delegation, who look like they've come for a potluck picnic in Haight-Ashbury.) Fighters from Hanoi parade with bouquets of red roses to chants of "Viet-nam! Vietnam!" Crowds make way for a fleet of miniature tractors donated to North Vietnam from the citizens of the Bulgarian city of Plovdiv. Delegates from Mozambique and Algeria parade in national costume. After the pageant, the film takes us to a meeting hall draped with a red banner declaring "Vietnam must win" in six languages. Here, Kendra Alexander, a leader of the American Communist Party, is speaking passionately about the war. Some in the audience are weeping. The camera moves along the front row and finds some familiar faces: Mark Shapiro, dressed in a neat jacket and striped tie, his face a mask of concern; Chuck Onan, his eyes unreadable behind shades; beside him, his flatmate John Picciano.

After the ceremonial burning of a draft card, we follow the deserter delegation out into the street. Bill Jones, looking impossibly boyish and happy, embraces a Vietnamese woman, who presses a red gladiolus into his hand. The ADC members introduce themselves on camera, reporting the details of their desertions as if they were giving name, rank, and serial number.

"We see our act of desertion as a concrete act of solidarity with the Vietnamese people," says Bill. "Ninety percent of the GIs in Vietnam are innocent," adds Mark Shapiro. "They were sent there by an aggressive nation, the United States." Chuck, though, makes the most radical remarks: "When the time comes to return to the States," he says, "I'll be ready to go back there and do my part to help others resist the system and fight the system." I couldn't help thinking that he had kept his promise—only he now expressed it in the language of the American alt-right.

The deserters enjoyed their visit to Bulgaria. There was something in the air: a new political energy as alien to the Soviet authorities as it was to their opponents in the West. When Bill Jones railed against the criminality of American policy in Vietnam, Soviet journalists scribbled happily. But, Bill recalled, they stopped when he accused the Soviets of using the war in Indochina as an opportunity to occupy the moral high ground. "The Soviet Union," he said, "is part of the problem, not the solution." To amplify the point, he walked around the city clutching a copy of Isaac Deutscher's critical biography of Stalin, enjoying the ripple of scandal it produced.

Once the applause and bouquet exchanging were over, Bill and Mark left Sofia for a ten-day tour of Europe, avoiding NATO countries in which they risked detention. They went to Prague, where Bill strolled through Wenceslas Square and saw a city thriving under Dubček's liberal reforms. ("It was like walking through Hyde Park," he said.) They went on to Warsaw, where Bill knocked at the door of the Cuban Embassy to ask if Havana would accept them if Sweden decided to turn them away. ("We could have ended up cutting sugarcane for the rest of our lives," he guffawed.) On August 16, they boarded a Polish airliner to Stockholm and prepared to face the music.

When they landed at Arlanda, Mark and Bill were taken briefly into custody, then sent on their way with fresh temporary residence permits.

They gave an impromptu press conference, in which Bill accused SÄPO, the Swedish security service, of harassing the ADC in order to hamper its campaign against the Vietnam War. Their joint statement was defiant: "The struggle of the Vietnamese people is more important to us than our stay here." But one reporter caught a more somber reflection from Mark. "I don't know where to go if I will be expelled," he said. Four days later, Soviet tolerance of Dubček's reforms terminated with the arrival of a column of tanks.

THESE MISADVENTURES DID not halt the travels of the ADC. In the revolutionary summer of 1968, the traffic remained heavy. Oda Makoto, the Beheiren leader who had helped smuggle Mark Shapiro and his comrades out of Japan, came to Sweden in July with news of more deserters ready to travel the high road via Moscow. Ray Sansiviero, a teenage marine from Long Island, and Ou Yang Yotsai, a twenty-four-year-old army sergeant, born in Shanghai, arrived a few days later. Both had seen action in Vietnam—Sansiviero had been wounded at the Battle of Khe Sanh—and both had gone on Soviet television to tell stories of plunder, torture, and rape.

Sansiviero did not remain in Sweden long. After eighteen months of fishing, moodily, on the embankment in front of Stockholm's Grand Hôtel, he disappeared. The ADC membership thought he had been kidnapped by the CIA. Actually, he'd given himself up to the authorities, to face court-martial and a year's hard labor. A third man, Randy Coates, had set out with Sansiviero and Yotsai but did not even make it to Sweden. After the usual rituals—museum visits, vodka binges, dinner with Yuri Andropov and Premier Alexei Kosygin—he went to the U.S. Embassy in Moscow and turned himself in. The intelligence men settled Coates down for a nice long chat: all the names he could remember were noted down and filed for future reference.

Routes from the West were also busy. GIs who came to the Club Voltaire in Frankfurt received Hans Göran Franck's phone number with their cup of coffee. In Britain, Michael Randle, an anti-nuclear activist who in 1966 had helped spring the Soviet spy George Blake from prison, printed thousands of deserter information leaflets and took them to the

European mainland stowed in the same hollow section of the camper van in which he'd smuggled Blake into East Germany.

Michael Vale was also on the move, cultivating deserter-friendly contacts in Britain and France. (He visited the campaigning actor Vanessa Redgrave, though this was not without its difficulties: he forgot to put on a belt, which obliged him to keep his hands in his pockets throughout the meeting.)

At 56 Queen Anne Street, headquarters of the Union of American Exiles in Britain, the runaway Hollywood agent Clancy Sigal dispatched deserters to Sweden under the supervision of his fellow expatriate Harry Pincus, a tall, elegant, acid-dropping medical student he'd met while working at R. D. Laing's radical therapeutic community in the East End. (The two volunteers had bonded when Sigal used a swift blow from a table leg to free Harry from the violent grip of a delusional resident.) They helped the deserving and the undeserving: Sigal remembered a deserter who arrived in London with his girlfriend, asking for funds to get them to Sweden: "We gave them the money—$600—and then we got a postcard from some desert island that said, 'There's a sucker born every minute.'"

Paris, though, was the busiest and most dramatic scene. Here, a complex constellation of GI welfare groups flickered into life, offering soft beds and hard Marxist literature to men making landfall in France. The noisiest and most radical was FUADDR, which sounds like something Steve Martin would say in *The Man with Two Brains*, but stood for the French Union of American Deserters and Draft Resisters. Its prime movers were a law student named Larry Cox—a future head of the American branch of Amnesty International—and a young American activist known as Arlo Jacobs, an expatriate member of Students for a Democratic Society, the most prominent radical youth organization in the States.

FUADDR's longer lived and more snappily named rival was RITA (Resisters Inside the Army), run by Thomas Schwaetzer, a breathless and disheveled Austrian who used the nom de guerre Max Watts and referred to his work as the "Baby Business." The hosts of RITA's safe houses were known as babysitters; the deserters were code-named Baby A, Baby B, Baby C, until four trips through the alphabet had been completed. Not all were easy charges. Baby A was a troubled Texas teenager who had joined the army to get out of a Waco orphanage: he was found a place in a psychiatric hospital in the Loire Valley, where he was classed as either a patient or a gardener, depending on who asked. Baby B had been a heroin addict since the age of twelve. Baby C had joined the army only to escape a prison sentence for stealing his thirty-first car. They both lodged with a Dutch woman in an apartment on the rue Saint-Jacques—from which they were briskly extracted when she disappeared to her bedroom and put a gun to her head.

Paris being Paris, some of RITA's friends had names worth dropping, and not all these details were shared with Max's glamorous patrons. His unpublished memoirs, stored in an archive in Amsterdam, furnished the details. Marguerite Duras, the novelist who scripted Mike Vale's favorite movie, *Hiroshima Mon Amour*, met Max at a table in Les Deux Magots, bringing a baby she had imported from New York—a hulking young specimen hot with glandular fever. The expatriate American artist Alexander Calder allowed Max's infants to lie low at his country home, where they gazed in bafflement at the mobile sculptures twisting in the garden. Jane Fonda, hugely pregnant, struggled up the stairs to Max's second-floor apartment with a carpetbag stuffed with her husband's cast-off clothes, and she invited the deserters to a preview screening of *Barbarella*. (They were unimpressed by everything except her zero-gravity nudity.) Max gained another famous sponsor when his downstairs neighbor arrived to complain about his habit of clomping over the flagstone floor in his boots. Catherine Deneuve accepted his apologies and was soon supplying him with donations.

France maintained careful neutrality toward the Vietnam War and was tolerant of its first seventy-five or so resident deserters and draft dodgers. Fourteen-day permits were easy to acquire and renew. But the events of May 1968 changed that. Paris became a battleground between riot police and student demonstrators. Barricades were built across the streets. Arlo Jacobs and the deserters of the FUADDR declared themselves allies of the new French revolution and preached the overthrow of de Gaulle. This defiance had consequences. When the smoke had cleared and the tear gas dispersed, all deserters found life measurably more difficult. Those who declined to renounce political activity were refused new paperwork—which meant that they had a choice between living underground in France or seeking humanitarian asylum in Sweden.

Bill Jones remembered the crisis. "When '68 happened they started to crack," he recalled. He and other ADC members traveled south and escorted new recruits up to Stockholm, sometimes collecting them from Larry Cox's safe house in the Paris suburb of Pantin, sometimes from a farm conveniently close to the Belgian border. "We got in touch with this guy called Arlo," he said. He winced as he said the name. "Not a guy to be trusted." I found Bill's attitude instructive. It said something about the atmosphere of suspicion that defined the culture of the deserter networks—a suspicion that seemed to swirl most thickly around its leaders and coordinators.

Like Michael Vale, Arlo Jacobs was a figure who inspired doubt that persisted long after he disappeared from the scene. Max Watts, for instance, considered him a villain. Watts's papers contained page after page of allegations. Arlo, said Max, "did more harm to RITA, us, than any agent, known, before or since." The two men disagreed on one of the great debates of the anti-war movement—whether GIs should desert their posts or resist the war from inside the army. Arlo's response, claimed Max, was to start a whispering campaign that RITA was a CIA front and that Max was tricking deserters into returning to base to face rough military justice.

Max had the opportunity to confront Arlo at a meeting of deserters in Paris's Latin Quarter. "When Arlo found me at the meeting, he became unhappy, wanted to leave," Max wrote.

Philip Wagner, an extremely pacifistic, but very big GI, 6 foot 4, and, although an intellectual, in very good physical shape, reached over and took Arlo's ear. He suggested Arlo sit on a table, so we could all hear his version, and when Arlo seemed unwilling, helped him up. It is the only time I have ever seen anybody lifted up by one ear, but I now know it can be done. Asked point blank, Arlo denied that he'd ever said Max was an agent, or that RITA was a CIA plot, and that in any case he wouldn't say it any more.

Arlo, it seems, failed to keep his promise. RITA had secured the help of the philosopher Jean-Paul Sartre, who agreed to let Max use his address as a poste restante for deserter mail. Once the CIA rumors reached him, the letters went nowhere. "That Arlo, deprived of an audience, by the evident success of 'our' line, turned to bad-mouthing, mongering, personal attacks and eventually sabotage—well, that may have been instructions from CIA Headquarters in Langley or just his own bad character. Unless someone else writes their memoirs, and we get to see them, I doubt we'll ever know."

Max Watts died in 2010. But Arlo, I discovered, was very much alive and happy to discuss his colorful past. His real name was Bo Burlingham. He was a California-based business journalist who wrote books with titles such as *Small Giants: Companies That Choose to Be Great Instead of Big*. I met him for coffee in the flower-filled courtyard of the Berkeley City Club and listened to a wry assessment of his radical years.

After leaving Paris in July 1968, he said, he'd stuck with the faction of Students for a Democratic Society that became the Weather Underground—a revolutionary cadre who were not averse to using explosives to advance their cause. (History shows that they were better at blowing up themselves than agents of U.S. imperialism.) "I didn't stay long," he said. "But it was long enough to get my ass indicted."

Bo was skeptical about the deserters. "There was nothing particularly admirable about them," he said. "These were not courageous people standing up on principle." He was also skeptical about Max Watts—and remembered entertaining the idea that he was the real CIA agent in Paris. His most generous thoughts were about Michael Vale. "He was an intellectual, I was an intellectual," he said. "But that's really giving us much too much credit. We were failed students is, I think, a better way to put it. We talked philosophical bullshit and ideological bullshit."

He warned me not to take my research too seriously and suggested that I view these intrigues as a form of 1960s performance art. "There was an awful lot of playacting that was going on," he said. "I was part of that. We were all sort of playacting, trying to be relevant. Aware that these big events were happening, and wanting to have some part in them."

THE LINE BETWEEN life and art is sometimes blurred. In my conversations with Michael Vale, he too played down the genuinely subversive nature of his activities, but it was easy to see why they might have given rise to official anxiety. Michael and his friends were building relationships with organizations dreaming of revolution: the SDS, British Trotskyists, Greek radicals living in exile after the military coup of 1967, a shadowy organization known as the Phoneless Friends—an underground network led by the Egyptian revolutionary Henri Curiel, who wanted the American deserters to live in the provinces and train as a guerrilla force. Some of these people only fantasized about taking up arms against the authorities. Some, like Curiel's followers, kept rifles under their beds.

Chuck Onan became an accessory to this plotting. After the Sofia festival he and the smooth-tongued draft dodger George Carrano went to Budapest to attend a conference with representatives of the American New Left, the North Vietnamese government, and the National Liberation Front. "The purpose of the meeting," said Chuck, "was to come up with strategies to create disruptive demonstrations in the United States that would create difficulties for the army." Vietnamese delegates made heartfelt speeches thanking American deserters and draft resisters for their support. Chuck offered a speech in reply, scripted for him by George Carrano. Everybody sang "We Shall Overcome."

Less formal contacts also took place. The Vietnamese asked for an explanation of a slogan then popular among U.S. radicals—"Up against the wall, motherfucker." At the bar of the Hotel Ifjúság, the founder of the Cornell University chapter of the SDS led the house band in a version of the Beatles song "Money (That's What I Want)," hoping that the audience would understand the irony. One of the Viet Cong's chief military strategists responded to some bad service in the hotel restaurant by announcing: "Next time, we attack."

The star of the show, Chuck recalled, was Bernardine Dohrn, a charismatic young lawyer from Whitefish Bay, Wisconsin, who had been elected to the leadership of the SDS in June. American radicals, she declared, had much to learn from the methods of the National Liberation

Front. A thrilling image took shape: a U.S. version of the Viet Cong that would take up arms in New York, in Los Angeles, in Washington, DC, and bring revolution to the streets of America. A global movement in which deserters, students, and Indochinese guerrillas might all play their part. "In effect," Chuck said, "we were collaborating with the enemy."

The American authorities had already come to the same conclusion. They knew about the contacts among these radical groups. They knew about the ADC's trip to Sofia. President Johnson had been briefed on Bill Jones's Bulgarian plans ten days before the World Festival of Youth and Students began. Obtaining the intelligence was easy. Somebody close to the American Deserters Committee was reporting everything back to Langley, Virginia.

In a community of radical exiles like the Stockholm deserters, the presence of spies was a constant source of speculation. "If someone new arrived and there seemed to be something a little out of place in their story, you always thought there might be something else going on," said Bill Jones. It wasn't said with regret. The ADC considered paranoia a useful weapon of self-defense. As the Jerum Affair had demonstrated, a sense of the enemy could keep members serious and vigilant. "I'm sure the CIA were running all kinds of operations," said Bill. "Interfaces to try and get a better picture of what was going on in the Soviet Union. Sweden has been a hotbed of intrigue since before World War Two."

To me, it seemed unenviable psychological territory: being nineteen, twenty, twenty-one, a long way from home, in a place where it was perfectly reasonable to suspect that one of your friends was probably also your enemy. Vincent Strollo, a deserter from Philadelphia, remembered the ADC leadership encouraging this thinking. "Michael Vale and Bill Jones propagated that kind of paranoia," he recalled. "Or maybe it wasn't paranoia. Maybe it was the truth."

Clancy Sigal observed its effects. "All deserters believed all other deserters were CIA," he said. "You could take that as a given. What they felt for each other was a curious mixture of brotherhood and mistrust." Clancy thought only a handful of real spies had slept on the beds and sofas administered by him and his collaborator Harry Pincus, and that most betrayed themselves with crude attempts to encourage the deserters to acts of violence. Most CIA talk, he suspected, was fantasy. "There was this sixteen-year-old from Tennessee who called himself 'Kid Blue,' " he said. "I had a call from him. He said he was in the U.S. Embassy and that the CIA had kidnapped him and were torturing him. He was making all this noise on the phone. 'Help! They're murdering me! Aaaarrgggh!' That was the last I heard from him."

"The levels of paranoia were ridiculous," said Steve Kinnaman, a deserter who came to Sweden on a false passport after months spent living incognito in Laos. "You could become a suspect for the slightest thing." The loyalties of a prominent ADC member named Desmond Carragher, Steve recalled, were questioned because he smoked dope without ever seeming to get high. At twenty-three, Steve was a little older than most deserters, and he firmly refused to play the game of hunt-the-infiltrator. "My attitude from the beginning was: Who gives a fuck? Spy on me all you want. I am in the newspaper. I am being interviewed on television. I am not going to hide what I think. We are the revolutionary forces that will go back to the States and set the country right!"

Others, though, could not resist the temptation to speculate. Half a century later, suspicions still smoldered. Most former members of the ADC were convinced that the CIA had a man inside their group. Many had theories about the identity of the infiltrator—or infiltrators. Chuck Onan was doubtful about Ou Yang Yotsai, whose Maoist ballyhoo sounded strained and overrehearsed. Bill Jones put the dope-smoking-but-clearheaded Desmond Carragher at the top of his list of suspects. The reason? Carragher wanted the ADC to take a more conciliatory attitude toward liberal Swedes.

A few weeks after seeing Bill I met up with Åke Sandin, an old Swedish peace campaigner who in 1968 had given his spare room to one of the Intrepid Four. Sandin's thinking ran in precisely the opposite direction. Bill Jones was his pick for the agency's inside man. The reason? Bill did all he could to prevent cooperation between the ADC and the Swedish anti-war movement.

Mark Shapiro, however, nursed the strongest suspicions. Ever since our meeting in a hotel parking lot in San Diego, he had been expressing them by phone and email. "George Carrano has been my friend for nearly fifty years," he said. "But I'm convinced that he was a member of an intelligence agency." Mark had spent many hours looking for inconsistencies in his old comrade's education and employment records, and had shared his doubts with other contemporaries. More surprisingly, he had also shared them with the subject of his inquiries. In 2005 Mark had challenged George to produce paper evidence of his draft resister status. But George had not risen to the bait. "It's only in response to personal attacks on my integrity," he wrote, "my 'credentials,' so to speak, that I'm even looking back on this."

Over the years, the mistrust between the two men never quite destroyed their friendship. Instead, it evolved into an uneasy running gag. Mark even stayed at George's home on Long Island, where, in long late-night conversations, Mark insisted that he was determined to crack his friend's shell and discover the truth about his Stockholm years. "I'll be hunting him down to my last dying breath," Mark told me. But it was impossible to know if the scent of guilt was genuine.

NEAR MY HOME in London is a public park with a thriving population of concrete dinosaurs. They were poured and painted in the 1850s by naturalists who wanted to give the nineteenth-century public a glimpse of a lost prehistoric world. Two iguanodons loom above the ferns and water: gigantic lizards with muscular bodies and sharp rhinoceros horns. The first models of their kind. In 1878 the discovery of several complete skeletons in a Belgian coal mine exposed an error in the London paleontologists' reckoning. The iguanodon horn was actually an iguanodon thumbnail—a bone stiletto protruding from a scaly reptile paw. My dinosaur neighbors were sharp in the wrong places.

Historians of espionage and surveillance are more like Victorian fossil hunters than they would choose to be. The secret state is under no obligation to preserve its own remains. Those who carry out its work may be answerable to God, but they are not answerable to historians. Suspected spies are not obliged to answer our letters or return our calls. So we work with what evidence we can turn over, spreading out the spare and scattered fragments, doing our best to deduce the shape of the monster.

The CIA has always had a passionate attachment to the shredder. Its habit of destroying documents was developed in compliance with U.S. legislation on data protection, but it has also obliterated evidence that would have been useful to anyone investigating its more serious transgressions of the law. Most of the extant CIA files on the deserters are accidental survivals—documents that escaped destruction because copies were made and dispatched to less amnesiac institutions.

One of the most tantalizing survivals is filed at the Nixon Presidential Library, in the personal archive of John W. Dean, one of the White House officials jailed for his role in the Watergate scandal. In a box of Dean's papers is a twelve-page report on the 1968 World Festival of Youth. Its writer, who was apparently a member of the American delegation, preserves some rich firsthand details. Border guards, he notes, ordered U.S. visitors to shave off their hippie beards before entering Bulgarian territory. The Laotian delegation presented their U.S. counterparts with rings forged from the remains of downed air force bombers. In addition to Kendra Alexander's speech about peace and unity, a young North Vietnamese woman spoke of killing eighteen Americans with twenty-six bullets, and another told how she had been captured by the U.S. Army and tortured by having acid poured down her throat.

The CIA's inside man also gives an account of an awkward meeting between the American delegates and the ADC: "The deserters seemed to have their own individual psychological and behavioral problems," he wrote. "They appeared generally agreed that they had never felt so clear in their thinking; that they found it impossible to kill; were pacifists; believed that war in general was immoral and that American participation in the war in Vietnam was illegal; and that they had no immediate plans or goals but wanted to return to the United States eventually, either under an amnesty or after a revolution."

TWO OTHER CIA documents demonstrated that the agency was using undercover operatives to inform on the deserters. A report from July 1969 included a CIA officer's account of a meeting with an informer inside the deserter movement who had been given the fragrant code name PETUNIA.

PETUNIA met his handler at the Café Batavia by the Dupleix metro station in Paris and laid his blossoms on the table. Most of his information had been obtained at the deserter safe house in the suburb of Pantin, rented by Larry Cox with funds supplied by the film star Catherine Deneuve and the Left Bank stars Simone de Beauvoir and Jean-Paul Sartre. I knew that both Michael Vale and Bill Jones had visited the place, and PETUNIA mentioned that he had also been up to Stockholm to meet the ADC. ("Said nobody likes Sweden," reported the spy. "Lousy weather, no work, lousy people.")

By PETUNIA's account, Michael and Bill had completed their mission of the summer. All deserters with revolutionary potential had been spirited out of Paris. Those who remained were "apolitical bums." He described their shortcomings with relish. One, he reported, amused himself by pulling a knife on visitors. Another had gone on a starvation diet to pay for false documents to get him out of France, then changed his mind and spent his savings on a pet monkey. A third spent his time writing letters to Mao Zedong, informing him that an army of Americans—one thousand exiles in Canada, fifteen thousand activists in Alaska, and others in France—were in training to take over the United States. Would the chairman, he wondered, care to contribute a few divisions to ensure the success of the invasion?

"Everyone displays the usual paranoia on the subject of CIA," PETUNIA added. "Larry and others are positive that there is an agent in the house. They are very suspicious of each other and play games trying to trip each other up." In an email Cox confirmed the basic accuracy of the report, and his own presence in Sweden. "Our main contact there was a shady guy called Michael Vale," he recalled. "There were a lot of shady guys."

Another report, from April 1972, clearly the work of someone trusted by the deserters, described a visit by a source code-named MHYIELD to the ADC offices in Stockholm. MHYIELD noted the committee's latest internal disagreements, its new enthusiasm for the ideas of the North Korean dictator Kim Il Sung, and the contents of its mailbag, which contained seventy-one typed anti-war statements purporting to be from American prisoners of war in Vietnam, as well as a letter from Harry

Pincus in London, asking for information on a U.S. Army deserter who was causing panic in the States by planting time bombs in safety deposit boxes.

The informer observed that the ADC leadership knew nothing of this terror campaign, but a reply would have been pointless in any case. Harry Pincus hanged himself the following month. He had money worries and was perhaps in some deeper kind of crisis. He had spent much of the previous year living in a commune in Primrose Hill, North London, under the supervision of David Cooper, a therapist who advocated the disarticulation of the family and the establishment of new social groups through bed therapy—"going to bed with the girl or guy—or child—you are most interested in."

These two documents bore the mark of the CIA operation that brought them into being: a project whose existence was known to only a handful of intelligence officers, secretarial staff, and government officials. The investigative journalist Seymour Hersh was the first beyond this circle to discover its existence. He observed its effects but could not name it, like an astronomer who suspects the presence of a black hole after noticing the distortion of the starlight. His sources told him about wiretaps and break-ins, about CIA infiltrators in anti-war organizations at home and abroad. Serious stuff, in contravention of the agency's own charter. Details, though, were scant. Even within the walls of Langley, this work was kept dark. "Despite intensive interviews," Hersh conceded, when he broke the story for the *New York Times* in December 1974, "little could be learned about the procedures involved in the alleged domestic activities except for the fact that the operation was kept carefully shielded from other units inside the CIA."

Now, though, we know its name. Its name was Operation Chaos.

6 / THE BIRTH OF CHAOS

BETTER TO HAVE called it something else. Something innocuous. Something unburdened with strong meaning. Something that didn't describe the screaming waste traversed by Satan in one of the scarier parts of *Paradise Lost*. Somebody with a sense of posterity should have spoken up. But they didn't, and Operation Chaos was born.

President Lyndon Baines Johnson was its daddy. In 1967, he looked across America and saw things he neither liked nor understood. That spring, boys on town hall steps, outside army offices, and in Central Park put matches to draft cards, or, more enterprisingly, burned them up with home-brewed napalm or soaked them in their own blood. In May, Black Panthers padded around the California state capitol in their berets and shades, shotguns pointed at the plaster ceiling. Their images competed for space with news from Stockholm, where American radicals had joined the Russell Tribunal to find the Johnson administration guilty of genocide.

Then, at the end of June, the president sat down for a $1,000-a-plate fundraising dinner at the Century Plaza Hotel in Los Angeles and discovered that the city had laid on a floor show: speeches by the boxer Muhammad Ali and the childcare guru Dr. Benjamin Spock; ten thousand protestors chanting, "Hey, hey, LBJ! How many kids did you kill today?"; LAPD officers swinging nightsticks; enough violent disorder to convince the commander in chief that his days of campaigning in public should come to an end. Convince him, too, that dissent of this intensity could not be entirely indigenous—that it had to have blown in on some cold wind from Russia or China.

By summer, Johnson had decided that this weather should be mapped and its patterns disrupted. On August 15, three senior CIA figures met to discuss how to grant the president's wish. James Jesus Angleton, a cadaverous poetry lover with a primly Anglicized accent, had been chief of the Counterintelligence Staff since 1954. Thomas Karamessines, deputy director for plans, had been in his job for only a fortnight—propelled there after his predecessor fell dead on the tennis court. Richard Helms, the director of central intelligence, was also a recent promotion, despite the failure of his attempts to assassinate Fidel Castro with a poison pen, a botulism-infected cigar, and an old-fashioned Mafia hit man. (The shoes laced with beard-killing thallium salts never progressed beyond the drawing board.)

All three men were examples of a now-vanished type: Ivy League graduates with good manners and clean fingernails who believed in their right to nurture a military coup, depose an elected leader, or offer a suitcase of cash to a gangster, if it retarded the spread of communism. Not because they were paranoid (though Angleton certainly was), but because they had been in freshly liberated Axis territory at the bitter end of the Second World War and had observed the brutal strategies by which the Soviet Union gathered Eastern Europe to its bosom. When they saw young Americans marching under anti-war banners, they imagined the smiles of satisfaction in smoke-filled rooms in Moscow and Peking. They imagined the hammer and sickle fluttering over the U.S. Capitol.

In selecting a leader for the operation, Angleton, Helms, and Karamessines chose one of their own. Two candidates were considered. Both had a strong scholarly background; both had worked as intelligence analysts at the CIA stations in Munich and New Delhi; both were career cold warriors.

The older of the pair, Harry Rositzke, was a crossword-loving scholarship boy from Brooklyn who had taught classes at Harvard and published a translation of the *Anglo-Saxon Chronicle*. His anticommunism had been confirmed in 1945, during an unauthorized jaunt into Soviet-controlled East Berlin, where he'd seen Red Army looters stripping buildings of bedding, toilet bowls, and electrical fittings, a column of doomed-looking German boys and old men being herded eastward by Mongolian troops wearing straw shoes.

Rositzke's CIA career had been audacious but not wholly successful. As chief of station in New Delhi, he had funded the activities of nationalist guerrillas in Tibet, used stink bombs to break up meetings of the troublingly electable Indian Communist Party, and, according to one colleague, given staff meetings "a certain Dickensian quality, like a colloquy between Fagin and his young pickpockets." As chief of Langley's Soviet bloc division, he had been responsible for the mainly disastrous attempt to get spies on the ground in Russian territory. (Most were greeted by armed welcoming committees before they'd had time to roll up their parachutes.) Defeat gave Rositzke a profound respect for the enemy. So profound that a family acquaintance wrote to the FBI to share her worries about his extravagant praise of the USSR.

Harry Rositzke's younger rival was a less flamboyant character. In a building full of professional secret keepers, Richard Ober was known as a man of few words. "Tight mouthed," they called him. "Close mouthed." He liked the people around him to be the same.

His academic qualifications were impeccable: history and philosophy at Harvard, a master's degree in international relations from Columbia, a year of further study at the National War College. But Ober's killer credential came from work in the field. He was already running a prototype for the kind of scheme President Johnson had in mind: a spoiler operation against the anti-war Left. Its target was *Ramparts*, a noisily countercultural magazine published in Berkeley, California.

The agency wished to squish *Ramparts* because its investigative reporters had begun to make a habit of uncovering Langley's most sensitive secrets. Its most recent scoop: revealing that since 1952 the agency had been funding the National Student Association, and was using its members to gather intelligence on campuses across the world. Ober failed to prevent *Ramparts* from running the story, obliging his colleagues to cut loose some of their paid agents. But the operation had allowed him to demonstrate a coolly pragmatic attitude to espionage techniques that were forbidden by the CIA's own charter. And it was upon these techniques that Operation Chaos was founded, with Ober as chief; Rositzke, slightly offstage, in an advisory capacity; and Richard Helms as the man who would take the fruits of their labor to the White House.

When the National Security Act of 1947 brought the CIA into being, it permitted the agency "no police, subpoena, or law enforcement powers or internal security functions." The *Ramparts* operation troubled the letter and the spirit of this law. It investigated the personal and financial affairs of the magazine's staff and backers, all of whom were U.S. citizens and residents. It put them under surveillance. It gathered material for blackmail. Years later, Edgar Applewhite, a member of Ober's staff, gave an interview about these activities. "We had awful things in mind," he said, "some of which we carried out." He also recalled the response of the deputy director for plans. "Oh, Eddie," he said. "You have a spot of blood on your pinafore."

FRANK RAFALKO NEVER asked to be part of Operation Chaos. What he really wanted was a place in the CIA's career training program. A chance to escape his desk in the records division and go out into the field, acquiring intelligence hot from the mouth of the asset. But the agency decided that a master's degree should be a requisite for this work. Frank didn't have one, so that was that. He did his best to resist the assignment, telling his interviewers that counterintelligence was a dead end. But they didn't pay much attention. By the time Frank got back to his desk in the basement, the job was his.

Frank and I arranged to meet in Wilmington, North Carolina, where he had business in town. An ice storm cleared his diary, but he came all the same, driving a careful forty miles through remarkable weather conditions: someone, it seemed, had taken the trees and dipped them in glass. He picked me up from the lobby of the Hilton and took me to his favorite restaurant, a seafood place beside the Cape Fear River, a popular venue for CIA reunions. Former agency employees, he explained, live tax-free in North Carolina; he hadn't received a federal tax bill since he retired here in the 1990s. We ate fish and chips to a smooth jazz sound track.

At first, Frank explained, Operation Chaos was run from three second-floor rooms close to James Angleton's office, in an area called the Black Section. Other colleagues on the project were scattered through the halls and corridors of the agency's headquarters. Angleton, said Frank, took little interest in the project. It was his habit to arrive when Frank and his colleagues were at lunch, and he would work late into the night in a shuttered office, the gleam of his little desk lamp faintly visible through the blinds. "He was a very mysterious person," said Frank.

Eventually the team migrated en masse to the most secure accommodation Langley could furnish: a suite of windowless rooms behind a cypher-locked steel door in the basement. "That," noted Frank, "was called the Vault." He traced a ghostly sketch on the tablecloth. Richard Ober's office. The New Left section. The Black Power section. The coffee area, with its large table next to the Xerox machine. His own office, and that of his colleague Jason Horn, deputy chief of the unit, each equipped with a two-drawer safe in which they stowed the contents of their in-trays. Desks occupied by staff who processed material supplied by the National Security Agency, a secret intelligence-gathering body that monitored communications all over the world.

And, to the left of the entrance, a second cypher-locked bulkhead, a vault-within-the-Vault that housed gray filing cabinets stacked with paper records. With Richard Ober in charge, correct security procedure was followed to the letter. "Ober was not so much an operations-type guy, but an analyst," Frank recalled. "Jason complained to me that he didn't know half the stuff Ober was doing, because he was so secretive."

The most impressive element of the operation lay in a room on the other side of the records division. This was the home of HYDRA—an IBM System/360 mainframe computer that marshaled files on 9,994 named subversives and was tended by a team of three technicians. HYDRA was an omnivorous beast. She devoured the name of anyone who had published an article in the *New York Review of Books*. She fed happily on information about Grove Press, because it had published Kim Philby's memoir, *My Silent War*, and distributed the Swedish sex-and-socialism film *I Am Curious (Yellow)*. Published reviews went into HYDRA's maw. "We were ahead of a lot of other people in the technology field," Frank reflected. "Everything was put on computers." Visiting men from the FBI would gaze upon these tape spools and punch cards and cathode ray tube terminals and suck their teeth in envy.

It was hard to picture Frank surrounded by this gleaming machinery. With his lantern jaw and bearlike physique, he had the air of a retired cop or football player. I wasn't surprised to hear him describe his delight at being assigned to monitor the sharp-dressed, gun-toting Black Panthers rather than the more drily academic New Left. "The Panthers were a bunch of thugs," he said, "but they sounded exciting." When Frank spoke of Eldridge Cleaver, the leader of the Black Panther Party, his tone revealed something of the intimacy that can grow between a counterintelligence officer and his quarry. "If he'd stuck around at home and kept out of trouble," said Frank, like the high school careers officer musing on the fate of one of the bad boys, "he might have ended up as the new Malcolm X." Years after Operation Chaos, Frank was out on a joint operation with the FBI and found himself in Cleaver's neighborhood. Had it not been a breach of protocol, he said, he might have called to discuss old times.

FRANK IS THE only CIA officer who has ever gone public about his work on Operation Chaos, the only person in the world you can ask for an on-the-record interview about its activities. His account is a minimalist one. The program, he insisted, was modest, not massive. It never had more than fifty-four people on staff, including the secretaries. It ran only a handful of assets in the field: additional eyes and ears were borrowed from other CIA divisions and other government agencies. Its scale and plenitude lay in the amount of data it harvested, more than it was ever able to process. CACTUS, a cable system separated from the mainstream agency wires, brought in reports from the police, the FBI, the National Security Agency, and CIA stations all over the world. Paid subscriptions to radical newspapers and magazines yielded another torrent of material, channeled by the ordinary U.S. mail.

Producing order from all this, Frank insisted, was the program's business. Not kidnappings or assassinations or messing with people's heads. "We never disrupted, we never interfered," he said. "All we did was collect and report." He paused. "The bureau, though. That was a different story. The military also got involved in disrupting things, but we didn't. It was hands-off for us." It was a picture of a billion-dollar brain: a nerve center that sent impulses firing into the muscles of other bodies—the FBI, military intelligence, the White House—which then twitched in response.

Our conversation had become one about cause and effect. About whether surveillance might not also constitute a form of disruption; whether the suspicion that your group had been infiltrated might not be as corrosive as the presence of an active agent provocateur. Frank accepted the principle: actions that appeared inconsequential in Langley might have wrought powerful effects upon individuals in the field. "Something could happen that affects that person's mind," he said. "That could lead to that person's death or serious illness. Maybe destroy his rational thinking. So you have to ask yourself, are you the cause of that death, directly or indirectly? Maybe some outside influence you know nothing about has caused it, but you always have that worry. Some of these people may have gone off at the deep end because they felt they were being persecuted. Even if they only *thought* it was happening to them. They're in a strange country. There's a lot of pressure on them. So do you blame yourself, or do you blame an outside force that is interfering with your mind?"

It was the chaos theory of Operation Chaos. A small action—a meeting in a café between a handler and an asset—might produce ripples or create waves; it might change the weather conditions as profoundly as the work of an army of salaried officers. The deserters already lived in a world of suspicion and paranoia. How much genuine interference would it have taken to trigger something spectacular?

FRANK DOWNPLAYED LANGLEY'S interest in the deserters. He had no recollection of discussing them in any meeting. But they were there in paperwork. In 1978 the agency declassified 2,662 pages of documents relating to Operation Chaos and other domestic spying operations. These contained mainly dross: countercultural tidbits about rock concerts, picnics, and teach-ins; humorless attempts to describe the taxonomical differences between hippies, Yippies, and Zippies; a story about a Catholic priest who threatened to kidnap Henry Kissinger and hold him hostage until the air force stopped bombing Cambodia and Laos.

It also contained the program's mission statement, which suggested that it was a countersubversion project with a long list of subversives to counter: "the extremist anti-war movement, extremist student/faculty groups, black extremism, Chicano extremism, Puerto Rican extremism, deserter/evader support and inducement, and international aspects of the domestic underground media." Beneath this was a long list of specific organizations, their names obliterated by the censor's ink. Details, too, about how assets were deployed in the field: "Americans with existing extremist credentials have been assessed, recruited, tested, and dispatched abroad for PCS assignments as contract agents, primarily sources offered for such use by the FBI. When abroad they collect information responsive to MHCHAOS program requirements, as well as other agency requirements." "PCS," I learned, stood for permanent change of station, and "MH" indicated that CHAOS was a worldwide operation. These were American agents living undercover among American subversives abroad. How many of them, I wondered, had I already taken out to lunch?

THE CIA WAS on the deserters' case right from the beginning, before the Intrepid Four had even left Japan. It was receiving information from an FBI tap installed on the phone of Howard Zinn, a Boston University historian and vigorous anti-war campaigner. When a member of Beheiren called Zinn to discuss the fate of the four sailors, someone pressed play and record. Through this surveillance, the CIA learned that Ernest P. Young, a history professor at Dartmouth College, had agreed to travel to Tokyo in order to check out the deserters on behalf of the U.S. peace movement. The tap may also have yielded another piece of useful information—that Beheiren had made arrangements with the Soviet Embassy in Tokyo through a colorful intermediary named Brian Victoria, a Buddhist monk from Omaha, Nebraska, who had burned his air force discharge papers and raised $5,000 for North Vietnam by begging on the streets.

As the story developed, Thomas Karamessines pulled in all he could on the activists who had helped the four defectors get to Moscow. He sent out a dossier to the White House, the FBI, Richard Helms, and a cluster of military intelligence agencies. Beheiren, Karamessines concluded, had seduced these sailors into defection. The Intrepid Four were "misguided youngsters gone astray in a foreign land and due to get slapped back in line with traditional Navy justice when they finally decided to stop the fun and go back to the ship. . . . But once the Beheiren people made contact they recognized the potential immediately and moved in for the kill."

Anti-war activity as a product of alien influence: it was a perfect fit for the narrative that President Johnson wanted to hear from the CIA, but it was wrong. The four had decided to desert days before they met anyone from Beheiren. They had formulated their opposition to the war in the roaring gray steel world of the USS *Intrepid*. It was working on the 27,000-ton aircraft carrier, watching planes depart and return—and sometimes fail to return—that pushed them toward desertion.

A day after Beheiren announced the four's defection, two investigators in regulation dark suits and fedoras came aboard the carrier to question men who had known the vanished sailors. Crewman Robert Doyon was summoned to the captain's cabin and given a grilling. Had his friends been brainwashed by Japanese communists? No, Doyon insisted. He could detect John Barilla's turn of phrase in the public statements issued by the four. Barilla had described the Vietnam War as "ugly," which was his favorite term of disapproval, and usually applied to the shipboard coffee or chow. This was not a view that the intelligence men wanted to hear. Doyon was kept away from inquisitive reporters with three weeks' cleaning duty in the chief petty officer's quarters. After that, he told me, his commanding officers made his life miserable.

THE AUTUMN OF 1968 brought a better harvest for the intelligence men. The juiciest fruit came in the form of Philip Callicoat, the hot-tempered teenage sailor who had been exported from Japan in the same boat as Mark Shapiro and Terry Whitmore. He seems to have been shaken from the tree by Bernice Foley, a globe-trotting, kid-gloved journalist from Cincinnati, author of *The Three Fs of Charm*, who rolled up in Stockholm looking for deserters to take out to dinner.

Callicoat accepted her invitation, giving her the fourth F of charm in the restaurant of the Strand Hotel. He told her the CIA was following him. He wanted it on the record that he was no pacifist. Having been sacked from his new job as a stevedore at the Oxelösund docks, he was considering leading a band of Swedish deserters into the Israel Defense Forces. Nor did he approve of any plan to halt the bombing in Vietnam.

"When you're on deck being attacked by the Commies you see your buddy's head blown to bits with its brains and eyes splattering you. Your own arm is suddenly in ragged and bloody tatters, then you hear and see overhead American bombers streaking out toward the Commies. Whether you're a religious man or not, you fall a moment to your knees knowing that you, a mortal man, have just seen a vision of heaven opening up to your scorched and suffering eyes."

He didn't go to Israel. Instead, he called his dad. On August 24, Edward N. Callicoat, the Pentecostal minister with the all-singing band of children, arrived on a plane from Canada to escort his son to the American Embassy in Stockholm. The following night they were both flown by military plane to an air force base in New Jersey, from which Philip was briskly transferred to the brig at the Naval Shipyard in Philadelphia.

Here he struck a deal and informed on everyone he had met since going underground in Japan. He dredged up details about Mark Shapiro, Terry Whitmore, and his other traveling companions. He named all the Beheiren activists he could recall and enumerated the physical characteristics of those whose names he didn't know, estimating ages, weights, and heights. He described the route through Russia, its people and places. He described the American Deserters Committee, spilling what he knew about Mike Vale and Bill Jones, their allies and enemies on the Swedish political scene.

Naval intelligence collated this information. It was turned into a report with flow charts, footnotes, and appendices. In return, there was no court-martial and no dishonorable discharge. Callicoat was allowed to rejoin the navy. But here his story took a stranger turn. After ten days back in uniform he made a run for the Canadian border in the company of a girlfriend who had followed him from Sweden. They flew back to Stockholm together, where Callicoat began filling out the forms that would make him the only deserter to have been twice granted asylum in Sweden.

The Swedes soon had cause to regret it. In July 1969 Callicoat attempted to rob a Stockholm bank using a water pistol. The teller pressed the emergency button, causing the glass bank door to close automatically. Callicoat crashed straight through it, which disoriented him sufficiently for a passerby to grab him and pin him to the pavement. All the papers printed her picture: Gunilla Norén, a fifteen-year-old with a passing resemblance to Velma from *Scooby-Doo*.

Because Phil Callicoat had made a clandestine arrangement with the intelligence men, few of the deserters knew about his boomerang trip to the brig and back. It remained a secret until 1976, when the navy gave evidence to a congressional committee on organized subversion in the armed forces. In the autumn of 1968, Mike, Bill, and their comrades were preoccupied with the fate of another member of the six-man crew of defectors who had traveled with Mark Shapiro—Edwin "Pappy" Arnett, the strange, somnambulant character whose horror stories had made him a nine-day wonder in the Soviet Union. Which is not to say that anyone liked him very much. Arnett's conversational habits made him a tricky houseguest. Fukumi Shinsuke, the Beheiren activist who gave him a room as he lay low in Japan, was so freaked out by his incessant atrocity talk that he considered leaving the anti-war movement. (The details seemed always to be shifting: the Russians were told about necklaces of ears; poor Shinsuke got a monologue about a sergeant who collected the eyes of his victims.)

His Swedish benefactors must have learned to live with it. When he arrived in May, Arnett found shelter under the wing of a peace group in the Stockholm suburb of Tyresö. Its founding member was Åke Sandin, the peace campaigner who had picked up the Intrepid Four from the airport in his little Renault car. "They thought it was very funny to see all the road signs with the word 'utfart' on them," he told me, as we sat in the studio of his local community radio station. "It means 'go out.'" The four, said Sandin, were just boys. Unlike Edwin Arnett. "He was special."

Sandin issued the euphemism with a sigh, recalling the preposterous game of chase that he and his wife had played with Arnett in the summer of 1968. One day in August they heard that the deserter was on his way to the U.S. Embassy in Stockholm. "My wife got in a taxi and said to the driver, 'Follow that car!'" Mrs. Sandin caught Arnett on the steps of the building and managed to persuade him to return to Tyresö. At the beginning of September he did it again, but this time it was too late to stop him. He was already on a plane to New York.

When Arnett landed at JFK on September 14, his army minders threw him to the press. It was a golden PR opportunity. Arnett seemed a perfect match for the military's textbook deserter type: slow-witted, unmuscular, self-involved. He also had nothing good to report about Sweden. Housing conditions were terrible, he complained. Employment prospects even worse. Was it true, asked a journalist, that the Swedish authorities expected deserters to live on $10 a week? "I'm not going to live like a tramp!" snapped Arnett. "Would you?" After this, he was sent straight to the stockade at Fort Dix to await his appointment with history, as the first Vietnam War veteran to be tried for desertion.

THE ADC HAD always regarded Arnett with wary contempt, but it knew a useful symbol when it saw one. If justice treated him roughly, then it would have a quietly positive effect on their cause: who would be tempted to leave Sweden if five years' hard labor was the penalty? It mounted a campaign to draw attention to Arnett's plight. Their expedience showed: they didn't spell his name right on the posters.

It took five months for Arnett to come to trial. He pleaded guilty to the lesser charge of absence without leave, but maintained his innocence of the charge of desertion—for which the penalty was dishonorable discharge without pay and half a decade of rock breaking. On February 26, 1969, a military jury of six men and one woman convened to hear Arnett's case. A comrade who had toiled beside him on his maintenance ship told them that although Arnett had spoken about deserting to Sweden, this was simply a way of expressing his boredom and frustration: really, he wanted a transfer nearer to the action.

Here, the story became more exotic. The defense argued that when Arnett left Cam Ranh Bay for nine days' leave in Tokyo, he had not intended to desert. The idea was put into his head by a glamorous young Beheiren activist who chatted him up in a teahouse, took him to a gam-

bling den, and then whisked him off in a taxi to a house full of persua-
sive Japanese leftists. The prosecution, however, had a compelling piece
of evidence. Ten minutes of color TV news footage taken in the international arrivals lounge of JFK airport, in which Arnett referred to himself
as a deserter over and over again. The judge decided to admit it, obliging
the defense to change its emphasis. One of Arnett's lawyers said that
his client was at "the bottom rung of dull" and waved the results of his
IQ test in the air—somewhere below 90. Arnett, he contended, was too
stupid to understand the legal implications of his words.

The jury took eighty-six minutes to decide that Arnett was responsible for his own actions. As the judge mulled over the punishment, the
defense presented medical evidence it hoped might soften the blow. A
psychiatrist had diagnosed Arnett as a borderline schizophrenic with an
"abnormal tendency to fantasy" and had learned of other mitigating circumstances in the course of a long interview with the deserter. Arnett's
parents had both been alcoholics. At the age of eight, he had witnessed
the violent death of his twin brother. The judge was not much moved.
The sentence was four years' hard labor. Perhaps the judge sensed that
Arnett's account of himself was as reliable as his stories of ear necklaces
and disemboweled infants. I looked long and hard through the records
to find evidence that Edwin Arnett had a twin brother who was killed in
an accident. There was nothing.

On the steps of the court, Arnett urged the public to write to the
president about his case—not least because there were others in Sweden
whose future depended on the outcome of his trial. In the Nixon archive,
only one letter is preserved. It was signed by a group of twenty-five soldiers on active duty in Vietnam, and it offers a stinging criticism of his
case. "We are all in agreement about the degree of punishment meted
out to Specialist Arnett. We feel that the court was lenient on Specialist
Arnett and he should be grateful that his punishment was not more
severe."

They also had a message to communicate to the other Stockholm
deserters. "It is our contention; as citizens of the United States and as
Servicemen in Vietnam; that our country does not need or desire this type
[of] individual. We should not solicit the return of those persons who
have no desire to conduct themselves by the standards of a True American.

If these deserters feel that Sweden is so much more advantageous to their standard of living . . . we feel it to our Country's benefit that they remain where they have chosen to live."

Nobody at the offices of the American Deserters Committee seems to have written a letter to the White House. They had their own problems to consider. In the time between Arnett's arrest and his court-martial, the ADC had torn itself apart.

7 / THE SPLIT

SO FAR, THERE have been very few women in this story. With the exception of Patton Hunter of the *Army Times* and the one-eyed Suntory whisky drinker who allowed Joe Kmetz to hide for sixteen months in her bedroom, they have remained indistinct figures. It reflects the nature of desertion: eleven thousand women served in Vietnam, and all seem to have stuck to their posts as air traffic controllers, clerks, doctors, nurses, and intelligence officers. But it also reflects the nature of the deserters themselves. They were not big readers of Simone de Beauvoir. Many arrived in Sweden believing it to be a country of depressive men and permissive women—and their unexpected celebrity status allowed even unprepossessing characters like Edwin Arnett to put that myth to the test. It took time for some men to treat exile as something more than a period of shore leave. "I'm a big, bad marine," wrote Terry Whitmore in his memoirs. "Always ready to help a lady in distress, especially if I think I can get a piece of ass out of the deal."

Whitmore had a wife and child at home in Mississippi. Some deserters had girlfriends back in the States, who became the source of mournful quotes in American local newspapers. Other men came to Sweden accompanied by young families. Many more found partners in Sweden. Chuck

Onan married Margarjan Gambell, a fearless teenager active in anti-war politics.

Margareta Hedman was still at school when she met her first American exile. "I was a political person and participated in several illegal operations," she told me. "The deserters were brothers-in-arms." She joined the Maoists at fifteen. By sixteen she was helping some of the first arrivals, like Ray Jones III, to hide from the Swedish police. At seventeen she met Bill Jones in Michael Vale's filthy apartment. At eighteen she married him. "Your questions," she told me, "have brought up a lot of thoughts and memories—mostly bad ones."

The same was true, I think, for a woman whose deserter spouse is the person with whom this story began: Michele Lloyd, whose old married name must remain a secret, not because she wished it that way, but because her former husband wanted to appear in these pages as Jim McGourty, the man he became in order to make a clandestine return to the States. Michele is a doctor, and she's the kind you'd trust. I met her at a metro stop in a suburb of Washington, DC, for a day that included meze at a café-cum-political bookstore, souvenir shopping for my children, red beer and Maryland oysters in a neighborhood bar. I liked her instantly: warm, intelligent, a responsible adult, impressively frank about the strange and bitter turns of life with the deserters.

For most men, the decision to go into exile was a lonely one. They made their choice, and their loved ones read about it in the newspapers. Not in Jim McGourty's case. His desertion was a family affair, and its impulse originated with Michele's father, a radar specialist who, as a navigator in the Marine Corps, had flown dozens of bombing missions over Korea. When the Vietnam War began he wrote a letter to his daughter in Anaheim, California, telling her that he could not participate in a repeat of the same carnage. Michele had not even realized that he'd had a role in the conflict. When one of her schoolteachers told the class, "We have somebody here whose father is in Vietnam," she was shocked to discover he was talking about her. "No," she said, "my dad is off the coast of the Philippines on an aircraft carrier." It had not occurred to her to ask where the aircraft were flying, and what each plane carried beneath its fuselage.

Warrant Officer Lloyd was not forced to declare his position: the death of his mother allowed him to take a hardship discharge from the marines. But by the time Michele left home to study bacteriology at UCLA, her father's dilemma had spread to her peers. UCLA was not a radical institution. Michele was faintly disgusted that the most dramatic protest of her college days took place when students blocked the free-way with burning cars because the football team had failed to reach the Rose Bowl. But she was accustomed to cutting against the grain: she was the only pupil in her high school to go to college; the only one to find a sympathetic history teacher pressing a copy of John Kenneth Galbraith's *American Capitalism* into her hands. She was better prepared than her boyfriend for the coming fight.

Jim McGourty, as we must call him, was also born a Californian, but this was all that fitted him for radicalism. His parents were Nebraska Republicans who opposed the Vietnam War because they thought isola-tion a splendid state and Asian politics an unworthy cause for sacrifice. "To them," Jim told me, "America was a fortress."

At first, he was content to remain within its walls. He attended a Catholic seminary, then studied pharmacology at Oregon State Univer-sity. When the math became too hard, he transferred to UCLA, where he met Michele. They were married in October 1966, a year before Jim was due to finish his degree. When his studies were over he enlisted in the marines, hoping to exercise some control over his posting. The power of nepotism was also invoked: Michele's father had a friend in the Penta-gon whose influence, they hoped, might keep Jim away from the fight-ing. Jim signed his papers in July 1967 and became an artillery clerk at Camp Pendleton, processing orders that dispatched men from training to the front line. The following summer, his in-tray was hit by an order that bore his own name. He was bound for Vietnam.

"He would have been a forward observer," said Michele. "He would have been killed. I knew enough to know that." So she researched how to desert and read about an activist group called RESIST, cofounded in September 1967 by the MIT linguist Noam Chomsky, upon the asser-tion that "every free man has a legal right and moral duty to exert every effort to end this war, to avoid collusion with it, and to encourage others to do the same."

Michele sent her husband to see the local RESIST representative, who supplied him with contact details for Hans Göran Franck, the ADC's helpful lawyer. Jim sold his car to his brother and spent the money on air tickets, flying in August 1968 from Canada to Copenhagen and then taking the ferry across to Malmö. "It was an open secret," said Michele. So open that before she followed her husband to Sweden, a group of marines came to implore her to use her influence to bring him back. There would, they said, be no penalty. Jim would even be free to change his military occupational specialty to something less dangerous. Michele knew the consequences of refusal. "Once you turn down an offer like that," she reflected, "the punishment is much worse."

Jim and Michele haven't seen each other for years. They don't write, they don't talk. Their memories of exile run along parallel lines. Michele recalled poverty, isolation, and the charmless sex-segregated accommodation into which she and Jim were placed. ("It was just like being in camps," she said. "You didn't feel like you were being integrated into society.") Jim, on the other hand, spoke wistfully about deserters landing in Stockholm like fallen leaves. Michele enthused about the attractions of the American Deserters Committee. "It was a group of people who were in the same circumstances. I really was sustained by an idea that we were part of something bigger and making a difference." She became its bookkeeper and administrator. Jim, however, insisted that he had been suspicious of deserter politics from the start, and even professed to have felt unease about Hans Göran Franck's association with Amnesty International, because some of its members were Communists.

It didn't stop him joining in. Almost as soon as they walked through the door of the ADC offices, he and Michele became converts to the Michael Vale project. "He asked me what I was planning to do," recalled Michele, "so I told him that I wanted to finish college." Michael's reply was quick and brutal. "Well," he said, "you could always be our contact *inside* the bourgeoisie." The criticism hurt. Michele reprimanded herself for not being a sufficiently serious revolutionary, and the idea was forgotten.

Michael's plans for Michele's husband were more unusual. "The first thing I heard from him," said Jim, "was that they were doing a movie, and I had gotten there just in time. So I could be in that." And that was how the American Deserters Committee members became film stars.

THE STOCKHOLM DESERTERS made a surprisingly large number of screen appearances, though some are harder to detect than others. When audiences watched Bo Widerberg's *Joe Hill*, a biopic of the Swedish American trade union activist who founded the Industrial Workers of the World, the credits did not tell them that Hill's comrades were played by a quorum of the ADC. And yet there is Walter Marshall, the reform school runaway, playing out scenes of personal and political humiliation that went to the heart of his own experiences: beaten up and thrown into the back of a police van, sluiced with human waste in a police cell, driven to a gibbet in the woods where he and his fellow prisoners are forced to kiss the American flag.

Terry Whitmore sustained something close to a career in cinema. His first paid job in Sweden was as an actor in *The Peace Game*, a dystopian science fiction picture by the radical British director Peter Watkins. Watkins was a species of exile himself, propelled from England by two bad experiences: the poor reception of *Privilege*, his feature about a pop star in the pay of a British totalitarian state, and the suppression of *The War Game*, a newsreel-like account of a nuclear attack on southeast England, unscreened by the BBC under secret pressure from Downing Street.

In the more sympathetic cultural climate of Sweden, Watkins took Whitmore and his cast to a disused brick factory outside Stockholm to film a story set in a future where war has been superseded by a TV game show on which small teams of competitors fight to the death. Whitmore, in U.S. Army fatigues, ran through the waterlogged corridors pursued by a Chinese People's Liberation Army major.

Soon after, he saw his name in the title of *Terry Whitmore, for Example*, a documentary shot by the Canadian filmmaker Bill Brodie, and in 1975 Peter Watkins put the deserter back in uniform for *The Trap*, a TV drama set in a Swedish nuclear waste dump on the last night of the twentieth century. Whitmore also got to play a version of himself; in *Georgia, Georgia*, a film scripted by Maya Angelou, he appears as the most talkative member of a group of African American deserters encountered by the white hero, Michael Winters, in a Stockholm bar. "We might get political asylum instead of this humanitarian bullshit we got," says Whitmore's character. But Winters (played by Dirk Benedict, future leading man of *Battlestar Galactica*) will not help.

BY 1972, THAT argument had been lost. But in the summer of 1968 it was a live issue, and one of the reasons why the ADC was so squarely in the public gaze. Journalists buzzed around its offices hungry for interviews. *Look* magazine made it the focus of a lavish illustrated article, which featured a full-page portrait of four members in moody rock-star formation on a Stockholm street corner. (In the photograph, Chuck Onan scowls; Bill Jones clutches a fat book about the Cuban revolution.)

The Italian film producer Carlo Ponti came talent scouting among the exiles and commissioned Gregory Vitarelle, a twenty-two-year-old army private from Texas, to develop a script called "The Denial." (Vitarelle drowned in a boating accident before his work was done: his father back in Texas, ashamed to acknowledge the desertion, told friends his son had been working undercover for the CIA.) The American intellectual Susan Sontag, then at the height of her influence, landed in Stockholm intending to make a film about a Vietnam deserter. She was thwarted. Her script, "Duet for Cannibals," had to be rewritten, as its production company had already signed a distribution deal for a different film on a similar subject titled *Deserter USA*—with a cast plucked from the ranks of the Stockholm exiles.

"The plot is about agents who try to infiltrate the ADC and break it up," Bill Jones told a reporter from United Press International. "But it is not a thriller." He was right. *Deserter USA* is an unclassifiable oddity: an agitprop picture with an espionage angle, in which the Stockholm deserters star as the Stockholm deserters, but not necessarily as themselves. There was a glorious precedent: a decade after the Russian Revolution, Sergei Eisenstein re-created the storming of the Winter Palace with a cast of thousands and successfully displaced our sense of a much less dramatic historical event. Using loans from their parents and a cast of nonprofessional actors, the two directors of *Deserter USA*—Lars Lambert, a new graduate of the Swedish Film Institute, and Olle Sjögren, a student researching a thesis on the French film journal *Cahiers du Cinéma*—made a modest attempt to do the same for the story of the

American Deserters Committee, creating a heroic account of its struggles against the American war machine, the CIA, and affluent Swedish liberals.

The film begins with the image that defined the deserter story for most of 1968: four young Americans getting off a flight from Moscow. But they are not Craig, John, Mike, and Rick. The Intrepid Four had spurned the ADC. John Barilla and Craig Anderson had become street buskers. Rick Bailey was living in Åke Sandin's spare room, where he painted the windows black and tended a pet boa constrictor named Olsson. The protagonists of *Deserter USA* are composite characters brought to life by four of Michael Vale's protégés.

John Ashley, the shock-haired speed-freak son of a Pentagon official, plays a GI named Alan Miller, who seems driven by Ashley's hedonistic impulses, but has also inherited war wounds and a Purple Heart from the backstory of Ashley's friend Terry Whitmore. Mark Shapiro's alter ego, Ben Rosen, shares a thoughtful manner and a Minnesota birthplace with his creator, but his ill-fated trip back to the States is a detail borrowed from the life of Ray Jones III. The leader of the ADC, however, has undergone the most dramatic transformation. Bill Jones plays John Lane, whose backstory is much more dramatic than that of a medical technician with a military career that took him no farther east than Frankfurt. "I was an interpreter working with army intelligence in the Delta," his character reports. "I came in close contact with the Vietnamese people and I realized what they were fighting for and what the National Liberation Front stood for."

Like the heroes of most propaganda films, John Lane talks in complete sentences and is always right about everything. He lectures middle-class Swedes on American imperialism, rattling off statistics about U.S. interests in the Venezuelan oil industry. He senses the treachery of a deserter named Fabian, deducing, correctly, that he is an intelligence plant. (One scene puts Bill on a sun lounger, reading David Wise's 1964 exposé on the CIA, *The Invisible Government*.)

Most perceptively, John holds his ground against a patrician figure called Lundberg, who lavishes hospitality upon the deserters, warns them against contacting the student Maoists, and then plots against them when they refuse to comply. Lundberg is an unsubtle caricature of the deputy chair of the Swedish Committee for Vietnam. When Bertil Svahnström saw the film, it killed the last of his goodwill toward the ADC. He procured a 16 mm print and kept it in his office like a piece of evidence.

"I didn't really have enough experience to make a movie," said Olle Sjögren, when I met him on a trip to London. "If you're a director you have to be strong, you have to be clear. And since we weren't paying anyone we couldn't expect them to be Marlon Brando." Despite these shortcomings, the deserters made a strong impression on him. John Ashley, he remembered, was a skittish figure bubbling with amphetamine enthusiasm. Bill Jones, he recalls, was strangely affected by working on scenes with the visiting American academic who had agreed to play the part of John Lane's father. The deserters' conversation, he remembered, was often a fevered discussion of who might be the resident CIA plant in the American Deserters Committee. A discussion led by Michael Vale.

"He was a very strange person," said Olle. "A little paranoiac. A little suspicious and unpredictable. But I really liked him for his energy and charismatic personality. He was a father figure to the deserters, and he gave them protection. He often hugged them. But they were also suspicious of him. It was very tense." Years later, he said, he watched Martin Scorsese's *Taxi Driver* and saw Mike reflected in Travis Bickle, the film's intense conspiracist antihero.

To his surprise, the distributors of *Deserter USA* sent Olle to the Cannes Film Festival, in the hope of securing a deal to screen the film in America. He succeeded, but the picture did not travel far beyond New York, prompting some of his more suspicious acquaintances to suggest that the buyer had acquired the picture in order to fillet it for intelligence of use to the Central Intelligence Agency. "I doubt it, though," said Olle. "That guy wasn't clever enough to be CIA. He wasn't even clever enough to distribute the film."

When *Deserter USA* opened at Andy Warhol's Garrick Theater in Manhattan, the *New York Times* film critic saved his fastest bullet for the final reel. "A climactic sequence," he wrote, "is so absurdly staged and played as to be laughable."

The source of his amusement was a dramatic reconstruction of the Jerum Affair, in which an American expatriate named Rudolph Pastor slipped into a suit like that of William Russell, the shady man from *Army*

Times. ("He was scared," recalled Olle. "He asked to sign a document saying that he was playing a fictional character and not a real person.")

His scene with a young African American deserter plays like a seduction. We are in a hotel restaurant in Stockholm. There is wine, salad, a lounge pianist, curls of cigarette smoke. "They want you back," says Pastor. "They want all you boys back. And I know they're going to make it easy." Then we cut to the offices of the ADC, where Bill Jones's character is receiving news of the elopement. "We've gotta do something to stop this man!" he declares.

Bill's voice-over introduces the ADC's secret weapon—"John, a crafty New Yorker"—and, like a knight-errant to the rescue, up rides Michael Vale in his Volkswagen Beetle. In an agreeably chaotic apartment, Michael calls the enemy to set up the con. As he speaks, he relieves an itch using a long wooden back scratcher with a candy twist handle. He also has a sidekick. Playing Robin to his Batman is a character named Walt, an effete young man with a Zapata mustache and a tilted beret, who looks on approvingly as Michael ends the negotiation by giving a middle finger to the phone receiver.

Moments later we see the sting carried out. Jim Dotson sits in a student's room, just as he did on the day. Michael Vale also reenacts his own life, sending away the taxi that has brought the embassy spooks to the green space of Gärdet. When the snapping and shouting and jostling are over, the final strophe of the film depicts the ADC at work: handing out newspapers, recording radio programs for broadcast by the Viet Cong, offering defiant words into the camera.

The film premiered in Sweden on April 14, 1969, to an audience composed mainly of ADC members and their friends. The screening was delayed by a bomb scare. The audience was asked to leave while the police made a fruitless search for explosives. "Some people read about that in the papers," recalled Olle Sjögren, "and thought we'd come up with a clever way of getting free advertising." The press also reported that a small knot of protestors got to their feet and shouted, "Long live the USA!" and "To hell with the Communists!" But Olle did not remember this. A different detail stuck in his mind. The premiere of *Deserter USA* had taken place at the Grand Cinema on Sveavägen. It was the same cinema from which the Swedish prime minister Olof Palme would walk on the night of February 28, 1986, into the path of his assassin.

WATCHING *DESERTER USA* in a glass-walled viewing room at the National Library of Sweden, it was hard to judge it as a piece of art. I could see it only as the record of a fragile moment in the lives of the men I was researching. A late summer moment, in which their moral and ideological confidence seemed precisely matched by their anxieties about spies and agents provocateurs. It was hard to say whether hope or fear sustained them more.

Olle Sjögren and Lars Lambert were so keen to speed the film into cinemas that they edited it on an exhausting twenty-four-hour shift system. But the political weather had altered before the film was off the cutting table. On September 15, 1968, the Swedes held a general election in which the Social Democrats achieved a landslide victory. In the year of the barricades, the Swedish electorate gave a firm endorsement to the status quo.

The Swedish Social Democrats played the game of 1968 more skillfully than other European governments. In France, the strikes and student demonstrations brought the country to a rancorous halt and sent President de Gaulle scurrying out of the country. Olof Palme, still a year away from becoming prime minister of Sweden, could walk into a hall of angry young protestors and be heard with respect. He may not have shared their relaxed attitude toward revolutionary violence, but he shared their instinct for activism. His uncompromising line on Vietnam demonstrated that. So did the presence of the deserters—the human evidence of the Social Democrats' opposition to the war in Indochina.

The election result put Michael Vale and his comrades in a delicate position. They had alienated Bertil Svahnström and the Swedish Committee for Vietnam. They had positioned themselves far to the left of potential supporters in the Social Democrats. They began to feel themselves slipping out of fashion.

"Now the initial fascination of desertion has worn off," wrote John Ashley, in a letter mailed to his mother in October 1968. "The slaps on the back in congratulating our unique protest have been forgotten. . . .

And every time a deserter goes back we can almost hear the Swedish Government hide in a closet and breathe a sigh of relief. Sweden only wanted a few deserters to show her humanitarianism, the same way American suburban socialites want one Negro at a cocktail party."

Some Swedes, however, were prepared to make more generous gestures. Sven Kempe, the owner of Linum, a successful textiles business in Uppsala, approached the ADC and professed his a desire to help its cause. Jerry Dass, a troubled former Green Beret, was given a live-in job at the Linum warehouse. More grandly, Kempe also gave the ADC the use of forty-four acres of farmland at the end of a long and winding forest road near Torsåker, a settlement best known as the location of a notorious seventeenth-century witch trial. He sank $10,000 into the project, purchasing equipment, seeds, and a pig named Porky.

The farm had been abandoned eight years previously and had no electricity or running water. But repairs and improvements were made, and twelve ADC members took up residence, pinned up their Che posters, played the *Hair* album very loud, and did their best to make something grow. "The work on the farm," declared an editorial in *Second Front Review*, "will provide many deserters with an opportunity for employment, and the feeling of community will form the basis of the therapeutic process that many new deserters need after months of being worn down by the military machine."

Despite the apparent good intentions, the soil produced nothing, and the farm at Torsåker gained a reputation among the deserters as a place of narcotic psychodrama. When I asked Michael Vale about the place, he remembered the presence of a dartboard bearing the face of Martin Luther King Jr., and a drug-addled deserter arriving in the middle of the night with the carcass of a deer he had caught and slaughtered in the woods. "He wanted to give it to his girlfriend," Mike told me. "The warmth of its dead body reminded him of her. That's so primitive, isn't it?"

THE WINTER OF 1968–69 was a season of struggle for the ADC—a struggle against the Swedish authorities, who had grown tired of its uncompromising politics, and a struggle against itself. One of the stars of

Deserter USA was a principal combatant in both. His name was Warren J. Hamerman, a smallish, round-faced college dropout who discovered radical politics while arranging bouquets at Sewall's flower store in Baltimore. In the film he is rechristened Walt, and he is seen storming into the Jerum building armed with a camera. Michael Vale called him Wally, mainly to annoy him. "He was an ass licker in a non-ass-licking environment," Michael told me. "He always had his tongue hanging out." In more generous moods, when imagining his closest comrades as their equivalent figures in the life of Trotsky, Michael thought of Warren as the ADC's answer to Zinoviev, the former shop assistant who helped to found the Bolsheviks and was executed on trumped-up conspiracy charges in 1936.

Warren wouldn't give me an interview for this book. The reasons for that will emerge in good time. They were the same reasons that several of his relations were so keen to speak to me. I talked to his brother in New York, who was still running the family's wholesale fabric business on Seventh Avenue. I had a pleasant but mournful dinner in Georgetown with his uncle Harold and aunt Rebecca. "You know the Yiddish word 'meshugenah'?" asked Rebecca. "That's what it all was. Crazy." When they spoke of Warren, it was as if they were describing a boy who had been lost at sea, long ago. "Another thing I remember," said Harold, "is that he was afraid of the moon."

Like so many involved in this story, Warren Hamerman endured an unenviable childhood. His father, Norman, had a violent temper, which went unpunished because the family's livelihood depended on his accountancy skills. Harold remembered a Thanksgiving dinner at which Norman quarreled with his wife and looked ready to settle the dispute with the carving knife. He also recalled that Norman screened blue movies in the home. Warren's mother, Muriel, could do little to improve the atmosphere: she was diagnosed with schizophrenia and would wander Manhattan, gate-crashing weddings, bar mitzvahs, and gala nights at the Metropolitan Opera. The positive elements of Warren's upbringing were supplied by Ray Pollack, his maternal grandmother, who had arrived from Ukraine after the 1905 revolution and was part of the generation who were born Orthodox Jews and grew up to be socialists. Her family nickname, "Cooky," was coined by Warren in recognition of her largesse with baked goods. It stuck so firmly that it was engraved on her tombstone.

Warren was a bright and idealistic boy. Bright enough to earn a place at Johns Hopkins University to study English and history; idealistic enough to join a project that sent volunteer tutors into deprived neighborhoods of Baltimore, then to drop out of college in order to devote his energy to protesting against the Vietnam War—in anticipation, perhaps, of the American socialist revolution of which Cooky also dreamed.

In October 1967, while he was working at the florist and on *Prisons and Zoos*, a self-published pamphlet of sub-Ginsbergian poetry, Warren was called in for a medical examination at Fort Holabird, the nearest army post, and pronounced fit for duty. His comrades in the local peace group picketed the gates. Knowing that he could be called up at any time, Warren went to France, hoping to claim asylum. His family's contacts in the rag trade helped him to find somewhere to live in Paris, where he made contact with the French Union of American Deserters and Draft Resisters and was present at a rowdy, foot-stomping meeting at which eight draft dodgers dropped their cards in an envelope addressed to General Lewis B. Hershey, director of the Selective Service System. Jean-Paul Sartre was there, and he identified it as a moment of romantic rebellion.

Someone else who was present supplied me with a more skeptical analysis. "The whole anti-war movement in the United States was filled with people like Warren Hamerman," said Bo Burlingham, who spent most of 1968 in Paris helping to run the FUADDR. "Intense people who were desperate to find some meaning in their lives through political activism."

The student uprisings of May 1968 gave Warren as much meaning as he could handle. As demonstrators fought running battles with the authorities, Hamerman felt the tear gas in his lungs; received a blow from a riot policeman's baton; woke up in hospital with a sore head. On his next visit to the police station to renew his fourteen-day permit of residence, the customary interview turned nasty. He was searched, and when his interrogators found a notebook in which he had written a list of anti-war organizations, they told him to get a job or leave the country. A plainclothes officer was put on his tail to assess his progress. Warren made none. Instead, he persuaded his family to wire him the money to get to Sweden, where he arrived in the middle of August. As he went, he sent a parting shot to the Parisian press: "The French government and its police tried to have us accept silence as the price of our asylum; this was a price we were not willing to pay and that we will not pay."

By the time his statement appeared in the papers, he was already in Stockholm with the American Deserters Committee and had begun applying for asylum. But there was a snag. The Swedish government had never offered asylum to a draft resister—only to deserters. (The exception was George Carrano, who, somewhat mysteriously, had received his papers in August 1968.) As Warren waited for his claim to be processed, something unwelcome arrived in the mail: an order to report to New York to begin his military service. Then the Swedish Aliens Commission refused his application for asylum.

His response was to go into hiding. And while he moved between the spare rooms and attics of friendly Swedish Maoists, the ADC and its student allies mounted a campaign on his behalf. On February 19, 1969, a rally was held in Stockholm, at which protestors waved placards bearing Warren's name. They handed out a leaflet that claimed he would be liable for a forty-eight-year prison sentence, as he had "refused to serve in an army committing genocide in Vietnam, as well as being deployed in armed actions in Negro ghettos in the U.S." (A weird muddled reference, perhaps, to his volunteer teaching in Baltimore.) "SUPPORT WARREN HAMERMAN!" insisted the flyer. "WE DEMAND that Vietnam refusers are granted political asylum in Sweden."

TODAY, WHEN THE Internet allows us to participate in every turn and tick of political argument across the world, it is hard to appreciate how difficult it was to follow a story like that of the American Deserters Committee in Stockholm. RESIST, for instance, the organization that put Jim McGourty in touch with deserter groups in Sweden, had only a vague sense of what it was propelling him toward. At the end of 1968, it sent Gerald Gray, an American postgraduate student at the London School of Economics, to find out. Gray's report remains a useful account of where the ADC stood at the end of a revolutionary year.

In December 1968, Gray flew to Stockholm to spend time with the deserters and their allies. It wasn't exactly a holiday. Bertil Svahnström gave him the evil eye for arriving late to a meeting. A weary Hans Göran Franck told him that he was sick of dealing with the deserters and wished they would stop coming. Michael Vale was sour and unfriendly and accused the visitor of being a snoop for U.S. intelligence. This was pure paranoia. But paranoia has its uses. Gerald Gray was not a spy, but everything he observed on his mission to Stockholm was relayed straight back to the CIA.

Just like the report on Bill and Chuck's Bulgarian adventure, the evidence has survived because the Nixon Library saved it from the shredders. The relevant document, "Swedish Deserters," is Langley's précis of a conversation with an informer who clearly enjoyed Gray's confidence, and it paints a portrait of a community in trouble. The Swedish government, Gray noted, had quietly decided to cap its grants of humanitarian asylum. Black deserters were faring less well than their white counterparts, and they were finding it hard to secure even the most menial employment. The big news, however, was the split in the American Deserters Committee.

The ADC, an organization still several months away from celebrating its first birthday, had wrenched itself into two unequal parts. A faction led by Michael Vale and Bill Jones had kept the name, the pure political aims, and a small core group of members. The overwhelming majority had decided to form a more moderate, less Isaac Deutscher–fixated organization called the Underground Railway—the faction that Gray thought deserved the financial help of RESIST.

Gerald Gray was easy to find. As founder of the Center for Justice and Accountability, an organization dedicated to putting torturers on trial and giving counsel to their victims, he was still in the anti-war game. I emailed him a scan of the CIA document. He sounded shocked to see it. Not least because it suggested that one of his friends had informed on him. Did he know who? He did, but he wouldn't say.

When your job involves investigating human rights abuses committed by your own country, you come to accept that the government will take a beady interest in your activities. Once, he said, he'd requested his personal files from the FBI. Between the redacted sections was a reference to his membership in the American Communist Party. Gray had never been a member. The closest he'd come, he said, was during his time as a student at Berkeley, when he'd gone along to hear a speech by the party's candidate in the 1960 presidential election.

"I suppose," Gerald reflected, "it was either a mistake somebody made, or it was an attempt to set a mark against me that would get in my way in later life." During the course of our conversation, he referred several times to changes of volume on the line. Evidence, he speculated, that his phone was still tapped. Just in case, we offered a cheery greeting to any silent party.

THE SPLIT IN the ADC was a revolt against Michael Vale. It was so clearly a consequence of his actions that some read it as a deliberate act of sabotage. All summer, he had been building bridges with radical organizations in Europe and the States, conducting meetings about which most ADC members knew nothing. He had been doing much the same in Sweden, cozying up to the young Maoists and increasing his opposition to more moderate figures. "The government didn't want us involved in political activity but had no way of neutralizing us legitimately," he told me. "But the [Maoist] groups were unpolluted. They were lovely. Sweet kids! They were so clean."

As he courted them, he went on the offensive against Bertil Svahn-ström. When Svahnström expressed disquiet about the ADC's support for a Viet Cong victory, Mike went to the public library to dig for dirt. He found articles filed by Svahnström when he was a foreign correspondent in wartime Berlin, and by wrenching quotes out of context Vale managed to suggest that he had expressed pro-Nazi views.

There was also an internal front in this war. As Michael pursued his campaign against Svahnström, he also took a harder line on his own members, intensifying his hostility toward deserters who failed to live up to the revolutionary values of the ADC.

"What most upset him," Bill Jones said, "were the guys who wanted to have a lush life, go to university and become professors. He thought that was something immoral. It pissed me off, too."

For Mike and Bill, the most egregious example of this tendency was a deserter who spent ADC meetings lying back in his chair with his glasses on the end of his nose, which made it hard to tell if he was listening, or even awake. Bill and Michael found him infuriating. They alleged that he had used the n-word in an argument with an African American deserter. The charge was flatly denied. But they kicked him out anyway.

In September, Michael made the declaration that broke his organization in two. A delegation from Students for a Democratic Society visited Stockholm, and Mike announced a merger. Henceforth, he declared, the American Deserters Committee would be an autonomous chapter of the SDS. He had a piece of paper to prove it: a letter of approval signed by Bernardine Dohrn, saluting the ADC as an integral part of the radical American Left.

An editorial in the *Second Front Review* explained why no debate was necessary. "The ADC is a working group. When a decision must be made, it is not necessarily to call for a general meeting to vote on it; it is not necessary to have a system of checks and balances to make sure that nobody usurps his authority." (An interesting Freudian slip.) "All these formalities, even if they do ring of democratic idealism, are impractical and tend to be divisive. A bureaucratic atmosphere creates mistrust among the deserters."

Mistrust, however, was already well established. In late October the dissenters raised their voices. Sixty came to a meeting at which the ADC was criticized from every angle. The committee, they argued, had become a zealous clique that had lost touch with its own members. Mike and Bill gave their opponents an ultimatum. They would leave the meeting, and anyone who wanted to work with them should follow. Only six did. And in that moment, the ADC completed its transformation from welfare group to political sect.

The breakaway faction, the Underground Railway, didn't object to politics. They liked to talk about Mao. They even acquired a library of Little Red Books. But they were also stirred by nonrevolutionary desires. They wanted to move out of their cold-water flats and student dormitories. They wanted jobs that did not involve dishwashing. They wanted to learn Swedish. They even had a rock band that had been offered an audition by the record company owned by the Beatles.

The ADC scorned such preoccupations. Vale and the others thought that if the deserters became too comfortable, they might lose their appetite for taking the war back home. It was a tough message to sell to a group of lonely Americans in their twenties. "These power hungry anti-socialist beings are known as opportunists," raged one loyalist on the pages of *Second Front Review*. "They are only interested in personal gain. Opportunists are not revolutionaries, they are sly manipulators and enemies of mankind."

Gerald Gray's report to RESIST predicted a bleak future for the ADC. Its hope for continued survival, he argued, lay in the links it had forged with organizations in the United States. "For a while," Gray wrote, "it can continue as a paper organization, so long as the situation is not known in the U.S." But the prospects were not good. "My own feeling," he concluded, "is that ADC is now on the way to collapsing under the weight of Vale."

But by the time Gray filed his report, Mike Vale had vanished.

8 / THE INFILTRATORS

NINETEEN SIXTY-NINE WAS the year of suspicion. The year of mistrust. The year the traffic reached its peak. Deserters, draft resisters, hangers-on, hacks, sociologists, spies: everybody came to Stockholm. It was the Casablanca of the Cold War.

Warren Hamerman helped to make it happen. On February 21, the Swedish Ministry of the Interior overruled the decision on his case and instructed the Aliens Commission to grant him humanitarian asylum. Americans opposed to war in Vietnam could now step straight from civilian life into Scandinavian exile, no dog tag required. Another condition was also relaxed. Conviction for a minor crime would no longer be considered grounds for expulsion: a great relief to those deserters who feared their next joint might become a pretext for being sent home.

These concessions had several effects. The ADC's campaign for political asylum lost its momentum: deserters felt their situations were less precarious, and most Swedes concluded that an enhanced form of humanitarian asylum was preferable to provoking America by declaring it a tyrant state. Exiles also began arriving in greater numbers. By the end of the year, the official figure edged toward four hundred, and the U.S. State Department was grumbling about the policy of funding the return journeys of men who had developed second thoughts. Perhaps its officials were worrying about their end-of-year accounts. But they may also have spotted something else. As the population of deserters increased, their prestige began to fade.

In the last days of 1967, the Swedish public had welcomed the Intrepid Four as living symbols of their distaste for American imperialism. But the hundreds who followed were not all quite so attractive. The Defense Department registered this shift in opinion and was keen to catalyze it. The day after *Deserter USA* opened in Swedish cinemas, a Pentagon press spokesman told the newspaper *Expressen* about a study conducted by his colleagues at the U.S. Embassy in Stockholm.

"The American deserters in Sweden are a sad collection," said the spokesman. "We made the research to pulverize the untruthful picture of the deserter as a young man of high ideals who fled because he detested the war in Vietnam. The facts are that the overwhelming majority chose Sweden for quite other reasons." The typical deserter specimen, the Pentagon concluded, was "a young man who finds it difficult to adapt, a thief, a drug addict, a cop-out."

The Stockholm exiles were accustomed to such insults, but this story brought a worrying new twist. The study had been carried out using data supplied by the Swedish Aliens Commission. Their hosts were cooperating with the enemy. The Swedish press remained sympathetic. The Pentagon's remarks were reported with skepticism, though as American names began to cluster in the crime columns of the Swedish newspapers, the pressure increased—and the deserters discovered that, like many migrant communities, they had been given collective responsibility for the transgressions of individual members.

From late 1968, the cases piled up. A Gothenburg judge convicted a pair of former soldiers for possessing forged passports, stealing five motorcycles, and relieving three elderly women of their handbags. Most deserter crimes were drug related, and of variable seriousness. Fred Pavese, a former artilleryman who deserted from Fort Sill, Oklahoma, was arrested by the Stockholm police for possession of marijuana—but the record suggests that he was too busy strumming his guitar and taking modeling assignments to become a menace to society.

In Malmö, two twenty-year-old Californians, Joseph Norwood and John Dowling, were jailed for dealing marijuana; they told the court they were trying to earn money for air tickets back to the States, but they did not seem particularly delighted to receive deportation notices.

Dowling, a dandyish young man from San Diego, had a signature trick that broke no laws: selling nonexistent blocks of hashish to credulous Swedish hippies. He and a Hungarian accomplice would take a prospective buyer to a locker at the Centralen railway station and give them a glimpse of the goods stowed inside. He would then sell the locker key for ten thousand kronor and be halfway to Budapest before the buyer discovered that he had purchased a wad of roofing felt wrapped in old newspaper.

"John Dowling had an excellent knowledge of people's behavior as well as a true love of being dishonest," remembered Rob Argento. "He was the Jean Genet of the deserter community."

More than one exile I interviewed believed that the American authorities were deliberately rolling bad apples in their direction. One summoned the image of an intelligence officer moving through the stockade, doling out plane tickets to the most unsavory inmates, and telling them to follow their desires.

Certainly, Sweden was the destination for a number of habitual criminals for whom desertion was simply a new way to feed their compulsion. Marshall Zolp, for example, was an air force pilot who ran several bombing raids over Vietnam before absconding to Sweden in early 1969. Having made himself disappear, he then did the same to large and small amounts of other people's money, aided by his killer charm and disarming resemblance to the film star George Hamilton. (He could, reported a former associate, "sell voodoo dolls to Catholic nuns.")

After his Swedish interlude Zolp returned to the United States, where he ran penny stock frauds in collaboration with the New York mafia, attempted to sell shares in a twenty-four-hour Nevada brothel under the pseudonym Archibald Spray, and founded nonexistent companies to deal in nonexistent products. (The most audacious was the Laser Arms Corporation, which made millions by selling worthless shares to investors who thought they were buying a stake in the future of ray guns and self-chilling beverage cans.)

FOR THE FIRST half of 1969, the two main deserter groups preserved an uneasy truce. The American Deserters Committee maintained a revolutionary stance appropriate to an overseas chapter of the SDS. It launched a newspaper called the *Paper Grenade* and waved the flag for the Viet Cong. The Philadelphia deserter Vincent Strollo remembered a comrade crashing into a meeting with a copy of an SDS newspaper that accused the Standard Oil Company of profiting from the carnage in Vietnam. "He had a Molotov cocktail in his hand," said Strollo, "and he was proposing to blow up the gas station over the road. Everybody ran out to stop him."

Cooler heads prevailed in the office of the Underground Railway. Its members organized role-play sessions with a visiting American psychiatrist, drew up a constitution, and designed a cute logo in the shape of a steam train. Some men retained membership in both organizations, though one leader of the Underground Railway told me that he thought George Carrano attended meetings of the more moderate group in order to keep an eye on the opposition.

IN THE SPRING of 1969, the exile community gained a figure who could bridge the gap between the two factions—a mentor whose job it was to listen to worries about drugs, housing, employment, and the folks back home. The Reverend Thomas Lee Hayes was an Episcopalian minister dispatched from the States by an anti-war group called Clergy and Laymen Concerned About Vietnam. He had a wife and two young children, a postgraduate degree in clinical psychology, and a strong track record in the civil rights movement. Around his neck he wore a pendant of his own design that combined the crucifix and the peace sign.

An impressive triumvirate blessed his mission by laying hands on him on the steps of the U.S. Justice Department: Rabbi Abraham Joshua Heschel, the Reverend Richard Neuhaus, and Coretta Scott King, the widow of Martin Luther King Jr. When Hayes and his family arrived at Arlanda, *Hänt i Veckan* magazine compared him to Father Flanagan, the Catholic priest whose delinquent-wrangling abilities had earned him the honor of being played by Spencer Tracy in the Oscar-winning movie

Boys Town. Except Father Flanagan never quoted Frantz Fanon or enthused about the Black Panthers.

Swarthmore College near Philadelphia houses the archive of CALCAV and the private papers of Thomas Hayes. Even the hate mail has been carefully archived. Some of its enemies just scrawled "bull" or "nuts" or "c/o Ho Chi Minh" across the envelope. Others were polite enough to enclose a letter. "I am concerned about Vietnam," wrote one correspondent, "and all the other small countries that are in the path of the ever-grasping tentacles of communism." Another wrote: "Your propaganda is sickening. Communist autocracy loves your unrealistic DISSENT." A message signed by a Real Concerned American argued: "Bomb the North Vietnam Commies out. Then complete the job by cleaning up the dirty Commies here in the U.S."

But friendly advice also came Hayes's way. Jim Walch, an American expatriate studying at Stockholm University, wrote to the new boy to sketch out the Swedish scene. It was, he said, one of "internal dissent and mistrust." "Besides the conflict of personalities, accusations, trumped-up CIA charges, slander, libel and general fear, which are all very real causes of dissension, I see sociological dissension."

Walch regarded the split between the ADC and the Underground Railway as a dispute between working-class and middle-class deserters— but he also acknowledged that the majority of men had little interest in politics. "In Sweden, as in contrast to France," he wrote, "the 'stable' persons, who could act as stabilizers on the whole group, get it made and isolate themselves, leaving heads, addicts, activists, paranoids and teen-agers, and the new guys of course."

Hayes arrived in Sweden on March 21, 1969, and moved into a modest but comfortable second-floor apartment in the Stockholm suburb of Solna. His papers showed that he wasn't merely enthusiastic about his new role. He was giddy. He was intoxicated. During his year in Sweden, he lived life with an intensity he spent the rest of his days trying to recapture. He read radical literature, went on marches, argued the deserters' case to the Swedish social bureau, made strong friendships with exiles of all factions. He stayed up until 1:30 a.m. with Jim McGourty and Bill Jones, discussing the future of the ADC.

When the Pentagon spokesman made his disparaging remarks to

Expressen, Hayes held a press conference to rebut them. He felt a kind of envy for the youth and vitality of the deserters, and tried to kindle it in himself. He fell a little in love with Jim McGourty's wife, Michele, and a little out of love with his own. He did not, like Michael Vale, allow deserters to sleep in his bathtub or roll up in a rug on the hallway floor, but more than three hundred houseguests passed through in the course of the year, and some nights there were eleven hungry young Americans crowded around the table.

Janet Hayes, whose attitude toward this new life was rather less fervid, had the task of making dinner stretch to feed the extra mouths. Not all these guests were taking advantage of the family's good nature. Swedish food was expensive. Most deserters were poor. Many subsisted on sacks of unwashed brown rice that could be bought cheap at the side door of the Chinese Embassy.

The Stockholm exiles had splintered into factions, but even those who scorned Hayes's liberal politics grew fond of the man. He deserved their respect. Nothing was too much trouble. He calmed the speed freaks. He wrote reassuring letters to parents back home in the States. When a deserter's car broke down, Hayes collected him—and a new radiator—from the junkyard.

There were some bitter disappointments. One deserter conned him out of $260 and vanished from Sweden, claiming to have foiled a kidnapping attempt by two CIA agents. Another turned out to be not a deserter at all but a sex offender on the run with his teenage victim.

But Hayes's protective attitude gave him common ground with his flock. He was as suspicious as Bill Jones of visitors asking too many questions. The pastor acted as a gatekeeper, performing background checks on reporters hunting for interviews, movie producers looking for script ideas, psychologists in search of experimental material. He dealt with hundreds of these inquiries.

In April, Gordon McLendon, a pirate radio entrepreneur and producer of the film *The Killer Shrews*, turned up in Stockholm and invited a group of seven deserters to his hotel suite. Hayes went with them, maintaining a fatherly eye as the visitor offered whiskey, salted nuts, and the company of a Swede named Lisa. ("I hope none of you have to ask why she's here," said McLendon.) Another unexpected presence in the room was the American television actor Ron Ely, who had joined McLendon's entourage after three years of swinging around in a loincloth as the star of NBC's *Tarzan*.

The deserters kept drinking until they discovered a hidden tape recorder whirring in the corner of the room. Someone plucked out the cassette and passed it to Hayes. The deserters demanded money for their stories. McLendon gave a long defensive speech about not polluting the journalistic process with cash. Ron Ely took McLendon off into the bedroom for a conference that ended with the producer unpeeling $300 from a roll of bills and sending the actor off to the currency exchange. "Five minutes later," wrote Hayes, "Ron was back and divvying up fifteen hundred crowns among the deserters in front of everyone. Two hundred crowns remained, and with that the group went out to dinner. But not before they had lifted their host's Scotch and rum."

In June 1969 an American sociologist, Michel P. Richard, contacted Hayes to ask for his help with a research project but made the mistake of telling him the title: *The Deserter as Political Deviant*. ("Ridiculous," fumed Hayes.) When Richard arrived in Sweden to look for subjects, he found the deserters forewarned. Nobody would speak to him. Crestfallen, he went to see Bertil Svahnström, who expressed his opinion of the ADC with an impromptu film show: his print of *Deserter USA* and news footage of Philip Callicoat's bungled bank robbery.

Toward the end of his two-month trip, Richard managed to persuade a pair of deserters in Uppsala to agree to an on-the-record conversation. But when he arrived at the meeting he found ADC members waiting to denounce him as a spy. Cutting his losses, Richard went home and wrote an article arguing that the old distinction between researcher and subject was breaking down; that the studied were now mobilizing against their interpreters. Half a century later, I found him looking back ruefully on the experience. "I am having trouble forgiving myself for not doing more with that study," he told me. "I let ego get in the way and failed to think outside the box."

REVEREND HAYES HAD moved among the deserters when they were in their teens and twenties. I was meeting them at retirement age. But I felt a strong sympathy with his position. We were both trying to understand the histories and motivations of these men; we were both trying to evaluate the truth of statements made in an environment that was shaped by threats both real and imagined.

The most puzzling story I encountered was that of Thomas Taylor, a former army private who spoke to me on the phone from his home in Hawaii. I found Thomas through his art. He is a prodigious producer of brightly colored oil paintings, which he describes as "the greatest body of art created during the first ten years of twenty-first century." He is also a prodigious drug user, and remains, I suspect, the only person to list all his narcotic experiences on LinkedIn. (His online CV also notes that his marriage ended because he spent the wedding night in bed with the best man.) Our conversations were as untethered as you might expect. "I think the Nazis won the war," he told me. "They came in through the windows and the doors of perception. All our weapons of war came off their drawing boards. I could go on and on. You know I do spontaneous poetry?"

It was hard to follow Thomas's account of himself, but that incoherence seemed to speak to the nature of the deserter experience. This was a life story with a psychedelic filter. During basic training at Fort Jackson, Thomas said, his instructor had tied him up in order to simulate a Viet Cong interrogation. The lesson included a sexual assault. "He passed out," explained Thomas, "and I kind of robbed him and took all money and gold rings and watches and went AWOL." His parents in Milwaukee were unsympathetic. "Every time I tried to tell them what happened, they looked at me like I ought to kill myself."

Later, at Fort Sheridan, Illinois, he got into a knife fight with a fellow soldier and attempted to make amends by offering him a marijuana joint. The cigarette became a piece of evidence: Thomas was sent to the stockade at Fort Leavenworth and put on a diet of raw potatoes, bread, and water. Never having completed basic training, he was surprised by the army's next move: shipping him out to Frankfurt and giving him a job as a van driver. His light duties allowed him time to develop a relationship with a young German woman who worked at a record store, and to add heroin and LSD to his narcotic regimen.

He was in the grip of this habit when he decided to make the journey north to Sweden—which seemed to explain the colorful complexity of the rest of his story. He was a founding member of the ADC, he said, but Michael Vale maneuvered him out of the organization. ("He was CIA," Thomas said, with confidence.) He did a screen test for Vana Caruso, assistant director of the proposed Carlo Ponti film about the deserters. ("She was also CIA," he asserted.) He played guitar as support to the visiting U.S. rock band Country Joe and the Fish—whose "I-Feel-Like-I'm-Fixin'-to-Die Rag" became the title music of *Deserter USA*. He became a medical guinea pig at a clinic in Uppsala, where he took part in a pioneering methadone trial. (Such trials, I learned, did take place.) In an email, he tried to convey the exhilaration of the moment. "We took Mandrax and Preludin crushed & soaked in water, drawn through a cotton or cigarette filter and shot into our veins. We were Rebels against The Machine! We wanted to save The Whole Human Race!"

From here the story became more dreamlike. Thomas claimed to have been kidnapped in Sweden by a pair of U.S. agents who flew him to Heathrow Airport. He managed to escape and find refuge among the members of an experimental art group who lived in a warehouse in Covent Garden. On a trip to Marseille, he said, he was detained by the French police and was transferred to Frankfurt, where he was reunited with his old company commander, who held him down and force-fed him a jar of confiscated LSD tablets. "I was tripping," he explained, "for forty-plus years." These experiences, he said, had convinced him to live as much of his life as possible beyond the purview of the state. He had joined a libertarian movement whose members shared intelligence on the dark web. "I wish I could go back to the America of my youth," he said, wistfully. "It was a great country then."

PARANOIA WAS A strong element in the atmosphere of deserter culture. Some men tried not to inhale; others filled their lungs and let it roar through their bloodstream. The effects could be fatal. They claimed the life of Robert Sylvia, a radio repairman with nine years' army service, a small part in *Deserter USA*, and two children back home in Fort Lauderdale. When he arrived in Sweden in March 1968, Sylvia told reporters that any CIA operative planning to take him back to the States might as well shoot him. The following July, sitting alone in a summerhouse belonging to his girlfriend's parents, he saved them the trouble. A few days before his suicide he had addressed a political meeting in the nearby town of Visby. He claimed that agents were on his tail. "I have," he said, "lived through a mental hell I hope you people will be spared from." He left no note. The reality of his fear is now beyond recovery.

Other anxieties had more visible causes. Mysterious mail began moving between Sweden and the United States. Deserters who had told no one back home of their whereabouts were surprised to get letters from their parents, begging them to return. In April 1969, the families of U.S. soldiers killed in action in Vietnam began receiving letters with a Stockholm postmark. They were purportedly from the offices of the ADC, and urged their recipients to press Congress and the president for the end of the war. Naturally, their recipients were outraged.

A bereaved mother from Xenia, Ohio, shared the message that she had already mailed to the White House. "If we cannot believe in our country and our merciful God," she told reporters, "what shall we believe in? Certainly not American deserters." A mourning father, himself a disabled veteran, declared his disgust for a similar letter received on the stationery of the ADC. "Anybody who can't serve their country belongs in Sweden or Russia or some place like that." These letters caused disquiet among the exile community. Who was their author? Nobody knew. And who had given those Swedish addresses to their families? Perhaps the Swedes, as well as the Americans, were spying on them.

MICHAEL VALE RETURNED to Stockholm in June 1969. The letters of Thomas Lee Hayes recorded the event. "Michael Vale is back in town after the word being spread around that the ADC had asked him *not* to return. I wonder what our meeting shall be like? Already I hear he is asking about me, why I don't like the ADC (not true), and what I am up to (who knows)."

Michael had been away on revolutionary business. Traveling Europe, meeting contacts in radical groups in France and Germany, immersing himself in Marxist theory in a library in Amsterdam. Without the knowledge of Hayes and the Underground Railway, he had also made a discreet visit to Stockholm. ("Forgotten but not gone!" said one ADC member who greeted him.) U.S. military bases near Frankfurt and Heidelberg were his new obsession. Perhaps, he reasoned, the men stationed there would turn out to be the foot soldiers of the revolution.

In Stockholm, his absence had made his legend grow. For many, it confirmed his status as a provocateur: Vale had formed the ADC, led it to extremity, broken it in half, and vanished. One subscriber to that theory, John Takman, a prominent Swedish Communist who had provided medical advice to the Russell Tribunal, encouraged Thomas Hayes to take the same view. "We now know that he was on the payroll of the U.S. Embassy or some agency with a money funnel through the embassy," Takman wrote. "But it will probably take some time before all the deserters are aware of this fact." Hayes ignored the accusation. He and Vale were soon on good terms.

Others could not put their suspicions to rest. Dan Israel, the son of the child psychologist Mirjam Israel, questioned Michael's financial weightlessness. "He was an enigma to me," he told me. "He had money. He had a lot of spare time. I never understood how he lived, just translating text for a chemistry journal." The records of *Chemical Abstracts* yielded no answers to that. Oddly, though, the journal did have a subtle role to play in Cold War counterintelligence. It employed an army of translators to fillet Soviet scientific literature for descriptions of freshly synthesized chemical compounds. The results were published in its pages and laid down on magnetic tape in its computer room in Columbus, Ohio. The CIA was an eager subscriber and used the information to monitor technological developments in the USSR. It also kept a keen eye on research that seemed relevant to missile production and looked for evidence of scientific espionage by comparing descriptions of new Russian compounds with those being made in American laboratories.

Michael Vale, however, was poor casting for a chemical cold warrior. One deserter with a high school science certificate found him ignorant of the basic facts of the field and remembered his bafflement when the subject of plastic polymers came up in the conversation. This, for him, was proof of Michael's perfidy.

When I raised these matters with Michael, he waved them away. His work for *Chemical Abstracts* had dried up, he said, with a speed that indicated official disapproval of his political activities in Sweden. The patronage of M. E. Sharpe, the publishers of *Soviet Psychology* and *Soviet Education*, had saved him from poverty. The story checked out: Sharpe's catalog contained dozens of his credits. Moreover, I had seen enough of him to know that he needed very little money to get by. He was entirely content with the cold comforts of revolutionary asceticism. In Sweden, he took his meals at the railway station snack bar. His whole life now fit in one rucksack. Michael was a loner and a wanderer. His reasons for being so might not all have been good, but the more time I spent with him, the more I doubted that he was something as simple as a CIA snoop. As for Thomas Taylor's story about a bag of Vietnamese cash handed over in a lavatory—I felt ashamed to have entertained it.

Perhaps I had been duped. Perhaps he'd done a Svengali number on me. But when old deserters told me they liked Michael but didn't trust him, I knew what they meant. Clancy Sigal offered some advice. "Don't worry whether Mike is helping or hindering," he said. "He's a character out of Dostoyevsky and himself probably doesn't know. He loves, or used to love, chaos."

One day, over lunch in the British Library, I asked Michael to name the man he thought most likely to be a plant within the American Deserters Committee. He, like Mark Shapiro, was putting his money on George Carrano. "A New York hustler. He was constantly advising us to do provocative things. Carrano said he'd been contacted by the Vietnamese to bring two hundred deserters to Sweden from Phnom Penh. If we'd announced that, it would have wrecked our situation." Might it have been an honest mistake? Mike shrugged. "At the time I didn't have the necessary paranoia that would have enabled me to dwell on it."

Michele, Jim McGourty's first wife, also had a story about George Carrano's reckless behavior. She told it with arresting clarity. She and her husband were visiting friends—a Swedish woman and her boyfriend, a former policeman from Algeria. Throughout the evening, their host kept refilling Jim's glass. "He got him really, really drunk," Michele recalled, "and then he came after me."

While Jim was unconscious in the next room, Michele suffered a violent assault. Fortunately the sounds of the struggle awoke others in the apartment. "The guy just slithered off," she said. The following day, as she was about to report the incident to the police, Carrano advised another course of action. "He wanted to go out and take charge of the situation. I just said, 'Look, we will just handle this through the police. What you are proposing is only going to make things worse and get everybody else into trouble, so leave it alone.' I remember screaming, yelling at him about all of that. I just said, 'This guy will get what is coming to him.'" He did. She reported it to the police, and her attacker was deported.

Right or wrong, theories about George Carrano's behavior were much discussed among his peers. They even inspired the plot of *Deserter USA*. Its featured infiltrator is a charming figure called Fabian, who supplies the exiles with cigarettes and alcohol and is later discovered rifling through papers in the ADC offices. Another member—played by Terry Whitmore—catches him in the act and administers a vigorous punishment beating. Carrano himself is a conspicuous absence from the picture.

"But they talked about him," said Olle Sjögren, the film's codirector. "They told me he was suspected. Mike said this, and some of the others." Olle felt around for the correct English expression. "They thought he was a guinea pig."

"A guinea pig?" I queried.

"A scapegoat," he said.

"A mole?" I asked.

"A mole," he replied.

MAPS OF THE Old Scandinavian world describe two kinds of territory. A known geographical space in which Vikings raided and traded, through which a captain could plot the course of his longship and expect to find, at the end of the journey, something he already had words to describe. And another space, where trolls and half-trolls watched and waited, where the backs of dragons broke the ice sheet. This space was not a void. Not an inconvenient blank patch filled with the mapmaker's monstrous doodles. It was geographical. It could be navigated. And as I tried to understand the story of the Stockholm deserters, the more they seemed to me like voyagers on these strange and hazardous seas. Some drowned; some reached the shore in safety. Some welcomed me and shared their sagas; others sat by the fire and refused to open the door. Many of the talkers, I discovered, could not give sure and certain accounts of their experiences. Much remained mysterious and unreadable to them—not least the true natures of old comrades who stayed silent about the past.

The official paper record both helped and hindered. The officers and operatives who kept it—or didn't keep it—were not the allies of posterity. They made records disappear and did their best to make themselves disappear. They bequeathed us a small percentage of the documents they generated, most dark with the ink of redaction. But that dangerous thing, a little knowledge, can be acquired from the surviving material.

In the records released by the American and Swedish intelligence agencies, evidence exists that a broad coalition of spooks was profiling individual members of the American Deserters Committee. A heavily censored FBI file shows that the Office of the Assistant Chief of Staff for Intelligence produced a substantial report on Mike and Bill's organization—though the Pentagon seems to have mislaid its copy. The same record notes that more information, and requests for information, were received from Stockholm by the FBI's Washington field office and its outposts in London, Paris, and Tokyo. The file also contains a bureau memorandum bearing five fat bands of censor's ink—beneath which clearly lurk the biographies of five ADC members. The list is preceded by the caveat "classified confidential to protect a source of continuing value."

The archives of SÄPO, the Swedish security service, yielded more explicit information. I saw one uncensored surveillance report from an undercover agent who noted the presence of Warren Hamerman and fifteen other deserters at a political meeting in Gothenburg. A much longer file contained information about the ADC that could only have been supplied by a member, or someone with intimate knowledge of its members. The names were blanked out, but it was possible to guess what the censor had obscured. One leading figure was "two-faced if not triple-faced . . . an intellectual opportunist who is generous out of pure vanity." Michael Vale seemed to fit that description. A deserter who risked arrest in late 1968 by coming out of hiding to attend a political meeting was surely Warren Hamerman—accompanied by a woman who was clearly Jim's wife, Michele. Another deserter was said to be "psychologically completely exhausted and . . . sitting with a gang of sympathetic sorts at the office smoking opium." John Ashley, perhaps, the doped-up son of a senior Pentagon official?

Most powerfully, the document recorded the climate of suspicion in which the exiles lived. "It is clear," said one, "that the American government has agents among the deserters. One must therefore protect oneself and the honest deserters. The Americans have two goals with their agents—in the first instance it is to gather intelligence and speed the breakup of the group, and for the second part to scare the others to silence with the mere knowledge that there are agents among them." It was easy to imagine a room full of marijuana smoke and young men looking into one another's eyes, scanning for loyalty or treachery.

At the beginning of 2016, I asked the Swedish National Archives if it held any documents relating to the ADC. It did. They were all classified, and too numerous to process in one batch. Perhaps, it was suggested, I could request the files of specific individuals, which could then be assessed on a case-by-case basis? Off went emails naming the deserters prominent in this story. Which is how I came to receive copies of heavily weeded dossiers on Warren Hamerman and Jim McGourty. How I discovered that SÄPO documents on Michael Vale and Bill Jones could not yet be released "for reasons of national security." How I learned that a file on George Carrano once existed, but had, at some stage, been removed from the archives. By whom, the archivist could not say. And with that, I was told that my requests would no longer be accepted.

FORTUNATELY, A REAL-LIFE SÄPO operative was happy to give me his angle on the story. He is Gunnar Ekberg, and he has the firmest handshake of anyone in this book. Eye-wateringly, bone-crunchingly firm, as befits someone who called his memoirs *They Would Have Died Anyway*. As the book explains, Gunnar's career in espionage came to a sudden end in December 1973, when a pair of investigative journalists from the magazine *Folket i Bild* exposed him as an operative of the Information Bureau, a SÄPO subdepartment so secret that the public had no knowledge of its name, still less its cozy relationships with the American, British, and Israeli intelligence services.

The story was a kind of Watergate: it showed that Olof Palme's fiery opposition to American foreign policy did not extend to the secret state. It also revised deserter history. Among the figures caught in the long lens with Gunnar was Sven Kempe, the textiles importer who had spent thousands of crowns encouraging the deserters to grow turnips at the farm near Torsåker. He was, said *Folket i Bild*, on the Information Bureau's "permanent staff of spies." To those who had turned its under-nourished soil, the project now seemed rather less altruistic than it had appeared.

The photographs in *Folket i Bild* depicted Gunnar Ekberg in a groovy turtleneck sweater and corduroy jacket with wide lapels. On the day we met, his dress was more causal. Tight black T-shirt, spectacles on strings, a little silver troll dangling from a chain around his neck. The habits of the old spy, however, remained steadfastly in place. We sat in the farthest corner of the restaurant. The table had a clear view of the street door. He kept a cool eye on my very un-Swedish habit of waving my hands around as I talk. He tailed me through the menu, following my choices, from risotto to espresso to limoncello. He was unobtrusively charming.

Gunnar began fighting the Cold War in 1964, when he was nineteen years old. It began when a friend from his diving club—also named Gunnar—called with some intriguing information. Long Gunnar, as the friend was known, owing to his height, had heard from a coastguardsman that a Russian submarine had sunk in Öresund, the strait that separates Sweden and Denmark. The boys went in a dinghy to locate its remains. They found them. They also found a boatload of Soviet sailors who were attempting to salvage the vessel. The Russians encouraged the boys to swim down into the wreck. The Gunnars emerged from the waves clutch-ing a red flag. When they handed it over, the captain rewarded them with vodka.

Someone, however, was watching from the coast. That night Long Gunnar received a visit from an authoritative stranger. "I come from a certain organization," he said, "collecting certain information for certain needs." The next day, under the supervision of these new employers, the boys descended once more into the wreck. They swam through flooded compartments, ignored the corpses of the drowned men, pulled out maps, papers, radio sets. The mission was fruitful. Thanks to the two

Gunnars, the Swedish security service learned of the existence of a previously unknown Russian submarine base on the Baltic.

Once he had completed his military service, other missions came Gunnar's way. "The first thing you have to do," said his SÄPO handler, "is to qualify yourself for the harpoon fishing world championship in Cuba." He did, and for a few weeks he was Stockholm's man in Havana—while resisting the attentions of a female Cuban agent who hoped to seduce him into being Havana's man in Stockholm. A more substantial assignment was waiting for him on his return. A job with the Information Bureau. Gunnar's mission was to live undercover in the student anti-war movement and sniff out the influence and money of hostile foreign governments: a Swedish equivalent of Operation Chaos, pursued in cooperation with the CIA. "The Americans wanted to run it," Gunnar recalled. "But we had to tell them no."

Gunnar began his new life in early 1968. He moved to Gothenburg with a company Saab and a generous tax-free salary. He read Karl Marx. He read Karl Popper. (Though not in the presence of his Marxist friends.) He went on marches, attended rallies, and joined the Communist Party of Sweden, a Maoist outfit run from premises that used an American flag as a doormat. ("Make sure your feet are really clean," said a notice.)

He resigned himself to once-a-year contact with his family. ("You couldn't fool my mother," he said. "She could see through everything.") He discarded his old friends, made new ones, and spied on them. It wasn't so hard. He had little time for the Maoists, who struck him as cultish, humorless, and absurdly middle class—and the job offered a satisfying element of drama. He installed listening devices. He kept a clay-filled matchbox in his pocket and used it to take an impression of the party's office key. (He remembered licking the key clean to remove suspicious traces.) He copied stacks of Communist Party documents and passed them on to his handlers. As a child, Gunnar had heard his Danish relations talking about their resistance work during the war. He felt as if he were fighting the same fight.

Gunnar had more sympathy for the deserters. "It must have been hell for many of them," he reflected. "They were people with no education, and they just ended up in a war." In this, he believed, he was more charitable than many of the Maoists. They had been expecting to meet a group of anti-imperialist heroes of the sort that might be sculpted in marble. Instead they were presented with a bunch of young men who were unkempt, unread, unsophisticated, and politically incorrect. Gunnar knew, however, what some of his radical friends only guessed—that some of these men were undercover agents, just like him.

"SÄPO placed people among the deserters, and they had a few reasons for it," said Gunnar. It was particularly interested, he believed, in the loyalties of men who had arrived in Sweden via Moscow. "The KGB are very skilled," he said. "Very good at reading people's personalities." Perhaps, he suggested, some of them had been persuaded to spy for the USSR.

AND HERE HIS story moved into more sensational territory. Gunnar told me that he had met one of these SÄPO infiltrators, an American who had been recruited to live among a small community of deserters in the Stockholm satellite town Tyresö. (It was, I realized, the group coordinated by Åke Sandin, whose spare room had been occupied by Rick Bailey of the Intrepid Four and Olsson the boa constrictor.) Gunnar showed me his notes on the conversation.

"My task," his contact claimed, "was to work out the relationships between the real deserters, who were commonly heroin addicts and quarrelsome, and CIA agents who were playing deserter to get into the left-wing movements and parties." These American operatives, claimed Gunnar's man, had been tasked with a mission that was much bigger than throwing a spanner in the works of a few exiled radicals. They were using deserter identities as a cover for an operation against the Soviet Union. The KGB, they believed, had placed its own sleeper agents in Sweden. Agents who would awaken in the event of the Cold War turning hot, and smooth the progress of a Soviet invasion by assassinating key figures in the Swedish government and defense establishments.

It was a plot out of a paperback thriller, but Gunnar, a veteran of this world, could not dismiss it. It was well documented that in the 1950s the CIA and NATO had cooperated on a project called GLADIO, a Europe-wide scheme to recruit and train a secret army that would spring into action in the event of communism achieving power, by either invasion or election. The Swedish section had been the responsibility of William Colby, a young CIA officer who would become director of central intelligence in 1973. His memoir *Honorable Men* describes the intense secrecy in which this work was conducted.

Sweden was a neutral country, which meant that neither NATO nor the CIA could operate openly on its territory. "Obviously," he wrote, "if the preparations ever leaked to the Russians, they would be in the position to destroy the nets directly after they occupied the country and so the whole point of the work would be lost." But the existence of this network also had to remain secret from all but a small number of trusted figures in Washington, NATO, and Scandinavia. "Public knowledge that the CIA was building stay-behind nets there in anticipation of a Soviet occupation would oblige the governments to put an end to the project forthwith," Colby wrote.

Gunnar told me that his contact was an old, sick man who had been part of this army and wanted to make a confession. There was one more detail: if the Soviets had activated their plan, American agents would have armed themselves with weapons stored in secret depots around the country and formed the resistance against the occupying force. "One of my tasks," Gunnar's man had told him, "was to pass keys to such a depot outside Stockholm if a critical situation should arise." He had even given Gunnar the name of the deserter entrusted to hold they keys. Gunnar peered at his notes and read out the name. Frederick Pavese.

Gunnar watched my jaw drop. The name meant nothing to him. But he had not spent several years reading through old newspapers, census records, and street indexes, scrabbling for biographical details about American exiles in Stockholm. I held dozens of these names in my head. Some were major figures, some minor. Fred seemed minor, but I knew I had some notes on him. I pulled my laptop from my satchel and began searching through my documents.

"His dad owned a delicatessen in Westchester, New York, and lost an eye in the war," I said. "Or maybe in the delicatessen. Fred played the guitar and smoked pot. He had a small part in a 1976 film called *I lust och nöd*." The trail, I told Gunnar, was pretty cold. It ended with Pavese's

2003 post to a website about insects, on which he shared an anecdote about a Thai neighbor who, by stamping her foot on the linoleum, would summon a cockroach that lived in her bathroom and feed it by hand.

A few days later I tracked down Larry Turk, one of Fred Pavese's high school classmates. "At the time of his desertion," he said, "we were more focused on those who saw Vietnam up close and were killed in action. We were very unimpressed with what he did." Larry sent me a copy of the souvenir brochure for their 1986 reunion. Pavese had supplied a photograph of himself in an open-necked wool jacket that revealed a luxuriant display of chest hair. Beneath this were a few upbeat remarks about his history. "Having the opportunity to live without confinement to work or family has given me the opportunity to partake in all aspects of society in many different parts of the world," he boasted. "I was in Iran and Afghanistan before their crises. I have known Afghanistan as a wonderful world of men who rode horses and people who were happy; it should have been left that way."

I'd hoped to find Fred Pavese. To ask him whether he was a guitar-strumming actor or a sleeper agent primed to break out the guns when Soviet tanks rolled over the border, or both. The Swedish Death Index revealed that my inquiries were a decade too late; Fred Pavese had died in Stockholm in March 2004. But the National Library of Sweden, I discovered, held a copy of what Google considers his most significant contribution to posterity, *I lust och nöd*. After a little throat clearing, the library agreed to make it available for viewing. It turned out to be a soft porn variant of Ingmar Bergman's 1966 film *Persona*. A faux-earnest psychodrama starring Elona Glenn as a woman tormented by her sexual appetite—which we observe her attempting to satisfy on a yacht, in a cinema, and at the Chat Noir club in Stockholm, where her partner is the British blue movie star Mary Millington. The credits compiled by the Swedish Film Institute list Pavese as "The Mechanic," but his scenes were missing from the library's print. It wasn't hard to guess where they should have been. At one point the heroine's car refuses to start. A little later the problem seems to be resolved. The services provided by Fred Pavese are lost to history.

9 / OUT OF LOVE

IN SIR ARTHUR Conan Doyle's short story "The Final Problem," Sherlock Holmes asks Dr. Watson if he has ever heard of Professor James Moriarty. Watson replies that he has not—and soon learns that his friend has developed an obsession with the man. "His career," explains the detective, "has been an extraordinary one." The world knows Moriarty as a gifted academic, but Holmes discerns something darker. "He is the Napoleon of Crime, Watson. He is the organizer of half that is evil and of nearly all that is undetected in this great city." Holmes is correct in his deductions. Watson travels with him to Austria for a fateful confrontation with his adversary.

In Nicholas Meyer's Conan Doyle pastiche, *The Seven-Per-Cent Solution*, Sherlock Holmes asks Dr. Watson if he has ever heard of Professor James Moriarty. Watson says that he has not, but this is a lie. Holmes has been banging on about him endlessly, particularly when under the influence of cocaine. "His career," explains the detective, "has been an extraordinary one." The world knows Moriarty as a gifted academic, but Holmes discerns something darker. "He is the Napoleon of Crime, Watson. He is the organizer of half that is evil and of nearly all that is undetected in this great city." But Moriarty is just a harmless old math teacher. Holmes is madly and spectacularly incorrect in his deductions.

So Watson takes him to Austria for psychoanalysis under Dr. Sigmund Freud.

Listening to competing theories about the infiltrator within the American Deserters Committee, I was often reminded of Meyer's revisionist tale of the detective with a damaging idée fixe. Åke Sandin had exclaimed "CIA!" as soon as I mentioned the name Bill Jones. Thomas Taylor was convinced that Michael Vale had taken a bribe from Hanoi. Mike Vale thought that George Carrano was not what he seemed. So did Mark Shapiro, who swore to keep investigating his suspect until his last breath. But if you were a protagonist in this plot, how would it be possible to tell whether you were in the Doyle story or the Meyer? I asked myself the same question as I tried to understand the motivations of the man around whom my own suspicions began to coalesce.

THE TRUE STORY of Dr. Clifford Garland Gaddy may be known only to Dr. Clifford Garland Gaddy. It's possible that even those closest to him have been denied some of the important details. Not that he has been hidden from view. The C-SPAN video library has archived three decades of his conservative wardrobe decisions and impeccably Washingtonian punditry. Political journalists, particularly those with an interest in Russia, have had many opportunities to sit in press conferences admiring his good cheekbones, tight, faintly equine mouth, and gray hair kept in the close cut of his school yearbook photograph. But Cliff Gaddy has never been part of any institution subject to the Freedom of Information Act, and, as most of his work has been done in collaboration, he has barely been obliged to utter a public sentence in the first-person singular. Which means that the official narrative of his life has never done justice to the weirdness of his biography—which incorporates desertion from the army, membership in the ADC, a senior position in a profoundly weird political cult, person-of-interest status in the assassination of Olof Palme, and a dazzling academic career achieved with financial support from the Pentagon. To me, it seemed inexplicable. Not least because he declined to offer any explanation for it himself.

Today, Cliff is known as one of the world's leading experts on Vladimir Putin, the former KGB man who became the president of Russia.

Cliff's book *Mr. Putin: Operative in the Kremlin*, cowritten with the British academic Fiona Hill, is the product of intense study of the known details of its subject's life, and careful deduction about the many strange blank spaces in his history. The book was a joint enterprise during the decade they spent as colleagues at the Brookings Institution, the prestigious think tank in Washington, DC. It offers a portrait of a figure whose primary identity is of an "operative"—a spy—whose instincts are always to conceal his own motives, to keep everybody guessing. It is pointless, Hill and Gaddy argue, to look for patterns in Putin's behavior. It is pointless to pursue a linear narrative. Putin adapts to any circumstance in which he finds himself, and this is the secret of his enduring power.

Diplomats, intelligence officers, and politicians have used the book to inform their dealings with Moscow. Former vice president Joe Biden and Sir John Scarlett, the former head of MI6, have sung its praises. In April 2017, the book received another flurry of publicity when the White House announced Fiona Hill's appointment to the National Security Council staff as deputy assistant to President Donald Trump and senior director for European and Russian affairs. Which is why there is a strong public interest case for shining a little light on the murky history of her coauthor.

CLIFF WAS BORN in Danville, Virginia, in June 1946. His father—also Dr. Clifford Garland Gaddy—ran a thriving medical practice in the city and owned a comfortable home near the bank of the Dan River. Clifford Sr. was a Rotarian and a pillar of his community, but one with a sense of fun—he was also a Golden Gloves state boxing champion and once hosted a rock festival on his twenty-seven-acre tobacco farm.

His eldest son—nicknamed Chip—was a boy whose abilities and achievements were absurdly numerous. He was a high school merit scholar, wrestler, track and field athlete, and champion of Babe Ruth baseball. At fourteen he was initiated into the Danville branch of the Order of DeMolay, a fraternal organization for teenage boys. In his senior year he became president of his school's chapter of the National Honor Society and won a thousand-dollar prize on a radio quiz show to find America's smartest high school student.

Though he earned scholarships to the University of Michigan and the University of Richmond, family tradition propelled him to Wake Forest University in Winston-Salem, North Carolina, his father's alma mater. Here, he joined the Kappa Alpha fraternity, a college organization whose local chapter was founded by Thomas Dixon Jr., author of *The Clansman: A Historical Romance of the Ku Klux Klan*, the novel from which D. W. Griffith adapted his film *The Birth of a Nation*. (Even in the 1960s, Kappa Alpha was known for staging Old South week, in which members marched around campus in Confederate uniforms, singing "Dixie" under the Stars and Bars.)

In October 1968, Cliff volunteered for the army. Here, he also dazzled: the assessors declared that he had the highest aptitude for languages they had ever encountered. He was quickly assigned to the Army Security Agency—the branch of the U.S. Army that dealt in intercepted enemy communications—and joined its training regiment at Fort Devens, Massachusetts. For this, there was also a family precedent. An uncle, David Winfred Gaddy, was a signals intelligence genius who monitored and decoded Vietnamese transmissions for the National Security Agency—a highly secretive organization whose existence was not acknowledged by the government until 1975. Anyone who wanted to build an intelligence officer would have been hard-pressed to find brighter and purer material than Clifford Garland Gaddy Jr. So why did he desert?

The reported explanation was a peculiar one. Cliff seems to have been the only man who went into Swedish exile because the army failed to advance his career at the pace it had promised. When the *Danville Bee* came asking Clifford Sr. why his son had disappeared to Europe, the response was that Cliff had gone because, after several months of waiting, the army had failed to assign him to a language school. A subsidiary claim asserted that Cliff was a "serious conscientious objector"— though not serious enough, it would seem, to have taken part in any protests against the Vietnam War.

The story of his defection broke at the end of July 1969, when the Swedish government gave him humanitarian asylum. Cliff wrote to his local newspaper with an account of his actions, perhaps to take some of the heat off his family. "My only excuse is that it takes some people a bit longer to open their eyes to conditions around them," he wrote. "Then too, when one has been taught to believe for over 20 years that America can only be right, it is rather difficult to abandon that illusion." He quoted Camus. "I wish I could love my country and love justice too."

MR. PUTIN: OPERATIVE in the Kremlin offers this advice on how to write about the president of Russia: "Every apparent fact or story needs to be regarded with suspicion," the authors counsel. "Very little information about him is definitive, confirmable or reliable." If we take the same approach to Cliff's life, several pieces of the jigsaw are hard to fit. He took five years to earn his bachelor's degree, rather than the customary four. During that time he was listed in only two of the Wake Forest University yearbooks, suggesting that he was more absent than present.

His brothers in the Kappa Alpha fraternity found him oddly hard to remember. One I contacted thought he'd run away to Canada. When pressed a little further, he emailed back a brief profanity. Another said he didn't know Cliff and that their careers at Wake Forest had not overlapped—but there they were, standing together in a photograph from their freshman year. For a boy whose achievements made national headlines while he was still in high school, his impact on university life was minimal. He seems to have joined no sports teams, triumphed in no quizzes or debates.

The press interviews with his father also produced an imperfect picture. Dr. Gaddy told the papers that Cliff had gone to Sweden using the passport he'd obtained when he was granted a Fulbright scholarship to study at the University of Würzburg in West Germany. Fulbright, however, could find no record of such a scholarship being offered. Dr. Gaddy also said that his son had boarded a flight from Boston to Stockholm on February 22, 1969. The record shows that he was granted humanitarian asylum on July 18. But the deserter Rob Argento remembered Cliff turning up on his doorstep in September, apparently straight off the plane.

When I mentioned Cliff to Michael Vale, he sounded a little heartbroken. "I thought of him as a best friend," he said. "We had intellectual discussions. I encouraged him to learn Russian, and he did." Michael recommended Cliff to the publisher M. E. Sharpe and brought him in on translation projects for *Soviet Psychology* and the *International Journal of Mental Health*. "Cliff was such a strong character," said Michael, wistfully. "Even at that young age. So thorough. So bright. So upright. He was *clean*." He sounded like Falstaff talking about Prince Hal.

DURING VALE'S ABSENCE, the ADC people had been arguing the case for political asylum. They screened *Deserter USA* to anti-war groups around Sweden, though they had to go without its codirector Lars Lambert, who was in jail for refusing to do his national service. Jim McGourty and Bill Jones went to plead their case to the voters of tomorrow, giving talks to Swedish schoolchildren about desertion. "What would happen if you went home now? Or if you were sent back?" asked a little girl named Ika, in a classroom not far from Stockholm. "We would get several years in prison," replied Bill. "And deserters in American prisons are treated very badly."

Book projects were also under way. Beacon Press, the progressive publishers of James Baldwin's *Notes of a Native Son* and Herbert Marcuse's *One-Dimensional Man*, commissioned the American journalist Susan George to compile a volume of interviews with the deserters. George was based in Paris, where her presence at anti-war meetings earned her a mention in the dispatches of the MHCHAOS asset codenamed PETUNIA. Mike Vale was pursuing his own deal with Grove Press, the company that distributed *Deserter USA* in the States, and arranged for Richard Bucklin, a gaunt and bug-eyed army private from Colorado, who seemed to survive solely on Coca-Cola, to begin conducting taped interviews with his comrades. ("Some of his questions were a little creepy," recalled Michele.) Neither of these works saw the light of day. However, several of the Swedish deserters did contribute to a book of interviews that was intended to advance their cause, but ended up doing the opposite.

At the end of 1969, the journalist and lawyer Mark Lane arrived in Stockholm, hungry for stories of atrocity. Lane was a celebrity of the counterculture: his bestselling book on the Kennedy assassination, *Rush to Judgment*, had founded the JFK conspiracy industry by attacking the view that Lee Harvey Oswald was a lone assassin. In 1968 Lane's fame had been amplified when he became the comedian Dick Gregory's running mate in a write-in presidential bid. When Nixon emerged victorious, Gregory denounced the process as corrupt and had himself and Lane sworn in as America's president and vice president in exile.

Lane arrived in Stockholm just as one of the great, grim news stories of the Vietnam War was breaking: the My Lai massacre, in which hundreds of unarmed Vietnamese civilians were murdered by U.S. soldiers in March 1968. The investigative reporter Seymour Hersh published the first account of this incident on November 12, 1969. As the world recoiled in horror, Lane hunted for similar stories among the deserters. The result was *Conversations with Americans*, one of the most incendiary books of the Vietnam period.

It is a collection of interviews, the first of which is with a Stockholm deserter who talks about his experiences as a member of an elite marine long-range patrol unit. Lane's interviewee describes how torture methods were high on the syllabus. "We were told to make use of electrical radio equipment," he said. "They had drawings on the board showing exactly how to clamp the electrodes into the testicles of a man or the body of a woman." Later classes, he said, included instruction in inserting bamboo sticks into the ears or under the fingernails of a prisoner. And in the case of female captives, other instructions were given: "to strip them, spread them open and drive pointed sticks or bayonets into their vagina." He adds: "We were also told we could rape the girls all we wanted."

The name of this interviewee was Chuck Onan, the weed-loving boy from the Chicago projects, and owner of Ninja the dog. Chuck had not been part of an elite marine squad. He had never received more than basic training. But the record suggested he had strayed from the facts. *Dagens Nyheter* placed Chuck at a press conference in December 1969, sitting beside Mark Lane and describing his instruction in "helicopter torture." "We learned how to tie up troublesome prisoners with rope under the helicopter and to then drag them until they confessed." Thomas Lee Hayes heard the same story. "Chuck," he wrote, "tells me of his training in various methods of torture as part of his duty with the Special Forces."

The veteran war correspondent Neil Sheehan read Lane's book for the *New York Times* and called the Defense Department to verify the details. He was told that Chuck's last job before his desertion was in a marine base stock handing out spare parts for airplanes. Sheehan also relayed official doubts about the massacre described by Terry Whitmore, another Lane interviewee. "Some of the horror tales in this book are undoubtedly true," wrote Sheehan. "Where there is so much stench, something must be rotting. Mr. Lane succeeds, however, in making it impossible to reach any factual judgment. Nevertheless, the naive and the professional moralists will derive considerable satisfaction from the book, if they can control their intestines."

Conversations with Americans was a PR disaster for the anti-war movement. Edwin Arnett had lied to the world about war crimes, but outside the Soviet Union his claims had been reported with skepticism. Lane's atrocity stories had been published between hard covers by a respected New York publisher, which was now refusing to print a second edition and asking the author to return his $75,000 advance. In Sweden, the deserters felt that their cause had been brought into disrepute. "Lane came looking for lies," recalled Rob Argento, the deserter from Miami. "That book did us a lot of damage. It cast doubt on other stories that were true."

I intended to ask Chuck about all this during my visit to his home in Eugene, Oregon, but failed to find my moment. On my last morning with him a young man came to the door to buy marijuana. He and Chuck went into the kitchen to do their deal. I sat on the sofa with Ninja, trying to formulate a question and feeling, in that house by the gravel pit, a very long way from home. When my airport taxi arrived, the customer was still mulling over his choice. Chuck and I were obliged to say goodbye in his presence. He hugged me hard, like a man standing on the edge of something.

Later, by email, Chuck gave his side of the story. He had, he said, never claimed to be part of an elite unit. Mark Lane had confused him with another interviewee. But he insisted that the part about the torture of women was true. "We were talked to about it," he said, "and told that we could do it." The drill instructor, he said, had presided over "a brainwashing event." "The Marines succeeded in turning me (a nice kid) into someone who would torture and kill women and children if ordered to do so. And I was proud of it! I was a terrible person. I was a perfect Marine."

BY EARLY 1970, the migratory patterns of desertion had shifted. The Soviets were no longer willing to smuggle deserters through Russia. Gloomy communications reached Hans Göran Franck about twenty deserters lying low in Beheiren safe houses, with no means of leaving Japan. "The former route to Sweden has been interrupted," read one plea. "Would it be possible to fly them in someone's private plane? Or someone's yacht?"

Old comrades were going their separate ways. Mark Shapiro left Sweden to study in Canada. Some deserters started families; others started college. The broader community gathered itself in less austere environments than Michael Vale's flat, including the Alternative Stomach, a social club and advice center that hosted poetry readings and vegetarian curry nights. (A magazine, *Internal Haemmorrhage*, was also produced.) George Carrano founded a group called the Stockholm Research Collective, whose members spent their evenings compiling a lengthy report on the problems of American imperialism, which was never published.

Beyond this warm circle, a substantial minority endured brutal economic hardship. Circumstances were toughest for the colony of deserters in Malmö. "I thought that I'd heard all about the bad scene down there but I still couldn't believe it," reported a visiting exile from Stockholm. "It was an American ghetto at its worst, and almost all that that implies." Among its most desperate inhabitants was John Babcock, a deserter who suffered from a serious kidney complaint. Four months behind in the rent, shoplifting to get food for himself and his pregnant girlfriend, he bought a pistol, took the ferry to Copenhagen, attempted to rob a bank, and got five years. His fate was memorialized in a song by a Swedish folk band.

MICHAEL VALE WAS now only an intermittent presence in Stockholm, and he concentrated his interests on a small cadre of people he regarded as trustworthy and politically wholesome. Among them were Cliff Gaddy, Warren Hamerman, Bill Jones, and Jim McGourty. They remained attached, nominally, to the American Deserters Committee, which still commanded the attention of a minority of politically minded deserters.

But Michael and his allies were making plans about which the rest of the ADC knew nothing. They were in touch with sympathetic activists in Frankfurt, and Michael had cultivated contacts in Britain, who moved in the orbit of a group called International Socialists.

Michael put a special effort into training Cliff Gaddy, the man who emerged as his most promising pupil. Cliff was smarter than the others and shared Michael's amazing facility with languages. He was fluent in Swedish and German and, with his mentor's encouragement, soon mastered Russian. Michael's contacts brought Cliff work from the publisher M. E. Sharpe and, with it, access to the latest Soviet academic literature.

In the early 1970s, sometimes in collaboration with Michael and sometimes on his own, Cliff translated scholarly articles on the future of Soviet-American relations, Moscow's view of the arms race, and the treatment of schizophrenia in Russian hospitals. He translated the essays of Yevgeny Preobrazhensky, an economist who had worked alongside Trotsky in the 1920s. Together, Mike's band of followers were planning a new revolutionary project. One based beyond Swedish borders.

In the summer of 1970, the ADC's collection of 16 mm news films disappeared from the office. So did Bill Jones. With its principal members absent or otherwise engaged, the organization entered a period of vagueness and lassitude. A small knot of activists kept it running, using modest funds that were still coming in from Thomas Hayes's CALCAV group. The principal figures were Gerry Condon, a former Green Beret with an impressive red beard and a psychology degree from the University of San Francisco, and Mike Powers, a Brooklyn-born activist keen on nurturing the ADC's links with North Korea and Albania. They became the voices of the political wing of the deserter movement—the ones to whom the press turned when they needed a quote on the latest crime or deportation case, or material for the customary, slightly Bergmanish piece on the loneliness of the American deserter in the long Swedish winter.

In October 1970, Michael Vale's faction tossed a paper grenade into their old office: a five-page communiqué entitled "Dissolution Statement of the American Deserters Committee." "An organization remains politically relevant as long as the situation and goals remain so," it argued. "As the situation changes or the goals lose their significance, it is also necessary that the organization undergo corresponding changes, or else dissolve as a viable political force, although perhaps retaining its name and form. But in such a case, the organization is a form without content, a mere chimera of political fancy." After much discussion, the statement said, the ADC had elected to disband. "The decision was based on a growing realization of the increasing political irrelevance of the ADC." The bottom of the last page bore the names of Bill Jones, Cliff Gaddy, Chuck Onan, and the deserter we know as Jim McGourty.

The first Gerry Condon heard about this was when he received a letter from CALCAV informing him that the ADC's funding would be frozen until the facts were clarified. He wrote straight back. "The statement," wrote Condon, "written, of course, by none other than our old friend Michael Vale and distributed by an unfortunately misguided Bill Jones, does not represent the opinion of anyone who has had anything to do with the ADC in the last eight months." Condon went tearing around town in search of the signatories. He found that most of them were no longer in the country. "All that's left of them here," he told CALCAV, "is bad memories, bad aftertastes." He hoped the document would be ignored. "If so, that crew will have given deserters in Sweden their last headache and we can get on with the business in hand."

THE CASH-FLOW PROBLEM happened just at the wrong moment. The winter of 1970–71 was a cold season for the ADC. In the summer of 1970, Jerry Dass, the former Green Beret who had become a protégé to their biggest donor, Sven Kempe, committed suicide by dousing himself in kerosene and setting himself alight.

In November, twenty-one-year-old Joseph Parra of New Orleans became the first deserter to experience forcible repatriation to the States. He was serving a prison sentence for smuggling LSD from Copenhagen to Stockholm and scheduled for deportation thereafter. As the moment came nearer, Parra became desperate. He attempted suicide. He married a Swedish woman, Sonja Lundström, in his cell. The ADC organized protests, sit-ins, and a ten-day hunger strike. None of it had any effect. At one of the protests an ADC member was charged with assaulting a police officer, sentenced to one month in jail, and told that he, too, would be deported upon release.

On November 25, 1970, Joe Parra was flown to New York by two plainclothes Swedish officers. His journey ended with a farcical flourish. Two U.S. Army military policemen boarded the plane as it sat on the tarmac at John F. Kennedy International Airport, but the Swedes and their prisoner walked straight past them, obliging the MPs to turn on their heels and dash back to arrest Parra in the arrivals lounge. "It's kind of tough to get out of jail this morning, fly across the Atlantic, and get picked up again on the other side," said Parra, before being bundled into a side room.

In the following fortnight, two more deserters were delivered from Swedish prison into the arms of the U.S. military authorities. Dick Fernandez, the head of CALCAV, responded in unclerical language. "We are absolutely blown out of our fucking minds here about these goddam Swedes sending three Americans back to this country to go to jail!" Why, he asked, could they not have been deported to Canada or Algeria? "I'm prepared to see if we can't really put some screws on Mr. Palme to move in this direction."

Max Watts, the old Paris stationmaster, observing the situation from Germany, reflected on the cases. "Sure," he wrote, "Palme wants only 'nice,' politically conscious deserters. Sorry, those we need right here in the army. If the Swedish govt is serious in its willingness to help the Vietnamese, it must be willing to take those GIs who can do little except kill, or smoke."

No killers had emerged from the deserter community. Not quite yet. But those who had joined the burgeoning drug culture now knew that they might be only one pill or cigarette away from deportation. "Generally," an ADC member wrote to CALCAV, "the situation is getting much tighter and there is much talk of going to Canada or going underground by several who feel themselves threatened." Some deserters had already made that decision. Among them was one of Sweden's star exiles—and his case demonstrates how hard the road could be.

THREE YEARS AFTER arriving from Moscow in a blaze of publicity, Craig Anderson of the Intrepid Four found that his exile had taken a Siberian turn. He was estranged from his American family and drifting away from the new one he'd started in Sweden. His most exciting experience was the hardest to communicate. In the winter of 1969–70, he saw his first UFO: a bright, low-flying object that scudded toward him through the Swedish night. Terrestrial life, however, was hard. Work proved elusive, save for a few odd jobs. But in the summer of 1970, he met a young street musician who had just arrived in Stockholm after a series of wild adventures on the hippie trail. Karen Fabec was good-looking, American, and also professed experience of a close encounter, having once witnessed a UFO hovering above her native Pittsburgh. She and Craig had been a couple for several weeks before she realized that she'd seen him before on the TV news. "I liked his quiet mysterious demeanor," she said. "I made a lot out of that. Young girls do that, right?"

I met Karen to hear the story of how she and Craig took the tough route home from Sweden—sneaking back into the States via Canada and living a life underground. Karen studies at a college in San Francisco; we had lunch in the cafeteria, surrounded by teenagers, and she told me about her exuberantly misspent youth. She was born a Catholic in Pennsylvania, but then the Beatles released *Sgt. Pepper* and, at the age of seventeen, she shouldered her guitar and set out for India in search of a guru. She never got there.

Instead, she wound up in the Moroccan city Essaouira, sharing a sprawling courtyard apartment with some sprawling hippie musicians. They meditated, smoked hashish, played drums all night. "Then," she explained, "somebody got the bright idea to go to Fez and get a bunch of kif and take it across Africa and sell it to Peace Corps workers in Tunisia. So we did it and we got busted and thrown into jail on a ten-year sentence." She was obliged to bribe her way to freedom, and after an interlude on a houseboat in Amsterdam she moved north until she met Craig in Stockholm.

In the warm summer months, she sang. People were generous with their coins. But the winter of 1970–71 was unkind to Karen and Craig.

They squatted in a disused puppet theater down a Stockholm alley with a name that meant "the end of the world." They warmed themselves at a wood-burning stove, talked about raising the airfare to go to India. A difficult proposition, when the only employment they could find was delivering newspapers. Neither of them had much enthusiasm for the four a.m. starts, trudging uphill, loaded with copies of *Dagens Nyheter*. Then an infected cut on Karen's thumb brought their efforts to an end. The doctor who prescribed antibiotics sent her to the visa office for paperwork that would secure her free treatment. The authorities decided that she had already overstayed her welcome and deported her.

She wasn't sure that Craig would follow. "I loved him," she said, "but I don't think I was really his type. I think he was with me because I was so emphatic." In her absence, however, he formulated a grand strategy—one that aimed to be as eye-catching as his decision to desert from the *Intrepid*. He would return to the States, make amends with his family, and give himself up to the authorities. He would turn his inevitable court-martial into a political act, use the dock as a pulpit to preach against the war. Perhaps that would be the end of it, and the end of President Nixon, too.

Rather than jetting straight back home to California, Craig chose a soft landing in Canada. In May 1971 he flew from Stockholm to Montreal and was reunited with Karen. She wasn't alone. On her return to the States, Karen had bought an old milk truck and converted it into a motor home. Four friends were on board for the ride. They crossed the entire breadth of the country to Vancouver Island, where they built an encampment out of driftwood, picked berries, harvested mussels, smoked dope, and watched for unidentified flying objects. When the weather cooled, they moved south to Seattle. At the border checkpoint, the guard demanded to see Craig's draft card. Someone made a joke about him being a notorious outlaw. The guard laughed and waved them through.

Their new underground life did not endure the winter. In February 1972, Karen went to the doctor with flu symptoms and discovered that she was pregnant. This, and the Seattle cold, sent them south to California. They sold the van and made the journey by Greyhound bus. Trouble followed them to new lodgings in San Francisco. Coming home early one day they found their apartment being used for a porn shoot.

"There were all these naked people and the man of the house was walking round in a jockstrap," Karen remembered. "Craig was really appalled. He had it out with the guy. I didn't want to be militant about it." Later that night, a more serious altercation took place. Karen was woken by sounds from the next room—one of the porn actors beating up his girlfriend. "At first it was arguing. Then I heard him punching her. I jumped out of bed and ran in, and he turned on me and pushed me down the stairs."

Shortly after this incident, the couple went to San Jose to see Craig's family. When her son and his pregnant fiancée visited, Irene Anderson said little. Once the couple had left, she picked up the phone and reported her son to the FBI. "I suppose," said Karen, "she was thinking of me and the baby. She wanted everything to be good for her grandchild, for Craig to take care of business and get it over with." On the morning of March 30, 1972, Anderson went to buy a newspaper and found the men from the bureau lying in wait.

They took him to the naval correctional center on Treasure Island, a rubble platform constructed in San Francisco Bay. When his fellow inmates realized who he was, the beatings and the threats began. When he protested, the guards set him scrubbing the cement floors with a toothbrush, then placed him in solitary confinement. When he went on a hunger strike, the prison doctor prescribed antipsychotic drugs.

On August 24, 1972, Karen Fabec had a memorable twenty-second birthday—a cloudless day that she spent in downtown San Francisco. At eleven o'clock, she was standing outside city hall, cradling her three-month-old baby, Shandra. At midday her fiancé turned up in a van from military prison, handcuffed, sedated, and accompanied by two guards, who helped him struggle up the steps and into the presence of Judge Joseph Kennedy.

The judge asked Karen if she took Craig W. Anderson to be her lawful wedded husband. "Sure," she said. Craig proved unable to muster a reply. Perhaps it was the lithium in his bloodstream. Perhaps it was the distracting sound coming from the street outside: the amplified voice of Jane Fonda, newly returned from Hanoi, telling a crowd of demonstrators about what she'd seen in North Vietnam—bombed schools, bombed churches, bombed theaters, bombed factories. The judge took silence for assent and pronounced Craig and Karen man and wife. The couple embraced, handcuffs were snapped on the wrists of the groom, and the van sped back to Treasure Island. Baby Shandra had slept all the way through the ceremony. A reporter asked the bride for a quote. "It's a drag," she said.

CRAIG NEVER MADE his speech about the war and Nixon. At the preliminary hearing for his case, he suffered a catatonic seizure and was rushed to the hospital. The intervention proved beneficial: the psychiatrists took the view that further confinement might cause irreparable damage to his sanity. Craig walked from the court with a three-year probation order and a dishonorable discharge from the navy.

Eight months in the brig, however, had already done their work. His mouth was a mess of abscesses. His skin broke out in boils. Noise and crowds distressed him—so much so that Karen allowed herself to be persuaded to move with him to a tent in the mountains of northern California. "He was becoming a recluse," she recalled. "He didn't want to see or talk to anybody. He always acted angry and bitter." Eventually, Karen lost her appetite for this life. The couple separated in 1975 and have barely seen each other since. Karen now lives modestly in San Francisco with her grandchild and her dog, catching up on the education she missed when she went on the trail to North Africa.

Craig's path, however, has been much weirder, and it demonstrates that even those deserters who were not interested in politics could end up living their lives by strange, conspiratorial ideas. A decade ago he adopted the pseudonym Will Hart, under which he writes books that mix biblical scholarship with speculation about the relationship between the American state and extraterrestrial intelligences. The Apollo missions, he thinks, encountered something sentient on the moon. The moon, he suspects, is an artificial object. He has no doubt that the CIA has alien bodies and alien equipment hidden in its labs, and that the last half century of U.S. foreign policy has been determined by these secrets.

He and I exchanged a few emails on these subjects. I was surprised that he seemed not to know that a coauthor of *The Roswell Incident*, the foundational text of UFO conspiracies, had identified Harry Rositzke of Operation Chaos as the head of Langley's aliens division. Craig was more expansive, I discovered, when the questions were asked by a true believer. One of his favorite interlocutors is a clairvoyant called Dr. Rita Louise, who offers "intuitive health readings" over the phone. ("Dr Louise," says her website, "infuses every engagement with both credibility and content.") She also hosts an Internet radio show on which Craig, in the person of Will Hart, is an occasional guest.

On one of these podcasts he described a visit he'd made to Mexico shortly after he had separated from Karen. Here, he made measurements that proved the ancient Mayans had access to alien laser technology. However, "very powerful forces" were preventing this information from emerging. Archaeologists were being discouraged from publishing their findings. Those who tried to add these details to Wikipedia found their revisions weeded out. "The power elites," he said, "don't want you to know about this."

IF THE CIA was doing its work with equipment borrowed from the inhabitants of the Zeta Reticuli system, then no surveillance technology was salvaged from the saucer. The agents of Chaos had to make do with making phone calls and knocking on doors. In April 1972, as Craig Anderson languished in the brig, the CIA asset code-named MHYIELD was sniffing around the offices of the ADC in Stockholm.

MHYIELD was on a tour of radical groups in Europe, with an itinerary that included Frankfurt, Copenhagen, and Belfast. In Stockholm, Mike Powers told his visitor that the organization was going through an identity crisis. The flow of deserters and resisters had slowed, men were returning to their bases in Germany, and the ADC, by now a tiny organization, had suffered another split. Two members had objected to Powers's growing enthusiasm for Maoism and had formed an even smaller group, the Revolutionary American People's Party. Those who remained included Mark Worrell, a California GI who had started a Kim Il Sung study group, and Mike Bransome, a deserter whose colorful past included time in the Baltimore city jail, an alarming interlude with the Moonies, and the donation of a pint of blood to a group who broke into a draft board office and spilled it over a cache of draft cards.

MHYIELD was trying to work out if the ADC was still plugged into radical networks that extended over international borders. He discovered that not only did they know little about what was happening on the army bases in Germany, or among deserters living underground in the States, they seemed barely aware of what was happening elsewhere in Sweden. They hadn't, for instance, talked to the ADC's representative in Malmö for over a month.

The depleted state of the ADC reflected a shift in public attitudes toward the deserters. The romantic enthusiasm that had greeted the arrival of the Intrepid Four was long exhausted. Every few weeks seemed to bring a fresh piece of bad publicity. In May 1971, a deserter was convicted of killing the three-year-old daughter of his Swedish girlfriend. The details shocked the public. Ten days later, Earl Pennington, a deserter who had lived in Malmö for seven months, took his girlfriend to Bull-tofta Airport, where he pressed a knife to her throat, burst through the gate, and climbed the steps of a DC-9. Pennington ordered the pilot to fly to the United States, but the captain told him that a DC-9 would never make it across the Atlantic. "Fly to Stockholm," said Pennington. "Or anywhere." The police moved in; Pennington was dragged away.

In June, Ray Jones III, deserter number one, surfaced again, in a maxi coat and silk shirt, imploring King Gustaf VI Adolf to protect him from the Swedish police, who, he believed, were harassing him on behalf of the U.S. government. "It is a hidden fact that the United States puts pressure on this country," he said. "I have had constant threats of physical violence against my wife and kids."

His examples were hard to interpret. The police, he said, had forced his car off the road, charged him with negligent driving, and assaulted him and his wife. They had allowed his creditors to remove property from his home in lieu of rent. "My two children sat naked eating a bowl of cornflakes," he said. "After one spoonful the authorities burst into our home and removed every piece of furniture we owned." Stories like this produced little public sympathy. The most common response in the press was to suggest that the Swedish benefits system was too generous toward American exiles.

One of many low points came in the small hours of October 10, 1972, when two deserters, Wayne Ellis and Rudolph Mitchell, began causing an uproar in a room at the Rex Hotel in Malmö. The assistant manager, Sven Persson, discovered the two men in a state of insane agitation. Believing there was a bomb in the room, they had cleared it of all flammable objects, hurling blankets and pillows out into the corridor. They had also removed their clothes, fearing that the imminent blast would ignite their plastic buttons and zippers. LSD was to blame, but so was their unusual relationship.

Ellis, the son of a middle-class Chicago family, had deserted his unit when his bank account was cleared of $3,000 by a woman he met on leave in Copenhagen. Mitchell, who had deserted via Amsterdam after a failed attempt to secure a false passport in Paris, promised to help his friend take revenge. Instead, they took drugs, began pimping, and became lost in a bizarre narcotic delusion. Mitchell decided that he was a prophet whose word was divine law. Ellis accepted this idea and began following his commandments. When Sven Persson came into the hotel room, Mitchell ordered Ellis to kick the man six times in the head with his bare feet. The attack proved fatal. With their victim lying senseless on the floor, master and disciple threw a mattress over the body and ran, naked and holding hands, out into the streets of Malmö, where they were quickly arrested.

Ellis and Mitchell were both African American, which added a racial dimension to the hostility provoked by the case—particularly when it emerged that they were living off the immoral earnings of Ellis's Swedish girlfriend, a hotel receptionist named Candy. The two-day trial was a circus. Ellis was too drug-addled to speak. Mitchell was adamant that the murder had been "necessary." A group of deserters who came to attend were arrested. A rumor spread around the city that some Yugoslav gangsters were planning to spring them from custody, after which the Yugoslav Embassy received a bomb threat. Both men were found guilty and told they would be deported after serving their sentences.

As if this wasn't bad enough, Vernon Boggs, a hip young sociology PhD from the City University of New York, turned up in Malmö to write an academic paper claiming that Ellis and Mitchell were typical cases. In "Black American Deserters in Sweden: From Desertion to Drugs to

Despair," Boggs wrote of men who'd earned a "degree in 'pimpology' in Copenhagen and then sought asylum in Sweden, where the racket was much easier to pursue." Like Michael Vale, Boggs had been reading the theorist Émile Durkheim. The deserter, he wrote, "is powerless, homeless, and very often despondent; he is truly living in a state of anomie. His anomic existence spirals downwards until he reaches rock bottom: drug addiction, desperation and imprisonment." Like Vale, he was fingered as a government spook. One interviewee taunted him: "You resigned from the CIA now, huh?"

Boggs may not have been a creature of Langley, but he did have help from a shadowy source: an enemy of Olof Palme in the Swedish civil service who, disgusted by what he saw as the "fondling and cringing position" toward the deserters, supplied Boggs with a secret report that toted up their crimes, from traffic offenses and smuggling to burglary and rape. The report asserted that only 3.7 percent of Sweden's new American residents were in any danger of being sent to Vietnam, and concluded that their presence was detrimental to Swedish society.

For Boggs, this was an academic question. At the beginning of 1973, that's what it became for the Swedish state. On January 27, America's war in Vietnam came to an end. America would send no more unwilling troops to Indochina. On April 2, the Swedish government announced that it had withdrawn its offer of humanitarian asylum to deserters and draft resisters.

But for many of those living in the moral and political space opened up by these changes, the struggle was far from over. Michael Vale and his band of allies had already decided that desertion had outlived its usefulness as a political act. For them, revolution was a goal now best pursued by those inside the army. They had to go where the GIs were and get the message out to them. And as soon as that decision was made, it was relayed back to Langley and to the head of Operation Chaos.

10 / THE NEXT STEP

ON MAY 24, 1970, a meeting was convened at the Club Voltaire, the Frankfurt coffeehouse that helped deserters on their way to Sweden. Michael Vale was in the chair. The others present were U.S. servicemen from bases in Germany, and members of Newsreel, a transnational network of filmmakers who produced 16 mm documentaries offering a revolutionary take on current affairs. (Instead of the Pathé rooster or the MGM lion, Newsreel viewers saw the collective's name appear in a volley of machine-gun fire.) Also in the room, either as part of the group or sitting at a nearby table, was a spy for military intelligence.

A hotheaded GI spoke in favor of bombing some German post offices or telephone exchanges. Nobody was very enthusiastic. Michael gave an upbeat assessment of a conference he had just attended in Copenhagen, where deserters had promised to comb the left-wing press for stories that might be of interest to Newsreel. But most of the afternoon's discussion was taken up with one job—the founding of a new revolutionary organization. The Next Step, as they decided to call it, would be an activist group. It would also be the title of a newspaper. These would share personnel, accommodation, facilities, and a common aim: to encourage soldiers on American bases in Germany to fight the army from inside the army. To give GIs a taste for revolutionary Marxism. The cover price, said Mike, would be ten cents. But if there were no takers, they would just give it away.

The report on Mike's meeting survives because it was forwarded to Ray Wannall, the FBI's chief of counterintelligence. His copy bears a covering note: "We would appreciate being advised as to your requirements for pertinent information on North Vietnamese and foreign radical involvement overseas with American deserter/draft evader groups and individuals." The name of the sender is typed below: Richard Ober, the chief of MHCHAOS. The name of the Next Step, we must presume, was soon punched into HYDRA.

THE *NEXT STEP* newspaper launched on July 4, 1970. Three stapled tabloid pages with a hand-drawn masthead above a quotation from U.S. Army Regulation 318-135 (D), which asserted a soldier's right "to read and retain commercial publications for his own personal use." Its lead story anticipated a large anti-war rally scheduled to take place that day in Heidelberg. The back page described the nature of the secret war it wanted its readers to join. "On almost every base, in Germany, in the USA, and everywhere else (even Alaska) where there are U.S. troops, there are unnamed groups of GIs quietly and skillfully doing a damned gutsy job. They're organizing GIs to fight while they're in the military, but for the people, and not for Nixon."

Most GI newspapers had a freewheeling, proto-punk aesthetic. They contained cartoons snipped savagely from other publications, pages laid out like ransom notes, expletive-filled copy. The *Next Step* was much more serious—closer, its makers hoped, to the kind of paper to which Trotsky was contributing in Vienna just before the First World War. It ran a campaign against the army's attempts to build better relationships among its men. Forums in which GIs could discuss their grievances with superiors were dismissed as "sycophancy" and "dull palaver." It recorded cafeteria scuffles within bases, the slashing of officers' car tires, the hurling of a smoke bomb through the window of the officers' club in Kirch-Göns.

In August 1970, the *Next Step* brought news that the U.S. Army stockade at Mannheim was "riot ripe": a white GI had thrown a glass of milk into the face of a black prisoner. Disturbances followed. The guard on the ammunition dump was doubled. Then dozens of men fell ill with food poisoning. The paper believed this was deliberate—that the brass had spiked the stew to ensure that the men were too busy vomiting to smash the furniture or help themselves to guns and grenades. Maybe it was true. Or maybe this reasoning was an indication of the shape of things to come.

MICHAEL VALE HAD always had his doubts about many of the men who came to Sweden. The exiles, particularly those who were resisting the draft rather than military orders, were too individualistic, too liberal, to submit to the kind of discipline he favored. From 1970, the American Deserters Committee lived on without him, in a much-reduced condition.

Those in its decaying orbit made their feelings known on the pages of its newsletter. "Let me say this as straight as I can," wrote one deserter who had been in Sweden from early 1968. "The ADC is a shit organization. It pontificates about 'unity,' but in practice promotes nothing but discord." Another longtime member agreed: "Some of the actions of the paper staff and ADC members tend to indicate that they want a monopoly on the action to insure that there won't be no action." The objects of this criticism replied with a quote transcribed from Pyongyang Radio, as interminable as a Swedish winter.

Michael Vale was glad to have left this behind. Relocating to Germany to cultivate resistance inside the army seemed a more promising plan. In this, he looked to Lenin and Trotsky rather than Kim Il Sung. Perhaps, he reasoned, another 1917 was coming. Perhaps the military could be forged into an instrument of revolution, as it had been in Russia during the Great War.

The *Next Step* tried to make it happen. "One of the biggest fears of the Pentagon," announced an editorial, "is that . . . it might soon have an army it cannot control." To that end, the paper developed a conspiracist, catastrophist vibe. Its articles insisted that there would be no jobs for veterans once the war was over: Nixon was closing industry and cracking down on union activity. Images reinforced the argument; the paper's pages bore photographs of long lines outside factory gates, striking miners in South Carolina, a little girl standing with her father as he signed for his welfare payment.

The paranoid style crept into the news pages. An early issue picked up a story about Nixon's psychotherapist Dr. Arnold A. Hutschnecker, author of a confidential report recommending government testing of young Americans for early signs of psychological disorders. Hutschnecker proposed that potential delinquents should be treated in camps. He was a Jewish refugee from Nazi Germany and was thinking of the sunny outdoor institutions of his Weimar childhood, but he lived to regret the unfortunate choice of words. The White House recoiled from the plan and the furor. But the *Next Step* used it to build a picture of an America gathering its energies to use psychiatry and austerity to manage its population. And that was a fantasy by which several of its members—Cliff, Bill, Warren, and Jim—would soon come to live their lives.

FOR MICHAEL, THIS time in Germany brought enjoyable skirmishes and maneuvers. "Oh God," he said, snorting with laughter, "it was so easy. I was older than everyone else by about a decade, so I would go in with a briefcase full of Newsreel films opposing the war and about the domestic situation. There'd be a young duty officer on guard, and I'd just say, 'At ease, Sergeant!' and walk right on through, and show these anti-war films in rooms filled with marijuana smoke. That was the American army in Germany." The Next Step was helped, he said, by a sympathetic major who spoke Vietnamese and had worked as an interpreter in Indochina. "He would give us advance warning of any action being planned against us," he said. "Very nice guy. A Catholic. Catholic kids were the easiest to turn into revolutionaries."

Not every member of the Next Step came to Germany, or lived there permanently. Cliff Gaddy shuttled between Stockholm and Frankfurt. Chuck Onan was a temporary recruit, passing through Germany after a spell enjoying the sun in Franco's Spain. Jim McGourty, however, decided to make a more dangerous journey. In the summer of 1970 he went back to the States to be with his wife, Michele. He traveled under his own name without arousing suspicion. The couple found an apartment in Hoboken, New Jersey, and jobs with AT&T, Michele as an overseas operator and Jim as an engineer. They were discreet and had no trouble. That winter, however, Michele became pregnant, and their semi-clandestine American life suddenly seemed less secure. They decided to return to Germany, using new travel documents secured with the help of their friends in the radical underground.

The paperwork was prepared in New York by Norm Fruchter, a novelist and filmmaker who worked for Newsreel. I found him happy to explain the process. A sympathetic doctor would write a letter authorizing a nurse to access death records, ostensibly for a study on child mortality. "We preferred a narrow age range," said Norm. "Zero to one." Norm would then use the information to obtain a birth certificate. "I had about a hundred across a whole range of races and ethnicities, so when people came I could offer them a choice about who they wanted to be."

So, in late 1970, Jim McGourty was born—or born again. In the spring of 1971, he and Michele cashed their savings and boarded an Icelandic Airlines flight to Luxembourg. On arrival they were met by a contact who escorted them to the railway station and bought them tickets for the onward journey to Frankfurt. He then left them sitting at a café while he took their money to the currency exchange. In his absence another man approached the table. He said he was from the U.S. Embassy and wanted to know if everything was okay. Their reply, recalled Michele, was too brisk to be convincing, but the man did not trouble them further. Neither did the figure who had taken their cash. Realizing they had been scammed, Jim and Michele boarded the Frankfurt train, penniless.

At first, the radical life was compensation enough. They gathered material for the *Next Step*, took the newspaper to army bases, and waited for their baby to arrive. For Michele, their new strategy was about giving active-duty soldiers the means to resist the war without having to enter the limbo that she and her husband were obliged to occupy.

"It didn't seem right to push people toward desertion because there was nothing to protect them," she said. "So why not dissent from within?" What most stuck in her mind from these days, however, was the unglamorous side of domestic life in a small revolutionary organization. The arguments over comic books. The bad cooking. When her son was born prematurely in the summer of 1971, her frustrations intensified—not least because Jim failed to turn up at the hospital, leaving it to Michael Vale to bring mother and baby home. Michael also persuaded a friendly German doctor to furnish the new arrival with a birth certificate unburdened by the fake McGourty name.

This, Michele told me, was the moment she began losing her enthusiasm for her husband and the life they were leading. As soon as she was able, she found a job in a nearby university research laboratory, determined to earn enough money to take her baby home to the United States.

SOME RELISHED THE recklessness that attended this kind of activism. Chuck Onan spoke warmly about his time with the Next Step. We were sitting in a diner in Eugene, Oregon, where the waitress had assumed that he was my dad. Chuck was much more interested in sharing his stories about Germany than he was in the burger on his plate.

"We were very disruptive on those bases," he told me. "After a while we became known and they started sending troops after us. We were chased in cars and on foot, but it was pretty easy to get away. It was dark, and we all ran in different directions." They had help, too, from local and American supporters. The journalist Mark Lane supplied them with a car to drive between bases. (It was lost in action and impounded by the authorities.) Chuck recalled a German woman who helped out for reasons of her own. "She was a cougar," he said, his eyes crinkling in nostalgia. "Michael and I stayed with her and that lady wanted both of us."

Michael Vale went more coolly over the same ground. He remembered a woman named Lynn who had convinced herself that a radio-controlled bomb had been inserted into her skull. "And," said Mike, "there was this guy called Engdahl. He was pretty unbalanced. He really needed a guru."

William Engdahl was a Minneapolis-born Princeton graduate who was at Stockholm University writing a thesis on social housing policy. He had attached himself to Michael's group in Sweden and traveled to Germany to be with them. Most people liked him. He was a good-looking, gentle soul with huge, burly arms and chest, pumped up by his reliance on crutches, a consequence of childhood polio. His family background also made him a good fit for a cell of radicals: the Minnesota Engdahls had produced Walfrid Engdahl, the secretary of the East of the Rockies subcommittee of the Industrial Workers of the World, and John Louis Engdahl, the first editor of the Communist *Daily Worker*, who was indicted on espionage charges for agitating against American involvement in the Great War. William's fate, as we will see, was much stranger.

Warren Hamerman's draft resister status made his visits to Germany less fraught with danger than those of the deserters in the group. He took responsibility for printing the newspaper in Stockholm and bringing copies south to Frankfurt, and he wrote pompous letters home about his revolutionary life. They produced a response. Michael remembered the day when Hamerman's grandmother arrived from New York to bend her grandson's ear. A tiny figure marched from the plane with a hand raised. "You don't have to say anything," she declared. "I know it already!"

In Warren's little apartment in Frankfurt, packed with deserter revolutionaries, Cooky Pollack told stories of pre-war radicalism. She spoke of her flight from Russia after the failed 1905 revolution. How she'd done political organizing among the cloth cutters and prostitutes of New York. She told the story of the 1911 Triangle Shirtwaist Factory fire, in which 146 New York garment workers, mostly Jewish immigrants like her, were burned or choked to death; how some had jumped to their deaths because the owner had locked the exits to prevent workers taking unauthorized breaks.

She told them of the optimism she had felt in the 1920s and '30s. ("We thought we had it in our hands!" she said.) And she told them of the great blow that came in the late 1940s, when the FBI indicted the leadership of the American Communist Party, and she and her husband went to a CP meeting in the Adirondacks, where a rented mob attacked the delegates. ("Max," she said, "it's going to be a long time.") Michael remembered Warren's astonished reaction to this speech. He knew almost nothing of her radical past. "Well," she said, "you never asked the right questions." Michael did not escape a tongue lashing, but he didn't mind: he was already a fan. "Cooky went round telling us all what to do," he said. "She transformed the organization."

As the months went by, however, the purpose of the Next Step fell into doubt. It was putting out its paper, screening its films, preaching revolution and resistance to the GIs. But the effects were hard to measure, and no battleship *Potemkin* moment seemed about to materialize in Europe or America.

The campus movement was in disarray. Students for a Democratic Society had, like the ADC, torn itself apart. A fundamentalist faction, the Weather Underground, had broken from the main body of the organization, and neither had survived the trauma. The Weathermen—whose number included Michael's old friend Bo Burlingham—were on the run, hunted by the FBI. On March 6, 1970, three members were killed in New York City while preparing a nail bomb they planned to detonate that evening at a dance for noncommissioned officers and their girlfriends at the Fort Dix army base in New Jersey. The explosion brought down the Greenwich Village town house they were using as a base. The actor Dustin Hoffman, who lived next door, escaped unhurt. The outrage altered the political climate. Revolution, violent or nonviolent, did not seem quite so proximate as it had in 1968.

"I'd got myself into a very existential situation," Michael told me. "Here I was, the leader of a group of people who depended on me, but who were still unproven in any political battle. We were primed, but we weren't part of any bigger organization. What could we do? Who could we join up with?"

THE ANSWER CAME from New York: the National Caucus of Labor Committees. It was a boring name for one of the few radical political organizations that seemed to Michael to be gathering energy rather than losing it. Its members were bright young people who had moved, like Mike, in the orbit of Students for a Democratic Society. Its leader, known by the pseudonym Lyn Marcus, was a charismatic economics lecturer whose free classes had been received with enthusiasm by the student Marxists of Greenwich Village.

"This guy Marcus was presenting some good theoretical analysis," said Michael. "And he'd gathered around him some real minds. In the law, physics, chemistry, the whole academic panoply. He'd formed a committed group around him. It was the only show in town."

The organization was looking to expand. It had explored alliances with British Trotskyists, with Greek socialists living in exile after the generals seized control of Athens, with a group of left-wing medical students who were making a noise in Düsseldorf. A delegation traveled from New York to Frankfurt to talk terms with Michael and his comrades. It was agreed that the Next Step would dissolve and its members would join the Labor Committees. Some would stay in Germany, others would return to Sweden to recruit more members there, and still others would be assigned to local groups in American cities. Cliff Gaddy and Bill Jones went north to Stockholm. Warren Hamerman returned home to Baltimore, though he retained a flat in Frankfurt. William Engdahl went to Chicago. Michele and Jim moved to Charlotte, North Carolina, and Michael to New York. The sympathetic major who had helped the Next Step evade detection paid for Michael's car to be shipped to the States.

In a modest apartment in Greenwich Village, Michael Vale met Lyn Marcus for the first time. A lanky figure in his early fifties, with thinning hair and a bow tie as prim and proper as his New England accent. A pipe smoker, whose tobacco habit also gave him a useful rhetorical prop. He smiled beneath a pair of dark glasses and welcomed Michael into the Labor Committees. Michael accepted. It was the biggest mistake of his life.

"Often I don't catch the signals of danger, or if I do I don't heed them," said Michael. "But I saw that one coming. It's a pretty eerie feeling to be in the presence of a psychopath."

"How do you detect a psychopath?" I asked.

"Ever heard of Pavel Câmpeanu?" asked Michael. I hadn't. "He was a Romanian sociologist. In the war, he was sharing a prison cell with someone else who had been fighting the Fascists. To pass the time, the two men played chess. Whenever Câmpeanu's cellmate lost a game, a strange expression would pass across his face. An alarming smile. The name of this bad loser was Nicolae Ceauşescu." Michael enjoyed my expression of surprise. "When they break down, people like this, they smile. They disintegrate. They go back to their true violent nature. Because they've been exposed. And Marcus would give that smile. It's horrible." He demonstrated with a flash of his teeth.

I knew the next part of the story, and the shadow that it had cast upon Michael's life. I knew that the man he called Lyn Marcus, and had once regarded as a potential political ally, was the villain of his biography. I also realized, as we spoke, that Michael Vale believed his old enemy was dead. We were sitting in a café at St. Pancras station in London. I flipped open my laptop and used the sluggish public Wi-Fi to load a website I thought Michael needed to see. The site had a red, white, and blue livery and the logo of an eagle rampant. After a few moments of waiting, the clip came up: a balding, bespectacled nonagenarian standing at a lectern flanked by blue curtains and patriotic flags. There were three large scabs on his forehead, as though he had recently recovered from walking into a door. In patrician, New England tones, he was giving a speech on one of his favorite subjects.

"The British Empire," he declared, "is our enemy. It's the enemy of all decent people on this planet. The British monarchy is an obscene satanic force. And I do not exaggerate when I say satanic. Because Zeus, who is the author of the Roman Empire, and also author of the British Empire, is otherwise known as Satan. Her policy is what? To reduce the population of the planet. Cause mass deaths. Starvation. Killing. Destroy crops. This woman is *satanic*!"

Michael squinted at the figure on the screen. "The enemies have changed a little," he said. "It used to be the Queen of England, Henry Kissinger, and *me*."

AMERICAN POLITICAL CULTURE of the late sixties gave life to scores of revolutionary groups. In New York, the Up Against the Wall Motherfuckers brawled with the Maoists and dumped uncollected refuse in the fountain at Lincoln Center; later they quit the city to try a hunter-gatherer lifestyle in the Rockies. In Chicago, the Yippies nominated a pig as a presidential candidate and spread the rumor that they had dropped LSD into the Chicago water supply. In California, the Symbionese Liberation Army used murder, kidnapping, and bank robbery as they struggled to live up to their slogan "Death to the fascist insect that preys on the life of the people." Some of these groups enriched American cultural life; some soured it with madness and cruelty. Most managed only a few years of existence.

The National Caucus of Labor Committees no longer goes by its original name. It has used many others, sometimes to bamboozle the electorate into voting for its political parties, sometimes to obfuscate its fraudulent and criminal activities. Its politics, too, have undergone a series of mutations—from adherence to the ideas of Karl Marx and Rosa Luxemburg to cheerleading for Ronald Reagan and Vladimir Putin. But it lives on to this day: a political cult that continues to suck the life out of its members on the promise that they are part of an intellectual elite that will, one day, acquire the power and the influence that is rightfully theirs. Its one fixed tenet is the infallibility of its leader, and his complex but essentially meaningless political theories. The man who wooed Michael Vale in that little apartment in New York in the winter of 1971, and who we watched together, more than four decades later, on my laptop in a London café.

"He was a hustler," said Michael. "The formula of his sick little universe was that anybody who has not yet been enveloped by the higher cause that only he represented was, by nature, subject to the usual vices. He flattered. He offered status. He co-opted me by putting me onto the Central Committee."

Why, I asked, did Michael not resist?

"I should have stood up to him," he conceded. "It was my duty to the people who followed me. But I was green. If I'd had another year I could have brushed up on my ideas. You could see it was going to lead to the moral dominance of one figure. That it would lead to the establishment of a series of rigid principles that could turn yes into no and no into yes. He had total dominance over everyone. He could reformulate the whole construction of the universe. What I don't understand on a personal level is why all those people stayed around him. Wally Hamerman. Bill Jones. Cliff Gaddy. They were my group."

To me, the answer was simple. Michael had answered it himself. They were his group. He had stripped them of their egos and, unwittingly, prepared them for servitude to another charismatic leader.

11 / BEYOND PSYCHOANALYSIS

UMBERTO ECO'S NOVEL *Foucault's Pendulum* is the story of a group of literary men who invent a conspiracy theory. "The Plan" is an incomprehensibly complex plot in which a huge number of interested parties—the Masons, the Nazis, the Jesuits, the Rosicrucians, and practitioners of Brazilian voodoo—are all working to harness a mysterious force called telluric energy, through which they hope to transform the world. In November 2015, shortly before Eco's death, I interviewed him for a BBC radio program. Afterward I asked his advice on dealing with real-life conspiracy theorists. "It's hard to protect yourself from this kind of thinking," he said. "To keep your skepticism. Many people who write about conspiracy theories don't believe in them." He chewed on his unlit cigarillo. "Well, not at the beginning."

To write about the history of the Labor Committees is to describe a body of thought that might have been invented by Eco—and to risk your own work becoming infected by its sickness. Intensely detailed, dramatic, and expansive, its mythography encompassed everything and meant nothing. Its adherents were intelligent, knowledge-hungry, articulate people who imprisoned themselves in a paranoid view of reality that was easier to construct than to escape. The principal figures in this story—Michael Vale, Bill Jones, Cliff Gaddy, Warren Hamerman, Jim

McGourty—all wandered into its labyrinth. Some took an early opportunity to turn back toward the daylight. Others became lost in it for decades. One remains inside, counting the bricks. Nobody, however, was more effectively entombed than the man who built it and sits at its center today. Lyndon LaRouche. The cult leader formerly known as Lyn Marcus.

To British readers his name may mean little. American readers will know him as the longest-running gag in U.S. fringe politics—an unlovable conspiracy theorist and eight-time presidential candidate. His most enduring contribution to the culture is probably the name-check he received in a 1996 episode of *The Simpsons*, in which aliens kidnap presidential candidates Bill Clinton and Bob Dole and immerse them in tanks of bubbling pink liquid. "Oh my God!" wails Homer, "Lyndon LaRouche was right!"

To his supporters, however, he is a colossus. To them, Lyndon Hermyle LaRouche Jr., born September 8, 1922, in Rochester, New Hampshire, is the world's greatest economist. He is also the rightful successor to Gandhi, Lincoln, de Gaulle, and Martin Luther King. His writings—*The Third Stage of Imperialism*, "Beyond Psychoanalysis," and *Children of Satan III: The Sexual Congress for Cultural Fascism*—are landmarks in the history of ideas. His thinking inspired the Reagan administration's Strategic Defense Initiative and the fall of the Berlin Wall.

"In only a few decades in the late twentieth century," said Warren Hamerman, in a speech at a 1990 Labor Committees conference, "the ideas generated by Lyndon LaRouche and our association, enriched by co-thinkers in every conceivable area of human knowledge and activity—from politics and physical economy to philosophy, natural law, the arts and sciences—have swept across the globe like seeds in a strong wind, and blossomed forth afresh from individuals on every continent on Earth."

If you're wondering why you've not heard this before, never seen LaRouche's portrait on the wall of any of our great institutions, or perhaps on the front of a postage stamp or the cover of *Time* magazine, it's because these glowing opinions have never penetrated beyond the membership of his own organizations. I'm pretty sure that number doesn't include you, because if you were a current member of the LaRouche group, you'd have no time for a book like this. You'd be standing on a street corner holding a poster of Vladimir Putin cuddling some kittens, or asking passersby to hand over their money to help prevent the Queen of England from blowing up the world.

IN THE BEGINNING, there was LaRouche. And he was a Quaker. But not the nice kind you see on the side of the cereal boxes. The Quakerism followed by his parents, Jessie Weir LaRouche and Lyndon Hermyle LaRouche Sr., was rigidly fundamentalist and strongly conspiratorial, and it provided young Lyndon with the playbook for his career in political cult building. It asserted the literal truth of the Bible. It considered Quakers who did social work in their communities to be Communists in all but name. It made trouble.

When Lyn was nineteen, his father was expelled from their local Friends Meeting House in Essex County, Massachusetts. "We believe Lyndon H. LaRouche is guilty of stirring up discord in this meeting," pronounced the Quaker Board of Overseers, "that he is responsible for circulating material injurious to the reputation of valued Christian workers; and believe that his conduct brings the Christian religion into public disrepute." The family's response was to print up more pamphlets and broadsides attacking the "pro-Communist" New England Quakers, and join a chapel in South Boston, which they soon took over and renamed the Village Street Society of Friends.

Young Lyndon was bullied by his father and bullied at school. His mother insisted that he should never return the blows, no matter how strong the provocation. He obeyed, enduring beatings at home and in the classroom. To compensate, he developed a vicious tongue, which only amplified the violence.

On America's entry into the Second World War, Lyn registered as a conscientious objector and was sent to an internment camp in West Campton, New Hampshire, where he took part in medical experiments that included being covered in lice and told not to scratch. It may have been this treatment that persuaded him to enlist in the army as a non-combatant medic. He spent the rest of the war in Burma and India,

The American Deserters Committee marches against the Vietnam War, Stockholm, February 1968.

Flanked by a pair of interviewers, the Intrepid Four—Michael Lindner, Craig Anderson, John Barilla, and Rick Bailey—explain their actions to a Soviet television audience in November 1967.

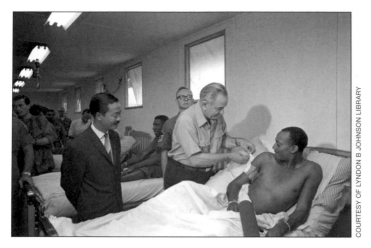

President Lyndon B. Johnson pins a Purple Heart medal to the pillow of Terry Whitmore—who will soon desert to Sweden, via Tokyo and Moscow.

Private Ray Jones, the first Vietnam deserter to arrive in Sweden, poses with his wife, Gabriele, on the eve of his trial in April 1968 for absence without leave.

Young American exiles in Sweden—Bill Jones, the chairman of the American Deserters Committee, along with Michele Lloyd and her husband, Jim McGourty.

Six deserters, smuggled from Japan to the Soviet Union, arrive at Stockholm's Arlanda airport, May 1968. From left to right: Kim Jin-Su, Mark Shapiro, Terry Whitmore, Philip Callicoat, Joe Kmetz, and Edwin Arnett.

The offices of the American Deserters Committee, housed in a building owned by Verdandi, a Swedish temperance society.

Olof Palme, Sweden's education minister, marches through Stockholm with Nguyen Tho Chan, the North Vietnamese ambassador to Moscow, on February 21, 1968, to protest the war in Indochina.

Bill Jones is besieged by reporters at the World Festival of Youth and Students in Sofia, Bulgaria, in July 1968.

Clancy Sigal, stationmaster of the London safe house for Vietnam deserters, at home in West Hollywood, April 2016.

Warren Hamerman, the subject of a successful campaign to persuade the Swedish government to extend humanitarian asylum to draft resisters.

The Stockholm deserters become movie stars.

COURTESY OF ROCKE ROBERTSON

Lyndon LaRouche lectures striking students on the lawn of Columbia University in April 1968.

PEOPLE'S WORLD

Using bare fists and nunchakus, members of the National Caucus of Labor Committees carry out Operation Mop-Up in Philadelphia in 1973.

Presidential candidate Lyndon LaRouche gives a press conference in Concord, New Hampshire, in September 1987. Among
his subjects that day was the evil nature of Senator Joe Biden.

Kerstin Tegin, leader of the European
Workers Party, the Swedish arm
of the LaRouche organization, in
Stockholm, September 1984.

Former Vietnam deserter
and LaRouche strategist
Clifford Gaddy speaks at
a meeting of the Valdai
Discussion Club in Sochi,
Russia, October 2014.

Blood on the pavement where Swedish Prime Minister Olof Palme was assassinated on the night of February 28, 1986.

Victor Gunnarsson, whose association with the European Workers Party helped to make him a suspect in the assassination of Olof Palme.

Michael Vale, the "Rasputin" of the American Deserters Committee, in a Paris café, May 2016.

bandaging wounds, applying iodine, reading Marx, developing a hostile view of the British, and learning to play chess against four opponents at a time.

The next phase of LaRouche's life is a story of failure and frustration. He studied physics at Northeastern University and dropped out after a year. He suffered periods of illness, which included two bouts of hepatitis and a problem with his immune system that required months of bed rest and treatment with bee venom. He traveled the country scripting radio commercials and spent his free time getting into barroom brawls. He tried to follow in the footsteps of his father, a management consultant to the footwear industry.

Success eluded him. He studied computer programming and offered companies advice on how to reduce labor costs through automation, but few wanted his services. He wrote a paper titled "Shoe Data Processing Comes of Age," but nobody published it. He joined the Trotskyist Socialist Workers Party and married Janice Neuberger, the secretary of its New York branch. They had a son, Daniel, in 1956 but the relationship did not endure.

In the early sixties, Lyn was struggling to find a job beyond the voluntary work he did for the SWP. Even there, he wasn't much welcome. "He was a loner," recalled the activist Clara Fraser.

> He was never active, never involved in any mass movement or internal
> organizational work. What he did was write—and write and write and
> write, until we all wished he'd be stricken by digital rheumatism. They
> said he was an economist, but nobody seemed to know where he
> worked or what he did. Sometimes I would feel sorry for him and go
> up and say hello; he never replied except in a mumble or a curt
> rejoinder. Once I mustered the audacity to ask him to explain his latest
> document. My polite interest evoked nothing but a look of utter
> contempt.

One member of the Socialist Workers Party, however, was more sympathetic. Carol Larrabee, a Brooklyn-born, NYU-educated math teacher, became LaRouche's lover and, by 1964, had allowed him to move into her apartment on Morton Street in Greenwich Village. The building had a history: her flat was directly below one that had served as a meeting place for the Soviet spy ring that included Julius and Ethel Rosenberg.

Carol was the breadwinner, though Lyn, like many male revolutionaries of this period, still expected his dinner on the table every evening. In 1966 they split with the SWP and formed their own Marxist group, the West Village Committee for Independent Political Action, whose membership fitted snugly into Carol's living room, or that of their friends, a pair of married Columbia graduate students named Nancy and Edward Spannaus.

In large groups, LaRouche had a tendency to fade into the background, but in small ones he could dominate—particularly if they were composed of people who were younger and less experienced. In 1966 he found his perfect niche: a neighbor pulled a few strings and secured him some teaching hours at the Free University of New York, a radical enterprise that ran five classrooms in a loft near Union Square.

LaRouche was a surprise hit. Those who attended remember him as a dazzling lecturer with a facility for making thrilling connections between far-flung ideas. ("Thoughts going off like bombs," one told me.) Lyn Marcus—as he had begun to call himself—quoted Rosa Luxemburg and Émile Durkheim. He drew lines between math and cybernetics and Hegel's *Phenomenology of Spirit*. He explained the falling profits of American companies with reference to the tool-making capacity of apes.

One former pupil, Nick Syvriotis, a Greek socialist exiled in New York, sounded awestruck five decades later. "He presented the most credible, most articulate and best-argued version of Marxist economics that I had ever heard," he told me. It was a prophecy of doom, but with a happy ending for everyone in the classroom. LaRouche argued that too much capital remained locked, unspent, within the financial system. American profits were declining, therefore wage cuts and government austerity were on the way. This, he said, would create a disaffected working class in need of intellectual leaders. With the right tutoring, a small cadre like theirs would be able to provide them, ready-made.

"The other thing that appealed to me very much," said Nick, "was that his interpretation of Marxist economics was not about redistribution. Every other Marxist organization that I knew was talking about giving the workingman his due and taking surplus value away from the capitalist and giving it to the proletarian. But he talked about missile production, high productivities, technological expansion. I was hooked. It was a love at first sight." Instead of telling his students to pity the exploited workers, Lyn Marcus asked them to imagine being the planners and thinkers of a high-tech future. He asked them to imagine them taking Marxism to Mars.

THE STORY OF Lyndon LaRouche's transformation from night-school lecturer to the leader of an international network of political radicals can be told in two ways. The first requires an understanding of how the West Village Committee for Independent Political Action used a joint protest against a proposed hike in New York bus and subway fares to build an alliance with the Columbia University chapter of Students for a Democratic Society, and then, during the tumultuous campus strikes of the spring of 1968, cooperated with and connived against the various SDS splinters to emerge in March 1969 as a new and more populous organization called the National Caucus of Labor Committees.

A less headachy way to think of it would be as a kind of fishing expedition, in which LaRouche, Carol Larrabee, and a small band of friends launched a successful campaign to poach members from the SDS, which was a deeply unstable organization teeming with clever young people looking for leadership and exciting new political ideas. When Columbia students occupied the campus in April 1968, LaRouche walked among them, giving impromptu lectures on Rosa Luxemburg and her theory of the mass strike. After the police had roared in with tear gas and billy clubs and cleared the demonstrators from the site, LaRouche gave more classes to those freshly discharged from police custody.

At a conference in Philadelphia in March 1969, the National Caucus of Labor Committees announced its existence, a group of men and women who would be the brains of the imminent workers' state. "The revolutionary intelligentsia," argued LaRouche, "is thus the embryonic representation of a new human species, a Promethean species which seeks to reproduce its own kind from the ranks of the working class. This includes, in part, the development of individuals as such, but more general and essential is the work of calling the new species of humanity into being."

How do you create a new human species? The answer is, of course, you can't and you don't. But it is perfectly possible to lose yourself in the mad task of trying. And in this, Lyndon LaRouche was entirely successful.

MICHAEL VALE HAD stepped out of the Next Step and into the National Caucus of Labor Committees out of pure political pragmatism. He began backing away from Lyndon LaRouche as soon as he joined. "I didn't trust him," he reflected, "and he didn't trust me." He sensed that the NCLC chair regarded him as a threat, "so I just shut up." It was, he admitted, an abdication of responsibility toward the men who had followed him: "When people, wrongly or rightly, are looking for your guidance, that's your burden. And I opted out. On the bogus argument that it was their decision. It wasn't their decision. It was my decision. It was a terrible thing to do."

Jim McGourty had no such doubts. For him, joining with LaRouche was a logical move—a kind of radical national service. "You've got to come back and take responsibility for the future of your country," he told me. "And what better way to go than with an organization that represented change and betterment for the United States? The Labor Committees weren't crazies like the Weathermen. We had policy. We were against drugs. We were for nuclear power. Laser technology. You wouldn't hear that from the Maoists, would you?"

It was my third trip to see him at his home in Loudoun County. The 2016 U.S. presidential election campaign was entering its final few months, and Jim, a Republican voter baffled and horrified by the rise of Donald Trump, was keen to discuss a more comprehensible period of American political extremity. He had something for me to read. A thick file of correspondence from the early 1970s, which, he said, would explain what was in his mind after his return from Sweden.

Most of the letters were addressed to his brother, an engineer who helped design communications systems for NASA. The subject matter was wide ranging, the tone urgent. Jim wrote about cybernetics and urbanization and political populism. He wrote about the NCLC's desire to recruit scientists for a campaign to hasten the development of nuclear fusion technology. But the address in the top right-hand corner of each page revealed the place to which all this had led him: Building 10140, Camp Lejeune, North Carolina. These little sheets of paper also told the story of the exposure of Jim's false identity, his arrest, court-martial, and imprisonment. Campaigning for a crash research program in fusion technology had not put him behind bars. He was propelled there by LaRouche's big strategy idea for 1973: Operation Mop-Up—the NCLC's scheme to achieve political dominance by neutralizing the competition on the American left. Using martial arts.

SOMEWHERE TOWARD THE end of 1972, the Labor Committees began preparing for the fight. In a gym on the top floor of a New York apartment building, members attended Saturday morning classes at which NCLC security officers shouted instructions: "This group has been brought together with one purpose in mind: revolutionary discipline. Within two months you will all be commanding cadres of several hundred workers apiece. You must be prepared!" Those who couldn't keep pace, or vomited before their eightieth jumping jack, received an angry earful. "Revolutionaries must be in shape!" they were told. "When the wars come, how do you expect the workers to follow orders like that?"

Elsewhere, the drill was even tougher. On rented farmland north of the city, recruits were shown how to cut throats and handle guns. (The training camp was disbanded after a state police team called at the property while investigating a local murder.) Most significantly, LaRouche's foot soldiers—most of whom were graduate students, young academics, and trainee social workers—were taught the street-fighting techniques that were going to help them achieve mastery over the Communist Party USA. Their weapons of choice were knuckle-dusters, clubs, and nunchakus—two solid sticks linked by a length of steel chain, familiar to anyone who had been to the cinema that year to see Bruce Lee in *The Way of the Dragon*. These weapons would ensure that when the collapse of capitalism came, no old-style Stalinist would be fit to take command.

The official declaration of war came in April 1973, when a front-page editorial in the NCLC newspaper, *New Solidarity*, announced its campaign to pulverize the American Communist Party: "We must dispose of this stinking corpse to ensure that it cannot act as a host for maggots and other parasites preparing future scabby Nixonite attacks on the working class." And in went the boys and girls of Operation Mop-Up. Forty NCLC members muscled into a meeting of mayoral candidates at Columbia University and charged the platform with wooden staves. Twenty steamed into a Third World Solidarity rally at Temple University in Philadelphia. "Chairs were overturned," said a witness, "and there was blood all over the floor."

Fifteen LaRouchians stormed into a conference of the Young Socialist Alliance in Detroit, pushing people to the floor and beating them with sticks. (Disabled delegates were not spared.) Victor Riesel, a journalist in Detroit, brought the news to the mainstream press. The NCLC, he explained, was "a new, virtually unnoticed, unreported revolutionary action network of young people, well dressed and well trained militarily. . . . It's so far to the left it makes Trotskyism seem like a flower power daisy-picking sect."

The most enthusiastic fighters were dubbed the Red Guard. Those who preferred an administrative role became known as the Ladies Auxiliary. They stayed in the office, logging the attacks, collating telephone numbers of Communist Party members, and making the occasional threatening call.

Unsurprisingly, this carnival of violence and intimidation did not cause the sudden evaporation of other left-wing groups from the political scene. Instead, there was uproar. American Communists wrote angry letters to the press alleging that the NCLC was controlled by police agents. (The NCLC, of course, said exactly the same about the Communists.) A correspondent of *Workers Vanguard* attacked the group as "a cult of demoralized psychotics engaged in a dance of death." Student bodies banned the Labor Committees from campus buildings. Communists attended meetings with blunt instruments secreted about their person, in case the enemy came crashing through the doors. But this mattered little to LaRouche: he was interested in revolutionary strategy, but he was just as interested in consolidating his own personal power.

The violence of Operation Mop-Up generated an intense camaraderie

among his followers. They had recaptured the thrill of the 1968 Columbia strike, only this time it was the radicals who were swinging the clubs,
and not the police. Tessa DeCarlo, who worked on Labor Committees
publications throughout the 1970s, described its exhilarations. *"We're
about to create a national Soviet!"* she exclaimed, recalling the thrill of
the moment. *"We're going to wipe the floor with these assholes!"*

Raw knuckles and split lips, however, were only the first part of
LaRouche's prescription. He also wanted to get under the membership's
skin. He fleshed out his approach in an essay called "Beyond Psychoanalysis," the product of a year of experiments on his own comrades. Most
Americans, he argued, lived in a world of illusion. They worked, watched
television, drank beer on the weekend, and went on vacation once a year.
This illusion, he argued, prevented them from seeing the pointlessness of
their existence and taking a logical step into suicidal despair.

Members of the Labor Committees, however, had the opportunity to
enter a higher state of being. "Over the period since September 1972,"
he wrote, "organizations of the Labor Committees in North America and
Western Europe have been given preliminary exposure to techniques
more advanced in some aspects than have so far been known to professional psychology. These approaches are being developed as indispensable auxiliary means for directly overcoming the fatal internal flaw of
all socialist organizations, Lenin's included, up to this time."

The prize was great. If members let go of their fears, then they stood
a chance of achieving a new status. They would be "world-historical
people." They would be "Cartesian beings." They would be fit to run the
new world that would be delivered by the coming collapse of capitalism. He used a term that was familiar to the Stockholm deserters:
ego-stripping.

It would be tough, he warned: "In respect of the mental processes,
absolutely nothing is secret; there is merely blindness. What you may
imagine to be only your private insight into yourself is accessible to
empirical demonstration for general knowledge. Not only that, but such
things within you as you may, for a brief remaining time, merely imagine
do not exist within you. Blindness will be ended; all the secrets will rap-
idly appear to become general public knowledge." Remarkable results,
he said, had already been achieved with a small group of followers in

Düsseldorf. "In Germany I am *Der Abscheulicher.* I shall soon be regarded similarly here." The title, plucked from *Fidelio*, Beethoven's only opera, meant the Abominable One.

THE DETAILS OF the ego-stripping process were later recorded by Christine Berl, a concert pianist who was a member of the organization's National Executive Committee. "According to Marcus," wrote Berl, in a document cosigned by her boyfriend, "the purpose of the sessions was to create a new kind of leadership based on the capacity to withstand psychological terror; but in reality the content of the sessions themselves was pure psychological terror. What the leaders were asked to withstand was described by Marcus as the stripping away of the persona before the entire group; but in actuality what was stripped away was their very identities."

LaRouche would attack the luckless subject of the session using foul and violent language. It was violence and intimidation disguised as love. "The procedure was brilliant and diabolical," wrote Berl. "After Marcus had himself reduced the leaders to a state of self-hate and terror . . . only then would he rescue them, in the name of self-consciousness from the terror which he himself had created."

Jim McGourty observed it, too—and wondered whether LaRouche had been taking lessons from Michael Vale. "The basic idea," he explained, "was that everyone is tortured by their mothers and has this creepy alter ego. A mother-image that will twist them and hold them back whenever they try to do something creative. The key to life is defeating the mother."

LaRouche impressed this point on members of the National Executive Committee, and they in turn did the same to those lower down the hierarchy. It even reached the children of NCLC members, who added "mother-dominated" to their repertoire of playground insults. "People would break down, cry, bring up stuff about their childhood, their mother and father, and how that was causing them to be weak and mistrusting," said Jim. "Some of this involved breaking up families. Husbands and wives. He would say the father was incompetent. Not aggressive enough. Pretty soon there were separations and divorces going on."

Jim's marriage was one of the casualties. He was prepared to stay loyal to Lyn Marcus. But his wife, Michele, had other ideas. They had been living in a rough-and-ready apartment in Charlotte, North Carolina, with a gang of NCLC activists, bringing the literature and the arguments they'd used on army bases in Germany to the gates of manufacturing plants in the city. The workers did not greet them with open arms.

"It was hard," Michele told me, "and we honestly did not know what we were doing." She no longer had the appetite for long debates about LaRouchian economics—or the much more alarming rigors of "Beyond Psychoanalysis" sessions. Since the NCLC delegation had arrived in Frankfurt, she had found excuses to avoid their company. "To get away," she said, "I would go upstairs and breastfeed my baby." On one occasion, she remembered, the wife of another NCLC activist came up to join her. She also had little love for the increasingly cultish character of the movement. "She asked, 'Is this baby important to you?' That was the nail on the coffin. I remember just crying."

After three months of this life in Charlotte, Michele asked Jim for a separation. "I realized I simply needed to go back to school and take care of my son," she explained. "It was time to stop playing at being a leftist. Contact with the Labor Committees crystallized a lot of things for me. They had no idea what they were asking people to do. Idiotic stuff. Violent stuff. Illegal stuff." Stuff entirely incompatible with the responsibilities of parenthood—which, she couldn't help noticing, LaRouche regarded with complete contempt. "Do you know what he once did?" Michele asked. "He took a cigarette lighter and waved it in my son's face just to see if he reacted. That's the kind of man he was." She moved back to her parents in Washington, DC, and enrolled in a course at George Washington University.

Jim McGourty had no such crisis of faith. Instead, he became one of the heroes of the movement. When he and Michele separated he went to live with Jose Torres, the NCLC security chief who led the organization's nocturnal raids on the Communists of Philadelphia. On May 6, 1973, Jim went out on a Mop-Up assignment in West Philly with a gang of NCLC activists. They bowled into a meeting of the Young Workers Liberation League and wreaked havoc.

Did you use nunchakus? I asked.

"Just karate," said Jim McGourty. "But the Communists had screw-drivers. One of them jabbed me in the head. And conveniently the police were right around the corner from the event, and scooped up all the Labor Committee members."

Jim and fifteen of his comrades were put in the back of a van, taken to the police station, fingerprinted, and sent home. Several weeks passed, and no further action was taken. On a day that he knows must have been June 25, 1973, Jim had a frank conversation about his past with Jose Torres. He told Torres that he wasn't a phone company employee named Jim McGourty but a Vietnam deserter born under an entirely different name. The following day, four FBI agents turned up on his doorstep. The fingerprint system, they explained, had detected his fraud, but Jim assumed that Torres had betrayed him. He was arrested and dispatched to Camp Lejeune in North Carolina to await his court-martial.

It took eighty days for his case to be heard. As he was married, he was permitted weekend and holiday leave. As his marriage was in trou-ble, he spent much of this time at meetings of the Labor Committees. "Ladies and gentlemen," he declared, "I know you came here because Jim McGourty is on trial. Well, I'm here to tell you that is not the rea-son. We are putting the government on trial." On one of my visits to his home in Loudoun County, he repeated this speech, mock heroically, in his own living room.

"That's when I fell in love with him," said his second wife, Christina. "I remember that line. Oh, what a man!"

The arrest, however, set alarm bells ringing in the organization. Ed Spannaus, the NCLC's head of intelligence, fired off a memo to his staff. "There is a strong possibility that the government will attempt to use the McGourty case as a springboard to frame up the NCLC for aiding and abetting deserters," he wrote. "We have to know the following informa-tion immediately: 1) if anybody claiming to be a deserter has approached us asking for help or simply establishing contact with members of the NCLC; 2) if any members of the organization are known or thought to be known as deserters. If we can get this information at once, we may be able to expose the government's plans before they can carry them out."

It is the first hint that the leadership of the Labor Committees had begun to think of Michael Vale's group not as a gang of comrades who had joined them in the revolutionary struggle, but as enemy agents. Agents who were not even conscious of their own destructive function.

This is what lay beyond psychoanalysis. A paranoia so potent that it turned the deserters against one another, and against themselves.

PARANOIA ADORES A network. During the summer of 1973, LaRouche was busy constructing one across a continent: connecting a constellation of tiny radical groups into a new organization called the European Labor Committees (ELC). His former girlfriend Carol Larrabee was in London, attempting to kick-start a British outpost of the organization with the help of her new British husband, Chris White. In Cologne, a knot of Greek exiles were ready for a formal alliance. In Düsseldorf, a cadre of Trotskyist medical students joined the cause. In Frankfurt and Stockholm, small groups coalesced around former members of the Next Step. They, too, studied LaRouche's theory of the revolutionary mind.

In this, Clifford Gaddy had an intellectual advantage. Michael Vale's influence had secured him the job of translating an entire issue of *Soviet Psychology*, and he had also begun a romantic relationship with a bright student in the field—Kerstin Tegin, a cool and self-possessed twenty-three-year-old graduate of the University of Stockholm. Everyone gathered in a beer hall near Düsseldorf to celebrate the birth of a new revolutionary organization and to discuss how the imminent collapse of Western capitalism would bring them, in LaRouche's words, "the successful seizure of world power within the decade."

At the end of the summer, however, rumors began circulating through the Labor Committees about a strange affair involving a member of the organization in Cologne. LaRouche had passed through the city on his way back from attending a conference in Yugoslavia. Buzzing with his new ideas on evil and motherhood and the revolutionary mind, he offered the German members his own form of marriage guidance counseling.

One of those members, Konstantin George, a Greek-American Trotskyist and recent recruit to the Labor Committees, was discovered to have been making secret trips to East Berlin. He was, it seems, conducting an extramarital affair with a psychiatrist on the other side of the wall. Rather than admit his adultery, he claimed to have mysterious gaps in his memory and insinuated that there was an espionage angle on his case. LaRouche ran wild with the idea.

"He wished to be interrogated, and stuck to it," LaRouche wrote in his autobiography. "I conducted a very hard interrogation, but a supportive one. It was like peeling away one layer of the onion after the other." Beer and cigarettes were supplied, and a story emerged. Konstantin George said that there was no girlfriend on the other side of Checkpoint Charlie: she was a fantasy constructed by his KGB programmers who had used hypnosis, drugs, and the photograph of an unknown woman to implant a series of false images in his memory. Those images concealed the real purpose of the treatment from his conscious mind—to assassinate Lyndon LaRouche.

This was, of course, impossible. But George played along with it, declining to contradict LaRouche's triumphant announcement that he had successfully deprogrammed a brainwashed enemy agent deployed to decapitate their movement. The membership, for whom psychological ordeal had already become part of the daily business of life, accepted the story without a murmur. Konstantin George had been a Manchurian Candidate. An unwitting enemy programmed to kill by a secret Soviet psychiatric technique. The intellectual universe of the Labor Committees had found space for nunchakus and ego-stripping. Now it found a place for the zombie assassin. So when LaRouche warned everyone to be vigilant for such beings, his followers concurred.

When they found them, war broke out.

12 / THE BRAINWASHERS

BILL JONES, CLIFF Gaddy, Warren Hamerman, and Jim McGourty risked their futures, their freedom, and their family relationships by taking a public stand against the Vietnam War. But they were willing soldiers in the war declared by Lyndon LaRouche. No draft was required, nor any boot camp. The rigors of Operation Mop-Up and "Beyond Psychoanalysis" had supplied all the training they required. The enemy was not a foreign state, but a nightmarish coalition of intelligence agencies, political figures, and their own comrades. The CIA. The KGB. Nelson Rockefeller, the governor of New York. Michael Vale. The stakes were high: if they lost, it meant the death of democracy, the death of the revolution, and the coming of a new world of prison camps, slave labor, mind control, mass starvation.

Though this war was a dream and delusion, the Stockholm deserters became its casualties. It turned them against their mentor and destroyed their relationships with one another. It enforced their loyalty to causes that were mad, meaningless, and immoral. It created periods in their personal histories that, in later years, they would be ashamed to acknowledge to employers, friends, family members.

The war broke out in suburban North London, five months after the Konstantin George brainwashing crisis. And, rather as any history of the

First World War must describe what happened to Archduke Franz Ferdinand and his duchess on a boulevard in Sarajevo in June 1914, the history of LaRouche's CIA-KGB psy-war must begin with an account of what happened to Chris and Carol White on Woodfield Avenue, Colindale, during Christmas 1973.

I FIRST MET the Whites at a Vietnamese restaurant in a strip mall on the edge of Leesburg, Virginia. Carol, a small, shrewd, birdlike woman in her eighties, was waiting outside. They did not disguise their unease. "We'll *hate* you when this is over," said Carol, ruefully. But I spent more time with them than anyone else in the story. We cooked for one another, swapped recipes and books, hung out in diners, went hiking through the Blue Ridge Mountains. I grew to admire them: unlike some of the deserters who acted beside them, they could name the madness in which they participated, honestly and on the record.

The Whites grew up years and a continent apart. Chris spent his early life in the English penal system: his father was deputy governor of HM Prison Lincoln. Academic success came early. Chris won a scholarship to Christ's Hospital, a venerable public school in Sussex. By the end of the sixties, he had embraced the radical life, and was working on a PhD about the peasant revolts in seventeenth-century Brittany. He was also organizing for the British Trotskyist group International Socialists, which—on a trip to New York in 1971—brought him into contact with the NCLC and with Carol.

Carol was born in Brooklyn a decade before her husband. Her family, the Kronbergers, arrived from Austria-Hungary in 1892. Her maternal grandfather was an organizer for the Communist Party who worked as an electrician at the Metropolitan Opera. He would sing as he worked on the lighting rig—so well that he was offered a job in the chorus, but without sufficient money to tempt him away from filaments and sparks.

Carol had been twice married by the time she met Chris. First to a fellow activist in the Socialist Workers Party; second to a cartoonist named George Larrabee, in a ceremony that turned out not to be legal, thanks to an administrative omission on the part of the priest.

When she spoke of her life with Lyndon LaRouche, Carol insisted that for all the weirdness that came later he was once a man capable of ordinary pleasures. He liked kayaking and rock climbing and country walks. He liked *Mission Impossible* and *The Man from U.N.C.L.E.* But, she conceded, he could be secretive, self-absorbed, and volatile. When they played chess together, he would abandon a game if he thought he was losing. When once she expressed a tolerant attitude toward homosexual relationships between men in prison, he gave her a black eye. When she bought his son, Danny, a set of racing cars, LaRouche and the boy hunkered down on the floor of the apartment to play. "But Lyn disagreed with him about how to set up the track," she explained, "and started screaming at him that his choices were immoral."

In early 1972, Carol broke off the relationship with LaRouche. He took the separation badly. "Now," he wrote in a savage little letter, "you are an empty, stinking hulk with a residual political value, which latter must be treated with the respect your person does not merit." Carol paid little heed to such insults. Chris, who was in Paris working on his PhD, invited her to join him in Paris. She accepted. The thesis remained unfinished, but a new relationship began.

A few months later the couple moved to London to recruit members to a British branch of the Labor Committees. They were married in March 1973, and celebrated with their fellow activist Tessa DeCarlo at a pizza joint by the Roundhouse theater in Camden. Carol taught math to private pupils; Chris gave history lessons at the Sir William Collins Secondary School near St. Pancras station. The pupils were unruly, and Chris dreaded each new working day. On the weekends they sold copies of *New Solidarity* on the steps of the London School of Economics, or did karate practice on Hampstead Heath. Although the Whites had little luck in attracting new members, the Colindale flat became a magnet for wannabe revolutionaries. One or two of their visitors were members of the Angry Brigade, an anarchist group responsible for bombing the home of a Conservative cabinet minister. Most of them were hungry. To avoid being eaten out of house and home, the Whites sometimes pretended to be out.

FOR THE HOLIDAY season of 1973, Carol organized a cadre school in London for members of the European Labor Committees. The venue was the Conway Hall, an atmospheric nineteenth-century auditorium in Red Lion Square, long associated with progressive politics. "There was going to be general Christmas cheer and turkeys," recalled Chris, "as well as classes and discussions." Delegates arrived from France, Germany, Italy, and Sweden. Cliff Gaddy and his Swedish girlfriend Kerstin Tegin were among them. So was a member named Michael Liebig, who had helped LaRouche in his interrogation of Konstantin George.

In the cold days between Christmas and New Year, the young revolutionaries of the European Labor Committees sat on plastic chairs listening to lectures about classical music and the relationships between the work of Hegel, Feuerbach, and Marx. The atmosphere was cheerful and anti-American. Everyone was having a good time. Then the Whites took Cliff Gaddy and a small group of NCLC friends back to the flat in Colindale and the phone rang.

The voice on the end of the line was Greg Rose, a new and rather pompous member of LaRouche's security staff in Manhattan. The Whites had been expecting some contact from the parent organization: Chris was booked to fly from Gatwick to New York the following day, in order to give LaRouche a personal progress report on NCLC activities in Britain. But this was not the subject Rose wished to discuss. He was calling from New York with more urgent information. There was, he said, a brainwashed infiltrator among the delegates in London. An unwitting agent, probably KGB. Chris was ordered to detect the spy, interrogate him, and deprogram him.

"It was a total paranoid intervention from the U.S.," said Chris. "They had us totally freaked out."

In situations like this, the finger of suspicion can point anywhere. That night, it pointed at Clifford Garland Gaddy. He was the only Russian speaker in the room. He had visited the Soviet Union. He seemed the most likely candidate. The room fell silent. Space was cleared for an interrogation, which would be carried out by Chris White and Michael Liebig. The questioning began. Was Cliff an infiltrator? Had he been programmed, like Konstantin George? Was he a creature of the KGB?

"It went on for hours," said Carol. "It got nasty. But Cliff just went silent." Perhaps this was his best policy. A denial would not have been accepted. This was a guilt that lay beyond the barrier of the conscious mind.

Eventually, the shouting stopped and the interrogation was abandoned. Cliff got up off the floor, an entirely unpeeled onion. Everyone went awkwardly to bed, knowing that a line had been crossed.

CHRIS WHITE IS a gentle man. He likes books and research. He likes cooking and bird watching. It was easy to imagine him coming to the end of this ordeal more shaken up than his victim; easy to see how his imminent trip to New York would have amplified his anxieties. What would he say when LaRouche asked him if he had exposed the spy at work in the European Labor Committees? That night, he barely slept.

The following morning, Carol, Cliff, Kerstin, and the others went back to the Conway Hall for more lectures and seminars, but the atmosphere had lost its jollity. Chris kissed his wife goodbye and set out for Gatwick Airport. He intended to be away for just over a week—long enough to attend the NCLC annual conference in New York before returning to London for the start of the new school term. At his kitchen table in Leesburg, Chris found it hard to describe his state of mind that day. Was he anxious about returning to the States to face Lyndon LaRouche, after his failed attempt to deprogram Cliff Gaddy? Perhaps. Did he expect to be criticized for having recruited so few members to the British branch of the Labor Committees? Maybe. Was he, as a former member suggested, fearful that LaRouche would punish him for having married Carol? Absolutely not, he insisted. This wasn't a story about a love triangle. So might he have suffered some kind of breakdown? Chris thought this quite possible, and he was willing to question the veracity of his own memories.

The preliminary details were surprisingly bright and clear to him. He described British Caledonian flight 221 taking off, gaining altitude, heading northward. He recalled looking through the window and seeing a knot of flames erupt from one of the engines; the captain announcing their return to Gatwick; the plane making awkward landfall at its point of embarkation. He could even remember the color of the upholstery, how he sat alone in a bank of three seats. But it sometimes felt—to both of us, I think—as if I were asking him to recall the events of a dream, or a half-remembered episode of *The Avengers*. And if flight 221 did suffer engine trouble on that day, it escaped the aviation industry's register of nonfatal accidents.

The next part of the story sounded like pure hallucination: the fantasies of a man who had entered a psychotic state. From Gatwick, Chris believed, most of his fellow passengers were bused to Heathrow to catch another flight—while he and two other refugees from flight 221, a Mr. Walsh and Mrs. Schroeder, were taken to the Copthorne, a nearby country club in forty acres of Surrey parkland. Chris recalled taking a short nap in his room, then coming down for tea—which he soon concluded had been spiked by Mr. Walsh. He remembered feeling a sudden pang of anxiety, handing his key to the concierge and ordering a taxi to the station, leaving Walsh and Schroeder behind in the tearoom. On the train back to London, he felt no better. "I was panicky," he told me. "Not really in good shape at all. Woozy, high heart rate."

Instead of heading home, he went to the Conway Hall, where the NCLC cadre school was in session. It was getting dark by the time he arrived. He stumbled through the door into a lecture on the Bach Passions and announced that he'd been drugged. Carol, sitting in the audience, was astounded to see him. "His face was frozen," she told me. "He looked really weird. He didn't want to be with me. He went off with some other people in the organization."

Those people might have taken him to a hospital. Instead, they interrogated him as Cliff Gaddy had been interrogated the night before. Later that day, they announced that Chris had identified the KGB spy. It was Carol.

Carol felt compelled to defend herself. If Chris had been brainwashed, then he may have been brainwashed to accuse his wife. But where could this process have been carried out? Only, replied Carol, at the place from which he had come home miserable each day. The Sir William Collins Secondary School in Camden. Her theory did nothing to defuse the situation. Instead, it had developed the story, and made it seem all the more real. The organization was hunting for brainwashed spies. Chris's breakdown was an unwitting audition piece for a role that could have been played by anyone in the group.

"Why did you say it?" I asked.

"I flipped," she said.

So did everyone else. Panic broke out in the group. Brainwashing was immediately accepted as the most likely explanation for Chris White's strange behavior. Cliff Gaddy and Kerstin Tegin packed their bags and returned to Stockholm. The German contingent fled back to Berlin. Chris's condition deteriorated further: he was noisy and agitated, hallucinating a halo of colors around his head. A call to British Caledonian produced no satisfactory account of events. A call to a British investigative journalist produced the claim that the mysterious Mr. Walsh and Mrs. Schroeder were MI5 agents. This doubtful assertion was instantly accepted as fact. British intelligence was now part of the narrative.

The panic then went transatlantic. Greg Rose, LaRouche's security chief, summoned the Whites and four of their American comrades back to Manhattan, warning them not to eat the airline food. The only member with a credit card booked their party on a flight to JFK. Sandwiches were made and wrapped in foil.

Carol tried to keep her husband calm as they boarded the plane. Her efforts, though, were undone by the in-flight movie. In his agitated state, Chris became convinced that the film was being screened in order to reinforce his conditioning. They watched an underwater sequence with frogmen rising from the sea. They watched a love scene between the hero and his girlfriend, a woman around ten years his senior. They saw the lover shot dead in her car, the hero avenge her murder by killing the old patriarch of the story, then commit suicide with poison. This, Chris believed, was the script he was required to follow on his arrival in Manhattan.

"We were too cheap to buy the headphones," Chris told me. "So that made the impression all the more powerful." As the plane landed, he yanked off his seat belt and got to his feet. "The CIA," he declared, adding another player to the game. "They're going to kill my wife!"

His fellow passengers assumed he was joking. Chris sat down again. By the time they disembarked, he had recovered enough presence of mind to pass through customs without arousing the interest of the immigration officials.

Outside the terminal building, three cars were waiting to collect them. It was the NCLC security team—veterans of Operation Mop-Up who had proven their skill in beating up American Communists with nunchakus. They drove the Whites to 65 Morton Street, Carol's old apartment. It was a small place, which seemed even smaller when packed with the gang that LaRouche had assembled to deal with Chris. Greg Rose. More heavies from the NCLC security staff. Gene Inch, a pediatrician from Long Island, a new recruit to the movement. And LaRouche himself—a man who had spent months readying himself and his comrades for some imminent but obscure form of psychological warfare. They were a receptive audience for the declaration Chris made as he came face-to-face with Lyndon LaRouche.

"I've come here to assassinate you," he said.

"Did you believe it?" I asked, forty years later. "As you walked through that door, did you really believe that you had been programmed to kill him?"

"No," said Chris. "All I can say is that in that moment, it seemed to me that was the quickest route to getting the whole thing settled."

It wasn't.

LaRouche and his team made Chris stand in the middle of the room. Someone pressed PLAY and RECORD on a reel-to-reel tape machine. The group bombarded him with questions—the same kind of questions with which Chris had bombarded Cliff Gaddy just a few days before. Had he been sent by the KGB to infiltrate the Labor Committees? Was he a spy? Was he a Russian agent?

"He can't be," said Carol. "He looks just like his mother."

LaRouche smiled at her naïveté. "You don't understand about cosmetic operations," he said. As with so much LaRouchian thinking, the first step of the argument was a triple somersault. But everybody jumped with him, and they jumped all night.

Dr. Inch tried hypnotism. LaRouche tried shouting. A breakthrough, the interrogators claimed, came between three and three thirty in the early hours of December 31—and the proof was captured on magnetic tape. The results are now lost but were heard by Paul Montgomery, a *New York Times* journalist who wrote up the story three weeks later. "There are sounds of weeping and vomiting on the tape, and Mr. White complains of being deprived of sleep, food and cigarettes," Montgomery reported. "At one point someone says 'raise the voltage,' but Mr. Marcus says this was associated with the bright lights used in the questioning rather than an electric shock."

At another point in the recording, Chris reacts to an excruciating pain in his arm. LaRouche seizes upon this as evidence for his programming. "The pain is real!" screams Chris. "I have to tell you what's real and stop this crazy fantasy world. Because it's not *my* fantasy." Sometimes, however, he loses the will to contradict his interrogator, and LaRouche expresses his satisfaction. "Now do you see, Carol? Do you believe?"

Montgomery concluded that whatever Lyn Marcus had cracked, it wasn't a brainwashing plot. "To a layman," he wrote, "it appears obvious that the elements of the conspiracy he claims to extract from Mr. White's mind are harmless bits of personal history or ideas suggested by Mr. Marcus himself."

Four decades later, Chris White thought this a reasonable assessment. "Someone knows what they want you to say, and they keep badgering at you until you say something like what they want you to say. Then when you say something like what they want you to say, they take that and go further with it."

Further they went. Greg Rose questioned Chris in Russian. Chris couldn't speak it—but to everyone's astonishment, he replied in what Rose reported was the Russian of a six-year-old with a heavy Ukrainian accent. (Rose, it later emerged, knew barely a word of the language, so what really occurred was an exchange of meaningless pseudo-Slavic noises.)

Chris's description of the in-flight movie proved a particularly rich source of material. From his ramblings about the film's underwater sequences, Marcus made one of the bizarre leaps of logic upon which his power over the group seemed to depend. A seven-strong squad of Cuban frogmen, he declared, was waiting beneath the Hudson to strike him dead, on receipt of a signal from Chris, relayed via a KGB middleman living in Greenwich Village. If this amphibian murder squad failed in its mission, Chris's programming would then compel him to lunge at Marcus with any available sharp instrument. Once the deed was done, the assassin would then execute himself by biting into a cyanide capsule planted into one of his teeth. Or possibly his bowel; LaRouche always favored the scatological angle.

LaRouche had created an environment in which all this seemed perfectly logical. His comrades thought they were being prudent when they took Chris to the emergency room at St. Vincent's Hospital and asked the staff to extract the cyanide capsule. Nothing, of course, could be detected. They thought they were doing the right thing when they dragged Chris into the consulting room of a psychiatrist in Brooklyn and asked him to confirm that they were dealing with a case of brainwashing. The doctor shrugged at the question and warned that Chris was in a psychotic state and required proper hospital care—a diagnosis confirmed when the patient suddenly emerged from his state of dazed passivity to declare, "Lyn, we've done it. We've defeated the unholy alliance between man and goat—the Popular Front."

CHRIS WHITE'S DEPROGRAMMING was a chamber drama that involved bright lights, sleep deprivation, and free association with Cold War imagery borrowed from the movies. But beyond its walls, a bigger production was being mounted. The curtain had opened on Saturday, December 29, 1973, the day before the Whites touched down in New York, as telephone messages about Cliff's interrogation and Chris's breakdown were crackling between Colindale and Manhattan.

Eight hundred delegates had been accredited for the opening day of the NCLC New York conference. Visitors from overseas and out of town were billeted with members who had apartments in the city. It was not a closed meeting. Attendees were encouraged to bring their parents. Day care facilities were provided.

There were two old Stockholm comrades in the audience. Warren Hamerman was present with his new girlfriend, Nora, who had just finished an art history master's at New York University. Another alumnus of the Next Step, Bill Engdahl, had arrived from Chicago and was staying with Molly and Ken Kronberg, a married pair of NCLC activists who had a place on West Seventy-Third Street.

Everyone had gathered to hear some confident Marxist analysis of the energy crisis. Instead, they received what their own newspaper, *New Solidarity*, described as "an actual battlefield report of the most devastating psychological warfare operation ever mounted in history." The parents in the room were not impressed.

"Jesus Christ," exclaimed Molly Kronberg's mother. "What's wrong with these people?" Others expressed their skepticism more quietly. But Warren Hamerman and Bill Engdahl swallowed the story in one gulp.

Molly Kronberg now lives near Chris and Carol in Virginia. On one of my trips we met up to discuss the events of that holiday season. Molly recalled that Bill Engdahl was a restless presence on their couch that weekend. LaRouche's speech, he said, had given him nightmares. In his most troubling vision, he saw the leader of the Labor Committees being throttled to death by an assailant with huge, muscular arms. Thanks to his use of crutches, Bill Engdahl himself possessed a pair of huge, muscular arms. The following night, with their guest sleeping in the next room, the Kronbergs went nervously to bed.

At some point in the small hours of Monday, December 31, Molly and Ken were woken by a phone call from LaRouche's intelligence chief, Ed Spannaus, reporting on the first night of Chris White's deprogramming. Ed urged Molly to assemble the press team and start alerting the media.

"Ken and I got dressed in our bedroom very quietly—sneakers, jeans, the whole thing," Molly told me, acutely aware that she was describing a scene from a farce. "Then Bill appeared at our bedroom door and we jumped back into bed, under the covers, fully clad."

The Kronbergs tried to pretend there was nothing amiss. Engdahl didn't buy it. Perhaps he saw their shoes sticking out from under the sheets. Wild-eyed and agitated, he began ranting about brainwashing and assassinations. Another element increased the atmosphere of hysteria. Molly and Ken Kronberg had never seen their friend without his leg braces. Now he was leaping around the apartment, propelled by his enormous biceps, as his crossed legs swung beneath him. Then came the pièce de résistance.

"I had this little pink polished ornament in the shape of a pig," Molly told me. "I guess it's quartz. It was on my bureau. Bill picked it up and stuck it in his mouth. I thought, 'Okay, that does it. Something very wrong is going on here.'"

The Kronbergs told Bill Engdahl that they were popping out to see their downstairs neighbors. "And this is one of the most chickenshit things I've ever done," confessed Molly. "We did not go back to the apartment. We did not say, 'Gee, he's in trouble; we need to help him.' We just were terrified. We were convinced he was going to kill us." As they crept down the stairs, they could hear Bill Engdahl crashing around their living room.

It was New Year's Eve, and the Labor Committees were at war. Its leader had inferred the existence of the conflict from the exhausted hysteria of a man in the throes of a psychotic episode. In doing so, LaRouche had abandoned his own sanity. Now it was time for his followers to do the same. The troops mobilized at the Ansonia Hotel on Broadway and West Seventy-Third Street. The Ansonia's unheated conference hall became the NCLC war room. The brains of the intelligence section pored over shipping reports and manifests, hoping to identify a vessel with a Cuban execution squad on board. (One member was dispatched to watch the docks.) Security staff searched delegates as they arrived. Molly Kronberg gathered her colleagues on the press team and took notes.

Once everyone had been pronounced clean, Ed Spannaus began the briefing. It was bad news. The brainwashed were among them. The KGB was planning to gain control of the Labor Committees by decapitating its leadership. Anyone in the room might be the unwitting bearer of the assassination program. Those present were invited to consider any gaps in their recent memory, during which conditioning might have taken place. Those who suspected themselves were invited to give their names to the security staff, then return home to await instructions. Using the telephone was forbidden—one call might be the means to deliver a lethal trigger word and end the life of Lyndon LaRouche.

"The message," said Tessa DeCarlo, "was 'Be afraid, be very afraid.' It was like some horrible seventies paranoid movie, starring us. I was terrified, my husband was terrified, and everybody else looked terrified. Some people now say that they didn't believe it, but in that moment, how could you not believe it?"

One event made the scenario infinitely more compelling. The appearance of Bill Engdahl, who staggered into the room, firmly convinced that he was an unwitting part of the conspiracy. "He couldn't account for certain days and assumed he was One of Them," Christina told me.

"Bill went berserk," recalled Tessa. "He was this amiable, levelheaded guy. He was ambling around, screaming, 'Cancel me, cancel me!' " In his panic, Engdahl lost control of his crutches and went crashing down a flight of stairs. Security staff picked him up, bundled him into a Volkswagen Beetle, and drove him off to Bellevue Psychiatric Hospital.

"It was," recalled Molly, "like an image from Hieronymus Bosch."

Ed Spannaus, however, seemed satisfied by the uproar. They had foiled the assassination plot. It was the greatest moment in their history. "This," he declared, "should be a time of joy."

Engdahl's spectacular collapse altered the flow of suspicion within the group. The new brainwash victim had been a protégé of Michael Vale. Michael Vale was an expert in Soviet psychology. In recent months, he had distanced himself from the Labor Committees. Perhaps the GI deserter network was not what it seemed. Perhaps it was a mechanism for delivering agents across continents, and programmed assassins into the presence of their targets. The security staff began taking the names of anyone who had recently visited Stockholm. Several people were ordered to isolate themselves in their apartments and await the arrival of a member of the intelligence staff. The rule also applied to those who had spent time with anyone who had been to Sweden. Soon, a dozen or so senior figures were under house arrest.

As the only close associate of Michael Vale present at the conference, Warren Hamerman ought to have been top of the list of suspects. His gung ho attitude, however, seems to have removed him from consideration. Nobody was keener than Warren to detect the enemy infiltrators. Molly Kronberg offered an explanation for his zeal: since returning to the States from Germany, Warren had been dissatisfied with his lowly position in the NCLC hierarchy. "All this brainwashing stuff," she told me, "was a great opportunity for promotion."

It was a smart move. Anyone who cast doubt on the Manchurian Candidate hypothesis was identified as a Manchurian Candidate. On Wednesday, January 2, 1974, six prominent members dismissed the whole business as a cynical power play. "In cases directly known to us the only conceivable substance of these charges is internal political opposition to the increasingly moronic policies of the leadership," they wrote. "In light of the latest spate of psychotic denunciations we have strong reason to suspect that all dissenters and critics will be hysterically singled out as KGB-CIA agents and the like."

They were right. The signatories were informed that they, too, had been brainwashed, and they were urged to submit to LaRouche to have the process reversed. "We," said the reply, "are the only people in the world who can. Why? Because we know how—slowly and painfully— to unlock the cage door and allow self-consciousness [and] humanity to re-emerge."

These dissenters were permitted to leave. But when Alice Weitzman, a twenty-two-year-old music student and recent recruit to the Labor Committees, expressed her skepticism about the brainwashing conspiracy, she was taken prisoner. A knot of members confined her to her apartment in upper Manhattan and attempted to deprogram her by using medicine prescribed by LaRouche—Beethoven's Pastoral Symphony, turned up to eleven.

After a few hours of this ordeal she scribbled a note pleading for help, folded it into a paper airplane, and launched it from her living room window. A child below picked it up and showed it to her mother, who called the cops. Forty minutes later, the police were running up the stairs of Weitzman's apartment building and snapping their handcuffs on six NCLC members.

Weitzman's testimony led to a second police raid, on the apartment of Ed and Nancy Spannaus. Molly Kronberg was present when it happened and remembers pandemonium, the Spannaus children cowering in their bunk beds, and the strong conviction that everybody present was going to be shot. But as Weitzman declined to press charges, nobody was incommoded for long.

CHRIS WHITE, MEANWHILE, was still being held in NCLC custody. By day he was left alone and given the Pastoral Symphony treatment. By night, in a series of different apartments across New York, his interrogation resumed, the invention and revision of the bizarre dream-narrative with which LaRouche had become breathlessly obsessed.

Lyn pushed harder, and Chris gave him the fantastic details he thought he wanted to hear.

Chris's position at the William Collins School in Camden was now identified as a setup from the start. There had been no job. There weren't even any children on the premises. Instead of teaching a class on American history, he had been subjected to a grueling fifty-two-day course of behavior modification.

On his arrival at school on September 17, 1973, Chris had been jabbed by two hypodermic needles and removed to the basement. Strange sounds were piped into his ears from a phone line connected to a remote computer. An interrogator taunted him about his father, and commanded him to eat his own excrement. An electric shock was the penalty for refusal.

Visual imagery was provided by a series of filmstrips projected on the wall. One showed Chris loitering outside government offices near Trafalgar Square and seemed to prove that he had been involved in a recent IRA bomb attack there. The most dreadful of these filmstrips, however, offered a record of the tortures supposedly endured by Bill Engdahl in Sweden. Images slid through the projector. Engdahl sitting on a chair with a ketchup bottle inserted into his anus. Engdahl consuming a dinner of his own feces. The mirror image of Chris's torture, occurring in some sister facility near Stockholm.

Chris was told that his conscious mind had retained no memories of this process because at three p.m. each day, he was disentangled from the apparatus, settled down, and shown another series of photographs. Rows of children looking back at him from their desks. Images of the normal school day that he would describe to Carol when he got home to Colindale.

Although his main contribution to the field had been the unpublished paper "Shoe Data Processing Comes of Age," LaRouche considered himself an expert in information technology. Under interrogation, he claimed, Bill Engdahl had babbled a series of coded commands. Numbers, letters, lines of Boolean algebra. Chris and Bill, LaRouche asserted, had been programmed like a pair of IBM computers. "Reduced," he said, in terminology that had gone out of fashion ten years previously, "to an eight-cycle infinite loop with a look-up table." (He would eventually transcribe the code for publication, though he always refrained from speaking it aloud, believing that it might alter the behavior of his audience.)

The discovery of this sequence of numbers and letters had turned the whole case on its head. This wasn't a plot by the Russian intelligence services to gain control of the Labor Committees and use them as a cover for their activities in the States. It was much worse than that. It was nothing less than a battle plan for the overthrow of democracy. A scheme to create a totalitarian America through the mass application of mind-control technology.

The KGB was a junior partner, possibly a dupe. The masterminds were the men of the CIA. But the CIA, LaRouche determined, was the tool of Nelson Rockefeller. And Chris, in his delirium, had called their project by its name: "Operation Chaos and Confusion." He'd plucked it from the air, but LaRouche liked the sound of it. It was certainly true to the spirit of their situation.

"Maybe," I suggested to Chris, "as he worked on you, trying to get you to crack, trying to get you to agree with his version of events, he cracked himself in some way? Maybe, in the act of trying to take you apart, Lyn managed to deconstruct himself?" Chris did not dismiss the idea.

AFTER SEVERAL SLEEPLESS nights of intrigue and alarm, the men and women of the Labor Committees were also beginning to show a few cracks. Perhaps that made it easier to accept the latest revelations. They were now at war with the CIA as well as the KGB. LaRouche, with an unerring instinct for colorful detail, decreed that no sleeper agent would be capable of hearing the phrase "CIA rats eat shit" without suffering a violent mental implosion. Members began shouting it at one another. Some rang up Alice Weitzman and yelled it over the phone.

Getting information through to the outside world proved more difficult. Two members of the organization went on a Manhattan radio station to spread the news: the host asked them if they were mentally ill. The press team called ABC, NBC, the *New York Times*, the *New York Post*, and the *New York Review of Books*. Molly Kronberg spent a peculiar few minutes on the line trying to stir the interest of the TV journalist Geraldo Rivera. When nobody bit, they produced a handbill claiming that the story was being suppressed on the orders of the CIA.

The only notable public relations success was, in part, the work of Warren Hamerman, who joined the task of recruiting an Emergency National Committee of Inquiry into the brainwashing of Chris White—a synod of authorities who would examine the case and act as custodians of the evidence if the CIA attempted to abduct, arrest, or murder any of its principals. Surprisingly, a number of prominent individuals agreed to consider participating. A lawyer, a union official, several church leaders, and a former IBM executive who had become president of Sarah Lawrence College and was probably persuaded because he was Tessa DeCarlo's worried father. The committee never sat, nor issued any report, but the names looked good on the press release, and within months LaRouche had rewarded Warren with a position on the National Executive council. "A decision to co-opt Warren Hamerman onto the NEC," he announced, "merely certifies the national leadership he has demonstrated since January, qualities that are well known to the membership throughout the continent." It was the beginning of a three-decade tenure as one of LaRouche's most trusted lieutenants.

On Thursday, January 3, 1974, flyers went out across the city for the showstopping finale of the brainwash affair. A public meeting at the Marc Ballroom, a shabby venue on the west side of Union Square, at which Lyn Marcus promised to enumerate the crimes of the CIA and the New York City police—"two insurgent government agencies . . . in the process of psychologically brainwashing extensive portions of the populations with the ultimate plan being the takeover by the CIA of the United States of America."

Molly Kronberg was asked not to attend. "A bunch of us were rounded up and taken to the Alternate Command Center. That was an apartment in the Bronx owned by a guy called Danny. We were told, 'If the Marc Ballroom gets blown up, you guys have to call the press.' " As she related the story, she burst out laughing. "And, of course, the thing is, we didn't bat an eye."

LaRouche's concluding speech that night was the maddest and most significant of his career. Even in its published form—edited and tidied up by the press team, and circulated in the organization's *New Solidarity* newspaper—it reads like a conspiracy theorist's attempt at a Samuel Beckett monologue, a breathless surge of paranoia, threats, and filthy talk, punctuated with the names of those he imagined were moving against him. As he went to the lectern, LaRouche hushed the applause and urged his audience to remain calm. Then he delivered a lecture calculated to scare them out of their wits.

"A man of great dignity, a comrade, was sitting on a couch sucking a pig one morning recently," he declared, turning Bill Engdahl's breakdown into a horrible bedtime story. "Why was he actuating a pig? Because his control was in the Russian language, and 'pig' in Russian is penis. He was receiving a reward—what's called 'freedom'—'svoboda'—for having completed a part of his assignment for the CIA."

The dubious Greg Rose must have briefed LaRouche on Slavic genital vocabulary. The Russian word for penis is nothing like "pig." There were probably people in the audience who could have corrected him. But nobody did. LaRouche was unstoppable, describing the visceral horrors of the brainwashing process—the products of his own imagination, fortified with images bullied out of Chris.

"I ask you to contemplate the high-voltage electro-convulsive shock therapy," he said. "I ask you to contemplate eating shit as a way of getting less pain. I ask you to contemplate sucking a penis as a way of getting less pain. I ask you to contemplate sitting for hours with a bottle shoved up your rectum as a way of easing pain." As he described the ultimate stage of the brainwashing process, his words collapsed into incoherence.

"There are some more real beauties," he promised. "The best of them all—you know what it is? *Svoboda*. How does the program end? *Svoboda*, you're free. The person goes into a final total caricature, sort of a Stepin Fetchit homosexual act. Pathetic. Worse. Like a dead cow. It begins to die. He's free. Automatic crematoria. No gas ovens required. The person is programmed to self-destruct. That's his freedom."

There was detail, too, on where this programming had taken place. "We have the scoop," LaRouche declared, "of one of the nastiest, most vicious CIA operations—the brainwashing institutes of Sweden. It's a great place to go for a vacation. But don't eat anything, don't drink anything. You may not come back a man, or a woman."

The mastermind of this program, he revealed, was a figure known to many present at the meeting. A charismatic intellectual who led the community of Vietnam deserters living in Swedish exile. An ideologue with a reputation for breaking men apart and rebuilding them as revolutionaries. A man who had encouraged the deserters to make common cause with the Labor Committees. "Mike Vale," said LaRouche, "is the bastard who . . . got poor slobs like us into this mess. Vale is the guy who ruined a lot of good men. A real crud."

Like much of the speech, this was pure improvisation. LaRouche thought he had uncovered a trans-European network of brainwashed agents. He might have named any number of potential villains. But Michael Vale's name was the one with which he began to riff.

Out came the story: Michael Vale was no ally in the struggle, but an agent of the CIA. He had connived to put Jim McGourty behind bars, in order to protect himself and his coconspirators. He had also been responsible for the mysterious incident the previous summer, when Konstantin George had been photographed at a meeting in East Berlin, and professed to have no conscious memory of the trip. Bo Burlingham, the former Weatherman who had run a deserters' group in Paris, was one of Vale's gang. More mystifyingly, so was the British poet Stephen Spender.

No alternative reading of these events was permissible. "Anyone who says this is a hoax—let him go down and look at Bill Engdahl. Let him hear the tapes of what Chris White went through, let him see what White has to go through to get out of this damn thing. Any of you who say this is a hoax—you're cruds, you're subhuman! You're not serious. The human race is at stake. Either we win or there is no humanity. That's the way she's cut."

LaRouche's elucidation of the plot against America defies synopsis. Its purpose, perhaps, was to be incomprehensible. A class war, he said, had started. The shooting would soon begin. People in the room could expect to be killed. Orwell's *1984* would become Sunday reading, a picture of prelapsarian paradise. Nelson Rockefeller would be the chief beneficiary, elevated to a totalitarian presidency by the machinations of the CIA, whose brainwashing program had already begun in America's prisons and factories. LaRouche was one of the few people alive capable of cracking this mental conditioning, which meant the Labor Committees were a threat to this plan. So the CIA had launched Operation Chaos and Confusion "to discredit the organization, and then create the conditions under which a hit could be done without much public furor."

Even LaRouche acknowledged that it was all insanely overcomplicated—this, he explained, was why he didn't understand the plot the moment Chris White landed in New York: "We've got a game of three-player Riemannian chess, among the world's three psychological powers: the KGB, the CIA, and the Labor Committees. Right. That's exactly what it is. The most fantastic thing you ever imagined. And the reason I missed the boat on this thing is I said, 'God, it can't be that. What's the matter? It's getting to me. It's impossible.'"

In this, at least, he was right.

13 / THE ZOMBIE ARMY

AS THIS MADNESS blossomed, Jim McGourty, halfway through his sentence for deserting from the marines, sat in a cell at Camp Lejeune, awaiting news from the New York conference. It arrived in the form of a telephone call from a breathless Warren Hamerman, who brought him up to date on the brainwashing, the killer frogmen, and the international conspiracy in which their former mentor, Michael Vale, had played the role of mindbender in chief. Jim did not understand all the details, but he believed them. When, three weeks later, Michael turned up to visit him in his confinement, Jim was forewarned and forearmed.

His old friend arrived with a piece of paper in his hand. An article cut from the *New York Times*: "How a Radical-Left Group Moved Toward Savagery." Its author, Paul Montgomery, had visited the offices of the Labor Committees and interviewed LaRouche. "He talked virtually nonstop about his life and his theories," Montgomery reported. "Only once did his reasoned, pipe-smoking professorial air vanish— when, with an explosion of spittle, he lunged with an imaginary knife to show how a CIA-programmed assassin might kill him." Jim read the piece, and listened as Michael gave him his assessment. "Marcus has initiated a test for total allegiance," said Michael. "You and me and Michele are included in that group and believed to be CIA agents—and you will never be able to convince them otherwise."

After his phone conversation with Warren Hamerman, Jim was determined to walk the LaRouchian line. Michael Vale was not to be trusted. Jim now blamed Michael for all his misfortunes, even the sudden cessation of his subscription to *New Solidarity*, which had prevented him from reading official accounts of the deprogramming of Chris White and Bill Engdahl. The books Michael sent were now construed as a form of attack. Jean Piaget's *Insights and Illusions of Philosophy* was an attempt to wean Jim off Marxism. Turgenev's *Fathers and Sons* was a choice "drawn from the pages of my psychological profile, which related to my lack of a relationship to my father during the crucial years of adolescence." Most of all, Jim was suspicious of Michael's Christmas visits to Michele, who was living with her parents in Washington, DC.

In February 1974, Jim left Camp Lejeune. He and twenty-eight other prisoners were flown north on a U.S. Navy plane and dumped, shivering, on an airfield somewhere in New Hampshire. They boarded a bus, on which they sat with their hands crossed and their heads pressed against the seat in front, to prevent them memorizing the route to their new home. The Naval Prison in Portsmouth. A new place for Jim to brood over Michael's apparent treachery.

THE CHRIS WHITE Affair, as it soon became known in LaRouchian lore, sent a surge of paranoid energy through the Labor Committees. Loyalists, like Warren, were rewarded with important-sounding job titles. Dissenters walked. Waverers were identified as spies or Manchurian Candidates and expelled. "Put simply," one former member told me, "the group lost its mind. It became a kind of Manichean cult."

The wider membership was kept informed by the NCLC's monthly magazine, the *Campaigner*. The February issue offered a landmark horror story. "On the Track of My Assassins"—an intense and detailed first-person account of Chris's ordeal—illustrated with the hideous image of a human head, a hemisphere of bone removed to expose the brain beneath. It told how Chris had been saved from becoming "a self-perpetuating mental zombie." It urged revolutionary war against the

CIA brainwashers. "These two-legged rodents are the men who condemned me, and others, to death. They are not, however, interested in me alone. They are after your mind as well. . . . That is why you will join with us to hunt my assassins down. You know as well as we do that you have no other choice. Your humanity is at stake."

"Did you write all that?" I asked him.

"That's Lyn talking," he said.

At the time, Chris didn't feel able to resist LaRouche's act of ventriloquism. Others did, however. In March, Christine Berl, the concert pianist who was one of the organization's biggest fundraising assets, voiced her concerns about the growing madness of the Labor Committees. She then received a three a.m. phone call informing her that she was a "potential traitor to the human race." Terrified, she and her partner set out their position in a document circulated to their friends, urging them to contact the authorities "in the event of our disappearance." Berl's principal conclusions were correct and clearheaded. Chris White and Bill Engdahl, she asserted, had never been brainwashed. Lyn Marcus's enemies were chimerical. The organization had "embarked on a process of autocannibalism."

Predictably, LaRouche had already taken another mouthful of flesh. In an internal bulletin headed "Why Christine Berl Could Be Turned into a Zombie," he explained that the pianist was particularly vulnerable to mental attack from the CIA thanks to her poor relationship with her mother and her interest in the atonal music of the Second Viennese School.

He issued another paper that formed a kind of contract with the remaining members of the Labor Committees, laying out the rules of the parallel universe in which they would now be required to dwell. He praised them for their "magnificent response" to the New Year crisis. He mourned the collapse of the British branch of the organization, particularly as the coming CIA takeover of the United Kingdom would have "permitted us to recruit fantastically, within the prisons and concentration camps in which our members would have been shortly prime pioneer candidates." He acknowledged the emotional impact of the brainwashing affair—though only as a spur to more sacrifices. "We are faced with the fearful infinity of a world in which we, tiny, virtually alone at the moment, must take responsibility for the very future existence of the human race," he wrote. "The mind reaches for comprehension of that, and withdraws with a shudder."

That shuddery feeling was one that members were ordered to resist, just as they were obliged to reject the doubt and skepticism of their parents and friends. Retreating into despair and depression was not an option. Nor was questioning LaRouche's bizarre contention that Nelson Rockefeller was an American dictator-in-waiting. They were to continue to fight—and to get out on the street to raise money for the war to come. Marcus underlined the most important part of the text: "*Unless the Labor Committees are able to deploy in almost a military exactness, with abrupt maneuvers, maintaining the financial level of activity necessary to function as an effective force, there will be no hope for the human race by the end of 1974.*"

IN HAPPIER TIMES before the CIA-KGB psy-war, Lyndon LaRouche liked to lie in bed with his son, eating potato chips and watching episodes of *The Man from U.N.C.L.E.* Perhaps the premise of that show inspired him at this moment. The agents of U.N.C.L.E. occupied secret headquarters on the Lower East Side, accessed through an entrance concealed inside a dry-cleaning store. From here they opposed the machinations of THRUSH, a shadowy outfit with an interest in mind-bending and world domination.

From 1974, the men and women from the NCLC mobilized against their enemies on three floors of offices above a furrier's on West Twenty-Ninth Street. Visitors stepped out of the elevator to arrive in a cramped hallway stacked with copies of *New Solidarity*. Here they were assessed by a pair of nunchakus-twirling security goons. If they passed muster, the receptionist behind a bulletproof glass window pressed a button and buzzed open the heavy steel door that led to the office.

Their new organizational structure was devised by Uwe Henke von Parpart, a philosophy lecturer at Swarthmore College who claimed to have worked at NATO headquarters in the early 1960s. (He is now in banking and occasionally pops up as a pundit on CNN.) Members were assigned to "sectors" and "files," each monitoring developments in a different part of the world.

In the International Telex Room, keen young people handled messages from NCLC outposts in America and Europe. The wall of the War Room bore an enormous laminated map of the United States, with LaRouchian centers of influence ringed in red and green crayon. In the Press Room, reporters reckless enough to enter were bombarded with the key points of the week. Charles M. Young, a future *Rolling Stone* writer whose cousin was ensnared by the Labor Committees, reported a short meeting in which he had been briefed by two members "on how Rockefeller caused or is causing the food crisis, the energy crisis, the impeachment of Richard Nixon, the assassinations of Malcolm X and John Kennedy, the flu, massive slave labor camps in the Arctic, the fall of Willy Brandt, heroin addiction in the ghetto, the counterculture, the overthrow of the constitutional government in Great Britain, the Arab-Israeli wars, the civil war in Northern Ireland, and the deaths of a billion people by the end of the century in order to save capitalism."

The daily routine was strict. Every morning someone would be sent out to buy armfuls of foreign newspapers from a news dealer on Forty-Second Street. These were filleted for useful stories, which were then translated, collated, and filed. Then members would hit the phones. They rang universities, hospitals, embassies, government offices, and Wall Street banks, sometimes impersonating journalists from more respectable outfits in order to get their calls put through, sometimes impersonating church ministers and rabbis. Whatever it took. They gathered data on politicians, terror groups, psychiatrists, the radical Right, and the radical Left. At the end of the afternoon this information was refined into a typed report, which was offered up to the National Executive Committee. The day's intelligence was then telexed to outposts in Stockholm, Copenhagen, Wiesbaden, Paris, and Washington, DC.

Don't imagine, though, some Manhattan version of the high-tech vault at Langley where Frank Rafalko wrangled IBM punch cards; still less the shiny world occupied by Napoleon Solo. Throughout the building, the atmosphere was fetid. Ashtrays remained unemptied, floors unswept, toilets uncleaned. Stuffing spilled from battered armchairs.

Members were obliged to bring their own toilet paper. The haphazard supply of equipment produced a daily rush for the small number of typewriters that possessed a full set of keys. The office culture generated other peculiarities. "There was a period," Tessa DeCarlo told me, "when wife beating was very on-trend."

LaRouche's visits to the office were rare. After the brainwashing crisis he became an indoor creature, rarely venturing outside without armed guards. Once, when he felt that his retinue was not putting enough energy into defending him from his enemies, he pointed a gun at his own head and threatened to do the job himself. For much of 1974–75 he was in Germany, holed up in an apartment in Wiesbaden selected for its assassin-proof qualities. ("Prometheus caged," reflected Chris White, "in a cupboard.")

In New York, he found secure accommodation in a series of increasingly expensive properties, including an apartment on West Fifty-Eighth Street previously occupied by Sylvester Stallone, and a huge town house on Sutton Place, a few doors down from the silent film star Lillian Gish. "When he did come to the office," said another former member, "you tried not to look him in the eye, in case he picked on you and said something horrible. But you also didn't want to look like you were deliberately avoiding his eye."

For all its lunatic intensity, this labor yielded results. The men and women who populated this sour-smelling world were smart, tenacious, and willing to work sixteen-hour days for minimal expenses. LaRouche told them that they were the chosen ones.

"There is no agency in the world to which we could look for approval of our work," he said, "and barely a handful of the world's leading figures and agencies which have the bare competence to act upon what we virtually alone can understand. . . . However queer your parents and miserable your feeling of yourself in your private fears and self-doubts, this 1,000-odd collection of seeming oddballs cannot be unfavorably compared with anything outside it today." Slowly, through its members' sleep-deprived toil, the organization transformed itself from a paranoid and introverted political sect to a paranoid and introverted political sect in control of a globe-spanning private intelligence agency. It became its own private CIA, with its own equivalent of Operation Chaos.

AFTER JIM MCGOURTY left jail, this world became his home. But not before he had spent one last summer with Michele. He was released early. Not for good behavior—though he did spend most of his time quietly learning German verbs and reading articles about nuclear fusion—but because, at the beginning of June 1974, the Portsmouth Naval Prison was closed down, its inmates dispersed or liberated.

Looking back on those months, one incident stuck in Michele's mind. It happened on the day that she agreed to accompany her husband to an NCLC meeting in New York. Warren Hamerman had arranged for the couple and their son to ride from Washington with a fellow activist. Everyone chatted pleasantly in the car. Later, Michele noticed that her passenger was not present at the meeting he had traveled so far to attend. She asked Warren what had happened to the man. Warren replied that he was a suspected police agent and had been brought to Manhattan only for an interrogation. The NCLC security team had just given him an enthusiastic pistol whipping. "I remember saying: 'If this is true, why would you let us talk with him as if he's a friend, and travel in a car with him for four hours?'" Hamerman was unrepentant. "Warren could be a sycophant around Michael Vale," said Michele, "but when he became immersed in the Labor Committees, he was just vicious."

A brief series of emails from Warren Hamerman rejected the story about pistol whipping. He professed never to have heard the expression before. Tales of dealing with hostile infiltrators were likewise dismissed as "false memories about events lost in the fog of time." I attempted to jog his memory with an article he'd written in 1976, describing the duty of NCLC security "to detect and investigate enemy deployments against the organization, and to plan and execute offensive counterthrusts." After that, he lost his appetite for our correspondence.

Of all the Stockholm veterans, Warren Hamerman was the most dedicated LaRouchian. "There was a tremendous amount of sucking up that went on in the Labor Committees," recalled Tessa DeCarlo, "but nobody was as sucky as Warren Hamerman." He would volunteer for anything. In 1974 he headed an NCLC investigation into the International Monetary Fund. In later years he would run LaRouche's political action committee and head his campaign to put American AIDS sufferers into quarantine camps. "He was a classic bureaucrat," one former comrade told me. "He was opaque in the sense that he had no charisma, always had short hair neatly combed, and as far as I can tell never entertained an original thought in his head."

Some of the viciousness noted by Michele was directed against a more unusual target. His own past. For the Stockholm deserters who remained in the Labor Committees—Warren and Jim in the States, Bill Jones and Cliff Gaddy back in Sweden—it was almost a condition of membership. They were required to delete their own histories and overwrite them with the paranoid fictions prescribed by LaRouche.

The American Deserters Committee was never a true part of the anti-war movement. The Next Step was not a real revolutionary cadre. Its members, from the beginning, had been the unwitting pawns of Michael Vale—whose sinister allegiances were revised, month by month, to fit the paranoia of the moment. Vale was a CIA agent. He was an operative deployed by the Tavistock Institute, a social science think tank in London that LaRouche had decided was a secret brainwashing laboratory. He was a member of "NATO's Schwarze Kapelle [Black Orchestra] West and East European-Japanese–North American network"—a mysterious body whose shifting membership also included Noam Chomsky, Stephen Spender, and Michael Vale's old friend Bo Burlingham.

In George Orwell's *1984*, Winston Smith, a clerk in the Ministry of Truth, is employed to edit old newspaper articles to fit the propaganda requirements of the present. But he is never asked to rewrite his own biography. The Stockholm deserters did just that. Their pasts became mutable, changing to accommodate each new obscure imaginary threat that LaRouche discerned.

In a *New Solidarity* article from December 1, 1975, "Why the Labor Committee Can't Be Taken Over by Agents," Warren Hamerman asserted that Joachim Israel, the former husband of the Swedish child psychologist Mirjam Israel, was a "Tavistock agent" who had used the deserters to launch a series of "hit and run 'probing' operations" against LaRouche. "Then The Next Step (TNS) American franchise of the network maintained by gutter operative Michael Vale was ordered to return to the U.S. for planting inside the Labor Committee."

In 1979, LaRouche added his explanation. During 1971–72, he wrote, "Vale was deployed by British intelligence to penetrate the U.S. Labor Party with 'sleepers,' acting in cooperation with the terrorist-linked section of the U.S. intelligence establishment." Jim McGourty, too, devoured and regurgitated these stories. Even by the time I got to know him, they still exerted an attraction. "So do you *not* think," he once asked me, "that Michael Vale was building a network of agents?"

ON ONE OF my visits Jim handed me a fat folder of papers that dated from the mid-1970s. He said they would explain his thinking during this time. He was right. They demonstrated how fully his personal and political life had become entwined, how the mythology of the Labor Committees altered his understanding of his own life story. One typewritten statement described a moment in November 1974 when Jim had spotted two old Stockholm comrades walking not far from his apartment on West Eighty-First Street: George Carrano, the former strategist and press officer of the ADC, and his friend Richard Bucklin.

"The first," Jim recorded, "has by now been determined to be one of the key operatives deployed by the CIA in the Spring of '68 when agents poured into Paris and later the rest of Europe, like locusts. . . . Carrano and Vale were deployed to Stockholm. Bucklin was one of the members of the CIA front group the American Deserters Committee."

The title of this document was "Concerning CIA Agent Vale's Recent Activities." It was, in effect, an account of Jim's divorce, written as a report from the front line of the war between LaRouche and the grand coalition of his enemies. In late 1974, LaRouche had urged his followers to beware "brainwashed gangs of zombies, deployed under direct or indirect control of covert operations agencies, as pseudo-leftists and zombie-fascist gangs and countergangs." Jim concluded that Michael had recruited Michele to such a group. He was driving her "to a paranoid schizophrenic state, ideal criterion for the zombie agents he is trying to create." For Jim, all the details pointed this way: Michele's choice to dissociate herself from the former deserters in the Labor Committees; her new will, which made Michael Vale guardian of their son; her decision to spend a few days in a beach house with Michael, reading Sylvia Plath.

Most striking, however, was the reason that Jim had compiled the dossier in the first place. It was not the basis for some NCLC internal communiqué, but notes for a court argument through which he hoped to win custody of his son. The paperwork suggested that LaRouchian loyalists were lining up to declare Michele a person of low morals. I recognized the names of the potential witnesses. Warren Hamerman and Bill Engdahl. Eugene Inch, the Long Island pediatrician who had assisted in the deprogramming of Chris White. These witnesses were never called. Jim's attorney's side of the correspondence showed why. Most of his letters were demands for payment, but they also hinted at a scene in which Jim had treated his lawyer to a long and serious tale about brainwashing, Michael Vale, and the CIA. "I strongly do not recommend that you pursue this custody case," wrote the attorney, "especially on the grounds you described in my office."

Jim lost his son and his marriage, but the NCLC provided a new family. LaRouche appointed Jim to its National Committee, the second tier of the leadership structure. Christina Nelson, the young activist who had admired the speeches Jim gave before his court-martial, also provided consolation. By the end of 1974 Jim had moved into her apartment in New York, where the pair ate, drank, and slept LaRouchian revolution. For two days a week they supervised the day care center for the children of NCLC members. The rest of the week brought other responsibilities. Jim worked in the Europe sector, for which he gathered intelligence on developments in Sweden and Denmark. Christina took on a more public role.

In September she ran for Congress in the Democratic primary against the incumbent congresswoman Bella Abzug, the pioneering feminist and women's rights lawyer. Christina's campaign poster featured a photograph of herself below a caricature of Abzug in stockings and suspenders. "Selling favors to Rockefeller is Bella Abzug's congressional career," declared the text, "*bumping* Nixon to make way for the CIA, *grinding* workers in 'full (slave) employment' resettlement programs, and *hooking* youth to be methadone zombies." (The image enjoyed a brief moment of exposure on the wall of the congressional canteen in Washington, DC.)

Christina's campaign generated more publicity than votes. When the election was over, she took to her bed, ill and exhausted. But there was little comfort in that. Their apartment was cold and crumbling. Cockroaches came up through the broken linoleum tiles and scuttered over the bed. The NCLC stipend upon which she and Jim lived was meager; a donation from Jim's brother got them through the worst of it. Christina wrote to thank him: "The check really helped us live like human beings and not rats in a dirty city for a very difficult period."

FOR STALIN, THERE was Trotsky; for the inhabitants of Airstrip One, there was Emmanuel Goldstein; for the LaRouchians, there was Michael Vale: the banished traitor around whom a mythology of terror could be built. Michael idolized Trotsky, but he had no desire to reenact this part of the story. "The Labor Committee was following me all over the place," he told me. "Taking pictures of me in restaurants." The columns of *New Solidarity* and its companion magazine, *Campaigner*, buzzed with weird accusations against him.

"Vale," argued a *New Solidarity* press release, "was also a key operative for Scandinavia and the Federal Republic in the British intelligence operation known as the 'GI Deserters Movement.' ... During 1971–2 Vale was deployed by British intelligence to penetrate the U.S. Labor Party with 'sleepers' acting in co-operation with the terrorist-linked section of the U.S. intelligence establishment." Mike found old associates were cold-shouldering him, not wishing to be incorporated into this growing conspiracist narrative. More painfully, new acquaintances also came under fire.

In 1975, Michael sought refuge in France, where he moved into the orbit of a French child psychiatrist named Stanislaus Tomkiewicz. Michael mentioned him on every occasion we met. Tomkiewicz was a charismatic doctor who worked with juvenile delinquents rejected by the French system. Instead of punishing them, he gave them more control over their environments. Instead of subjecting them to analysis, he gave them cameras and told them to make photo stories about their lives. Instead of pacifying them with pills, he stimulated them with five-minute doses of pure oxygen. They found it exhilarating. So did Michael. He

wanted to be part of it, to become Tomkiewicz's amanuensis and translator. He might have devoted his life to him.

"This guy trusted me to be his emissary in America," said Michael.
"And I was so impressed by these techniques that he had." But the Labor
Committees intervened to wreck the relationship. A member named Mark
Burdman wrote to the doctor and told him that Michael was a CIA agent
who had come to spy on him. The doors of the French National Institute
of Health and Medical Research slammed shut. Jim McGourty's notes
explained the Labor Committees' line of thinking: "[Vale] is now working
for a network which transports psychotics back to their homeland, once
proclaimed to be in that state by a mental institution in Paris. With the
escalation in terrorist activity by brainwashed zombies, there is little
doubt where these victims will make their homes."

Michael attempted to rebut these accusations. "I went to the newspapers," he said. "But they didn't do anything about it. Mud sticks," he
said.

Who threw it?

"Marcus. Because he was out of his mind."

The madness of Lyn Marcus was easy to accept. It was a phenomenon like the wind, always howling somewhere. Mike's difficulty was with
the idea that the men he regarded as comrades had begun howling in
unison. "Why did all those other people relay it?" he asked. A note of
emotion entered his voice. "Bill Jones? Cliff Gaddy? Warren Hamerman?
They lived with me, like revolutionaries do. We *bathed* together."

This was, in part, a set of rhetorical questions. He'd worked most of
it out for himself. Jim McGourty's behavior, he thought, could be
explained by the violence of Operation Mop-Up. "It's a technique of
political psychological warfare. You make people do things that mean
they can never go back to their original moral position. And they're
trapped. So he denounced me."

Bill Jones, he believed, was embarrassed by the whole affair. "I met
him at a World Health Organization conference in Copenhagen in 1975,
and he was pretty sheepish. So he has a conscience." Warren Hamerman
was an open-and-shut case. "We were always humiliating Wally," said
Michael. "We didn't take him seriously. This little pipsqueak of a per-

sonality. Those little men, those little guys, it seethes inside them and they have to have their revenge."

Cliff Gaddy's role, however, was much harder to explain. Michael had been a mentor to him. He had encouraged him to pursue his studies in the Russian language, and secured him his first gigs as a professional translator. Cliff's earliest publication credits were joint efforts with Michael Vale. In 1973 they tackled a long essay on adolescent schizophrenia, a subject with which Cliff then struck out on his own, carrying Michael's preoccupations with him. Looking over these essays in the yellowing pages of old academic journals, it was strange to think of Cliff and Michael rendering all this psychiatric jargon from Russian into English—"enhanced excitability, motor disinhibition, uncontrolled instinctual drives"—while the leader of their organization was ushering the members into a zone of madness.

At the end of this came a moment in Mike and Cliff's relationship that would be familiar to anyone who had seen the ending of *Henry IV, Part 2*. At the end of 1975, Mike, harassed from his place with Tomkiewicz by the conspiracy theorists of the Labor Committees, called Cliff to tell him he was coming back to Stockholm.

"Why?" asked Cliff, coolly.

"I got the message," Mike told me. Cliff had rejected his old mentor and pledged himself to Lyndon LaRouche.

They never spoke again.

THE LAROUCHIAN EMPIRE was run from New York. Its Wiesbaden office became its European headquarters—where French, Swedish, and Italian members went for firearms training and "Beyond Psychoanalysis" sessions. Its outposts, however, had a fair degree of autonomy.

The Stockholm organization was founded by Bill Jones and Cliff Gaddy. Gaddy's girlfriend Kerstin Tegin also took a leadership role and gave up her studies in order to devote herself to the group. Almost immediately, it established a position on the local political landscape— marginal, noisy, ideologically unclassifiable, mysteriously flush with cash. It acquired offices, telex machines, and computers—made possible, according to its newspaper, by "considerable collections of money, conducted by the USA working class."

Like its parent in Manhattan, the Swedish group directed its energies into maintaining a great flood of printed material, much of it screamingly paranoiac. Its members leafleted employees at the Saab car factory in Trollhättan, warning them that their workplace was being turned into a "laboratory for depression" where they might expect "the same treatment the German working class received under Nazism." Its press bureau churned out articles and communiqués that described how Sweden was being primed for a totalitarian takeover.

Swedish readers learned that their country had been identified as "the most appropriate choice for the Rockefeller forces to use as a laboratory for their 1984-style experiments." They heard that Sweden was on the point of economic collapse, that "medieval hordes of rats" were invading its towns, that "a two-tiered labor force now exists on the Third Reich principle, dividing the population into a dwindling number of older, skilled workers and a growing mass of robot-like laborers." They heard—more than once—that Joachim Israel had been working since the 1960s to identify the neurotic weaknesses of the Swedes, and that the CIA and the Swedish prime minister Olof Palme intended to exploit these to create a "model for social fascist society." They also implied that Israel had lied about being a Jewish refugee from Nazi Germany.

Who wrote this stuff? At first, much of it went out under the byline of the International Press Service—a company established by the Labor Committees in order to acquire media accreditation for its members in Europe and America. But its representatives were such a weird and disruptive influence at press conferences that they were soon declared a bogus organization. Henry Kissinger ordered them banned from the White House in March 1975. ("Fascist pressure exerted by the CIA," said the Labor Committees.)

In time, LaRouchian publications began to acknowledge individual authors and editors. Cliff Gaddy was named as Stockholm bureau chief, with ultimate editorial responsibility for the stories it issued. He stayed in the post for over a decade. Bill Engdahl and Bill Jones acquired their own bylines. In 1974 the Stockholm organization had only fifteen members, of whom only seven were full-time Swedish residents, so it seems reasonable to assume that most of the articles published in this period were the work of this triumvirate.

Like the fabulists of *Foucault's Pendulum*, Cliff, Bill, and Bill discovered that any event, no matter how irrelevant, could be absorbed into their master narrative and made to thrum with mysterious energy. In May 1974, an ex-convict walked into a pharmacy in Gothenburg with a machine gun, taking five hostages. LaRouche's Stockholm bureau announced that this incident proved that "the CIA's international terrorist network is now being activated in Sweden." A month later, Bill Jones made a nuisance of himself at a conference on occupational stress held at the University of Uppsala, accusing puzzled academics of being part of the CIA's secret behavior-modification project. He handed out copies of "On the Track of My Assassins" and called for a delegate to be indicted for crimes against humanity. "When challenged," he wrote, "these doctors quickly reveal their own insanity."

In December 1974, a few words in a Swedish newspaper editorial were transmuted into proof that Olof Palme had been instructed by Nelson Rockefeller to increase Sweden's offensive capability against Russia. LaRouchian hacks became masters at this kind of distortion: they could spin any innocuous remark into evidence for a plan of genocide. In 1975, the West German Embassy in Stockholm was bombed: LaRouche publications pronounced it a false flag operation by International Socialists—with whom Palme and all the journalists working on the story had collaborated. Those involved should "expect to answer to these actions with their lives."

These bizarre outpourings were not limited to the printed page. The organization was a disruptive presence at all kinds of public, professional, and political gatherings. "I have not been to a single meeting the last two years without this company making their presence felt and sabotaging proceedings," said Inga Thorsson, Sweden's representative at the United Nations. Gösta Bohman, leader of the center-right Moderate Party, found himself bombarded with strange questions at his own party conference. The Social Democratic MP Birgitta Dahl once shouted at them from the platform: "Hold your own meetings instead of coming to disrupt ours!"

Palme's party was so concerned about the behavior of NCLC activists in Sweden that they commissioned Håkan Hermansson, a journalist from the Malmö paper *Arbetet*, to write a pamphlet about the organization. "They appear at public party gatherings and conferences where the most regular tactic is to destroy every attempt at a meaningful discussion or exchange of ideas," reported Hermansson. "This occurs through an unrestricted venting of impossible vocabulary in seemingly endless propositions, by posing intentionally provocative questions, breaking off, making accusations and even threats."

There was little point, he suggested, in trying to follow their arguments. "Their political lingo," he wrote, "is to all intents and purposes impossible to understand. Their argumentation builds on fantastical claims presented as uncontested truth. The fanatic conviction makes it impossible to conduct any meaningful discussion. Their worldview is complete, true, and indivisible, and every attempt at criticism risks being taken as evidence that the critic is a brainwashed victim of the organization's enemies. Or a hired double agent."

Trouble for critics usually followed: Hermansson was harassed in his office in Malmö; European Labor Committees members came up to the newsroom to tell him that he was a CIA agent who should face trial as the Nazis did at Nuremberg. Klas-Örjan Spång, the owner of a Stockholm bookshop that declined to stock LaRouchian literature, was denounced on the pages of *Ny Solidaritet* as "Agent Spång" of Langley. When *Aftonbladet* ran a story comparing the European Labor Committees to the Children of God, a California cult that separated children from their families and became notorious for its toleration of sexual abuse, Kerstin Tegin declared that Olof Palme was behind the smear and threatened him and the paper with a $5 million libel suit—which never materialized.

In later years, journalists who investigated the Labor Committees reported physical attacks by members, but their preferred methods were much less conventional. The American organization threw a foil-wrapped hunk of liver at a Catholic archbishop, coordinated a telephone campaign to accuse Boston's FBI officers of abducting dogs for sexual gratification, and confronted the actor Peter Fonda at an airport with a banner reading FEED JANE FONDA TO THE WHALES. The German group in

Wiesbaden published a cartoon of Chancellor Willy Brandt in Nazi uniform. (Brandt sued for libel and won, but the European Labor Committees found themselves an unlikely ally in the form of the conceptual artist Joseph Beuys, who declared that this was art.)

The Stockholm chapter developed weirdnesses all its own. More than one of my interviewees remembered Sweden's happy band of LaRouchians making bizarre and incomprehensible interventions at meetings addressed by Olof Palme. A favorite stunt was a three-person operation: one member would sit near the stage and begin a loud diatribe against the speaker; a second would feign some kind of learning disability, like a character in Lars von Trier's *The Idiots*; a third would then shout at them for being too noisy. It was a good strategy, if the aim was to cause chaos and confusion.

BILL JONES WAS a well-educated middle-class boy who had been destined for the priesthood. Most people who encountered the teenage Cliff Gaddy considered him one of the brightest blooms of his generation. Bill Engdahl was a Princeton graduate. How did the Labor Committees persuade such smart young people to do such strange and nasty things? Partly by insisting that black was white.

"Take, for example, the person who describes the NCLC as being 'paranoid' because we have identified the Rockefeller conspiracy as governing capitalist politics today," wrote Ed Spannaus in a 1975 article for *Campaigner* magazine.

> What such a person is actually saying is that there is no coherence or lawfulness to events, that everything is discrete and arbitrary. Such an individual must himself deny the coherence of external reality in order to satisfy his internal authorities who tell him that there can be no such thing as a conspiracy—with its implication that one would have to act upon reality in order to stop it. Thus he demands that reality be adjusted to "fit" his internal fantasy-map, just as the child magically attributes events outside himself to his imagined omnipotence. In a child, such paranoia is a normal feature; in an adult, it is pathological.

Parlor tricks also helped. LaRouche would make furious insistence on the critical nature of some obscure technicality. One week he told his acolytes, "Anyone who doesn't understand the isoperimetric principle is not qualified to save the human race." Members who hadn't listened in their high school geometry class scurried back to Pythagoras and attempted to deduce why this was so important. The following week LaRouche announced, "If you don't understand the ablative absolute, you can't think properly." The ablative absolute is a Latin grammatical term. *With these words having been said, Caesar departed.* It had no particular significance. LaRouche just liked the sound of it, and the fact that most of his followers had to go and look it up.

One former member, the Greek exile who used the nom de guerre Nick Syvriotis, told me, "He would take people who had at some point in their lives done serious work on serious topics and put them together with these nutcases, thereby keeping everybody off-balance. What was common in both groups, the cranks and the serious people, was the need for parental approval. Lyn supplied it to both. He would promote a crank to a position of authority, and the genuinely authoritative were left with their mouths hanging open. But they wouldn't challenge for fear of losing his parental approval. That's how the game was played." He spoke from his own experience: "I had to break with my need for parental approval to quit," he said. "Then I saw the extent of the insanity. What I learned from being in the Labor Committees is that insanity is curable."

Some of the damage they inflicted, however, was not so easily healed.

IN MAY 2016, Michael Vale summoned me to Paris. He'd decided to sell his flat and invited me to stay for the last few days of his ownership. The furniture had gone; the carpets had been taken up; the cupboards dismantled. I helped him carry lumber down to the street. The place was pretty filthy. When I went to bed that night, I wrapped a T-shirt around the pillow to avoid inhaling the sourness of the bedclothes. The next morning, in the eviscerated kitchen, Mike presented me with a stack of documents. Old copies of the *Next Step*. Paperwork recording his unsuccessful attempt to claim back a car confiscated by the German government. A collection of press clippings, saved as an actor might save his old reviews—but these were paranoid ramblings from Labor Committee publications, written by friends who had turned against him, or exposés on the Labor Committees from the Swedish and Danish papers. Attacks on all fronts, most accusing him of being an agent of the CIA.

At the bottom of the pile was the letter that ruined his life. As Mike was neither its writer nor its addressee, it was hard to understand how he had acquired it, but there it was, a brittle photocopy on the notepaper of the French National Institute of Health and Medical Research. It was addressed to Mark Burdman of the Labor Committees and signed by Stanislaus Tomkiewicz. "Cher Ami," wrote Tomkiewicz, "you earn my respect and my sympathy for having been the first (after me) to have understood the relationship of Michael Vale with supporters of order on a planetary scale." The CIA again.

On my last day, I accompanied Michael to his doctor. He was awaiting some test results. He emerged beaming from the appointment, clutching an envelope of X-rays that were the evidence of his good news. To celebrate, we went for lunch at Les Deux Magots, the famous haunt of Jean-Paul Sartre and Simone de Beauvoir. Mike had quiche, most of which made it to his mouth. A splot of mozzarella became lodged in his stubble, and remained there four hours later, when we said goodbye at the Gare du Nord.

As we were walking on the street, Mike asked me if I knew what had happened to Mark Burdman. Having read so widely in the lunacy of the Labor Committees, I knew the answer. In 1980 he had taken a position at its German headquarters in Wiesbaden, where his writing passed completely through the LaRouchian looking glass. His magnum opus—which now enjoys a quiet afterlife on websites with names like "Jew World Order"—was an essay asserting that the British prime minister Benjamin Disraeli was the founder of both Zionism and Nazism.

"Did I outlive him?" asked Mike.

"Yes," I told him. Burdman had died in July 2004.

Mike's eyes lit up. "Good," he said. "Good."

14 / OPERATION DESTRUCTION

OFTEN, WHILE WRITING this story, I felt as if I were recording a series of dreams. Dreams of distant homes, where baffled parents sat, thinking of lost sons. Dreams of Vietnam, where officers in khaki and Ray-Bans may or may not have ordered men to burn the huts with villagers inside them. Dreams of revolution, in which Rosa Luxemburg's mass strike came to 1970s New York, and young American Marxists built colonies on the Red Planet.

Apocalyptic dreams, too, with electrodes and pigs and ketchup bottles, and Michael Vale and Nelson Rockefeller wandering through a landscape built by Hieronymus Bosch. Those were LaRouche's favorites. The ones he hoped would steal upon his followers when they closed their eyes at night. "The most optimistic view of AD 1990 under the Rockefellers' program would be the reduction of earth's population to no more than a few hundred millions of psychotic cannibals, scavenging a wretched subsistence from the wreckage of the collapsed civilization." That was Lyn's Christmas message of 1974. The same Christmas that the existence of Operation Chaos was revealed to the American public.

Radicals and revolutionaries are supposed to be dreamers. The best of them bequeath their visions to us. Nothing to lose but your chains. Nothing to kill or die for. Little black boys and black girls joining hands with little white boys and white girls. But during the period of MHCHAOS, the forces of established order also seemed to enter this untethered state.

Lyndon Johnson had a dream. He dreamed that the KGB was joining hands with the youth of America and leading it onto the streets to protest against the Vietnam War. His successor, Richard Nixon, shared that illusion. Operation Chaos was established to turn fantasy into prophecy. Richard Ober, the taciturn Harvard man assigned to run the project, did his best to make that happen.

But no matter how much energy its operatives expended, no matter how much money it spent, or how many files it opened, Johnson and Nixon's vision remained insubstantial. HYDRA chuntered through the data on its 9,994 names, but it couldn't detect a ruble of Moscow gold. American radicals, it seemed, were as self-reliant as Ralph Waldo Emerson. They had decided to hate LBJ and Nixon and the Vietnam War without anyone from the Kremlin encouraging them to do it for cash.

Harry Rositzke, the crossword-loving Anglo-Saxon scholar who had been attached to MHCHAOS in its earliest days, woke up to this before many of his peers. He left the CIA in 1970 to raise crossbred Angus calves on a farm near Middleburg, Virginia, but maintained a parallel career as a sympathetic commentator on agency affairs.

In the early 1970s, American intelligence personnel felt in need of sympathy. First, a series of troublesome reporters and activists began exposing their unconstitutional habits. Military intelligence spying on civilians. The FBI sending its agents provocateurs into the Black Panthers, the Communist Party, and the civil rights movement. The Watergate burglaries.

Then, government responded by setting up a series of inquiries into the morals of America's spooks. The Pike Committee attempted to discover the cost of the CIA and the true scope of its activities. The Church Committee investigated the CIA's tampering with the U.S. mail and its plots to assassinate foreign heads of state. The Rockefeller Commission, headed by the bête noire of the Labor Committees, heard evidence on MKULTRA, Langley's failed attempt to develop chemical and psychological techniques for manipulating human behavior.

In response to all this, in 1977 Rositzke published *The CIA's Secret*

Operations, an attempt to set the record half-straight on the agency's clandestine activities. But the book also diagnosed the defining malaise of all intelligence outfits.

"They form a society of their own, with purposes and standards distinct from those of the nation. Prolonged immersion in the segregated, self-contained, and self-justifying world of deception and secrecy tends to erode links to reality," he argued. "The misuse and abuse of the CIA may have been as much the result of the inner momentum of an isolated and hallucinatory bureaucracy as of the interference of Presidents." He might have been describing the workings of a cult.

A HALF CENTURY has passed since the creation of Operation Chaos. In the beginning it was nameless, hidden in the field of the CIA's Special Operations Group. At this stage, few within the CIA knew of its existence, and those who did were uneasy about its activities. That unease grew. Rumors circulated around Langley that Richard Ober and his colleagues were doing something illegal down in the basement.

In December 1971, Thomas Karamessines, the CIA's deputy director of plans, felt obliged to fight this fire. He assembled his junior staff and listened to their concerns. "The group," he noted, "mentioned Dick Ober's unit and said that there was a lot of scuttlebutt that the purpose of this unit was to keep book on Black Power adherents." Karamessines told them not to worry. He also told them not to believe anything they read in *Ramparts* magazine. He failed to put their minds at rest.

Early in December 1974, Seymour Hersh, the investigative reporter who had brought the first news of the My Lai massacre, heard whispers about Langley's biggest secret. His anonymous sources could not put a name to it, but they told him about wiretaps and burglaries, infiltrators and data banks. They told him about a well-funded, high-tech, and illegal surveillance operation against American citizens at home and abroad. They even told him who was running the show. Hersh dialed a number in Fairfax, Virginia. "There's nothing I can say about this," said Richard Ober. It was the most honest and expansive public statement that Ober made in his life.

Hersh's story ran in the *New York Times* on December 22, accompanied by photographs of the three most recent directors of central intelligence—Richard Helms, James Schlesinger, and William Colby. The headline read: HUGE C.I.A. OPERATION REPORTED IN U.S. AGAINST ANTIWAR FORCES, OTHER DISSIDENTS IN NIXON YEARS. Hersh's source, a former CIA officer, reported the same suspicions that Karamessines had heard at his meeting. "Ober had unique and confidential access to Helms," said the informer. "I always assumed he was mucking about with Americans who were abroad and then would come back, people like the Black Panthers." By the time the story was in print, however, it was already too late to write the comprehensive history of Operation Chaos. The CIA had shut it down, Richard Ober had been kicked upstairs to the National Security Council, and the Chaos files had gone to oblivion.

FRANK RAFALKO, the man who mucked about with the Black Panthers on Ober's behalf, was there when it happened. "People say they never cut out the Chaos program, but they did," he told me. "It was cut out even before Colby. He shut it down officially, but it was already shut down before that. There were very few people left." An officer named White was assigned to destroy the files. The undertaking was so vast that it gained an unofficial code name: Operation Destruction.

White was a blunt instrument. How long, he asked Frank, would it take to get rid of data stored on a computer tape? "Ten seconds, I told him," said Frank. "You just had to erase them or write over them. It's the hard copies that take the time. But he didn't believe me." So the tapes were unspooled and fed to the incinerator, along with shredded letters, telegrams, newspaper cuttings. All were made intangible by fire.

As Frank was keen to point out, fires were started in accordance with the law. To retain such records would have been against the instructions of Congress. Obliterating them, however, had an unintended consequence. It created a space in which fantasies about the power and the reach of the Central Intelligence Agency could thrive. It opened up another space in which to dream. Lyndon LaRouche closed his eyes and gave it the full *Kubla Khan*.

DURING THE SLEEPLESS panic of his deprogramming, Chris White had cried out in the night about "Operation Chaos and Confusion." It was a lucky guess, and one reason why the CIA should never have given its campaign against the New Left such an obvious and melodramatic code name. Another piece of luck followed in February 1975, when President Gerald Ford appointed his new vice president, Nelson Rockefeller, to head a new inquiry into the intelligence services. His report revealed the operational name of CHAOS and described its scale and scope.

For LaRouche and his followers, these events seemed to support their own interpretation of recent American history. Encouraged, they added more to the story, placing themselves at its center. "Beginning in January 1974 with the attempted assassination of International Caucus of Labor Committees Chairman Lyndon H. LaRouche and the activation of a wave of National Security terrorist operations," claimed *Executive Intelligence Review*, the new glossy LaRouchian magazine, "Nelson Rockefeller launched 'Operation Chaos'—a program of escalating terrorism, economic destabilization, and red scare hysteria directed at creating a condition of 'accepted' military police-state rule throughout the advanced sector."

Why had the Rockefeller coup not happened? Because the Labor Committees had saved the day. "Millions of leaflets permeated every major industrial center in both the U.S. and Canada. Extraordinary public meetings were held on an ongoing basis until the cumulative effect of this mass 'inoculation' campaign forced Rockefeller to place Operation Chaos in a state of suspension."

New Yorkers might have faintly remembered a brouhaha at the Marc Ballroom, or the moment when two NCLC members went on a radio program and were asked by the host if they were drug users or psychiatric patients. But this did not matter in the Labor Committees, for whom the facts never stopped mutating.

In September 1978 an *Executive Intelligence Review* article by a member named John Sigerson announced that British intelligence had masterminded Operation Chaos and launched it at Heathrow Airport a few days after Chris White arrived in New York. The following year, when LaRouche published *The Power of Reason*, probably the world's most inappropriately titled memoir, he described how Chris, Bill Eng-dahl, and Alice Weitzman were drugged in "an extensive operation of the sort catalogued by spooks under the name of 'Chaos.' The clear objective was to sow such chaos and paranoia-ridden confusion into the Labor Committees, as to destroy the organization to all intents and purposes." In a sense, the opposite was true. Operation Chaos had sustained Lyndon LaRouche. It was the glue that bound his followers together.

THE INCINERATOR MADE its files disappear, but the greatest vanishing act of Operation Chaos was performed by its chief. Among the senior intelligence figures of his generation, Dick Ober remains the invisible man. In early 1975, when the CIA was under the most intense scrutiny it has ever endured, his name appeared in every newspaper in America from the *Manitowoc Herald Times* to the *Emporia Gazette*. But no reporter ever tickled a useful quote from him, or even persuaded him to confirm his date of birth. Silence was all he bequeathed to the archive.

In June 1975 he wrote to Nelson Rockefeller to signal his disgust for the conclusions of his report: "I have made no public statements regarding allegations concerning my activities with the CIA and I have no present intention of doing so," he stated. "Lest silence on my part be interpreted as agreement with the text of the report . . . I am writing to you to make my disagreement a matter of record."

Two decades later, when the investigative reporter Angus Mackenzie was researching the history of the CIA, he discovered that "it was a breach of the code when one associate gave me a rough description of Ober as a big man with reddish skin and hair." Ober's love of biographical blank lines outlived him: when Frank Rafalko wrote his official history of MHCHAOS, the CIA refused permission to print simple details that had already appeared in Ober's *Washington Post* obituary. As I write this, Ober doesn't even have a *Wikipedia* page.

"Ober was disliked by people," said Frank, listing some of his detractors within the agency. "But I liked him. He treated me very fairly. He took care of his people. Always backed us up."

I pushed for an example. Frank told me about the day that a case officer came into the Vault to brief them about an asset he was running in the field. As they sat in Ober's office, the officer pulled out a pack of cigarettes. Frank was trying to kick the habit and objected. "So Ober said, 'Okay, don't smoke here. He doesn't want you to smoke.' So he didn't. That's the kind of guy Ober was." As the record stands, Richard Ober's only documented act of kindness is the one described in this book. Telling someone not to smoke in a windowless room. It's not much of a legacy.

A fact of Ober's family history, however, means that a wealth of detail about his early life has lain on the record for decades, unnoticed by historians of spying. In 2016, another source of information emerged—a thick file compiled in the 1950s by the FBI. Its pages tell the story of how the future chief of Operation Chaos was investigated for his own suspected connections with the radical Left. Let us put this on the record, and fill that empty space he did so much to preserve.

RICHARD OBER'S FATHER was an agent, though the term made him uneasy. Harold Clark Ober preferred the term "author's representative." H. G. Wells, William Faulkner, J. D. Salinger, and Agatha Christie were the authors—though F. Scott Fitzgerald was the one who gave him the greatest glory and the greatest grief.

Ober showed a paternal interest in his writers. He sometimes took in their laundry, though he drew the line at taking them to the psychiatrist. With Fitzgerald, the line became blurred, and thousand-dollar loans were wired frequently across it. In 1937, when Fitzgerald was drunk, broke, and disconsolate, Ober secured him a contract with MGM, dispatched him to Hollywood, and took in the Fitzgeralds' sixteen-year-old daughter, Frances—known as "Scottie"—as an "instant sister" to his two boys.

Richard was her exact contemporary, Nathaniel three years her junior. Neither boy welcomed the intrusion until they saw how it was changing the culture of the family. Suddenly, there were frequent trips to the movie theater in White Plains and visits to Schrafft's for a Dusty Miller sundae—a confection of vanilla ice cream, marshmallows, chocolate sauce, and powdered malt. ("Well, we sure don't much like having you here," confessed Nat, "but I'll say this for you: Father's a lot nicer to us when you're around.") When Scottie was married in February 1943, the Ober boys were her ushers.

Thanks to Scottie Fitzgerald and other memoirists, it's possible to construct a detailed picture of the world into which Richard Ober was born. His mother, Anne, was the daughter of Northern Irish Catholics and a journalist for *Suburban Life* magazine. She met Harold in Paris during the Great War—Anne was a Red Cross nurse; Harold had been sent by the U.S. government to investigate the wartime uses of Airedale terriers.

Home was a converted barn at the end of a wooded road in Scarsdale, New York. There was shrimp curry for dinner, Prokofiev and Shostakovich on the gramophone, asparagus and peas growing in a luxuriant garden. Tennis was played on the court belonging to their neighbors Robert Haas, a founder of the Book of the Month Club, and Merle Haas, the English translator of *Babar the Elephant*. Prize-winning dogs scurried around the house and—to the disgust of the servants—were sometimes allowed to lick the dinner plates. Fixed to a beam in the living room was the crimson oar commemorating Harold Ober's rowing days at Harvard, carefully turned so as not to expose the exact age of its owner. (His sons, who also made the varsity crew, would move it, maliciously, to expose the date.)

Richard Ober registered as a Harvard freshman in September 1940. He studied philosophy and history, volunteered as an air-raid warden, and joined the Reserve Officers' Training Corps with enough enthusiasm to earn a medal from the Sons of the American Revolution. By August 1944 he was training in southwest England with the 681st Glider Field Artillery Battalion; by the winter, he and his comrades were moving through the snows of Belgium and Luxembourg and on to the rigors of Operation Varsity, in which they made military history by forming the first glider crews to land in territory not already secured by paratroopers.

The experience must have been terrifying: dropped by towplane, flying blind through the drifting Allied smoke screen, strafed by German antiaircraft guns, crash-landing amid ditches, barbed wire, and hostile enemy troops. Back home in Scarsdale, Harold Ober sat by the radio with Scottie Fitzgerald, hoping for the best. He got it. Richard Ober survived to return home and exchange his first lieutenant's stripes for the postgraduate degree that helped him acquire a desk at Langley.

Harold Ober may have disapproved of his son's choice of profession. On his commute to the city, he would always avert his eyes when the train chugged close behind the houses of Harlem and the Bronx. "I don't like prying into their private lives," he told Scottie Fitzgerald.

THE CIA DOES not declassify the personnel files of its officers. Its culture reveres the shredder. The FBI, however, abhors the destruction of paper: its archives might comprise the richest history of the American people ever compiled. So we must thank its director J. Edgar Hoover for the knowledge that Ober joined the CIA in December 1948 as a foreign affairs analyst and that by the spring of 1952 he had graduated to a spookier role—an intelligence officer working out of a CIA office concealed inside the U.S. consulate in Munich, where Harry August Rositzke was his boss. The bureau put these details on file in the second half of 1956, a sour patch in Ober's life, when a team of FBI agents was appointed to determine whether he might be a risk to the security of the American state.

The doubts about Richard were really doubts about his father. Harold's name had been turning up in the papers and conversations of too many suspected Communists. It was spotted in a pencil note written by Stephen Laird, a journalist and movie producer alleged to be an asset of the KGB; on the mailing list of the United Committee of South Slavic Americans, who were unacceptably friendly to Marshal Tito of Yugoslavia; in a notebook that had been seen in the house of a Communist Party member in Los Angeles when a naval intelligence officer had been rifling through her papers all the way back in 1936.

Harold's friendship with Inez Munoz, a Hollywood writer who had recently been questioned before the House Un-American Activities Committee, was also perceived as potentially compromising. Another connection caused alarm bells to ring: Ober had friends in common with

Jack Soble, a KGB agent who had been inserted into Leon Trotsky's entourage and would be arrested by the FBI in 1957.

Richard Ober was suspended from his duties and questioned by his colleagues. What were his father's political views? How many Communists did his father know? Was it true that Harold's assistant Ivan von Auw was homosexual? Ober told them that his father was a "liberal in the strict sense of the word, and an individual who was personally very interested in civil rights, government security standards, and similar issues." He also professed to know little of his father's professional life, and acknowledged that writers sometimes had "peculiar political views."

The case was passed to Hoover, whose special agents checked out Richard Ober's background as if it were a crime scene. They quizzed his neighbors, his rowing coach at Harvard, alumni of the foreign affairs course at Columbia, and the proprietor of the Dew Drop Inn Store in Fairfax, Virginia. But it was his colleagues at Langley who gave the sharpest assessments. Ober, one said, was "the type who wants to make all the decisions rather than delegating in that respect to his subordinates as a result employee works himself to the point where he has to take sick leave." This instinct was the secret of his success as a CIA officer, and the source of his hubris.

Frank Rafalko knew of one officer who regarded Ober as "a nincompoop who went way beyond his charter." "Autocratic," judged another. "Truly evil," said a third. But the agency looked after its own. "They didn't fire him," explained one of Hersh's anonymous sources, "but they didn't want him around. The CIA had to get rid of him—he was too embarrassing, too hot."

A new job on the National Security Council kept him safe. So did the White House. A memo from Henry Kissinger to Donald Rumsfeld, chief of staff to President Gerald Ford, sent two days before Christmas 1974, gave advice on how to handle awkward questions about Ober. If a journalist asked if he was to be suspended, the preformed answer was there on the page: "I am not prepared to discuss further Mr. Ober's duties on the staff." But nobody asked.

That silence continued until his death. Even after that, a sharper picture failed to emerge. A brief obituary in the *Washington Post* noted

Ober's CIA postings in India and Mexico, but MHCHAOS and Hersh's exposure went unmentioned. More space was devoted to Ober's horticultural pursuits—his second career as the owner of a thirty-two-acre Virginia farm that supplied herbs to the French restaurants of DC; his membership in the Herb Society of America; his editorial role on the guidebook to the National Herb Garden. Nobody took the opportunity to dig a little deeper. On the day that Richard Ober died, journalists with an interest in espionage had their eyes on a different story. The chief of Chaos breathed his last on September 11, 2001. The CIA had kept Richard Ober in obscurity for decades, but al-Qaeda provided the final ministrations.

His last recorded sighting, as far as I can tell, was logged by the French chef Jean-Louis Palladin. One day in 1979, Richard Ober appeared at the back door of Palladin's restaurant at the Watergate hotel in Washington, DC. He was clutching a handful of mint, a bunch of thyme, and a seed catalog. He told the chef that he worked at the State Department and was bored of his job; that he'd made a bet with a friend that his garden could yield produce fit for the best restaurant in DC. Palladin recorded the moment in one of his recipe books.

"I looked at him and said, 'Did God send you to me? You're exactly what I've been looking for.' " A year later, Ober's farm was sole supplier of herbs to Palladin's restaurant. Their quality reminded the chef of the produce grown on land owned by his family. "My father owned an orchard he worked in every Sunday," said Palladin. "He had cherry, apricot, apple, and peach trees, and the fruit he got from those trees was fantastic. Why? Because under his orchard was the old cemetery."

IN OCTOBER 1973, an American novel was published that pictured the United States transformed by the ideological forces that Chaos had been established to frustrate. *Left On!* is set in a parallel post-Nixonian universe, where Republicanism and every conservative certainty lie crushed, and an entirely new political culture has been brought into being. Its architect is a charismatic Democratic candidate who has revitalized and radicalized his party using techniques that would have been familiar to any member of the National Caucus of Labor Committees.

"The practice of criticism and self-criticism," asserts President Mack, "is the only means of changing men's minds, of washing old brains and curing sick thoughts." With the White House gained, he begins his cultural revolution. Mack curbs the powers of the FBI and fires 70 percent of its staff. Intelligence files on leftist agitators are closed, and new ones opened on their right-wing equivalents.

Out in the political wilderness, Ronald Reagan, the deposed Republican governor of California, forms a covert resistance group called the Secret Center. Mack's intelligence services fight back with a computer project that analyzes the activities of any Americans earning over $50,000 a year, and soon identifies the ringleaders. Found guilty of "conspiring to incite reactionary riots across state lines," Reagan submits to a program of moral and political reeducation. At the end of the process, public tears of contrition demonstrate that he has seen the error of his ways. "I envy the young, because I am old, and I have persecuted them," Reagan confesses. "I can't relate with the blacks and the browns because my white skin is my only heritage. I have been selfish, boastful, and hard of heart. This Committee, to whom I am eternally grateful, has shown me to myself as I am."

There are at least two remarkable things about *Left On!* The first is that this isn't a shivery dystopia of the *Red Dawn* variety—the novel greets this new world with full-throated pleasure. The second is that its author is Harry Rositzke of the CIA.

Rositzke's mischievous proposition is that the wiretappers, snoopers, and black-bag men of the intelligence agencies are the principal financiers of the left-wing groups they are working to discredit and destabilize. When President Mack orders the spooks to end hostilities against the organizations on their watch list, those organizations are thrown into crisis. The 3,385 FBI informers paid to join the Communist Party USA resign simultaneously, creating a perilous black hole in the accounts of *Daily Worker*. Student bodies and black welfare groups falter. "Sit-ins, love-ins, think-ins, police-baiting and dean-hustling, the stump-oratory of Maoist fustian, Marxist folderol and Marcusan fog had ended."

As a Dear John letter to the secret state, it was stinging. As a satire for the general reader, it was pleasingly zeitgeisty. But sometimes the real world can do better. In February 1975, Lyndon LaRouche made the decision that would seal his reputation as one of America's canonical crackpots, and allow him to become a gag on *The Simpsons* and a character on *Saturday Night Live*.

It was time, he concluded, to build his own political party and run for high office. It was time for President LaRouche to save the world from the zombies and the nuclear warmongers.

And in Sweden, Cliff Gaddy's fiancée would do the same.

15 / THE BELIEVERS

MY FIRST RESEARCH trip to Stockholm coincided with the final two weeks of Sweden's 2014 general election campaign. As is traditional, a stretch of concrete near the entrance to the Sergels Torg metro had been turned into a political village. Sergels Torg is a creation of the Palme years. A large public square attacked from above by a surging concrete road system and skewered by a great tower by the sculptor Edvin Öhrström. Election time adds a touch of kitsch to all this brutalism: a cluster of garden sheds and summerhouses occupied by the contending parties. Social Democrats. Christian Democrats. Greens. Moderates. The Swedish tabloid *Expressen* (slogan: "It stings!") also has a space, on which I watched the deputy prime minister Jan Björklund being hugged by a man dressed as a six-foot wasp.

On the other side of the street, the smaller parties were accommodated. A young, cheerful crowd was having a sociable time in the pink kiosk staffed by Feminist Initiative, the women's party supported by Jane Fonda and Benny Andersson of ABBA. Next door, in a red hut stocked with Marxist-Leninist literature, a little knot of Communists maintained a more somber tone. Beside them, in a white shed under a brown plastic gable, were activists from *Europeiska Arbetarpartiet*—the European Workers Party. Judging by their hand-drawn posters, their main business was cheerleading for the Kremlin. "Sanctions on banks, not Russia!" declared one placard. "Stop Carl Bildt's war against Putin." Nobody was paying much attention, so I decided to cheer them up by accepting a free copy of their newspaper. It contained one English-language article, which argued that the financial crisis of 2008 was a manufactured catastrophe. "Call it Tonkin Gulf Syndrome," it said. "It's what the British Empire did to suck the U.S. into the Vietnam quagmire." The author of the article was Lyndon LaRouche.

Issues that unite all commentators across the political spectrum are rare. But for the past five decades, the European Workers Party has provided one for Sweden. Everybody from SÄPO to the Communists to the Social Democrats to the libertarian Right has a long-held and consistent view on the EAP—it is profoundly, mystifyingly weird.

In 1978, the conservative magazine *Contra* reflected that there were many parties with unattractive ideologies, "but at least they accept that a horse is a horse and that a cow is a cow. You can't say this about the EAP. They have a language all of their own." A government report from the mid-1980s made this assessment:

> The EAP is in all likelihood the most peculiar political organization to have appeared in Sweden in the post-war era. Through outlandish episodes, conspiracy theories, and focused attacks on individuals the party and its associated bodies have to the highest degree invalidated any influence they could have held over the political landscape. EAP has in national elections never polled more than a few hundred votes. To not have come further after 25 years' struggle would be enough to leave any one person downhearted and ready to quit. But not the EAP, who tirelessly push onwards, apparently with the conviction that the world cannot manage without the insights they so eagerly wish to communicate.

Sweden's Lyndon LaRouche party was founded at a conference in Stockholm in May 1976. Delegates chose a tractor for a logo and Kerstin Tegin for a leader. She was enthusiastic, articulate, and presentable. She had neatly cut hair and followed the group's conservative dress codes without looking like she was selling double glazing door-to-door. She could mimic one of LaRouche's most distinctive rhetorical habits—sustained speechmaking that combined Marxist jargon and vulgar personal attacks—and had dropped out of further study to spend more time with LaRouche's theories.

The birth of the new party did not abolish the existence of that older entity the European Labor Committees; the LaRouche organization has always found it helpful to maintain a confusing plethora of identities. In her maiden speech as leader, Kerstin described the size of the prize. The Social Democrats, she said, were losing voters. The Communist Party was also in decline.

"How could any worker," she asked, "support their ass-licking of Palme?" The first objective of the new party, she declared, should be to secure a 4 percent share of the vote. "We need 250,000 votes to get into parliament. This is something that Palme and his Maoist countergangs cannot prevent except by fraud." In that summer's elections, the EAP fielded as many candidates as it could muster. Across the whole of Sweden, the party received 108 votes.

In 1979, Bill Jones ran for office in Malmö, and he urged its people to support his vision: the city's shipyards converted to the production of giant floating nuclear power stations that could move around the world to meet the energy needs of developing countries. Looking through the campaign literature, it was strange to see the shaggy radical of *Deserter USA* all tidied up and grinning from the page in a suit and tie and plastic glasses, enthusing about the power of the atom. "Don't throw your vote away!" he implored. "Vote EAP!" That year, the party's total rose to 158.

But dismal performances at the ballot box never deterred a LaRouchian candidate. Like Scientologists and pod people, they have always been more interested in bodies. Bill Jones donated his. So did Cliff. For a while, Chuck Onan, the deserter with the tough Chicago childhood and the tall stories of torture training, loaned them his.

By 1976 the furor over Mark Lane's book *Conversations with Americans* had died down. No second edition appeared. A few disparaging mentions of Chuck's name in American newspapers did not impede his progress. He settled back in Stockholm and married his teenage girlfriend, Maggie, who was studying for a degree in political science. Chuck had become a textbook hippie—long hair, Lennon glasses, bell-bottom jeans. When he got back in touch with his old comrades from the ADC and the Next Step, he found them oddly changed. They had become evangelists for LaRouche. They invited Chuck to meetings at their headquarters in Södermalm and gave him the hard sell on nuclear power, Rockefeller, and the CIA.

"Bill and Cliff were the authorities," Chuck told me. "They had all the best arguments. And they talked about Lyndon LaRouche as if he was the new Jesus Christ." Chuck could never think of a clever comeback. He looked through an issue of *Campaigner* and raised an eyebrow at all the articles written under absurd pseudonyms such as Hermyle Golthier Jr. He sat puzzled through a lecture in which the speaker demonstrated the safety of nuclear power—and the contemptible nature of the environmentalist movement—by taking a chair and banging it down on the ground. The chair, said the speaker, also contained atoms. Therefore atomic power was safe.

"LaRouche had an explanation of history and science that Cliff and Bill bought," said Chuck. "A worldview that included everything. Even Beethoven. They were always talking about Beethoven." The pressure was intense. Pretty soon, Chuck was also talking about Beethoven. "It was my wife who really saw it for what it was," said Chuck. "A cult."

Chuck's ex, Maggie Gambell, told me the story from her point of view. "All of a sudden, he changed. He started wearing a suit and tie. He cut his hair. He changed his glasses. He was only to listen to classical music. If something or somebody has this kind of influence on you, you have to beware." One afternoon, Maggie came home from class to find her small living room crammed with people. Chuck and five or six members of the EAP. Serious men in suits and ties. "Come on in here," said her husband. "We want to talk to you."

The visitors talked at her. "They wanted me to stop whatever I was doing," recalled Maggie. "I was going to get rid of my dogs. I was going to stop studying. I was going to stop working. I would join this party and everything would be great." She found their attitude threatening, but took a diplomatic approach and promised to consider their ideas. "I sort of managed," she said, "and they left, but I realized that these guys were really dangerous."

The experience spelled the end of her marriage. She asked Chuck to stop attending EAP meetings. He refused. She asked him to move out of the flat for a few days while she gathered her thoughts. He turned pale with rage. The LaRouchians, concluded Maggie, had done nothing for her husband's temper. "They were appealing to young intellectual people who for some reason felt lost. They were sucking them up into this organization."

I asked her about the men who'd invaded her flat. Were they Swedes or Americans?

"Americans," she said.

IF A MEMBER of the Swedish electorate does not wish to vote for one of the main political parties, she can write in the name of her preferred candidate—which provides an infinite number of ways to spoil a ballot paper. Historically, "Donald Duck" has outpolled the European Workers Party.

It made the group's tenacity and financial weightlessness all the more puzzling. How could such a tiny organization afford to rent offices and venues for their meetings? Hire telephones and telex machines? Put up almost as many election posters as the Christian Democrats? How could it fund a news agency that supplied Swedish media outlets with an unending stream of free stories? Or the production of a newspaper with a print run of eight thousand, half of which were given away?

"It is hard," wrote the journalist Håkan Hermansson, "if not impossible, to conclude other than that the majority of the ELC's operations in Sweden must be financed externally." As leader, Kerstin Tegin often found herself answering questions about where the party found its money. They were not, she explained, as rich as they seemed. Sometimes they were obliged to turn off the telex machines in order to avoid getting cut off. But they were never cut off.

The party's literature claimed that its expensive equipment was bought with money raised by working-class supporters in the States. This was a fantasy. The Labor Committees had very few working-class supporters in the States or Sweden. Much of its cash came from its own members, who signed over their trust funds and legacies to the cause. And thanks to a series of prosecutions made in the 1980s, we know that some of the NCLC's resources came from fraud. One of LaRouche's favorite films was *The Producers*, Mel Brooks's 1968 comedy about two Broadway mountebanks who fund a musical about Hitler by conning rich widows out of their savings. The Labor Committees shared some of the same methods. Jim McGourty told me how fundraisers would spend long hours on the phones, fishing for donations, sometimes actually using that line from the Bible about camels and needles. One boiler-room Stakhanov favored soft persuasion. Jim impersonated his honeyed voice: "*Your name is on a list of very special people who have the intellectual capability to understand the problems that we face today. . . .*" Others just yelled that humanity was on the brink of nuclear destruction and the only way to do something about it was to hand over a credit card number now. Chris White recalled another pitch: "Rockefeller is going to start World War Three! Sell your house before the crash!"

Fundraisers were obliged to stay in the office until they had met their targets and sometimes made up the difference from their own pockets in order to go home and get some sleep. Those who failed were punished with all-night ego-stripping sessions. Military language was deployed. Cold callers were told to think of themselves as Patton's army, taking beachheads, taking the landing places—with the collapse of civilization as the price of failure.

For the U.S. organization, the object of this toil was to get Lyndon H. LaRouche into the White House. LaRouche's eight bids for high office are his principal claim on the historical memory. (A ninth, in 2016, may not count, as even his followers barely registered his declaration.) The 1976 contest was his first, but his electoral vehicle had already been constructed: yet another LaRouchian body—the U.S. Labor Party, launched in 1973 to allow NCLC activists to run for congressional seats, mayoralties, and state governorships.

When LaRouche announced his candidacy, the revolution was put on hold. He could not, however, dispense with the apocalyptic narrative. Nelson Rockefeller, by now vice president to Gerald Ford, retained his Sauron-like power in the story. Badges were struck and posters printed that read: IMPEACH ROCKY AND STOP WORLD WAR THREE. But when Jimmy Carter won the Democratic nomination, the old mythology required substantial revisions. LaRouche performed them live on prime-time television. The Labor Committees bought half an hour of air on NBC-TV and paid the fee with a paper bag containing $95,000 in cash. Picking his fingers and wiggling in his swivel chair, he told a tame interviewer that a Carter presidency would usher in an age of nuclear war and "genocidal austerity," and claimed that Carter's intellectual puppet masters were research fellows at the Brookings Institution, the venerable Washington think tank.

It was a new twist on the old Manchurian Candidate story that had once starred Chris White and Mike Vale, and the detail was provided on the pages of LaRouchian publications. The brainwashing institutes of Sweden were mothballed. Now the subbasement of the Brookings Institution housed a laboratory in which a team of doctors were reprogramming Jimmy Carter's brain.

"Parroting such code words as 'trust,' 'love' and 'unity' in a linguistician's computer," claimed an NCLC press release, "Carter's empty hulk is being transported around the country to preach the virtues of fascism to the population." This time the brainwasher in chief was said to be an American-educated Englishman named Peter Bourne—"a key agent creator of the CIA's terrorist gangs now being activated by Lower Manhattan's insurrectionists to overthrow the country's Constitutional government and to install a completely manipulable zombie like Carter in the Oval Office."

Peter Bourne is now a visiting senior research fellow at Green College, Oxford. Earlier in his career he was awarded the Bronze Star for his work as head of the U.S. Army's psychiatric team in Vietnam. He was a senior medical adviser to the White House and assistant secretary-general at the United Nations. In 1972 he persuaded his friend Jimmy Carter, the governor of Georgia, to run for president, then held a senior position in his successful campaign in 1976.

"But there was no psychological manipulation," he told me. "Just a clear statement of the facts and my faith in him that he could make it." The Labor Committees, however, were committed to their paranoid reading of Bourne's résumé. "I have been harassed by these people off and on over the last forty years," he said. "Throughout the campaign and on into the White House years the LaRouchies showed up with placards and pamphlets to hand out every time I spoke in public. Sometimes they would completely disrupt the events. They inflicted this only on me and not on any other of Carter's staff. I never understood their political philosophy or what they believed in."

Their interest in him may have had an unanticipated literary consequence. When Robert Ludlum wrote a bestselling thriller about an amnesiac assassin shaped by a secret CIA brainwashing project, he borrowed Peter's name for his hero, along with a few biographical details. The Labor Committees were energetic in their dissemination of their flyers and press releases. Perhaps Ludlum picked one up, and *The Bourne Identity* has its roots in one of their fictions.

CIA CONSPIRACY THEORIES sustained the Labor Committees. They were also used to explain their activities. In Sweden, the combative nature of the American Deserters Committee led many to suspect that it was a front group intended to create conflict and disunity on the left. Even Hans Göran Franck was telling friends, mournfully, that he thought Michael Vale and Bill Jones had been spooks from the start.

For the ADC's successor organization, that suspicion was doubled. Olof Palme's press officer defined the EAP as "an agency of North American origin whose behavior corresponds perfectly to a group tied to some sort of intelligence organization." The deputy chairman of the Danish Social Democrats agreed: "I cannot deny that it is an American intelligence organization," he said, "but it is impossible to say whether it is CIA or others behind it."

The renegade agency man Philip Agee, in Stockholm to promote his confessional memoir *Inside the Company*, told journalists that the Labor Committees were a right-wing organization masquerading as a left-wing one. "That it is now expanded to Europe," he said, "fits the pattern of a normal CIA operation." Few in the Swedish media took issue with the explanation; the idea that EAP members were Langley's paid provocateurs was the most orthodox interpretation of their existence. The title of Håkan Hermansson's 1975 pamphlet spelled out the consensus: *Moles in Socialist Disguises*.

In recent years the CIA has released a large number of documents relating to Lyndon LaRouche and his political empire. They suggest that the agency found it as weird and alarming as everyone else. More so, perhaps, as the CIA was the focus of so many of its beliefs. Among the declassified papers put online in the first days of 2017 is the agency's copy of a letter sent in late February 1974 by William Colby to the newspaper editor Ben Bradlee, complaining about the *Washington Post*'s coverage of the Chris White Affair.

Colby protested that readers could be left with the impression "that the CIA, through its refusal to comment, indeed might be involved in the kinds of activities the NCLC alleges. Our recollection is that we told your reporter that the NCLC appeared to be a domestic organization, so he should ask the Federal Bureau of Investigation rather than the CIA for information about it. While it appeared self-evident that the NCLC charges are only twisted fantasy, your circulation of them forces the CIA to deny them flatly as false."

Seymour Hersh's articles on Operation Chaos were eleven months away. After that, such protests would be pointless. And the archive now shows that, contrary to Colby's letter, Langley accumulated a substantial dossier on the Labor Committees and their international offshoots: handbills about the brainwash plot, a leaflet urging action against Rockefeller's Nazi doctors, a copy of LaRouche's telegram to President Nixon, warning him that the agency was plotting to remove him from office. Handwritten annotations suggest that files were also kept on individual members.

In the mid-1970s, the CIA file on the Labor Committees was maintained by Michael Schneeberger, a counterintelligence officer in the Security Analysis Group at Langley. This should have remained a secret, but when the CIA declassified the file, someone forgot to redact his name. Schneeberger retired from the agency in 1998 but was happy to reminisce by email—and to confirm that his suspicions were an extension of those upon which MHCHAOS was founded. The CIA feared that the Labor Committees were working with the guidance and encouragement of Moscow.

"We were concerned," he told me, "that the KGB was taking advantage of anti-war movements and organizations to infiltrate their ranks and use the principal movers and shakers as agents of influence." Schneeberger and his colleagues busied themselves identifying contacts between members of the Labor Committees and suspected representatives of the KGB. "I'm not precisely sure of the genesis of our counterintelligence interest," he told me, "but strongly suspect that there was some degree of credible information from Soviet defectors and recruited agents suggesting that the KGB had an interest in using domestic American anti-war organizations for intelligence purposes since they were typically ripe for recruitment given their progressive platforms." The anxieties were manifold: the Russians might use the Labor Committees to spread propaganda, or, more seriously, "to identify any existential threats to U.S. intelligence or military establishments and facilities" or "create violence to disrupt and discredit Vietnam War efforts."

Operation Chaos had been closed, its files incinerated. But its job was still being done, and the same blanks were being drawn. In 1976, as LaRouche gathered his skirts to run for president, the CIA conceded that there was no Russian money in his purse, or the detectable influence of any other government.

JIMMY CARTER WAS sworn in as president on January 20, 1977, having secured just over 50 percent of the popular vote in the election the previous November. Lyndon LaRouche had scraped 0.05 percent, trailing many thousands behind the Libertarians, the Communists, and the Socialist Workers. But this did not deter him. His aggressive campaign against Carter had won him a number of wealthy right-wing supporters. And he also sensed opportunity in Carter's skeptical attitude toward the intelligence men.

In March 1977, Carter appointed Admiral Stansfield Turner to reform the CIA. Turner had commanded a destroyer, a guided missile cruiser, and a naval fleet before he assumed the captaincy of Langley. On his first day in the job he asked for a report on Operation Chaos. His initial inspection found that the super-secret, highly compartmentalized bureaucracy that produced efforts such as MHCHAOS had evolved into a mechanism for obscuring unethical activities, from the toppling of the Allende government in Chile to the maintenance of assets who were actually the mistresses of CIA officers, or arms dealers with whom they were doing business on the side.

Turner's first move was a swift one: he sent out a computer-generated letter informing 820 case officers that their services were no longer required. Then he set about redefining the business of spying. Espionage under Turner was oriented away from blackmail, cyanide capsules, and exploding cigars and toward more academic activities. Rather than trying to cultivate moles in the Kremlin, a new breed of officer would investigate the enemy by analyzing public and private opinion in their field of operations. "Undercover case officers or agents . . . with the polling skill of George Gallup," Stansfield proposed, might "take the pulse of a foreign country."

Lyndon LaRouche was ready to offer his services. He was in an upbeat mood. He was the head of an intelligence-gathering body with offices all over the world, staffed by zealous operatives who would work for starvation wages. Perhaps the Labor Committees could take up the slack? Charles Tate, a security aide to LaRouche, described the thinking. "I'm not suggesting that he was advocating that the security staff storm Langley and take over," he explained. "I just mean that we were to aid and abet the CIA and other intelligence agencies which had taken a body blow from Stansfield Turner."

It was quite a switcheroo. In the space of three years, the organization's official line on the CIA had changed from seeing it as a malign counterinsurgency plotting to depose the president and zombify America, to an essential state apparatus that required defending from reformers. The CIA's enemies were now their enemies—the Soviet Union and President Jimmy Carter.

The shift caused disquiet among some of LaRouche's followers, who began to ask questions. One former member described his unease: "What if the results of all this research were being passed on elsewhere? To the CIA or the FBI or the KGB? To rightist governments who might appreciate an assessment of, say, networks of oppositional figures within their own sphere of influence?" It was his cue to leave. But other Labor Committees members had grown accustomed to performing ideological backflips and had learned to see them as tests of their loyalty.

"It's what Michael Vale would have called a necessary deviation," said Jim McGourty. "In order to retain control of the executive portion of a political organization you have to abruptly and overtly change its direction." People noticed: in Sweden, Cliff and Kerstin's European Workers Party began to attract the attention of journalists and researchers who kept tabs on the European Far Right. One, Stieg Larsson, the future author of *The Girl with the Dragon Tattoo*, opened a file on them.

When Larsson died in 2004, he left behind a large personal archive, much of which related to his long career as an investigator of Swedish political extremism. Going through this material, I was amazed to find swathes of notes on the European Workers Party. Biographical sketches of Cliff Gaddy, Kerstin Tegin, and Bill Jones—referred to, cutely, as "Billy." Pages that showed Larsson engaged in the pointless task of trying to reconcile the disparate elements of the LaRouchian world picture. His conclusion was that the party was not a CIA or KGB front, but "a fascist group in its classical concept; it has its own ideology, its own organization, and is fully autonomous from outside interference." Most intriguingly, Larsson had drawn a rough plan of the EAP's offices, on which he'd scribbled speculations about the position of its unseen entrances and exits. It was the kind of diagram you'd make if you were planning a burglary.

ONE OF PRESIDENT Carter's first acts in office was to sign Executive Order 11967, pardoning men who had avoided the Vietnam draft. Its terms did not stretch to deserters. In March, however, the Defense Department threw them a bone. If a deserter reported in person to the military authorities, he would receive an undesirable discharge. He could then apply to upgrade his status to a general discharge. The offer would expire on October 4, 1977.

The scheme made many uneasy: a court-martial and prison sentence were still possible. It was a game of Russian roulette in which the players were not permitted to know how many bullets were in the gun. That summer, however, many of the Stockholm deserters took their chances. Bill Jones flew home and was met at the airport by two military policemen. He shrugged when I asked him if he had been nervous: the process, he said, had been brisk and painless.

Chuck Onan admitted to a feeling of trepidation. He reported to Camp Pendleton and was amazed to find that nobody wanted to give him a hard time. He walked into the waiting room in a cool blue Swedish suit, and the envious looks of marines in fatigues, back from a last tour of duty, told him that he'd made the right decision.

Cliff Gaddy also made a trip home that summer, which would have given him the opportunity to turn himself in at Fort Meade, Maryland, the headquarters of the U.S. Army Security Agency. Old LaRouchians to whom I spoke remembered Cliff and Kerstin going on an NCLC road trip in the summer of 1977. They had recently been married: perhaps it counted as a honeymoon. The couple spent time at the organization's headquarters in Manhattan. They visited a local group in Houston, Texas, where Kerstin reinforced the official message on birth control: true revolutionary women were obliged to reject motherhood. (In the New York branch, pregnant members were offered a free ride to the abortion clinic, courtesy of its so-called coat hanger brigade.) The couple also spent three weeks in Cliff's hometown of Danville, Virginia, where a LaRouche lifer, Alan Ogden, was running for governor on a U.S. Labor Party ticket.

The campaign, like everything to do with the Labor Committees, was noisy and confusing. Ogden had eleven arrests for trespassing and similar offenses on his record hanging over him: some of his campaign was conducted from prison. (An FBI setup, said Ogden.) Then the press obtained bureau documents that described the candidate as "a dangerous international terrorist." The skinny, bespectacled pipe smoker seemed an unlikely bomber. He did nothing more offensive than take his soapbox to the state's parks and street corners and shout through a megaphone about Jimmy Carter's "fascist labor front" and the probable imminence of nuclear war with the Soviet Union. "And so it goes for the U.S. Labor Party," reported the *Danville Bee*, "the freak show of Virginia politics, a party consigned by the news media and the political establishment to ridicule, or even worse, obscurity."

Cliff and Kerstin joined the campaign trail in August. Kerstin toured Danville in a neat gingham dress and told reporters about the importance of impeaching Jimmy Carter and forming a "Whig coalition" of farmers, factory workers, and industrialists against "the entire Rockefeller banking interests." She brought the same message to the gates of the local textile mill. Not everyone was pleased to hear it.

"It was only through President Carter's intervention that people like

'Chip' Gaddy could come home," complained one reader of the *Danville Register*. "'Chip' Gaddy's past actions clearly show that he has no regard for the U.S. and Virginia." The electorate may have agreed: Ogden secured only 0.8 percent of the vote. Fraud at the polls, said the LaRouchians. But that didn't stop the Gaddys from returning to Sweden in triumph and going on a lecture tour to tell their fellow citizens about "the real America"—one ripe for a U.S. Labor Party victory.

IN DECEMBER 1977, the Labor Committees had something to celebrate: LaRouche's marriage to Helga Zepp Ljustina, a German journalist who had reported from Beijing during the Cultural Revolution. (Her first husband, a Yugoslav sailor who worked on container ships, had transported her on a literal slow boat to China.) But his real romance was with the CIA. Like a besotted suitor who acquires a new haircut and wardrobe to impress a potential partner, LaRouche primped and pomaded his organization to attract Langley's attention. Many of his gentleman callers were con men.

Edward von Rothkirch was a chancer who presented himself as a freelance agency contractor working undercover behind the Iron Curtain with an anti-Soviet sabotage unit called the Freikorps of Barbarossa. Roy Frankhouser was a grand dragon of the Ku Klux Klan who courted LaRouche by claiming to be a former CIA operative whose glass eye was the result of an injury sustained during the 1961 Bay of Pigs invasion. It was hogwash, but LaRouche was impressed and signed him up on a $700 weekly retainer. He did little to justify the fee. On one occasion LaRouche dispatched him on a spying mission to Boston. Instead he went to a *Star Trek* convention in Scranton, Pennsylvania. Frankhouser did not admit his deception, but called from the hotel to warn the organization that he had just discovered that the FBI was tapping its phones.

The most elaborate and costly scam was perpetrated by a group of hustlers led by a figure code-named "the Major," who announced himself as a CIA officer who wanted to cooperate with LaRouche and his security team on a top-secret project. He persuaded them to buy a large farm south of Washington, DC, on which special agents would be trained for old-school missions of the sort discouraged by Stansfield

Turner's reforms. In exchange, the Major would supply LaRouche with agency intelligence on the latest assassination attempts against him. Then a call came through that the Soviets had got wind of the plan. To allay suspicion, hundreds of thousands more dollars would be required to stock the farm with animals to disguise its true function. Excited by this intrigue, LaRouche instructed his acolytes to hand over the cash.

Not all of LaRouche's contacts with power were imaginary. When Ronald Reagan won the 1980 presidential election, the organization made eyes at the new president's advisers. The more respectable members of the Labor Committees invited Republican officials to policy seminars on Capitol Hill. Favored parties received free subscriptions to the glossy LaRouche magazine *Executive Intelligence Review*, and to *War on Drugs*, a title founded as an echo chamber for Reagan's views on narcotics. Amazingly, the strategy worked. With loyal Warren Hamerman at his heels, LaRouche met with representatives of the Reagan transition team. He also had coffee with Admiral Bobby Ray Inman, the new deputy director of the CIA—an embarrassing fact that would dog Inman for years afterward.

The great prize of this effort, however, was something LaRouchians still celebrate today as their leader's great achievement—a modest consultative role in the development of the Strategic Defense Initiative, Reagan's plan to win the Cold War by putting laser cannons in space. With the blessing of the National Security Council, an NCLC intelligence specialist met with a contact from the Soviet mission in New York to convey a reassuring message: America intended to share this embryonic technology, and had no intention of using it to launch a nuclear first strike. When Reagan went public with his plans in March 1983, the Soviets backed off and these meetings withered away. But LaRouche barely acknowledged the failure. He kept on smiling, as if his relationship with the Reagan administration were close and warm.

Around this time LaRouche chose to move his headquarters from New York to Leesburg, a pretty little town in Loudoun County, Virginia, in order to breathe the same air as its population of government officials and Pentagon types. (He'd also heard that Washington's nuclear bunkers were located in Loudoun County.) In August 1983 he took the lease on an estate that had once been the home of the ballet dancer Rudolf

Nureyev and encouraged his followers to find homes in the vicinity. About two hundred did. Among them were Warren and Nora Hamerman, Jim McGourty and Christina Nelson, Chris and Carol White, and Molly Kronberg and her husband, Ken. From here, everyone proselytized for "Star Wars" technology—though as LaRouche believed that science fiction was morally pernicious, the popular nickname for the project rarely passed his lips. SDI became an inescapable subject for his publications, in America and beyond.

In Sweden, Cliff and Kerstin were not visibly troubled by this ninety-degree turn. The conflict with Eurasia was over, and they were now at war with Oceania. Their party launched its own antidrug campaign, which mimicked the official Swedish equivalent so convincingly that several prominent celebrities—among them Björn Ulvaeus and Frida Lyngstad of ABBA—were fooled into giving their support. SDI was added to the party's list of prescribed obsessions: the Gaddys became cheerleaders for space weapons and the end of Swedish neutrality.

In December 1983, they held a conference in Oslo at which they urged delegates to celebrate the opportunities brought by this new extraterrestrial frontier. Cliff spoke in favor of space-mounted lasers. Kerstin delivered a tirade against the peace movement. Their colleague Michael Liebig, who, a decade before, had tried to extract a confession from Cliff in the Whites' bedroom in Colindale, urged NATO to open a front beyond the earth. The event did not go smoothly. Anti-war protestors occupied the conference hall and chained the doors. Once they had been ejected, they cut off the electricity supply to the building. The LaRouchians declared that the demonstrators were controlled by Moscow.

It's worth stopping to imagine what it must have been like to inhabit the mind of Cliff Gaddy at this moment. He had once been part of an anti-war movement suspected, wrongly, of being funded by the Soviet Union. Now he was urging Sweden and its neighbors to join NATO and take human conflict beyond the limits of the earth—to fight the next Vietnam War in space. As he gave the opening speech, mixing enthusiasm for orbiting laser weapons with the usual goggle-eyed catastrophism about the imminent collapse of Western civilization, the irony must have struck him. It was a moment from the last page of *Animal Farm*.

THE ORGANIZATION'S SHORT affair with the Reagan administration did not dilute the weirder aspects of the LaRouchian project. As the CIA were now the good guys, and Nelson Rockefeller had dropped dead of a heart attack in January 1979, his network of slave labor camps unestablished, new obsessions were required. LaRouche saw conspirators everywhere. Even the Leesburg Gardening Club was a nest of KGB agents. ("Clacking busybodies in this Soviet jellyfish front . . . oozing out their funny little propaganda and making nuisances of themselves.")

But he required a more prominent enemy. His pick was both astute and insane. He chose Her Majesty Queen Elizabeth II, then commissioned a book contending that the British Empire had never fallen but had reinvented itself as a covert body of power and influence. *Dope Inc.* argued that the queen controlled the world's illegal drug markets and was fighting a secret opium war against the United States. It had been a long campaign: the British had drawn the United States into the Vietnam War and had also encouraged the development of the student anti-war movement. But it had prevented that movement from achieving its revolutionary potential by keeping it supplied with hashish and LSD.

Inevitably, the Tavistock Institute was incorporated into the royal master plan: Her Majesty had charged it with the task of popularizing and weaponizing a minor rock group called the Beatles, who, under the guidance of the philosopher Bertrand Russell, were dispatched to the States on a mission to ruin American youth. "Once caught in the environment defined by Russell and the Tavistock Institute's wartime psychological warfare experts," asserted *Dope Inc.*, "their sense of values and their creative potential were snatched up in a cloud of hashish smoke."

Some became instant enthusiasts for this idea. Warren Hamerman supported it because he supported anything that LaRouche said, no matter how peculiar. For those who retained a better sense of how LaRouche was perceived beyond his own organization, the principal response to this royal conspiracy theory was embarrassment.

Chris and Carol White remembered that those who campaigned for

LaRouche in 1979, when he dissolved the U.S. Labor Party and made the first of seven attempts to secure the Democratic nomination for the presidency, saw their hard work evaporate when LaRouche turned up for the 1980 New Hampshire primary and started making speeches about the Satanic influence of the House of Windsor. The audience soon realized that it was in the presence of a crackpot.

OVER THE YEARS, NCLC members have expended as much energy thinking about the queen as the makers of Royal Wedding souvenir mugs. They have put her, headscarfed and grim, on the covers of their magazines. They have published tracts describing Her Majesty's desire to murder billions of people. They have hired lecture halls to express the view that she had a jeweled hand in the 9/11 attacks. One member, even today, likes to pull on a gray wig and tiara and troll around Manhattan, making regal statements in a voice that owes rather more to the Wicked Witch of the West than the head of the Commonwealth. (I'm not convinced that Elizabeth Windsor has ever used the phrase "Fly, my pretties.") But the queen is of limited use to an organization of provocateurs. LaRouche has always preferred enemies who answer back, in order that their annoyance or bafflement can be quoted in the pages of his publications and spun into evidence of guilt. Her Majesty's public statements about her own feelings are rare. And unless she sits up late at Buckingham Palace, tapping her own name and "green genocide" into Google, it is doubtful whether she has even heard of Lyndon Hermyle LaRouche Jr.

So the silent Elizabeth had to be teamed with another, more vocal supervillain. The role was given to former secretary of state Henry Kissinger. In his case, NCLC members were much more hands-on. They disrupted his diary by impersonating his staff over the phone and canceling engagements. They ordered pizza to be delivered to his home. They harassed him in public. In February 1982 a pair of LaRouche activists accosted Kissinger as he passed through Newark International Airport on his way to triple-bypass heart surgery in Boston.

"Is it true," yelled a member named Ellen Kaplan, "that you sleep with young boys at the Carlyle Hotel?" An enraged Nancy Kissinger reached for Kaplan's throat, and found herself up on an assault charge.

The judge dismissed the case. So did the press. ("Nancy Kissinger made one mistake in etiquette," reflected a newspaper columnist. "Mrs. Kissinger did not stomp on the woman's face.") LaRouche publications, however, recorded this dismal event as a major victory.

The organization produced a Kissinger joke book full of obscene cartoons that depicted him as a cannibal and a pervert. They planted stories in the overseas press that accused him, variously, of murdering the Italian prime minster Aldo Moro and braining a Romanian waiter with a whiskey bottle during an orgy in Acapulco. When Kissinger spoke at a meeting in Germany, a LaRouchian prankster dressed as the former secretary of state disrupted the event by insisting that the man on the podium was an impostor.

LaRouche issued a press release entitled "Henry Kissinger, the Politics of Faggotry." "His heathen sexual inclinations," argued LaRouche, "are merely an integral part of a larger evil. . . . Kissinger is the kind of homosexual personality who ordinarily makes a potential professional assassin, a gangland thug for hire." He ended with a catastrophist flourish. "That kind of faggotry destroyed Rome. Will you permit it also to destroy the United States?" In documents for internal distribution within the cult, he used even less attractive language: "I wouldn't want Kissinger dead. I'd want him in a pit to come out once a day to be pissed on by the widows and orphans of the world."

LaRouche's obsessions with Kissinger and Elizabeth II made him a national joke. *Saturday Night Live* began "Lyndon LaRouche Theatre," in which Randy Quaid, in a bald wig, bow tie, and spectacles, narrated the latest melodramatic twists and turns of the conspiracy. "Next week in part three," he hooted, "diabolical Kissinger and miscreant Elizabeth engage KGB agents to assassinate me while continuing to sponsor attacks in the media which attempt to foster one of the most monstrous lies of the twentieth century—that I am insane!"

It seemed a fit subject for farce, but according to Dennis King, an investigative journalist who has studied the organization for five decades, violent action was also on the agenda. In 1983, LaRouche's security team called a meeting and told the gathered membership "Kissinger must die." LaRouche's chauffeur was asked to consider putting a bomb under Kissinger's car.

"But this rage," writes King, "ultimately was just sublimated into more nasty leaflets and articles in *Executive Intelligence Review*. The LaRouchians had come to believe that really clever conspirators never carry out an assassination themselves, but simply spread hate propaganda about the targeted person that might trigger an attack by some disturbed personality or fanatic. That way, they can never be held legally responsible."

IN SWEDEN, OLOF Palme was the target. He was a good choice. Palme had enemies at both ends of the political spectrum, many of whom shared LaRouche's taste for violent fantasy. The right-wing *Contra* magazine produced a dartboard bearing an image of Palme's face. Maj Sjöwall and Per Wahlöö, the crime-writing Communist Party members whose Martin Beck books invented the genre of Scandinavian noir, made their last novel, *The Terrorists*, a political thriller in which the girlfriend of an American deserter assassinates the Swedish prime minister, blaming him for her partner's suicide.

The first dark blossoms of Cliff and Kerstin's hate campaign against Palme appeared in the same year, when the Stockholm edition of *New Solidarity* declared that "Sweden's population is led by a madman, a demented murderer who turns up out of the dark, cold winter nights and sneaks toward his victims with an ax ready." In case readers found this picture hard to envisage, the paper provided a portrait of a mad-eyed Swedish premier shouldering an ax dripping with blood. It became the EAP's favorite image—printed in its literature, blown up to placard size for use at its card-table shrines—and far more memorable than its boring logo with the tractor.

"Behind the Democratic mask," read the handbills, "we find the true Olof Palme, a raging beast, an ax killer, the Devil's devil. . . . The worker who tolerates Palme as his leader at this point in history . . . does so because he is terrified by the thought of leaving his world of impotent, deathlike fantasies."

LaRouche offices across the world ensured the spread of this rhetoric. "Palme was one step below Satan," recalled one former member of the U.S. organization. "We had never-ending articles, exposés and cartoons about him and whipped everyone into a frenzy about how he must be stopped. This one guy was among the most important participants in enslaving humanity."

When the Stockholm paper *Aftonbladet* ran a series of investigative reports on the EAP in October 1975, LaRouche sent a telex to its editors:

GENTLEMEN: ARE YOU AND OLOF PALME SO ENTIRELY INSANE THAT YOU BELIEVE THAT SUCH HASHISH-SCENTED GOSSIP WILL DETER SERIOUS PERSONS WHO KNOW THAT THE CRUSHING OF THE ATLANTICIST FACTION IS ABSOLUTELY ESSENTIAL TO SAVE THE WORLD FROM A TAVISTOCKIAN FASCIST NIGHTMARE AND TOTAL THERMONUCLEAR WARFARE?

There was an obvious one-word answer to the question. But anyone turned on by such language could expect a welcoming hug from the EAP—particularly if that person had money in the bank.

Victor Gunnarsson, a braggartly fantasist of the Far Right, who liked to boast that he had served in Vietnam and worked for the CIA, signed up for membership and went home with an armful of anti-Palme literature. A better catch was Alf Enerström, a wealthy doctor who had broken with the Social Democratic Party in 1974 over its liberal policy on abortion. Enerström was a strange and damaged individual. In 1976 he was accused of beating his teenage son and, when the boy was taken into care, decided that this was part of a state operation against him, orchestrated personally by Palme. He made his case in a series of full-page advertisements in the Swedish press. The depth of his pockets and of his hatred made him an attractive ally for the EAP, for which he coughed up around $150,000 and a torrent of anti-Palme bile.

The Gaddys were relaxed in his company. During the 1982 election campaign Kerstin stood beside Enerström at rallies and public meetings as they railed against Palme and accused him of collusion with the KGB. Cliff accompanied Enerström to a community radio station, where they presented the case for Palme's fascist modus operandi: the evidence included conspiracy theories about the hidden Nazi history of his family and an account of his plan to give Swedish officials the right to commit murder with impunity. ("Freedom of speech in Stockholm community radio reaches far beyond our own galaxy," wrote a perplexed journalist who tuned in.)

The LaRouchian accusations became increasingly weird. In May 1982, William Engdahl wrote a piece for *Executive Intelligence Review* asserting that Palme was part of a heroin-smuggling syndicate that also included a group of Turkish neofascists that had plotted to assassinate Pope John Paul II. The following month LaRouche produced an essay entitled "Olof Palme and the Neo-Nazi International," which argued that the Swedish prime minister was part of a secretive and powerful network known as the Black Guelph. "They are presently the single wealthiest political force in the world, the dominant rentier-finance interest centered in such places as Venice, Trieste, Liechtenstein, Switzerland, Amsterdam, and London," he wrote. It was as insane as it was meaningless, but any nut with a copy of *The Protocols of the Elders of Zion* would have read between the lines and nodded in agreement. They may even have felt compelled to do something about it.

SWEDEN IS A small country. Its politicians are not distant figures. In the 1960s and '70s, they were even more proximate. The home number of Palme's predecessor Tage Erlander was listed in the phone directory; if you rang, he would pick up. Olof Palme liked to walk through the streets without a bodyguard. When Cliff, Kerstin, Bill, and their comrades distributed literature that suggested Palme was a paranoid schizophrenic, or, more colorfully, a "foul-smelling excretion from a dead world, the progeny of a lunatic military-aristocracy," they must have calculated that its target would be among their readers. But this did not give them pause for thought. On at least one occasion, a member of EAP approached Palme and tried to sell him some of this literature.

Eventually, the leader of the Social Democrats felt moved to comment. In May 1979, the EAP circulated a letter that purported to be from a group of union leaders, denouncing Palme's nuclear energy policy. The letter was a hoax, but this was not discovered before it had run on the front page of the main Swedish evening newspaper. "This CIA organization," said Palme, wearily, "has been after me for several years."

The psychology of stalking would probably explain the party's reaction: when the object of its fantasies acknowledged its existence, it was Christmas for the EAP. It gave them an opportunity to issue lengthy communiqués calling for a government inquiry into the harassment of their party, and declaring how wounded its members felt by the false accusation that it was an instrument of the CIA.

As leader, Kerstin always signed these, but their use of distinctly English idioms suggests that Cliff may have been the one sitting at the typewriter. They achieved their aim: publicity. By the early 1980s, the Swedish media treated Kerstin as an entertaining if faintly unsavory political curiosity. Her sullen good looks and tight smile made regular appearances in the press, usually when her party was accused of extremism or electoral misconduct.

In early 1982 the Channel TV-2 program *Magasinet* put its reporter Larsolof Giertta on Kerstin's case. He interviewed her, attended a party meeting, caught a few shots of Cliff, shuffling papers and looking mistrustfully at the camera, and concluded that the EAP was a "Nazi-influenced" organization of the Far Right. A quote was obtained from Palme himself, who described the party as "a tiny fascist-like sect." Predictably, the EAP was not delighted. Just as predictably, a pair of intense Swedish LaRouchians appeared on Giertta's doorstep to tell the journalist that if he went to Wiesbaden to investigate the European headquarters of their organization, he should beware of fast-moving cars on the autobahn.

Magasinet invited Kerstin Tegin-Gaddy into the studio to explain her political position and her strange beliefs about Olof Palme. She was not in a conciliatory mood. Kerstin argued that *Magasinet* was part of Palme's smear campaign against the EAP. "Okay, Olof Palme," said Kerstin, as if the prime minister were in the room. "Let's take this discussion. You or me, which is it who is pushing a fascist politics?"

It was a fairly cranky performance, but the EAP claimed it as a great propaganda victory. "The general response everywhere is the same," enthused a party report to the mother organization in Leesburg. "Great relief and joy that finally somebody is able to challenge the Social-Democratic-Greenie-Fascist power-structure." Invigorated, Kerstin announced a national speaking tour—apparently convinced that by 1987, Palme would be toppled and she would be the new prime minister of Sweden. Half of the prediction came true.

LaRouchian fantasies about Palme became so intense and omnivorous that they began to devour the biographies of the people who constructed them. Bill Engdahl identified Palme's policy of granting humanitarian asylum to Vietnam deserters as a smoke screen to make Sweden a safe haven for terrorists and gangsters. LaRouche contended that the GI movement in Sweden was "a front organization using unwitting Vietnam War opponents and critics as a diversionary cover for an evil operation against the United States." (The illustration featured Olof Palme as a vampire and Bo Burlingham as a gun-toting frogman with a cigarette in his mouth.)

For LaRouchians who had entered the movement through the American Deserters Committee and the Next Step, this was the most baroque, prog-rock concept-album phase of their incorporation into LaRouchian mythology. For a decade Bill Jones and his former comrades had been obliged to accept that they had not, after all, been the leaders of a group that had fought for the rights of deserters and grabbed the attention of the world. They had been the dupes of some Cold War intelligence operation. Now they were part of a conspiracy that went back centuries—part of a master plan designed by Bertrand Russell and the Tavistock Institute and executed by Michael Vale and his allies, to preserve the dominance of Olof Palme, the House of Windsor, and an Illuminati-like organization founded by the East India Company and a group of old Venetian banking families. My lunchtime conversations with Bill suggested that, decades later, he remained loyal to this mad, fake version of his own life story. Bertrand Russell, he told me, had once sent a letter of support to Michael Vale, and that was evidence enough.

Bo Burlingham, whose life also furnished the material for these fantasies, offered me the best explanation of their power. As we sat under the blossoms in the courtyard of the Berkeley City Club, he described how the Labor Committees became a sticky-doll trap for a certain kind of radical.

"The LaRouche blandishments have this pseudo-intellectual quality," he said. "It's all smoke and mirrors. Ultimately, to get involved in that you're a fool, an agent provocateur, or somebody who has a need of some sort that leads them to get involved in a cult. The Weathermen were a cult, so I'm not saying this with any great sense of superiority, but the

LaRouchies are generally cultish. You adopt a certain orthodoxy from which it becomes a grave sin to stray. There are mechanisms inside to make sure it gets reinforced, reinforced, reinforced, to the point where you're detached from reality. You're living in this bubble."

That bubble burst on the night of February 28, 1986. It happened when Olof Palme, his wife, Lisbet, and their son Mårten walked out of the Grand Cinema on Sveavägen, in the heart of Stockholm. They had watched a Swedish comedy called *The Brothers Mozart*. It had been a last-minute decision: Lisbet had wanted to see Lasse Hallström's picture *My Life as a Dog*. Despite the bitter cold and the slippery conditions, Palme and his wife began walking home to their apartment in Gamla Stan. On the way they passed an arts and crafts shop called Dekorima. Its illuminated windows cast a bright light on the icy street.

At 11:21 p.m., a man grabbed Olof Palme by the shoulder, pulled a large handgun from his coat, and fired a single shot into the prime minister's back. Blood ran into the snow. The assassin stood for a moment, gazing down upon his victim, then bolted into the darkness.

At six minutes past midnight, Palme was pronounced dead. A description of the perpetrator was constructed from impressions gleaned from passersby. The dread news spread through the early hours. A radio bulletin at 1:10 a.m. A television report at 4:00 a.m. A government press conference an hour later. Sweden reeled in horror.

In the offices of the EAP, they opened a bottle of champagne. In the offices of the investigating detectives, the phone rang. An anonymous caller supplied the name of a man he thought might be responsible for the assassination. The man answered the description of the assassin and had been heard speaking about Palme with memorable viciousness. The man was Cliff Gaddy.

16 / THE ASSASSINS

AFTER A DECADE of vitriol throwing, it was hardly surprising that the European Workers Party should find itself under suspicion. It had portrayed Olof Palme as a vampire, an ax murderer, and an Iranian ayatollah. It had put hatred for him at the heart of its discourse and its policies. It had made the suggestion, in public, that the death of the prime minister would be a welcome event.

Cliff Gaddy was not the only EAP member to be mentioned by a tipster. An usher at the Grand Cinema said that he had seen someone who looked like Kerstin Tegin-Gaddy loitering outside the building on the night of the murder. More than two hundred members of the public telephoned the investigation with information and theories about the party's involvement in Palme's death. The Swedish consul in New York and the Swedish ambassador to the United Nations also urged the detectives to put the EAP in the frame.

The investigators began interviewing the party's principal members. They were easy to find. There were very few of them, and SÄPO had kept their names and addresses on file since 1975. The police spoke to a *New Solidarity* contributor whom an informer had overheard saying that the EAP had a plan to kill Palme. But he had been in the office that night. They contacted a member named John Hardwick and discovered that he had left the organization three years previously, after an unpleasant meeting with LaRouche at the European Labor Committees office in Wiesbaden. (Hardwick was now worried that his former comrades were spying on him.) They interviewed the EAP's sugar daddy Alf Enerström, but his girlfriend Gio Petré (an actress who had appeared in Ingmar Bergman's *Wild Strawberries*) furnished him with an alibi.

They did not interview Cliff or Kerstin, despite receiving more calls mentioning their names. The focus of the investigation had already moved to another individual on the EAP membership register: Victor Gunnarsson, a volatile eccentric with a Burt Reynolds mustache and links to the Swedish Far Right, who made a fitful living as a language teacher. (One school had sacked him for habitual lateness, another for punching a boy who had irritated him.)

Detectives found some of the EAP's nastier anti-Palme literature in his apartment. On the night of the murder, he had been close to the scene. That evening he had made a nuisance of himself in a Stockholm restaurant called Mon Cheri, where he had pretended to be an American tourist and railed angrily against Olof Palme and his politics. "If you say what you think in Sweden today," he had declared, "you'll get shot in the back." Failing to impress his audience, he left the restaurant. He told the police that he'd gone to see *Rocky IV* at the Rigoletto Cinema. No witness, however, could verify this. The next confirmed sighting was at 1:10 a.m., when he annoyed the staff in a branch of McDonald's not far from the murder scene.

Gunnarsson was taken into custody. He seemed utterly unbothered by the experience, infuriating his interrogator, Detective Börje Wingren, by laughing at his questions and replying in the voice of Eddie Murphy in *Beverly Hills Cop*. Gunnarsson's attitude cooled only when a witness was produced: a cabdriver who claimed that the suspect had jumped into his taxi not far from the murder scene and told him to drive away as fast as he could. The driver picked Gunnarsson from a police lineup. But just as the suspect was about to receive a formal charge, the prosecutor learned that Detective Wingren had coached his witness to settle on the prime suspect. The case collapsed, and Gunnarsson was released. The wasted time, and Wingren's unethical behavior, dealt the investigation a blow from which it did not recover.

The Swedish press does not print the names of criminal suspects until conviction is secured. It referred to Gunnarsson as "the 33-year-old"—a nickname that still has resonance for Swedes who remember the assassination. But interest was so intense that the newspapers broke their own rule, and Gunnarsson's name and photograph were printed. When he was released from custody, he discovered that he had become notorious. Work was impossible to find. People shouted at him on the street, calling him a murderer and an assassin. Newspaper reports continued to mention him in connection with the LaRouchians, and the police recalled him several times to take part in lineups. He still hated Palme. Now he also hated the European Workers Party for having brought the inquiry to his door.

His prospects had been ruined because his apartment was littered with obnoxious LaRouchian literature. But the people who published it had fled Sweden and were already building new lives for themselves in the States. By mid-1986, it would be fair to say, the names of Cliff and Kerstin Gaddy would not have filled Victor Gunnarsson's heart with joy.

CLIFFORD GARLAND GADDY was an academic whiz kid who enlisted and deserted in quick succession. He was a political exile who joined a cult and married its leader. His organization's violent hatred for Olof Palme had brought him to the attention of the Swedish police. A dangerous right-wing thug had acquired reason to resent him. And yet, from this not inconsiderably deep shit, he would leap, unbesmirched and unstinking, into a fancy job in a Washington think tank. The Brookings Institution, which, his comrades once insisted, had used its subbasement to brainwash the president in mind-bending sessions straight out of *The Parallax View*. How was this possible?

Mr. Putin: Operative in the Kremlin, the book on Russia's election-proof president, written by Cliff and the British academic Fiona Hill, is an object lesson in how to write about somebody who declines to give interviews, and about whom biographical data are scant. ("When there is no certifiably real and solid information," they argue, "any tidbit becomes precious.") It compares Mr. Putin to Mr. Benn, the quiet hero of a 1970s

BBC children's TV show who frequents a costume shop where the changing room is a magic portal to other times and places.

Each week, Mr. Benn slips into a diving suit, a zookeeper's uniform, or a wizard's robes and is transported to an adventure appropriate to his dress. Mr. Putin's adventures required other identities, and the authors give them names: the Outsider, the History Man, the Statist, and the Case Officer. In a video on the Brookings Institution website, Cliff explained the importance of the last identity. "That was his profession in the KGB, and it shines through in so many different ways. In the way he conveys this image. *I'm actually nobody. I'm not going to let you know who I am.* In a way he's everybody. He's anybody."

Cliff's own life was similarly divisible. He, too, comprised a small constellation of different people. The Prodigy. The Deserter. The Cultist. The Expert. And, like Putin, his biography contained a number of silences and mysteries. His official résumé, circulated by Brookings, bore a blank space where his work in the 1970s and '80s should have been. Only the Prodigy and the Expert were represented. The Deserter has been preserved in the local newspapers of Virginia and North Carolina and in the recollections of his friends. The Cultist is to be found on the pages of *New Solidarity* and *Executive Intelligence Review*.

Cliff's own book offers advice on how to interpret such a life. A person's behavior in the past, it argues, is a poor predictor of his action in the future. Instead, we should look to the moments when his behavior changes, as he adapts to new circumstances. These are the moments when a person reveals his essential nature. Deserting the U.S. Army, for instance.

Cliff's alma mater, Wake Forest University, was a conservative campus, and Cliff's fraternity was one of its most conservative institutions. The Kappa Alphas were given to marching around in Confederate uniforms during visits from the National Association for the Advancement of Colored People. Perhaps their extremity explained Cliff's sudden change of heart. Perhaps Cliff had enlisted in the army out of peer pressure and then, beyond the influence of his "Dixie"-singing comrades, had come to regret it? Or perhaps a more exotic explanation was possible. Perhaps he had never committed the crime of desertion in the first place. Perhaps his uncle at the National Security Agency, the master code breaker David Winfred Gaddy, had introduced him to the world of intelligence and arranged for him to be dispatched to Sweden. It seemed far-fetched, but not by the standard of weirdness established by the verifiable facts of Cliff's life.

When I discussed Cliff's case with Bill Jones, he remembered that in late 1974, when President Gerald Ford proposed conditional clemency for the deserters, David Gaddy had called Stockholm to persuade Cliff and his comrades to accept its terms: honorable discharge in exchange for two further years of public service. Nobody took up the offer. Bill considered it a trap.

At the time, a reporter from the *Washington Post* called Cliff's parents to discover his views. Inez Gaddy gave a careful account of her son's position. "He said, belief is not a belief unless I act the way I believe," she reported. "In order to act the way I believe, I have to leave the country." But what did Cliff Gaddy believe? Six impossible things before breakfast, as LaRouche demanded? Or something else that he kept hidden carefully from view?

"He's not going to be so eager to speak about all this," said Bill Jones. "Cliff is working his way up through the bureaucracy. Probably he doesn't talk too much about his past history. It may have hindered his movement forward."

He was right about the first part. Emails, letters, and registered letters to Brookings produced no response. Writing to Kerstin at her office at the Catholic University of America yielded nothing. The university declined to comment. A Brookings spokesperson told me that the institution took no view on the activities of its fellows. It simply gave them a place to work and study. "Brookings has no views," she said. It was as if I had called a hairdresser and asked for the salon's opinions on the political activities of a stylist who rented a chair on the premises.

Only one of Cliff's past colleagues would talk about him on the record: Bruce Blair, a former U.S. Air Force Minuteman missile launch control officer who is now a highly regarded expert on nuclear security. Blair worked alongside Cliff when he first arrived at Brookings in 1991. "I recall Cliff mentioning on a number of occasions working for LaRouche in Stockholm, which did seem strange but I discounted it as youthful wandering and a search for mission and identity." I supplied him with some of the stranger details of Cliff's LaRouchian life. The Rockefeller conspiracy. The hate campaign against Palme. "He is a person of character," Blair concluded. "I am sure he followed his conscience wherever it led him."

A FEW WEEKS after the Palme assassination, conscience, or some other force, took Clifford Gaddy out of Sweden, the European Workers Party, and the LaRouche organization. He and Kerstin had been loyal and enthusiastic NCLC members for almost fifteen years. They gave no public hint that their commitment to the organization had faltered. For Cliff, the previous year had been particularly busy. Since July 1985 he had been making trips across Europe to promote a report cowritten with a small group of NCLC researchers entitled *Global Showdown: The Imperial Russian War Plan for 1988*. It comprised 366 eccentric pages of scaremongering, warmongering, and bad statistical analysis that insisted that the Soviet Union was preparing a nuclear first strike.

One of his fellow authors was Webster Tarpley, a shrill, rotund conspiracy theorist who would make headlines in 2017 when Melania Trump sued him for the false claim that she had worked as an escort. Another was Konstantin George, the LaRouchian whose phony story about an East Berlin brainwashing triggered the crisis of 1973–74, as well as Cliff's experience of being interrogated as a KGB infiltrator in Chris and Carol White's bedroom in Colindale.

Cliff Gaddy and Konstantin George formed a double act. They went to London, Paris, Bonn, Rome, West Berlin, Copenhagen, Geneva, and Lisbon. In each city, the message was the same. The Soviets, they announced, had already declared war on the United States. They had also declared war on LaRouche and considered him "very dangerous" and a "principled adversary."

Reading through the report, I was struck by the persistent presence of the story of Michael Vale and his army of deserters. The names had faded away, and the sinister controlling forces had been recast, but the story remained intact. "Soviet deployed 'sleepers' were sent into LaRouche's environment," the dossier asserted. The CIA was nowhere.

This was now an East German job. "These Stasi operations were run during 1972–74 in conjunction with the Palme-Brandt faction of the Socialist International, and elements of British intelligence, including the London Tavistock Institute, which were then and now heavily penetrated by Soviet intelligence." Who in their audience, I wonder, realized that the two men leading the presentation were selling a strange dream version of their own shared past?

Cliff's final public act as a LaRouchian was to chair the *Global Showdown* conference in Stockholm. Here, he warned delegates—and the Swedish edition of *New Solidarity*—that Palme's murder was the herald of a new world of Soviet-inspired political instability. Shortly afterward, he and Kerstin boarded a plane for the United States.

What made Cliff leave so suddenly? Many in the U.S. organization assumed that he had been shipped out of Stockholm to avoid questioning by the Swedish police. Had the Palme inquiry made Sweden too hot for him? Were he and Kerstin afraid of bumping into a vengeful Victor Gunnarsson? Had they experienced some kind of awakening about the true nature of the Labor Committees?

There was no shortage of material to bring them to their senses. In the first week of April 1986, *Newsweek* ran a four-page exposé on the organization—triggered by the surprising success of a pair of LaRouchian candidates in elections in the state of Illinois. The controversy even reached the pages of the *Old Gold and Black*, the newspaper of Cliff's college, where a student columnist condemned LaRouchian tactics as "a form of terrorism, one which involves no guns or bombs but seeks to destroy established institutions nevertheless." (That columnist, Rogan Kersh, would become provost of Wake Forest in 2012.) Whether Cliff and Kerstin fled from fear, guilt, disgust, or with the satisfaction of a job well done is a secret that only they know.

IN CLIFF'S ABSENCE, Bill Jones was promoted to Stockholm bureau chief. It was left to him and Bill Engdahl to coordinate the organization's official response to the Palme assassination. Lyndon LaRouche gave them the task, and he thought up a portentous title.

Under Operation Edgar Allan Poe, the two Bills produced a theory attuned to their own paranoia and narcissism: that the Soviets were behind Palme's killing and were now working hard to achieve their second objective: "laying the blame at the doorstep of the ELP [European Labor Party], as a first step in dismantling the LaRouche movement globally." LaRouche liked this theory, because it was all about him.

Their hefty report, *A Classical KGB Disinformation Campaign*, proved nothing about the assassination, but contained much evidence that the LaRouchians inhabited a Ptolemaic universe with themselves as its center. Legitimate press interest in the European Labor Party was "a coordinated wave of lies and innuendo" unleashed from Moscow. Journalists who described the party's gruesome methods were subject to personal attacks. (Paranoid schizophrenia, for instance, was diagnosed in a newspaper columnist who made the reasonable observation that "the public activities of the ELP have long passed the limits of decency.") The report speculated that Victor Gunnarsson might have been a KGB agent provocateur who signed up for party membership in order to bring suspicion on the LaRouchians once the assassination had been carried out.

The dossier was published in October 1986. And it would have received much more attention had the Labor Committees not had a more urgent problem to attend: a raid on their headquarters by four hundred armed agents.

IT HAPPENED BECAUSE of a federal investigation in Boston, where a grand jury was examining the financial arrangements of the Labor Committees and the group's tangle of subsidiary organizations and shell companies. The investigators found evidence of fraud on a massive scale. Loans solicited with no intention to repay. One million dollars skimmed from credit card accounts. The LaRouchians knew trouble was coming. Ed Spannaus and his security staff had already begun a counteroffensive. They shredded documents and made plans to fly indicted members to Germany, beyond the reach of the court. Roy Frankhouser, the former Klansman who was LaRouche's security adviser, had floated another bright idea: killing the prosecutor in charge of the case.

These tactics, however, were their undoing. Obstruction of justice was added to the charge sheet, and at seven a.m. on October 6, 1986, the FBI descended on LaRouche's 172-acre property in Loudoun County, Virginia, search warrants ready, guns loaded.

His home was well protected. There were sandbagged guard posts at the gate, cement barriers and metal spikes in the driveway, a retinue of ten guards armed with semiautomatic weapons, employed to patrol the barbed-wire perimeter. The FBI took no chances. The agents brought helicopters and armored cars, strapped on bulletproof vests, and massed in the early hours on a field above the estate. When the signal was given, an army of agents and law enforcement officers surrounded the property. Inside his redbrick antebellum mansion, LaRouche told his staff that any attempt to arrest him should be considered an assassination attempt. It fell to the obedient Warren Hamerman to relay LaRouche's response to the FBI and the wider world. "I will not submit passively to arrest," said the statement, "but in such a scenario I will defend myself." It sounded like a threat of armed resistance.

LaRouche went on to accuse the KGB of masterminding the operation against him. "Mikhail Gorbachev," he declared, "has demanded my head." Nobody, however, was much interested in LaRouche's head. They wanted his bank statements, account books, and dud promissory notes. LaRouche meekly withdrew his threat of violence. For three days, the police, the FBI, and the Internal Revenue Service searched the mansion and the offices of *Executive Intelligence Review* in downtown Leesburg, looking for evidence of wrongdoing.

Four hundred boxes of papers were wheeled away for examination. Records of credit card details used without the consent of their owners. Memos describing the cases of donors who had been persuaded to mortgage their homes and lend the proceeds to the Labor Committees; pensioners who had signed over the contents of their bank accounts on the understanding that they would be repaid in full. If they asked for their money back, they were stalled or bullied, told they were a troublemaker or a psychotic. The paperwork referred to these people as "hardship cases." The material was so damning that IRS officials were seen toasting one another over the ransacked filing cabinets.

The first documents to make headlines, however, had nothing to do with conning old ladies out of their life savings. They were a set of notebooks compiled by a member of LaRouche's counterintelligence staff that contained forty-five references to Victor Gunnarsson and the assassination of Olof Palme.

The *NBC Nightly News* broke the story on December 4, 1986, and had more intrigue to add. Its reporter spoke to Irwin Suall, chief fact finder at the Anti-Defamation League of B'nai B'rith, an anti-Semitism watchdog organization based in New York. Suall revealed that he had made a recent visit to Sweden while compiling a report into LaRouche's activities.

The report concluded: "The potential threat to America's democratic values and institutions posed by the LaRouche political cult derives from the movement's thriving on secrecy, deception, disruption, fear and hostile confrontations, and its peculiar brand of erratic, bigotry-laced extremism, cunningly camouflaged by the outward respectability of front groups and business suits." Since the assassination, said Suall, the Swedish authorities had asked for his assistance in locating two of those business-suited acolytes: Clifford Gaddy and his wife, Kerstin Tegin-Gaddy. He proved unable to help, but he seems to have tried. The ADL archive still holds his files of press clippings, with the Gaddy name ringed in red ink.

The Swedish police did not declare their interest in the couple until the spring of 1987. The line of inquiry was opened shortly after Hans Holmer, the Stockholm police commissioner who had headed the inquiry since the beginning, resigned his post and was replaced by a new chief.

Ulf Karlsson kept a low public profile and allowed his detectives more independence than his predecessor. The European Workers Party returned to the agenda. Detectives announced that a woman answering Kerstin's description had been spotted outside the Grand Cinema on the night of February 28, 1986; they used the press to appeal for information on her whereabouts. The papers granted her the favor extended to all criminal suspects. Although Kerstin was the leader of a national political party, they kept her name and her face out of the coverage. Front pages ran censored photographs of Kerstin, her face as smooth and blank as a figure from a Magritte picture.

The appeal worked. A few days later the Swedish police learned that Kerstin and Cliff had taken refuge in a deafeningly quiet suburb of Raleigh, North Carolina. Three detectives flew to the States to interview them, but a Swedish journalist found the house first—a nondescript gray bungalow, empty and bolted, its lawn unmown and correspondence piling on the doormat.

"The area is fenced off and a sign says it is guarded by private security guards," he reported. "In the South this generally means that blacks should keep away if they do not have good reason to be there. It also means that those who live here—many pensioners—prefer to be left in peace." The reporter asked an elderly neighbor if the couple had moved. "Not moved," she said. "Maybe disappeared. If they've got the police on their tails then they may well have disappeared. That happens."

Farcically, however, while Swedish detectives crossed the Atlantic to follow her trail in North Carolina, Kerstin had moved in the opposite direction, flying back to Stockholm to spend the Easter holidays with her family. As the Swedish papers printed faintly sinister photographs of her rented bungalow and her talkative neighbor, another group of detectives simply drove to the Tegin family home to interview her.

They spoke for an hour in a police car parked outside the house. The detectives asked her whether EAP members had weapons training like their comrades in Leesburg, but she professed to know nothing about this. She also claimed that she and Cliff had been planning to quit the party months before Palme was assassinated. The usher who thought he had seen her outside the Grand Cinema must have been mistaken. On the night of the murder, Kerstin insisted, she had been at home with her husband. They had eaten dinner, watched a TV program about the Israeli conductor Zubin Mehta, and gone to bed. The alibi was not perfect, but one fact of their domestic life made them unlikely assassins: on January 17 that year, Kerstin had given birth to a son.

A couple of weeks later Kerstin was back in the States, where she and Cliff were interviewed by another Swedish detective. An FBI agent was also present. Cliff described his work as Stockholm bureau chief for *Executive Intelligence Review* and his interest in military development in the Soviet Union and Europe. He was also asked about his attempts to communicate with a Swedish naval commander who, like the EAP, disapproved of Palme's desire to maintain friendly relations with the Soviet Union. He repeated Kerstin's description of a quiet night at home with Zubin Mehta on the TV, and her assertion that they had both been looking for a way out of the EAP. The detective seemed satisfied but would not grant Kerstin's request to make a public statement about eliminating them from the list of suspects.

The scandal, however, had been ridden out. Unlike Victor Gunnarsson, Cliff and Kerstin were not shouted at in the street. They could now settle in North Carolina, rebuild their lives, and forget past associations with the Palme inquiry and the European Workers Party. Bizarrely, that is precisely what Victor Gunnarsson also did.

IN THE FIRST weeks after the raid, the LaRouchians were not downhearted. A hysterical good humor overtook the organization. They began producing novelty T-shirts with the slogan I SURVIVED THE GREAT LEESBURG PANTY RAID. They put out their own local paper, the *Loudoun County News*, which blamed everything on the Russians. They held a Halloween costume party, to which one guest came as the AIDS virus and another as Warren Hamerman, complete with plastic pig snout.

But the trials of Lyndon LaRouche ensured that this mood passed. Like so many things in his life, they were tortuous, peculiar, and long-winded. Over the course of four years, cases involving grand larceny, securities fraud, unpaid fines, and conspiracy to obstruct justice were heard by judges in New York, Boston, and Alexandria, Virginia. Dozens of NCLC members were indicted, among them Ed Spannaus and Molly Kronberg.

LaRouche's lawyers tried to dissuade their client from getting on the witness stand. Not just because he would start talking about KGB assassination plots and the coming apocalypse, but because he could not be trusted to keep quiet about many other doubtful activities that were not even on the charge sheet. But Warren Hamerman, whom LaRouche had appointed to head the legal team, overruled them.

"LaRouche didn't care about what happened to any of us," said Molly. "But he did want to exculpate himself. I think he believed it would help his appeal if he could show that the rest of us were guilty as sin." LaRouche also forbade his followers to plead guilty, which, when the verdicts came in, meant longer sentences for everyone.

In December 1988, LaRouche and six of his associates were convicted of conspiracy and mail fraud amounting to $34 million. LaRouche was defiant. "The purpose of this frame-up is not to send me to prison, it's to kill me," he told reporters. "If this sentence goes through, I'm dead." It did go through. He didn't die. Instead, he served five years of a fifteen-year sentence at the federal prison in Rochester, Minnesota, where, for a time, he shared his cell with the disgraced televangelist Jim Bakker, freshly jailed for similar crimes. The prison authorities were generous. They had heard that LaRouche was a computer genius and gave him the job of overseeing the new IT system they had installed in the library. But it soon became clear that LaRouche barely knew how to switch it on.

LaRouche's five years in prison saw Warren Hamerman rewarded for his years of unquestioning loyalty. He was appointed the organization's chief spokesman. He endured the sniggers of reporters as he insisted that his master was an American Dreyfus, the victim of "a political dirty operation carried out by the parallel government." He issued proclamations when LaRouche ran for president from his prison cell in 1992. It also fell to Wally to tell the world about the latest assassination attempt on the leader of the Labor Committees. Agents of a hostile power, he announced, had tried to kill LaRouche during surgery to remove some anal polyps. The scheme had been foiled by canceling the operation. None of this nonsense caused Warren Hamerman the least bit of embarrassment.

In 1985 he had taken on the running of the Labor Committees Biological Holocaust Task Force, in which capacity he advocated putting AIDS patients into quarantine camps and insisted, against scientific evidence, that the disease could be spread by insect bites and casual human contact. (He made a panic-mongering tour of Europe, recycling stories about the synthetic nature of the virus, a theory born in a disinformation campaign by the KGB.)

His most operatic act of fealty occurred in September 1990, when delegates from the Labor Committees took over the Hyatt Regency Hotel in Arlington, Virginia, to listen to a speech recorded by LaRouche in his cell. During this period the organization decided, under the influence of LaRouche's wife Helga, to make overtures toward right-wing Catholic organizations.

This policy produced a number of spiritual conversions: Warren turned obediently from Judaism to Rome; Jim McGourty, born Presbyterian, did the same. Jim's wife, Christina, a lapsed Catholic, followed her husband back into the Church. LaRouche's rhetoric also took a religious turn. As the official account noted, his taped speech "traced those efforts through the Ruskin circle at Oxford University and their satanic co-thinkers around Friedrich Nietzsche and Aleister Crowley, who sought to revive the cult of Dionysus and the Age of Aquarius, through the rise of the ugly twins of Bolshevism and fascism, and into the Frankfurt School, which launched the rock-drug-sex counterculture."

Warren Hamerman followed this with an aria of flattery and wishful thinking entitled "The Role of the LaRouche Movement in World History." "Anyone's list of great leaders of our last two centuries would certainly include Martin Luther King, Lincoln, Gandhi, and de Gaulle," he declared. "There is an unmistakable pattern. Like LaRouche, each was an explicit warrior against the slavery and racist genocide which emanated from British imperialism, basing themselves on the notion that all men are created equal." Everyone applauded.

But when LaRouche came out of prison in March 1994, he showed little gratitude for Hamerman's loyal service. Wally and his wife Nora were expelled from the organization shortly after its Labor Day conference. They were purged along with other members thought to have been disloyal during Lyn's imprisonment, and were denounced as "stay-behind agents" of "Buckley family-style Carlist Gnosticism."

Similar charges were made against Jim McGourty and Christina Nelson. In 1998 they had thrown themselves into a passion project: the establishment of a private Catholic school in a local community center. With Jim as headmaster, the St. John Bosco High School was a success, and soon it moved to permanent premises above the Leesburg branch of Subway. Fourteen pupils studied Latin and Shakespeare with the smell of baking bread in their nostrils.

In 2000, however, the LaRouche organization reversed its position on Catholicism. "Sunday activity," announced an internal memo, had caused "the repeated sharp deterioration in intelligence and morale of the Leesburg Labor Committee." The truth lay in the opposite direction. "LaRouche stepped in it when he began to write about Church history and doctrine," Christina Nelson told me, "because some members took these issues seriously. It amounted to a loss of control for him over a portion of the cult members." She and Jim chose God over Lyndon LaRouche.

They knew the process would be painful. Members moving for the exit had many unpleasant experiences to share—threatening letters, a hearse sent to their parents' house to collect their bodies—but most were subjected to a process called the Shunning. "First they would call you night and day to try to get you back in," Jim explained. "Come over to your house and try to convince you. If you left, then the Shunning began. If they saw you walking down the street they'd turn their heads. If you called on the telephone they hang up." Once that process was exhausted, the denunciations began. *Executive Intelligence Review* attacked St. John Bosco as part of the "spreading slime-mold of tiny pro-Carlism-polluted schools" that aimed "to bring fascism to power throughout the Americas."

It meant nothing. But what had any of it meant?

WHILE THE LEADER of the Labor Committees sat in his cell discussing the Bible with Jim Bakker, the Gaddys were in North Carolina, building their post-LaRouchian lives. Both enrolled at Duke University. Kerstin began a master's thesis on the German playwright and poet Friedrich Schiller. (This was an intellectual inheritance from LaRouche, who had conferred bogus respectability on his organization by setting up an institute in Schiller's honor.) And Cliff started postgraduate work in the economics department, working under a professor named Vladimir Treml. A fairly unsensational development, you might think. But this, like Cliff's desertion, is a shift of the kind that *Mr. Putin: Operative in the Kremlin* asks us to examine.

Cliff's doctoral work was not an ordinary PhD on an obscure subject. He was joining a group of economists on a project funded by the Office of Net Assessment, a think tank within the Pentagon. Their job was to examine data harvested from interviews with recent defectors from the Soviet Union in order to produce a picture of Russia's black economy—from which the real economic strength of the Soviet Union might be deduced.

Cliff was assigned to estimate the worth of the Russian prostitution market. (Gross revenues of 300 to 1,800 million rubles, it turned out.) Other scholars studied the sales of home-distilled alcohol, fruit and vegetables from private allotments, illegal gasoline, and illegal drugs. The CIA took a strong interest in the work. The project's supervisor, Vladimir Treml, was a member of its Military-Economic Advisory Panel and had been sharing his findings with Langley since the mid-1970s.

What, exactly, did Cliff say at his interview or put on his application form? Did he admit that he had spent a decade as a senior member of an organization that was proscribed by the FBI, put under surveillance by SÄPO and Swedish military intelligence, and suspected of involvement in the assassination of Olof Palme? Did he mention that his most recent publication was a LaRouchian farrago claiming the existence of an Imperial Russian War Plan for 1988? Was he greeted, perhaps, as an undercover operative back from the field? As a prodigal son, returned from a long, mad, misguided interlude? Or did Cliff, like many ex-LaRouchians taking their first steps out of the madhouse, present the association in a positive light and hope for the best? "If you come from a 'good background' and come across like a smart and reasonable person," one told me, "most people don't care what you've been up to."

Whatever the case, his LaRouche years did not retard the progress of Cliff's career. He was awarded his PhD in May 1991 and was speaking on behalf of the Brookings Institution by the summer. In the turbulence that followed the collapse of communism, he went to Russia to visit collective farms and advise local government officials on their tax affairs. He also found work as an adjunct lecturer at Georgetown University, where he taught a course on Russian military economics. By 2015, he had reached his professional zenith, as a senior fellow at Brookings and a key contributor to "Order from Chaos," its project to produce foreign policy ideas for the post–Cold War world.

Cliff's reinvention as an expert on the Soviet economy did not go unnoticed by his former comrades in the Labor Committees. In documents intended for internal consumption within the cult, he was cast as the protagonist of a bizarre pornographic fairy story that depicted a number of former members as sex workers in a German brothel. "Cliff

Gladly," we're told, "went on to fame, for having made the leap from empirical experience . . . to enlightened theoretical studies, a fame properly earned with his scholarly study on Soviet prostitution cash flows, and later, his ground-breaking theory on the necessity for the Russian mafia in guaranteeing contracts in the free market."

Snide paragraphs about his disloyalty made occasional appearances on the pages of *Executive Intelligence Review*. A 2002 article referred to him as "a former LaRouche associate who has sold out himself." After he joined the Brookings Institution, NCLC representatives would sometimes turn up to see him at seminars and press conferences. It's hard to imagine that he felt particularly delighted when they got to their feet to ask him if he was aware of the latest turn of LaRouche's political thinking. Particularly when the questioner was the NCLC counterintelligence staffer who compiled the notebooks that put the Palme detectives on his tail.

Over the years, there may have been many such moments of discomfort for Cliff and Kerstin. In March 2003, when the British student Jeremiah Duggan was found dead on the autobahn after attending a series of LaRouche meetings in Wiesbaden. ("Mum, I'm frightened," he said, in his last call home, fifty minutes before his body was discovered.) Or in November 2003, when the EAP's sugar daddy Alf Enerström was back in the news for shooting a female police officer as she tried to evict him from his rubbish-strewn Stockholm apartment. (Enerström came running at her with a saucepan on his head and a Smith & Wesson revolver in his hand. He was sent to a psychiatric hospital, where he covered the walls of his room with aluminum foil to prevent the authorities using beam weapons to give him an "electromagnetic lobotomy.")

Or in January 2017, when, somewhere beneath a memorably gruesome *tableau vivant* depicting Donald Trump warming up for Miss World 2013 by watching a sex worker relieve herself on the soft furnishings of a Moscow hotel room, a doubtful dossier compiled by a former MI6 officer claimed that the Kremlin had recently paid for a delegation of LaRouchies to visit Russia.

Unpleasant reminders of the world they had left behind.

But the first of these moments came closest to home.

ON JANUARY 7, 1994, a surveyor from the North Carolina Department of Transportation was walking through the woods in Deep Gap, Watauga County, when he discovered the body of a man lying in the snow. The corpse was several weeks old and completely naked. Despite the cold, it had begun to decay. But the cause of death was not obscure. Two bullet wounds to the head.

Thanks to the presence of a signet ring and fake gold watch, the police identified the victim with ease: Victor Gunnarsson, the first serious suspect in the Olof Palme case. He was four thousand miles from Stockholm, but less than two hours' drive from Salisbury, the town in which he had settled in order to escape the notoriety conferred by the assassination, and where he had been reported as a missing person one month before.

At the moment of his death, Gunnarsson was no longer of interest to the Palme investigation. He had been supplanted by Christer Pettersson, a petty criminal and drug user who was convicted of Palme's murder in 1988 but freed on appeal the following year.

Gunnarsson's emigration was the product of a chance encounter on a Swedish ski slope, where a sympathetic American businessman offered him a room in his apartment in North Carolina. Gunnarsson accepted. But changing continents didn't change his personality. In Salisbury, he acquired a reputation as a drinker, a braggart, and a womanizer. He traded on his exotic status, his air of mystery. He liked to tell people that he worked for the CIA. A clerk at the Hop In convenience store said that he had shown her seven different passports in seven different names. Another witness claimed to have heard Gunnarsson boasting, drunkenly, of being responsible for Olof Palme's murder, describing how he ran up behind the prime minister and shot him in the back. Gunnarsson was also unaccountably wealthy. He professed to make his living teaching private language classes, but that did not explain the thick wads of cash that some had seen him flourish from his wallet.

On the evening of December 3, 1993, Gunnarsson had a dinner of baked potatoes with his girlfriend Kay Weden at the home of her seventy-seven-year-old mother, Catherine Miller. At eleven-thirty he drove Weden home, kissed her good night, and went back to his apartment. She was the last person to see him alive. That night someone abducted Gunnarsson from his home, gagged him with a length of duct tape, tied him up, and put him in the trunk of a car. He was driven eighty miles to Deep Gap, then forced from the roadside into the forest, where he was executed with two bullets from a .22-caliber rifle.

Five days after her last dinner with Gunnarsson, Kay Weden received some terrible news. It was not about her boyfriend's disappearance. That had yet to be discovered. Her mother, Catherine Miller, had been murdered. Shot twice in the head as she cooked at her stove.

Kay Weden knew of only one person who bore her family a grudge— Lamont Claxton Underwood, a retired homicide detective to whom she had once been engaged. Underwood had reacted badly to the breakup. Once, Weden recalled, he had spotted her at a restaurant on a date, marched in, and tipped iced tea into her lap.

The State Bureau of Investigation began examining his case. Its agents discovered that on the night of the murder, Underwood had phoned a former colleague at the Salisbury police station and asked him to run a check on a license plate. It was Gunnarsson's car. Underwood's house was searched. His typewriter was identified as the source of some anonymous threatening letters received by Weden earlier in the year. The most compelling evidence was forensic. Underwood's car, like his house, was spotlessly clean, but strands of hair were found embedded in the mat in the trunk of his car, and they proved a good match for Gunnarsson's.

At his trial in 1997, a jury took seventy-five minutes to find Underwood guilty of Gunnarsson's kidnap and first-degree murder. He was handed a life sentence without parole. No trial for Miller's murder ever took place. But Underwood did not accept the guilty verdict. He appealed his conviction on the grounds that his attorneys did not have sufficient experience to handle the case. In 2011, his appeal was rejected: the forensic evidence was so strong that the greenness of his lawyers was ruled irrelevant to the outcome of the trial.

But he had supporters. Many of them were conspiracy theorists who believed that Underwood was the victim of a CIA plot. Gunnarsson, they argued, had murdered Olof Palme on the orders of Langley, which then disposed of its talkative assassin with a bullet. Voodoo history. Like another idea that was suggested to me over breakfast one morning by a mischievous Michael Vale. "There was a rumor," he said, "that Gunnarsson came back to the States for revenge. To get rid of the people who had got him mixed up in the assassination." He meant Bill, Cliff, and Kerstin. I looked at him and thought of the swing of Foucault's Pendulum.

WHEN SURVIVORS OF the LaRouche cult find success in the real world, former comrades rejoice. When I appealed for memories of Cliff on LaRouchecontinued.org, the principal online forum for ex-members, a debate broke out on the morality of my request.

"It's creepy," wrote one. "He's made a new life for himself and been successful at it; isn't that the mantra of some here? To me it's McCarthyism." Cliff and Kerstin, I assumed, felt the same. But they had placed themselves beyond the reach of any witch-hunter. Until I had dealings with the Brookings Institution, Duke University, and the Catholic University of America, I hadn't understood how defensive and unaccountable such bodies can be. I'm used to dealing with their equivalent British institutions, which tend to be public, and are therefore obliged to answer questions from journalists. I wondered if Cliff's career had been shaped by the closed nature of such places. He had never worked anywhere that a Freedom of Information request would penetrate.

Cliff and Kerstin failed to respond to my letters, not even to decline the opportunity to talk. I could have taken no for an answer, but the silence led me to hope that I stood a chance of persuading them to be interviewed. Their musical interests gave me the opportunity.

They were both, I discovered, members of a folk band called the Kensingtones. Cliff played the cello, Kerstin the flute. I decided to go to one of their gigs. "Make sure you have all your documents to back this up," said a tough Washington journalist I contacted for advice. "Brookings will steamroller you." I came equipped with a sheaf of clippings tracing the Gaddys' relationship with LaRouche from the mid-1970s to the official Swedish government account of their interviews with the Palme investigation detectives.

My journey from London acquired an appropriately LaRouchian tinge. There had been a security alert at JFK airport. Someone had reported gunshots. Flights were grounded, and mine was one of the casualties. After hours of hanging around at Gatwick, I was assigned a seat on a charter flight that touched down in New York at two a.m. and was then kept waiting on the tarmac for an hour. Having missed my connection to Washington, I took a shuttle bus to the nearest hotel.

At around four a.m., the bus crashed into the metal railings outside the Days Inn. There were two other passengers on board. We got out to peel the fence away as the driver extricated his twisted bumper. When I finally reached my bed, sleep proved elusive. And I realized that I had entered that exhausted and overimaginative state in which paranoid thinking blossoms: the state in which the tiled edge of a bath looks fit to crack a skull, and a knock from the chambermaid seems to portend a reenactment of that scene from *Michael Clayton* in which two assassins murder Tom Wilkinson and cocoon him in plastic.

The Kensingtones' gig was at Gypsy Sally's, a waterside venue in Georgetown. The audience was small—seven friends and colleagues from the Brookings Institution and the Catholic University of America. Perhaps the bad weather had put people off. I sat at the bar and ordered a beer. Cliff, in cargo shorts, bare feet, and a Panama hat, bowed the cello, strummed the ukulele, and sang somewhere down at Lee Marvin level. Behind him, Kerstin played the flute, sometimes sweetly, sometimes so flatly that the barman cast me a pained glance and redoubled his concentration on the women's wrestling playing on the TV.

I'd intended to approach them at the end of the night, but because the audience was so minuscule, I found Kerstin bounding over to me at the interval to ask me what I thought of the music. For me, it didn't feel like a first meeting: I had been reading her weird speeches about Olof Palme's fascist master plan for years.

"I like it," I said. "I have your album." She was a bit surprised. I explained that I was hoping to have a word with her and her husband. Ice formed on Kerstin's upper slopes.

"Then I know who you are," she said. "We have no interest in this. Do you respect that?" I began to answer, but every time I opened my mouth she fired out the question again. *"Do you respect that? Do you respect that? Do you respect that?"*

I said that after two years of silence, it was good to have a reply. She walked away. In the meantime, Cliff had come to the bar. I introduced myself. "I know it's your job to write about an enigmatic man who won't give you an interview," I said. "And you're an enigma to me." He smiled so wide his face seemed in danger of cracking. "Can I ask you one thing?" I said. "Were you a real deserter, Cliff? Or were you something else?"

Cliff began nodding and smiling. But not because he was pleased to see me or giving an answer to my question. It seemed to be for the benefit of observers. Anyone in the room looking in our direction might have assumed that Cliff was basking, delighted, in the compliments of an admirer.

During the second half of the gig, the humid DC weather broke. Rain sluiced down on K Street. Lightning carved the sky. The Kensingtones were obliged to compete with the thunder. "You're stuck with us now," said the band's chief vocalist.

In his deep bass voice, Cliff began a Leonard Cohen number.

Everybody knows that the dice are loaded
Everybody rolls with their fingers crossed
Everybody knows the war is over
Everybody knows the good guys lost
Everybody knows the fight was fixed
The poor stay poor, the rich get rich
That's how it goes
Everybody knows.

As the song went on, I was struck by how its bitter pessimism spoke to the lives of the people in this story. The men I had come to know were players in the game of history. They had hoped to win the new world that had seemed so proximate at the end of the 1960s. Their refusal to fight in the Vietnam War was a respectable first move. But the game was rigged, and some of the other players weren't even real. And despite the struggles, the upheavals, and the head-banging madness of all they had endured, the outcomes of their lives seemed more shaped by the circumstances of their births than the momentous choices they had made in their twenties.

Half a century later, they had found ends that were very much like their beginnings. Chuck Onan, the poor kid from Chicago who shined shoes on his way from school, was still living hand to mouth, one small step away from penury. Michael Vale, that clever, unloved boy from Cincinnati who drifted from town to town talking to strangers, was still on the road, though it no longer wound through America. After a flirtation with revolutionary violence, Jim McGourty had returned to the staunch conservatism of his parents. Cliff Gaddy, the son of the kind of comfortable and well-educated family the establishment adores, was playing his cello, among friends, as a diversion from his respectable job in a Washington think tank. Untouched and apparently untroubled by his decade and a half of attachment to a batshit crazy cult. Still letting his wife do the talking.

LET US END this chapter in North Carolina. One bright afternoon in February 2016, I found myself behind the razor wire of the Alexander Correctional Institution, a citadel of colorless concrete boxes built over a landfill site in the Appalachian foothills. The deputy superintendent, a thoughtful, thirtysomething dad with the close-cropped hair favored by prisoners and guards alike, was taking me to meet Lamont Claxton Underwood, the man convicted of the murder of Victor Gunnarsson.

But just as my escort was leading me through the remote-controlled bulkhead of the interview room, an announcement buzzed through the public address system. The midday head count had produced the wrong number. Life in the prison froze as its officers restarted the tally. The deputy superintendent and I waited, making conversation. He told me about his love of the British sitcom *Are You Being Served?* I complimented him on the shininess of his floors. The polish, he explained, was manufactured within the North Carolina prison system. So was the paint on the walls, the furniture in the rooms, the clothes and shoes worn by the prisoners, and much of the food consumed in the refectory. The prison sector, he said with pride, was leaving the taxpayer almost untroubled. It was an economy within the economy, in which boom and bust, debt and credit had been eliminated—along with the freedom of its labor force.

After half an hour, the alert was over. Lamont Underwood shuffled into the room, dressed in the colorless clothes produced by the prison workshops. The TV footage from 1997 had shown him as a tanned man with a neat side part. Inevitably, prison and the passage of time had changed him. He winced as he moved, and his hair was patchy on his skull. Once he had settled into his plastic chair, I asked him about his childhood in Winston-Salem. His mother, he said, worked in an ice cream factory. His father had a job in construction. There were complexities: Lamont was the product of his father's relationship with another woman, and in the end, Mrs. Underwood decided to keep the son but rid herself of the husband. L.C., as he was always known, left home to join the army, but got out, went into law enforcement, and stayed until back pain forced him to take early retirement. He looked around the whitewashed walls. "And here's how I'm spending my retirement," he said.

Underwood placed a heap of brown envelopes on the table between us. He was going to present his case to me, and I had been assigned the role of the jury. For two hours he gave me his theories about who really killed Victor Gunnarsson and how the crime had been pinned on him. The forensic evidence was faked, he said. He'd seen the lab report on the hair teased from the mat in his car. It was dated Sunday, and the lab was closed on a Sunday. His lawyers, he said, were not up to the job. "You could tell they were both idiots. One sat in the courtroom and was throwing candy behind him to the crowd. Whoever paid for his law school deserves a refund."

One line of his defense would not have pleased the conspiracy theorists who believe that Victor Gunnarsson was murdered by the CIA. The killing, Underwood said, was a botched job. "I was a homicide detective," he reflected. "I worked all kinds of major crimes. At the trial they said: *He was a detective, he would know about all this.* And that's true, absolutely that's true. But I also wouldn't have left that trunk mat in that car if Gunnarsson had been in there, too. I wouldn't have. If I had killed Victor Gunnarsson, they would never have found his body. Never."

"What would you have done?" I asked.

"What would I have done to get rid of him?"

"Yes."

"Probably found an old well somewhere," he said. "And I know where a bunch of them are. They'd have never found him. They'd still be looking for him on Judgment Day."

I asked him how he felt about Gunnarsson. A man he never knew and said he never met, and yet, thanks to his conviction, the reason for his two decades in jail.

"He's like the mist," said Underwood. "He's like the mist to me." His next remark surprised me. "But I do think he killed the prime minister," he said. "There's no doubt in my mind."

THERE WAS PLENTY in mine. But not so much, perhaps, about the justice of L. C. Underwood's conviction. It is hard to make the case that Victor Gunnarsson was Olof Palme's assassin. Gunnarsson was a fanatic and a fantasist. He liked the idea of CIA intrigue, and he liked anyone who hated Olof Palme. That's why he signed up for the European Workers Party and took its vile literature back to his apartment. There are many hypotheses that link him to the crime, but no convincing piece of evidence.

In November 1995, the Swedish prime minister Ingvar Carlsson attended the funeral of Yitzhak Rabin, the Israeli prime minister assassinated by a right-wing extremist. On his return, he told *Aftonbladet* how the tragedy had brought back memories of the killing of Olof Palme. "Far to the right," he said, "there was the EAP, which in its leaflets were calling Olof Palme 'mentally ill' and 'murderer.' . . . I will never get rid of the thought that the act of the murderer, be it spontaneous or planned, was influenced by the hatred which, after years of campaigning, was permitted."

Only the gunman bears true responsibility for the act. But if I were an alumnus of the Stockholm LaRouchians, this is the idea that would keep me up at night. If it were possible to alter time, if we could remove the European Workers Party from history, then Olof Palme would still have been gunned down in the snow, and by the same assassin.

But I think it more likely that we would know the identity of that killer. A world without the EAP's paranoid speechmaking, its poisonous rhetoric, its baroque and meaningless opinions, is one in which the detectives investigating the murder did not waste their time following Cliff and Kerstin Gaddy halfway across the world or trying to understand the political ideas upon which their party was founded. There was nothing to understand. It was founded upon chaos, and Cliff and Kerstin were its agents.

17 / THE END OF THE WORLD

I CAN CHART the progress of this book against the mental and physical decline of Lyndon LaRouche. At first, I watched his weekly webcast on the website of the LaRouche Political Action Committee. Every Friday night he gripped the lectern in a tiny TV studio in Leesburg and addressed the middle distance with faux-presidential grandeur. "The British Isles has been the British Isles," he would say, with thunderous authority. "Which has been a sick department of humanity." He was a niche act, but impressive.

On Monday lunchtimes he would treat his fans again, convening the LaRouche Policy Committee to debate the most urgent issues of the day. I became a regular viewer for a couple of years—partly because these roundtable discussions illustrated the ideological milieu that claimed many of the protagonists of this book, partly because the "A Mad Tea-Party" has always been my favorite chapter of *Alice in Wonderland*.

The structure was always the same. The chair asked Lyn to make some opening remarks. LaRouche, blinking, puffing, and finger wagging, riffed on themes that have been his comfort and joy since the time of the Chris White Affair. We were only weeks away from nuclear war—or *thermo*nuclear war, as he called it, because that sounded worse. In order to save ourselves, we were obliged to follow his plan of action. The president must be impeached. The president's British puppet masters must be restrained. The solar system must be colonized. Putin must have the Ukraine. The Chinese must mine helium-3 on the moon. The new human paradigm must be achieved by studying the ideas of the fifteenth-century German theologian Nicholas of Cusa. Pragmatism was the enemy of progress. A raven was very much like a writing desk.

"You don't define the behavior of mankind based on given facts," insisted LaRouche. "That doesn't work." On this point, he always practiced what he preached. "Well," he announced, on a broadcast in 2016, "Schwarzenegger is a sex maniac. He was the world's leading sex maniac. He was promoted directly from Ireland, but not from the Irish; and he was shipped into the United States to become the leader of California. And what he did is he turned the whole California into a bunch of degenerate sex maniacs. What we're trying to do is get rid of the sex maniacs out of California."

As LaRouche plucked concepts from his mental tombola, two or three hollow-eyed colleagues beside him would make furious notes. As if they hadn't heard it all before. As if it made the faintest sense. He once gave some advice on how to deal with dissenters: "Well it's very simple! He has that opinion? Kill him! Then we won't have a problem." Everyone laughed nervously at that but wrote it down all the same.

When Lyn fell silent, the committee would flatter him by attempting to paraphrase his remarks. They had their work cut out. Between exquisitely awkward silences, they constructed a tapestry of phrases calculated to elicit his approval. The Kepler Question. The Eurasian Land Bridge. Energy-flux density. Zeusian genocide. Man is not an animal. Bertrand Russell was satanic.

By the end of the hour, they had usually managed to encircle their guru in a cyclorama that depicted a world where world events were shaped by his contentions; where their organization was a vigorous and influential political movement. This done, he would beam at them, the happy inhabitant of a world that had no existence beyond the group's own meeting rooms and lightly visited websites.

As the months went by, LaRouche's appearances became less frequent. In 2015 his Friday night show was canceled and replaced with an audio-only Thursday night phone-in, billed as a "fireside chat," in imitation of Franklin D. Roosevelt. The format required LaRouche to answer questions from members of the public. He didn't seem very keen on this. "Don't let any screwballs get on this week," he told the moderator.

As calls were sparse and screwballs his core constituents, the moderator relayed a question from me. I asked if LaRouche thought his ideas would ever gain any traction in Britain. "If you get Royal Family out of the picture, you can actually make miracles in the Scottish areas," he said. "I know my Scottish ancestors. I didn't know all of them, personally, but I do know a great deal about all of them. And that would be my opinion."

By the middle of 2016, this kind of thing was clearly too much for him. His online appearances dwindled to a weekly Saturday afternoon interaction with the faithful in the basement of a Manhattan hotel. Not in person, but over a video link, like the science-fiction dictator who cannot appear in public because he is actually a corpse whose actions are controlled by a giant alien arthropod lurking just out of view. The frequent technical glitches were blamed on interference by the FBI.

No such excuse could be found for the condition of Lyndon LaRouche, who, in the space of two years, had declined from being a man capable of extemporizing conspiratorial join-the-dots from an upright position to a man sitting in a high-backed chair who couldn't quite see where the dots were, but kept on talking anyway. Sometimes he pitched forward to shout his remarks into the carpet, allowing his bald skull to fill the screen. Even his small congregation seemed disengaged. Just before Christmas 2015 he announced that the world was going to end on January 2, 2016. Nobody seemed that bothered. And yet his acolytes still celebrated his greatness.

Bill Jones, alone of all the deserters, was among them.

I KNEW IT would end badly with Bill. Our first lunch had reached a friendly conclusion because I did nothing to disrupt the fantasy he invited me to enter—that he was the long-standing Washington correspondent of a respected magazine, and not one of the last survivors of a dying political cult. Our second meeting took place at the same venue, the Old Ebbitt Grill beside the White House. This time, no Red Army hat was necessary. Washington was overpoweringly hot. We were grateful for the air-conditioning.

As I wanted to ask him about his life after the American Deserters Committee, I expected the conversation to be tricky. But it went well at first. He spoke happily about his anti-green activism, sniggering at the mention of the Hog Farm collective, a peripatetic peace group that arrived in Stockholm for the 1972 United Nations Conference on the Human Environment. The hippies, he recalled, led by a clown-suited activist called Wavy Gravy, marched through Stockholm behind a truck wrapped in plastic to represent the body of a whale. The Labor Committees organized a counterdemonstration.

The first wobble came when I asked him about Michael Vale. He admitted that he'd bumped into him at the 1975 World Health Organization conference in Copenhagen. He didn't mention that the meeting had produced an article in *New Solidarity* accusing his old friend of being part of the latest CIA plot. Or that he had accused Michael of posing as a member of the EAP in order to bring the party into disrepute—"at a time when our programmatic influence among Communists and left-wing Social Democrats is explosive." Bill even told me that he'd like to meet up with Michael, though I didn't believe it for a second. Then I asked him about his duties for the EAP, the nature of his position in the party.

"Writing articles," he said.

When I pressed further, the temperature in our booth at the Old Ebbitt Grill fell suddenly. Paddington Bear could not have given me a harder stare. "Switch that off," he said, indicating my voice recorder. "I've been in this game a long time, you know." I did as he asked.

"What is this all about?" he asked. He was not pleased to hear that I knew about the brainwashing affair. Horrified when I mentioned that I'd talked to Carol and Chris White. He seemed on the point of leaving the restaurant. But I stopped him. By talking about his favorite subject.

"This stuff about the queen, Bill," I ventured. "You don't really believe it, do you?"

Bill smiled. Did I know, he asked, what Prince Philip had said in 1989? I did know it, because I'd read dozens of references to it in *Executive Intelligence Review*. It was one of the most overworked out-of-context quotes in the history of his organization, and Bill had committed it to memory. "In the event that I am reincarnated, I would like to return as a deadly virus, to contribute something to solving overpopulation."

This, Bill claimed, was more than a bitter joke. It was a hint of the secret project that the royals have pursued for decades through their manipulation of the Commonwealth, the European Union, and the global financial system—a conspiracy to reshape the world with a brutal form of laissez-faire economics adapted from the ideas of the British philosophers Thomas Malthus and Jeremy Bentham.

"You mean utilitarianism?" I asked.

"*You* may want to call it that," he laughed. "Maybe 'fascism' would be a better word." And he reflected on a state visit to Germany that the queen had made that June. Did I think it was a coincidence that she had gone to meet Angela Merkel just a few days before the Greek referendum on a financial bailout from the European Union? These two events were connected. Her Majesty had gone to Berlin to give Merkel her orders, just as, a few months before, the British prime minister David Cameron had delivered the latest royal instructions to Barack Obama. "You don't think she was just being friendly, do you? She's an *operator*."

Why, I wondered, if Britain was run by a secret cabal of Malthusians, does it have the National Health Service and the welfare state? "Well," said Bill. "There are always factions."

It was like talking to someone lost in a dream. Perhaps, at his stage in life, it was too dangerous for him to wake up. Better to die in it than endure the thought of having squandered a lifetime on such ideas.

He drained his iced tea and left. I watched him go. "My Way" was playing on the restaurant sound system.

THERE IS NO such thing as brainwashing. Not in the way we see it in the movies. Not in the way it was envisaged by Lyndon LaRouche, who thought that filmstrips and electric shocks and sexual humiliation could soften a mind into behaving like a 1960s computer.

But it is possible to train yourself to accept the impossible. To incorporate so many unfounded ideas into the way you view the world that you come to mistrust the processes of ordinary empirical inquiry. It was strange to think of Bill, shuffling through the streets of Washington, DC, pushing his shopping cart through a Leesburg supermarket, with this magical, paranoid universe turning in his head. One in which Bertrand Russell was the most evil man in history, Jimmy Carter was a programmed zombie, and the inhabitants of Buckingham Palace spent their evenings plotting nuclear Armageddon.

"Paranoid delusion," writes the philosopher John Gray, "is often a reaction against insignificance—the sense, often well-founded, of counting for nothing in the world." But Bill did count for something. Or at least he did in 1968, when he deserted from an unjust war and became one of the leaders of a movement that wanted to bring that conflict to an end and build a more just and equitable world. And then he met Lyndon LaRouche and kissed reality goodbye.

As I neared the end of my work, I hoped to have a final conversation with Bill. I thought, foolishly, that I might be able to crack his shell a little, present him with the facts that might inspire him to leave the organization. I began mailing him material that would remind him of the person he had been before he became a LaRouchian drone. I sent him the document announcing the dissolution of the ADC. I sent him a photograph of his younger self, with bright eyes and bright buttons, at the Christian Brothers School in St. Louis, Missouri. Weeks later, a reply arrived from Loudoun County.

"I sincerely hope," he wrote, "there is more to your life than chasing these moonbeams you seem to be obsessed with," he wrote. "A mind is a terrible thing to waste." I replied:

Dear Bill,
   They might be moonbeams, I suppose. Certainly something bright and insubstantial. But I prefer another metaphor. I've realized, I think, that I'm writing a history of a collective dream, from which some people awoke and some didn't. First the dream was of revolution—a dream inherited from Trotsky and Lenin. Then it became something else. A dream about brainwashing and the CIA. About Rockefeller and Olof Palme. We know how that one ended. After which, the queen and Bertrand Russell took their places. That kind of substitution only happens in dreams.

When we last had lunch together, you told me how the queen had gone to Berlin to give Angela Merkel her orders; how she and Prince Philip were in the business of plotting genocide; how the British Empire was still exerting its power over America and was attempting to start World War Three with Russia. Did you really believe it, Bill? I looked you right in the eye, and I couldn't tell.

And, to pursue the question back to your Swedish years, did you really believe the equivalent stories of your first years with LaRouche? That Mike Vale organized the mental reprogramming of Chris White and Bill Engdahl? That, as *EIR* reported, Olof Palme had allowed "the Rockefeller forces to use [Sweden] as a laboratory for their 1984-style experiments"?

I wonder if the LaRouche project is really quite as attractive today as it seemed to you in 1972? Could you leave it now, do you think? Or are you now with him to the end—whatever form that takes?

You're right. A mind is a terrible thing to waste.

I think you deserve more.

All the very best,
Matthew

On one of my visits to Virginia, Chris and Carol White gave me the tour of LaRouchian Loudoun. They pointed out Cardinal Park, where the group had planned to build a spanking new headquarters—until the loan company discovered the organization had no books to examine. We drove through Woodburn, the antebellum estate that, once Rudolf Nureyev had moved out, had become LaRouche's first headquarters in Virginia. We looked at the pond installed by LaRouche as a security measure, the barn used for mass meetings, the elegant manor raided by SWAT teams when LaRouche declared that fraud investigators would be repelled with bullets. All occupied by others now. But after dinner at a sushi place in Reston, Molly Kronberg joined us to scope out LaRouche's present official residence. Another mansion on elevated ground, called Windy Hill.

Finding the place was harder than anticipated. In the last decade, ugly million-dollar houses have sprouted in the fields like fiberglass mushrooms. After a right turn down an unmarked road, the landscape looked suddenly familiar to Chris. There, at the end of the lane, was a five-barred gate to the estate. A pair of sculpted hounds stood guard on the posts, beside which was planted an archaic-looking intercom system. A security camera gazed in our direction. Up on the hill, the vague shape of a house was discernible through the trees. I wondered about getting out to take a photograph.

"I don't know whether that's a good idea," said Molly. "They have guns." We paused, taking time to watch a family of deer peering back at us from the other side of the fence. They held our gaze for a while, then skittered off into the trees. Chris restarted the car and we made our way back up the road. A large black Saab was coming the other way. As it passed us, we saw the occupants. Two unfriendly young men in black suits, who shot us a suspicious look and thankfully nothing more.

THE WHITES HAVE been out of the LaRouche cult for twenty years. They would have left sooner, but felt obliged to remain while their comrades served out their prison sentences. Just as they were formulating an exit strategy, Chris fell seriously ill. A blood clot on his intestine required emergency surgery. His recovery was slow. With no savings and no health insurance, he and Carol relied on the patronage of the organization. With no employment history, they knew it would be hard to find work out in the real world. But Chris went first, setting up as a real estate agent and gradually developing a base of clients in the Leesburg area. Carol followed a year later. They managed to make a modest living—enough to buy a home of their own and a place to put all their books. They also made peace with their families.

Some former members feel compelled to follow the fortunes of the cult they left behind. The Whites are not among them. So when I told them I was planning to attend one of LaRouche's Saturday afternoon meetings in Manhattan, they told me to wear a padded vest. I felt pretty sure that the organization's nunchaku and pistol-whipping days were over, but I did take one or two precautions.

I downloaded the first draft of this book and all my documents onto a USB stick, and I stowed my laptop, camera, and notebooks in the luggage room at Penn Station. I texted my wife and a couple of friends with details of where to find them. I took a taxi to the venue, and when we reached the destination, I popped the memory stick through the glass with the fare and a ten-dollar tip. "If you hear about anything weird happening in the basement of this hotel," I told the driver, "would you take this to my publisher's office in the Flatiron Building?" Being a New York cabdriver, he didn't bat an eyelid. "Sure," he said.

The Hotel Beacon at Broadway and West Seventy-Fifth Street has a fancy lobby. The LaRouchies paid a weekly thousand-dollar charge to use its facilities and were made to enter through the side door. By the time I arrived, a couple of dozen people had already gathered in the basement conference room. Some looked familiar from the webcast. An enormous bearlike man with a copy of *China Daily* and a prodigious plumber's crack. A red-faced, choleric senior with a dozen ballpoint pens tucked in the front pocket of his lumberjack shirt. A loaf-haired woman who lined up her medications in a row as she squinted at a copy of *Executive Intelligence Review*—not the glossy magazine of old, but a stapled and photocopied fanzine.

There were a handful of younger members, too: intense, eager to please, as yet unhusked by the experience of living la vida Lyndon. One, a man with sweetly imperfect English, announced that he had just acquired American citizenship. He was carrying a celebratory sponge cake. Everyone applauded and tucked in.

After I'd filled out my registration form and coughed up $25 for a seventy-page report on the queen's plans for global genocide, two LaRouche ladies came over to chat. Margaret Scialdone, a friendly sixty-something who told me that in 1985 she'd quit her job in computer programming to devote herself full-time to the organization. Renee Sigerson, a hare-eyed figure who I later watched on a YouTube clip, proudly displaying a poster depicting Barack Obama as Hitler. ("He got that mustache," she told a heckler, "when he kissed the butt of the Queen of England.")

Renee informed me that there were LaRouche groups all over the world, but that some of them were probably MI6 operations. She might have said more, but up at the front Diane Sare, the leader of another LaRouche front, the Schiller Institute New York City Chorus, was firing up her Casio synth and announcing that we would now all join together to sing the opening of the Mozart *Requiem*. A score was provided.

Margaret guided me through the soprano part. "Solfège first," she said. "*Do re mi*. You remember *The Sound of Music*?" About half the room showed willing. The rest sat silently munching crackers or mulling over the latest LaRouchePAC handbill. I read it over someone's shoulder.

"In 2018," it announced, "a Chinese mission will reach the far side of the Moon—provided that we can succeed in defeating the British Empire's forces of chaos."

Once Mozart had been successfully murdered, the webcast began under the chairmanship of Dennis Speed, an NCLC lifer who, forty years ago, had led the African American Students Association at Swarthmore College. From beneath a necktie so huge it made him look like he'd stepped from the middle reel of *The Incredible Shrinking Man*, Dennis shared some bad news. LaRouche was in Germany and would not be participating in the day's discussion. Margaret thought that this was his wife's doing. ("Helga," she whispered, "keeps him on a tight leash.")

In his absence we watched a fuzzy twenty-year-old video of Lyn giving a lecture about Chinese railways. Nobody even pretended to make notes. This was followed by disquisitions on why the public were shamefully unaware of recent developments regarding trans-Eurasian refrigerated freight trains, and why Bertrand Russell was the most evil man of the twentieth century. People fussed with their papers and nibbled bits of cake. Their behavior seemed a little against the spirit of the thing. There they were, the new intellectual elite, poised to revive classical culture and defeat Elizabeth Windsor's plans for thermonuclear population management—and they were bored and listless. As I was ushered to the microphone to make my contribution, I did my best to change the temperature.

I began by apologizing for being from London. A ripple of interest moved through the basement. I pushed on with a brainwashing gag. "I can assure you," I said, "that I haven't been sent on some secret mission from Her Majesty. To my knowledge, at least."

They laughed. This, I suppose, was a bit more fun than berating Americans for their ignorance about how long it takes a head of lettuce to get from Moscow to Beijing. An enterprising stand-up could probably have run with it further, but I had to produce an actual question.

A few weeks before my trip, the world's press had been preoccupied by the story of the Panama Papers, a massive leak of private information on the dodgy tax and business affairs of some of the world's most influential people. The papers contained a small amount of dirt on the Russian president. Therefore, LaRouche declared, this was an attack on Vladimir Putin, coordinated by the West. By which, of course, he meant the British.

However, LaRouche's former ally Cliff Gaddy had published an article on the Brookings website that argued exactly the opposite. "Does this strike anyone else as a very fishy story?" he asked. "It's like something out of a cheap spy movie." The material on Putin, Cliff argued, was harmless trivia. It would be water off a duck's back. The release of the papers was, he suspected, a warning shot, signaling that the Kremlin had blackmail material on "real targets" in the USA. "You *reveal* secrets in order to *destroy*; *conceal* in order to *control*," wrote Cliff. "Putin is not a destroyer. He's a controller."

As I asked Dennis for his opinion on the competing theories of Gaddy and LaRouche, he smiled at the mention of Cliff's name. He pushed against the lectern and reminisced about a trip he'd made to Stockholm in March 1984, when he'd listened to Cliff and Bill Jones squabbling about what their respective families had done in the Civil War. "Well," said Bill to Cliff, "at least my family fought for the United States when it *counted*." Dennis chuckled indulgently, then embarked on an upbeat speech about the glory of the present Russian regime.

London feared Putin, said Dennis, because he was the most credible threat yet to the British East India Company, which had ruled our planet since 1763. "We don't automatically condemn you for your origins," he said, generously, "but we would wish that you might think through the deeper importance of what is actually happening. The final death of the British Empire is about to occur! And we are going to be very happy about that when we are responsible for it!" Everybody applauded furiously. Everybody, at last, was awake. What's the point of being in a cult if you can't enjoy yourself from time to time?

Twenty-four hours after the meeting, I was driving with Chris and Carol White for lunch at the Silver Diner in Reston, Virginia. An email from Bill Jones pinged onto my phone. "I told him to stop 'chasing moonbeams' and do something productive for mankind," it read. "Here is his response." He had shared my last email with a third party. It was impossible to see the identity of the recipient—LaRouche? The FBI? His sister in Missouri? Who knew? But the message was clear. I'd been found out.

I emailed back, describing what I'd heard at the meeting.

Bill replied: "How's that 'book' going?"

And at that moment, I knew that I had been assigned a place in the vast and senseless narrative of LaRouchian history. Bill thought that the book was a cover story, a pretext to spy upon him and his comrades. He thought that I was an infiltrator. And now he was tapping away at his keyboard, sharing his thoughts with the only people in the world who could take the idea seriously.

"Our lives were fiction, you know," Carol said to me as we drove. "A series of fictions." Chris, at the driver's wheel, made eye contact in the mirror.

"You hear that?" he said. "You'd better write that down."

Nearby, in a bungalow in Leesburg, the former leader of the American Deserters Committee added another twist to his own impossible story.

18 / CLIFFHANGER

HALF A CENTURY ago, the men at the heart of this story went into exile in Sweden. Their details were recorded in the press, and recorded again on the punch cards and magnetic tapes of HYDRA, the computer in the vault-within-the-Vault beneath CIA headquarters in Langley, Virginia. Most of these men are now back on American soil. But not all are at ease with their homeland, or their shared history, or themselves.

In late 2016, Chuck Onan left his house by the gravel quarry in Eugene, Oregon, and moved with his dog, Ninja, to cheaper accommodation on a farm twenty miles south of the city. For a while, email and social media provided me with a picture of his shifting moods. He filled my Facebook feed with his increasingly extreme anti-Islamic views, supported by videos of ISIS beheadings and links to white nationalist websites. "Soon there will be neither Sweden or the Swedes," he wrote. "The Islamists will rip your throat by 2020." But from time to time, he would send me lyrical messages about Scandinavian literature; when my favorite sitcom was canceled, he wrote a post urging his alt-right friends to sign a petition to save it. It looked deeply incongruous on a timeline full of paeans to Marine Le Pen and Geert Wilders and Patriots Against the Islamization of North America.

Of the deserters who traveled with Mark Shapiro from Japan to Moscow to Sweden, two are now dead. Terry Whitmore returned to Mississippi in 2001 and lived there among his family for six more years. His memoir, *Memphis Nam Sweden*, remains the best firsthand account of the Swedish deserter experience. Joe Kmetz, who lost his words after months of hiding in a little room in Tokyo, breathed his last in New Jersey in 2004.

Mark Shapiro's health remains fragile. When we speak on the phone, the expression "ironing my last shirt" is often on his lips. He has yet to find a piece of killer evidence that will prove his theory that George Carrano was the intelligence mole within the deserter community. He knows that he is unlikely to find it. The object of these suspicions is now retired and engaged in charitable works in his community, after a career in the management of the New York transit system, where, in the late 1970s, his boss was a former CIA officer once employed on Richard Ober's campaign against *Ramparts* magazine. Another fact for Mark to compute. The uneasy friendship between these two old ADC comrades continues. Mark tickles him with enquiries about his past. George supplies answers that fail to satisfy the questioner. And so their dance goes on.

I JOINED IT, much to my surprise, in September 2017. The invitation came by telephone.

"I have George on the line," said Mark. "He wants to talk."

On the phone, George was not the confident, silver-tongued character described by his former comrades. His tone was mild and apologetic. If he resented the fact that Mark and I had spent several years speculating about his loyalties, then he did not betray it. Indeed, he admitted that some of the details of his biography were rather hard to swallow—how many people in the world had been in both the merchant marine and the SDS? For an hour and a half we examined the wrinkles in his story. During his Stockholm years he had claimed to be a graduate of the Columbia School of Journalism. This, he conceded, was untrue—he had invented the detail to protect a Swedish girlfriend who had procured him a journalist's visa. "It was just a convenience," he said. "I was under a lot of stress." What about his relationship with the Swedish Aliens Commission? How, I wondered, had he obtained humanitarian asylum in August 1968, six months before draft resisters became eligible? George did not recall any such process, and was baffled when I sent some newspaper clippings that reported his change in status. "It's a simple story," he said, "made confusing because the bureaucracy made, and continued to make, classification errors." He intended to take up the matter with the Swedish government.

We discussed the doubts entertained by his friends. Michael Vale's principal charge against George was that he had risked provoking a diplomatic incident with a phony story about a great gang of American GIs who were ready to be shipped to Sweden with the help of the North Vietnamese. George's explanation was like a vignette from a spy film. The tale, he said, was fed to him on a trip to France, where he made contact with Max Watts and Arlo Jacobs, the bitter rival leaders of the Parisian deserter scene. Max, he recalled, was overseeing "a crazy Punch and Judy show" in which journalists interviewed GIs who were hidden behind a sheet to protect their identities. Arlo, conversely, had no such men in his charge. He was running a deserter group without any deserters. Instead, he took George on a cloak-and-dagger tour of the boulevards. "We went to three different cafés," said George. "I suppose he wanted to check if we were being followed." In the final venue, George came face to face with a French revolutionary whom Arlo wanted him to meet. A dark-haired, seedy-looking figure who used the code-name Adrian and talked about his connections with Che Guevara. It was the mysterious Adrian, said George, who urged the ADC to treat with the enemy and bring two hundred men from Indochina to Sweden. "But he was talking in whispers," said George. "And his English was very poor. In the end I thought maybe I'd misunderstood." The punchline was one calculated to appeal to my interest in old British movies. "I felt," George said, "like the casting director on *The Man Between*."

I asked George for his own theories about infiltrators within the ADC. He was sure that there were American expatriates living in Stockholm who sent intelligence back home, but he didn't believe that any ADC members were among them. "Michael and I had our falling out," he said, "but it wasn't over me thinking that he was some kind of agent." Their disagreements were about strategy—the attacks on Bertil Svahnström, the trip to Bulgaria that turned the ADC into the stars of a Soviet propaganda film.

He did confess, however, to feeling disturbed by Michael Vale's psychological dominance of some members of their group. "He liked to break people," he said. To George, the men who followed Michael into the Next Step and the LaRouche organization seemed the most broken. "The way they were was a lot the result of Michael's intense dealings with them. They took on this harsh character themselves. They became his acolytes in a strange sort of way. They were almost like Jonestown people, ready to go for the Kool-Aid."

THE SURVIVORS OF the Next Step—Bill Jones, Cliff Gaddy, Warren Hamerman, and Jim McGourty—live within forty miles of one another in the commuter belt around Washington, DC. They do not hold reunions. Warren is particularly keen to avoid contact with witnesses to his former life as LaRouche's most loyal retainer. His reasons may be professional as much as personal. He spent his post-LaRouchian career as a technical writer and IT consultant, and his clients included the Department of Homeland Security and the U.S. Citizenship and Immigration Services. Perhaps he figured these government agencies would have been unhappy about employing someone who had once been a member of an organization proscribed by the FBI. He and his wife Nora now live in a 1980s condominium in Reston, Virginia, where Nora teaches piano to private students.

Like many who left the cult in middle age, the Hamermans used their freedom to adopt children. LaRouche discouraged reproduction among his followers. "The moment the leadership discovered a pregnancy," Christina Nelson told me, "spouses were isolated from one another and sessions started until the woman caved in and agreed to terminate it." Once they were free of the organization, she and Jim McGourty also contacted the adoption agencies. On one of my visits, I met their teenage son, a polite young man who had grown up in that large house in their quiet corner of Loudoun County, surrounded by prints of Italian Renaissance masterpieces.

Jim retired from St. John Bosco High School in 2007. He now offers his services as a private math tutor. He and Christina worry about big things—the moral decline of America, the liberality of its abortion laws—but life for them is settled, quiet, and comfortable. Jim would like to be reconciled with his son from his marriage to Michele, but he's not holding his breath. The young man was married in August 2007. Jim was not invited to the ceremony and has yet to meet his grandchildren.

THERE IS SOME good news, however, from Loudoun County. Its residents no longer have Lyndon Hermyle LaRouche Jr. for a neighbor. During the summer of 2016, the leader of the Labor Committees left his mansion on Windy Hill, with its barbed wire and its armed guards. His wife Helga Zepp-LaRouche took him to live with her in Germany, where, when the time comes, she will bury him with all the ceremony that befits the greatest statesman of our times. That moment, however, may be years off. Only the good die young, and at the end of 2016 LaRouche, despite his age and frailty, showed that his opportunist instincts were still intact and successfully executed one of the nimblest ideological somersaults of his long career.

Like much of the rest of the world, LaRouche and his followers spent that year sniggering behind their hands at the Republican candidate for the U.S. presidency. The organization even recorded a satirical song suggesting that the candidate's core constituents were mentally ill. "He's a festering pustule on Satan's rump!" trilled the singer. "Don't you be a chump for Trump!" But when Hillary Clinton conceded defeat, the tune changed. Suddenly, Donald Trump was not, as had been previously thought, a maniac poised to legalize heroin and govern on behalf of Wall Street, but America's best chance to defeat the British Empire and forge a new alliance with Russia.

The LaRouche membership, inured to every kind of switcheroo, sang from the new hymn sheet without protest. Fresh articles and handbills warned that Barack Obama and the financier George Soros were plotting a "color revolution" against the victorious candidate. Heroic work was done by LaRouche pundits, who transmuted Trump's solecisms into art: "In the way he used the term 'the failing *New York Times*,'" declared one, "I sensed a note of poetry." When a leaked intelligence report by a former MI6 officer listed the LaRouche Political Action Committee among the recent recipients of Kremlin hospitality, the cult made hay—it was more evidence of British perfidy.

Then, in February 2017, I was watching a live feed of one of the first White House press briefings of the Trump administration when the camera focused on a familiar face: Bill Jones, bowling a softball question in the direction of the president's spokesperson Sean Spicer. It was shocking to see him standing in the press room among all the real journalists from real publications. But the Trump White House was at ease with conspiracy theorists, and 2017 was a year of shocks.

ONE CAME, UNHERALDED, in January, when Clifford Gaddy left the Brookings Institution. No announcement was made; no press release was produced. References to him on the think tank's website were simply shunted into the past tense. The "Senior Fellow" became a "Former Expert." Where Cliff had gone, or why he had left, the Brookings press officer declined to say. He was simply "not giving interviews at the moment." Other sources, however, suggested that he'd been silent for some time. Cliff, I was informed, had barely been seen in the building for the past six months. He'd not even RSVP'd for the Brookings centenary party.

Perhaps his reasons were personal. Cliff had reached his seventieth birthday in June 2016. On December 27, his mother, Inez Chapman Gaddy, died in Danville at the age of ninety-two. But at the beginning of March 2017, the story acquired another twist. Reports began to circulate that Fiona Hill, the coauthor of *Mr. Putin: Operative in the Kremlin* and Cliff's staunch intellectual collaborator, was to be made Donald Trump's chief adviser on Russia.

In Washington, the news was received with surprise. Hill was a hawk on Putin and no fan of Trump. She had wondered aloud about the Kremlin's influence over the president. "Are they," she had asked a reporter from the *New Yorker*, "trying to turn him into the Manchurian Candidate?" On March 28, Hill's place was confirmed. The official announcement might have come sooner had her prospective boss General Michael

Flynn not resigned in disgrace after admitting to a series of compromising conversations with Russian officials.

Newspaper profiles discussed Hill's experience as an intelligence officer under George W. Bush and her modest childhood in the northeast of England. Most commentators noted that her reputation was founded on the book she had written with Cliff Gaddy. A researcher who was one of the world's most authoritative experts on Vladimir Putin at a moment when expertise on Vladimir Putin was urgently required—and yet was now sitting at home, apparently unemployed.

Had Cliff withdrawn to do intelligence work behind the scenes? Was he, perhaps, busy examining links between the U.S. president and the Russian state, just as, fifty years ago, the snoops of Operation Chaos had gone looking for Soviet influence on the deserters? Or had my inquiries played some small part in his disappearance?

Fiona Hill's appointment to the White House was bringing new scrutiny to her character and background. For years, Cliff's weird LaRouchian past had lain quietly in old copies of *Ny Solidaritet* and *Executive Intelligence Review*. Once released from those places, it would be a gift to Hill's enemies. The brainwash plot, the Palme assassination, the drug-pushing Queen of England. None of these stories would amplify the authority of the authors of *Mr. Putin*.

Hill was soon under attack from conspiracy theorists and alt-right apoplectics. A blogger in Moscow declared that she was a KGB sleeper agent and superimposed her face on the cover of an old horror comic entitled *Return of the Zombies*. Roger Stone, Donald Trump's former campaign adviser and a man happy to describe himself as an Agent of Chaos, went on the Infowars channel to accuse her of being a mole for George Soros. "Disgusting," said Strobe Talbott, the head of Brookings, as dubious online theorists ran with the idea.

IN THE MIDDLE of April 2017, I attended a lecture at the Brookings Institution. Its little bookstore was piled with fresh new paperback copies of *Mr. Putin: Operative in the Kremlin*. "Is this one of your bestsellers?" I asked, picking up a copy. The assistant pulled his ask-a-stupid-question face. "I hoped," he said, "he would do another book before he went."

Cliff, he confirmed, had left the think tank suddenly and unexpectedly. Nobody knew why he'd gone. "The news didn't go down well here," he said. "It's kind of a mystery."

Two days later, on Good Friday, I walked through the suburbs of Washington with a letter in my hand. The blossoms were out. The people weren't. Cliff's street, I noticed, shared a name with the road in Colindale on which Chris White had made his ill-fated attempt to expose a spy and an infiltrator. On that night, Cliff had maintained a policy of silence. Just as he had done with me.

The Gaddys' place was a corner house on a grassy slope. I climbed the cement steps up to the front door. It was ajar. I could hear voices coming from inside. My letter laid out two interpretations of Cliff's life. Two hypotheses on which I had settled, but between which I had been unable to choose, despite several years of trying.

Cliff was a deserter who got involved with a cult but found a lucky, Pentagon-funded escape into a fancy Washington think tank. Or Cliff was an operative, and always had been. An operative in the American Deserters Committee. An operative in the Next Step. An operative among the LaRouchians. An operative in Brookings. An operative now having lunch at home, with a journalist standing on his doorstep, who knew that his own work was unlikely to reduce the amount of chaos in the world.

I put the envelope on a chair on the veranda. It was a beautiful spring day. Perhaps later, Cliff would come out to watch the sunset and find he had something to read.

WHEN I GOT back to London, I met up with a friend for a drink. I told him about my trip to Washington. I was going to end the book, I said, with the image of my letter sitting on Cliff's chair. Not, sadly, a rocking chair, but you couldn't have everything. It was American enough.

He burst out laughing. "You've seen the film, haven't you?" he asked. We were in the Edgar Wallace pub, named in honor of England's most prolific thriller writer. The back of our booth was a wall of yellowback crime and espionage novels. "Don't you remember the ending of *The Parallax View*?" I did. Warren Beatty thought he'd exposed the villains, but realized, in the closing moments, that he'd become part of their operation. Then he got shot.

"Who benefits," my friend asked, "if Cliff gets into a load of trouble about cults and brainwashing and a dead Swedish prime minister?"

"Well," I said. "Vladimir Putin, obviously. But I can't do much about that. I just had to follow the story."

"No," he said. "Someone you've talked to. Who wanted you to write it this way?"

WHEN I BEGAN this story, I thought I might crack its code, experience the thrill of exposing a CIA mole inside a group of isolated and troubled young men. Instead, I had written a history of their agonies, an account of how it felt to live life in a cloud of suspicion and uncertainty. Some of these men had told me their secrets. Some had lied to me. But all those who talked had a reason to talk. Jim McGourty craved reconciliation with his son. Bill Jones wanted to feel important in a fancy Washington restaurant. Mark Shapiro wanted an ally in his obsessions. Chuck Onan wanted to defend the reputation of his old mentor. His own, too, perhaps.

I had failed them all. Jim's testimony could not sweeten a relationship poisoned by LaRouchian paranoia. Bill's need to be interviewed like a real Washington correspondent had brought us, inevitably, to a row about his entrapment in a life-sapping cult. I stood no chance of satisfying Mark's desire for a deathbed confession from George Carrano. (Mark's deathbed, not George's.) As for Chuck, I knew the lies he'd told about the Vietnam War, and that had reduced us both to silence.

Michael Vale, however, was a different case. In the beginning, I assumed the rumors about him were true. I thought he was the villain of the piece. A CIA operative charged to bring discord and division to the deserter community in Stockholm. I had seen his cruel side. I had observed the delight with which he'd recalled his ability to reduce impressionable young people to tears. He'd never tried that on me. But this crumpled little guy I'd been meeting, on and off, for the past three years had exerted his influence. Without really trusting him, I had grown to like him and to feel sympathy with the strange narrative of his life.

He was a man who had used his knowledge of psychology and politics to prepare the deserters for revolution, and then found the tide of that revolution turned against him. His loyal comrades had defected to a cult that sabotaged his career, harassed him in restaurants, and assigned him a role in their paranoid view of the world. Michael had considered himself a mentor to Cliff Gaddy, Warren Hamerman, Bill Jones, and Jim McGourty, and they had betrayed him. Through me, however, he had achieved a kind of justice. Lyndon LaRouche had stolen his protégés. But in telling this story, they had become his once more. The Stockholm deserters and their Gray Eminence, bound together in the pages of a book.

I emailed him. His reply came from the Philippines. "I've finally begun to get a purchase on some understanding of this vile, repugnant place," he wrote. "I'll be back in the summer. Probably London. My hearing aids are playing up."

I'd sent him a list of questions to clarify some details of his early life. His travels. His education. His reading in Soviet psychiatry. He answered them fully and generously. But at the end of his email he wrote: "Matthew, to tell the truth, what exactly and specifically this book of yours is about still eludes my grasp."

"We'll discuss it when you come to London," I replied. "Let's meet where we first met. Islington Green. Last bench on the right."

NOTES

All quotations from individuals are from interviews conducted by the author, unless otherwise indicated.

INTRODUCTION: DEEP SNOW

3   the influence of a cult: For the cult nature of Lyndon LaRouche's organizations, see "Judgment Is Reduced in NBC Libel Case," *New York Times*, February 24, 1985; Dennis King, *Lyndon LaRouche and the New American Fascism* (New York: Doubleday, 1989); Robert Mackey, "Visitors from Planet LaRouche," *New York Times*, August 25, 2009; Alexandra Stein, *Terror, Love and Brainwashing: Attachment in Cults and Totalitarian Systems* (London: Routledge, 2016).

4   "the takeover by the CIA of the United States of America": "Injunction Against CIA and NYC Police for Insurrection Against U.S. Government," handbill, National Caucus of Labor Committees records, Manuscripts and Archives Division, New York Public Library.

1: THE HIGH ROAD

11   "It's them, man": For the source of much of the information in this chapter, see Terry Whitmore, *Memphis Nam Sweden: The Story of a Black Deserter* (Garden City, NY: Doubleday, 1971).

13   "gooks" and "slant-eyed bastards": Thomas Hayes, *American Deserters in Sweden: The Men and Their Challenge* (New York: Association Press, 1971), p. 94.

13   a $1,000 stipend from the Kremlin in their pockets: Johan Erlandsson, *Desertörerna* [The deserters] (Stockholm: Carlsson, 2016), p. 39.

14   They had been smuggled into Russia by an outfit called Beheiren: Thomas R. H. Havens, *Fire Across the Sea: The Vietnam War and Japan 1965–1975* (Princeton,

NJ: Princeton University Press, 2006), pp. 54–76. The name is an acronym for Betonamu ni Heiwa o! Shimin Rengō, or Citizens' Federation for Peace in Vietnam.

14   Joan Baez had performed: Ibid., p. 116.

14   full-page ads in the *Washington Post*: *Japan Times*, "Reasons for Placing Ad in U.S. Paper Explained," April 5, 1967.

14   preparing hiding places and airing the spare bedding: Havens, *Fire Across the Sea*, p. 144.

14   Oda Makoto: Peter Kelman, "Protesting the National Identity: The Cultures of Protest in 1960s Japan" (PhD diss., University of Sydney, 2001), p. 168.

15   having saved Ed Sullivan from humiliation: Michael Harris, *Always on Sunday: An Inside View of Ed Sullivan, the Beatles, Elvis, Sinatra . . . and Ed's Other Guests* (New York: Meredith Press).

15   the "Moron Corps": See Thomas Sticht, "Project 100,000 in the Vietnam War and After" in *Scraping the Barrel: The Military Use of Sub-Standard Manpower, 1860–1960*, ed. Sanders Marble (New York: Fordham University Press, 2012), pp. 224–68.

15   a Christmas bedside visit from President Lyndon B. Johnson: See Whitmore, *Memphis Nam Sweden*, pp. 85–88.

16   a four-minute film: "Anti-Yanks Sneak Griggs from Japan," *Idaho Free Press*, February 28, 1968.

19   "For those of you on the battlefields": "Six Real Men," *Win*, June 1, 1968.

19   he gave testimony that shocked and baffled the world: UPI, "Deserter Tells Weird Tales on Moscow TV," *Greenville (SC) News*, May 9, 1968.

19   Edwin C. Arnett had been an army cook: Erlandsson, *Desertörerna*, p. 156.

20   the possibility of becoming an unwitting combatant in the propaganda war: Yuri Andropov, head of the KGB, to the Committee for State Security of the USSR Council of Ministers, February 24, 1968, Library of Congress, http://lcweb2.loc .gov/frd/tfrussia/tfrhtml/tfr032-1.html.

21   *Knet, Arnet, Kollikot*: Ibid.

21   "I thought he was dead": "Stunned Family Hears Navy Deserter Filmed," *Salem (OR) Statesman-Journal*, May 5, 1968.

21   "If it's true, we disown him": "Nyack Man Listed as Defector to Soviets," *White Plains (NY) Journal News*, May 10, 1968.

21   Arnett's tales dominated the headlines: Reuters, "U.S. Deserters in Moscow Tell of "Atrocities' in Viet," May 4, 1968; UPI, "Six Deserters on Moscow TV: U.S. G.I.s Called More Brutal Than Hitler's SS," *Cincinnati Enquirer*, May 5, 1968.

22   In the shots from that day: "Deserters Reach Sweden," *White Plains (NY) Journal News*, May 27, 1968; "More Deserters Arrive in Sweden Seeking Asylum," *Long Beach (CA) Independent-Press-Telegram*, May 26, 1968.

22   A press conference was coalescing: Whitmore, *Memphis Nam Sweden*, pp. 172–73.

23   "At least Sweden ain't Mississippi": Ibid., p. 175.

23   UPI sent out a story by Virgil Kret: Virgil Kret, "GI Deserter Changes Tune on Moscow TV," *Chicago Tribune*, May 27, 1968.

23   "he spoke English like a Japanese bar girl": Ibid.

24   a California charity dinner attended by Mr. and Mrs. Zeppo Marx: "It's All Over, Even the Shouting," *Desert Sun* (Palm Springs, CA), November 5, 1964.

24   "time poem": Paul Krassner, "The Assassination Hotline," *Berkeley (CA) Barb*, November 4, 1976.

24   *The Obituary of the World*: Virgil Kret, *The Obituary of the World*, http:// icnews360.blogspot.co.uk.

2: THE COMMITTEE

28 "They call you a man": Hayes, *American Deserters in Sweden*, p. 63.

31 "this violent indignation of alienated people": Bill Jones, typewritten speech, April 20, 1968, Papers of Hans Göran Franck, Arbetarrörelsens arkiv och bibliotek [The Swedish Labor Movement's Archive and Library], Stockholm.

32 a private tribunal to investigate American war crimes in Vietnam: Bertrand Russell, *War Crimes in Vietnam* (London: Allen & Unwin, 1967).

32 a notorious article entitled "Sin and Sweden": Joe David Brown, "Sin and Sweden," *Time*, April 25, 1955.

32 "Ten percent of the infected boys": Alfred Zanker, "Life in a Great Society," *U.S. News & World Report*, February 7, 1966.

33 "The goal of democracy": Olof Palme, speech, February 21, 1968, http://www.olofpalme.org/wp-content/dokument/680221c vietnamdemonstration.pdf.

33 police batons drawing blood outside the U.S. Embassy: "FNL-demonstranter och polis är överens om 20 december-väg" [FNL demonstrators and police in agreement over 20 December route"], *Dagens Nyheter*, December 17, 1968; "3000 visade snällt sitt förakt för USA, Nilsson och Wallenberg" ["300 kindly showed their contempt for the USA, Nilsson and Wallenberg"], *Dagens Nyheter*, December 21, 1968.

33 "leftist mob": *U.S. News & World Report*, February 19, 1968; Noel Grove, Newspaper Enterprise Association, "Swedish-American Relations Go from Neutral to Reverse," *St. Cloud (MN) Times*, May 26, 1968.

34 a barrage of hate mail and rotten eggs: Associated Press, "U.S. Recalls Ambassador in Stockholm," *Baltimore Sun*, March 9, 1968.

34 The U.S. State Department threatened: Carl-Gustaf Scott, *Swedish Social Democracy and the Vietnam War* (Huddinge, Sweden: Södertörns högskola, 2017).

34 The International Longshoremen's Association warned: Victor Reisel, "Union Plans to Hit Sweden," *Montana Standard* (Butte, MT), April 11, 1968.

34 The NBC anchorman Frank McGee: *The Frank McGee Report*, NBC, February 25, 1968.

34 "They are bums": Associated Press, "G.I. Deserters Called Bums," *Pittsburgh Post-Gazette*, January 26, 1968.

35 the man was loaded into a van and driven away: Michael Vale, email message to the author, April 13, 2017; Dan Israel, telephone interview with the author, February 23, 2016.

35 the landmark study *There Are No Naughty Children*: Joachim and Mirjam Valentin-Israel, *Det Finns Inga Elaka Barn!* [There are no naughty children!] (Stockholm: Norstedt, 1946).

36 "Vietnamese people": UPI, "Reports of GIs Deserting," *Cincinnati Enquirer*, September 10, 1967.

40 an attempt to induce neurosis in laboratory apes: G. M. Cherkovich, "Experimental Neurosis in Apes Induced by Disturbance of a Daily Stereotype," trans. Michel [Michael] Vale, *Soviet Psychology* 8 (1969).

40 the effects of "conflict situations": G. O. Magakyan, "Neurogenous Hypotension in Apes as a Model of Neurocirculatory Hypotension (Human Hypotension)," trans. Michel Vale, *Soviet Psychology* 8 (1969).

40 *Forensic Psychiatry*, a textbook: G. V. Morozov and Ia. M Kalashnik, *Forensic Psychiatry*, trans. Michel Vale (White Plains, NY: International Arts and Sciences Press, 1970).

40 the Serbsky had begun to acquire a reputation as a psychiatric gulag: Peter Reddaway, "Five Years in the Life of Piotr Grivogenko," *The Listener*, February 20, 1969.

40   "You've got to admire him, though": Lucinda Franks, *Waiting Out a War: The Exile of Private John Picciano* (New York: Coward, McCann, Geoghegan, 1974), p. 136.

41   Margareta Hedman: email message to the author, July 28, 2015.

41   Sigal had been an army observer: Clancy Sigal, *Black Sunset: Hollywood Sex, Lies, Betrayal, and Raging Egos* (Berkeley, CA: Soft Skull Press, 2016), pp. 31–32.

41   The FBI tapped his phones: Clancy Sigal, "The Problem with Clint Eastwood's Hoover," *Counterpunch*, December 15, 2011, http://www.counterpunch.org /2011/12/05/the-problem-with-clint-eastwoods-hoover.

42   Pristine, unfingermarked copies: James V. Werstch, *Recent Trends in Soviet Psycholinguistics*, trans. Michel Vale (White Plains, NY: M. E. Sharpe, 1978); Pavel Câmpenau, *The Genesis of the Stalinist Social Order*, trans. Michel Vale (Armonk, NY: M. E. Sharpe, 1989).

42   Ralph Miliband, the father: See Philip Wallace, "Critique: More Than 30 Years of Socialist Theory," *Critique,* April 2007.

42   "independent scholar": American Association for the Advancement of Slavic Studies 41st National Convention, November 12–15, 2009, https://aseees.org /sites/default/files/u29/2009program.pdf.

3: THE TRANSLATOR

48   "The abstract, humanitarian, moralist view of history is barren": Isaac Deutscher, *The Prophet Armed. Trotsky: 1879–1921* (Oxford: Oxford University Press, 1954), p. 202.

52   when the real Jesus Zeus Lorenzo Mungi was killed in action: Shelley Marshall, telephone interview with the author, August 25, 2016.

52   he was jailed in 1970 for dealing in LSD and died in prison: "Desertör fick 3,5 år för knark" [Deserter got 3.5 years for drugs], *Dagens Nyheter*, April 4, 1970.

52   a witty memoir of his desertion: John Ashley, "The Deserter," *Washington Post*, February 3, 1969. The article quotes a letter Ashley sent to his parents from Cincinnati, Ohio, in January 1968: "Not smoking, not drinking or taking LSD." But all those with whom I discussed his Swedish years told me he did not remain abstemious.

53   two American eavesdroppers were found hiding in a cupboard: Barry Fockler, interview with the author, April 4, 2012.

53   "The Swedes have a natural prejudice against black people": James Helbert, "America's Critics Rebuked," *Pittsburgh Press*, March 19, 1968.

54   "I am here," Russell announced: "*Army Times*-redaktören: Avhoppade USA-soldater utnyttjas av Sverige" [*Army Times* editor: Deserting USA Soldiers are being exploited by Sweden], *Svenska Dagbladet*, March 15, 1968.

54   "All these men are still enlisted": Ibid.

54   "Despite our concerted attempts": Ibid.

55   "This is a clear indication": "A Statement by Bill Jones on the Jerum Affair," March 1968, Papers of Hans Göran Franck, Arbetarrörelsens arkiv och bibliotek [The Swedish Labor Movement's Archive and Library], Stockholm.

4: THE JERUM AFFAIR

57   a transcript of the call between Russell and Vale: "A Statement by Bill Jones on the Jerum Affair," March 1968, Papers of Hans Göran Franck, Arbetarrörelsens arkiv och bibliotek [The Swedish Labor Movement's Archive and Library], Stockholm.

59 "stormy operation": See "CIA-försök tvinga desertörerna hem," *Svenska Dagbladet*, March 21, 1968.
59 "There is evidence for close collaboration": Bo Hammar, "Hur LBJs agenter arbetar i Sverige" [How LBJ's agents operate in Sweden], *Tidsignal*, March 1968.
59 "See how we love our country?": Hayes, *American Deserters in Sweden*, p. 65.
61 court-martialed for going absent without official leave: UPI, "First GI to Flee to Sweden, Back with Unit, Faces Trial," *Amarillo (TX) Globe-Times*, April 3, 1968.
61 a bad conduct discharge and four months' hard labor: UPI, "G.I. Who Returned from Sweden Gets 4 Months," *Los Angeles Times*, April 4, 1968.
61 "Ray will now be free": "Declaration of Ray Jones III to the Aliens Commission," Papers of Hans Göran Franck, Arbetarrörelsens arkiv och bibliotek [The Swedish Labor Movement's Archive and Library], Stockholm.
61 Ray Jones's deposition to the Swedish Aliens Commission: Ibid.
62 "One of the first days of March": Ibid.
62 acting executive secretary of the Fair Play for Cuba Committee: See Bill Simpich, "Fair Play for Cuba and the Cuban Revolution," *Counterpunch*, July 24, 2009, http://www.counterpunch.org/2009/07/24/fair-play-for-cuba-and-the-cuban-revolution/.
62 His declassified FBI and CIA files: Richard Gibson CIA file 1994.04.26.09:35:40:220005, https://www.maryferrell.org/showDoc.html?docId=55454&search=richard_gibson#relPageId=1&tab=page; Richard Gibson FBI record 124-90148-10001, https://www.maryferrell.org/showDoc.html?docId=118699&relPageId=1&search=124-90148-10001.
62 "to penetrate the ranks of the international revolutionary movement": *La Révolution Africaine*/Richard Gibson, CIA file 104-10217-10204, https://www.maryferrell.org/showDoc.html?docId=108725&search=104-10217-10204#relPageId=1&tab=page.
63 a letter typed by Gibson: Richard Gibson, CIA file 1993.07.09.18:45:58:460330, https://www.maryferrell.org/showDoc.html?docId=57826&search=460330#relPageId=1&tab=page.
63 Gibson had made similar overtures to the FBI: FBI memorandum 124-90147-10095, https://www.maryferrell.org/showDoc.html?docId=121828&relPageId=1&search=124-90147-10095.
65 "a weasel-like character": FBI memorandum 124-90147-10095, https://www.maryferrell.org/showDoc.html?docId=121828&relPageId=1&search=124-90147-10095.
65 The information was supplied by Ray Jones IV: Ray Jones IV, email correspondence with the author, May 2017.
65 "A prominent Swedish figure": Bill Jones, speech, April 20, 1968, Papers of Hans Göran Franck, Arbetarrörelsens arkiv och bibliotek [The Swedish Labor Movement's Archive and Library], Stockholm.
66 "We have chosen a side in the struggle": "A Statement by Bill Jones on the Jerum Affair," March 1968, Papers of Hans Göran Franck, Arbetarrörelsens arkiv och bibliotek, [The Swedish Labor Movement's Archive and Library], Stockholm.
66 "We'd rather not take a chance on foul-ball soldiers": "Army Says 'Rotten Few' Were Already in Trouble," *Washington Post*, January 16, 1968.
67 "He was wrong": *Sekai Waga Kokoro no Tabi* [My heart travels the world] (Japan: NHK, 2002).
68 "The man with the guts": "Coward," *Second Front Review*, n.d., 1968.
68 "The more shit you will take": Ray Krzeminski, "Now Hear This," *Second Front Review*, n.d., 1968.

69   "Hello, all you happy defenders of freedom": Mark Worrell Collection, Arbetar-rörelsens arkiv och bibliotek [The Swedish Labor Movement's Archive and Library], Stockholm.

5: PETUNIA

72   The protagonist is a naïve man named Matthew: Tarjei Vesaas, *Fuglane* [The birds], trans. Torbjørn Støverud and Michael Barnes (London: Peter Owen Publishers, 2013).

75   a 2005 Swedish television documentary: *Ramp om historia: Tillbaka till Vietnam*, [Ramp on history: Back to Vietnam], utbildningsradion, June 7, 2005.

76   The World Festival of Youth and Students: Karin Taylor, *Let's Twist Again: Youth and Leisure in Socialist Bulgaria* (Vienna: Lit Verlag, 2006), pp. 53–56.

77   committed the evidence to celluloid: *A Time to Live* (USSR: Soviet Documentary Film Unit, 1968).

79   They gave an impromptu press conference: Associated Press, "Two G.I.s Denied Swedish Visas," *St. Louis Post-Dispatch*, August 17, 1968.

79   "I don't know where to go if I will be expelled": Ibid.

79   he'd given himself up to the authorities: "Deserter Given a Year in Prison," *Arizona Daily Star*, September 11, 1968.

79   all the names he could remember: See *Organized Subversion in the U.S. Armed Forces: Hearings Before the Subcommittee to Investigate the Administration of the Internal Security Act and Other Internal Security Laws of the Committee on the Judiciary, United States Senate* (Washington, DC: U.S. Government Publishing Office, 1976), pp. 59–60.

79   Michael Randle, an anti-nuclear activist: Max Watts, unpublished typescript, "The Randle Factor," TORD 58, Brünn-Harris-Watts Papers, Internationaal Instituut voor Sociale Geschiedenis [International Institute of Social History], Amsterdam.

81   Baby A was a troubled Texas teenager: Max Watts, unpublished typescript, "Baby A," TORD 54.4, Brünn-Harris-Watts Papers, Internationaal Instituut voor Sociale Geschiedenis [International Institute of Social History], Amsterdam.

81   a Dutch woman in an apartment on the rue Saint-Jacques: Max Watts, unpublished typescript, "Baby A," TORD 74, Brünn-Harris-Watts Papers, Internationaal Instituut voor Sociale Geschiedenis [International Institute of Social History], Amsterdam.

81   Marguerite Duras, the novelist: Max Watts, unpublished typescript, "Mononucleosis and Marguerite Duras," TORD 19, Brünn-Harris-Watts Papers, Internationaal Instituut voor Sociale Geschiedenis [International Institute of Social History], Amsterdam.

81   The expatriate American artist Alexander Calder: Dick Perrin with Tim McCarthy, *G.I. Resister* (Victoria, BC: Trafford Publishing, 2002), p. 89.

81   Jane Fonda, hugely pregnant: Max Watts, unpublished typescript, "Fonda You," TORD 75.1, Brünn-Harris-Watts Papers, Internationaal Instituut voor Sociale Geschiedenis [International Institute of Social History], Amsterdam.

81   her zero-gravity nudity: Perrin with McCarthy, *G.I. Resister*, p. 87–89.

81   Catherine Deneuve accepted his apologies: Watts, "Fonda You."

81   allies of the new French revolution: Perrin with McCarthy, *G.I. Resister*, p. 107.

82   "did more harm to RITA": Max Watts, unpublished typescript, "Was Arlo a Real Agent?," TORD 77.7, Brünn-Harris-Watts Papers, Internationaal Instituut voor Sociale Geschiedenis [International Institute of Social History], Amsterdam.

82 "When Arlo found me at the meeting": Max Watts, "Agents? Arlo Mongers and Starts Real Trouble," unpublished typescript, TORD 77.5, Brünn-Harris-Watts Papers, Internationaal Instituut voor Sociale Geschiedenis [International Institute of Social History], Amsterdam.

83 "That Arlo, deprived of an audience": Watts, "Was Ardo a Real Agent?"

84 "Phoneless Friends": Gilles Perrault, *A Man Apart: The Life of Henri Curiel* (London: Zed Books, 1997).

84 George Carrano went to Budapest: Frank Rafalko, *MH/CHAOS: The CIA'S Campaign Against the Radical New Left and the Black Panthers* (Annapolis, MD: Naval Institute Press, 2011), pp. 151–52.

84 the founder of the Cornell University chapter of the SDS: Bruce Dancis, *Resister: A Story of Protest and Prison During the Vietnam War* (Ithaca, NY: Cornell University Press, 2014).

84 "Next time, we attack": Ibid.

85 President Johnson had been briefed: "Weekly Summary Special Report: The Ill-Starred Ninth World Youth Festival," CIA file RDP79-00927A0065000 70002-4, https://www.cia.gov/library/readingroom/docs/CIA-RDP79-00927A 006500070002-4.pdf

87 "It's only in response to personal attacks": Email from George Carrano to Mark Shapiro, July 10, 2005.

88 a twelve-page report on the 1968 World Festival of Youth: *Report on the Ninth World Youth Festival*, September 17, 1968, John W. Dean Collection, Richard Nixon Presidential Library and Museum, Yorba Linda, CA.

88 "individual psychological and behavioral problems": Ibid.

88 A report from July 1969: CIA 1993.07.13.19:42:04:280400, http://www.mary ferrell.org/showDoc.html?docId=59385&relPageId=1&search=petunia.

89 "Our main contact there": Larry Cox, email message to the author, February 22, 2016.

89 Another report, from April 1972: CIA file 104-10071-10026, http://www.mary ferrell.org/showDoc.html?docId=27605&search=MHYIELD#relPageId =1&tab=page.

90 planting time bombs in safety deposit boxes: "1971 Radical Pleads Guilty to Planting Bombs in Banks," *New York Times*, April 29, 1987.

90 Harry Pincus hanged himself the following month: Alessandra Stanley, "Most Likely to Succeed," *New York Times*, November 22, 1992.

90 "going to bed with the girl or guy—or child": Linda Wolfe, "The Doctor's Dilemma," *New York Magazine*, February 28, 1972.

90 "Despite intensive interviews": Seymour M. Hersh, "Huge C.I.A. Operation Reported in U.S. Against Antiwar Forces, Other Dissidents in Nixon Years," *New York Times*, December 22, 1974.

6: THE BIRTH OF CHAOS

91 In May, Black Panthers padded around the California state capitol: Joshua Bloom and Waldo E. Martin Jr., *Black Against Empire: The History and Politics of the Black Panther Party* (Oakland: University of California Press, 2016), pp. 57–62.

92 his days of compaigning in public should come to an end: Kenneth Reich, "The Bloody March That Shook LA," *Los Angeles Times*, June 23, 1997, http:// latimesblogs.latimes.com/thedailymirror/2009/05/crowd-battles-lapd-as-war -protest-turns-violent-.html.

92 On August 15, three senior CIA figures met: Rafalko, *MH/CHAOS*, p. 15.

92   The shoes laced with beard-killing thallium salts: Fabian Escalante, *Executive Action: 634 Ways to Kill Fidel Castro* (New York: Ocean Press, 2006).

92   published a translation of the *Anglo-Saxon Chronicle*: H. A. Rositzke, trans., *The Peterborough Chronicle* (New York: Columbia University Press, 1951).

93   an unauthorized jaunt into Soviet-controlled East Berlin: Harry Rositzke, *The USSR Today* (New York: John Day, 1973), p. xi.

93   "a certain Dickensian quality": Duane Clarridge, *A Spy for All Seasons* (New York: Simon and Schuster, 2009), p. 78.

93   So profound that a family acquaintance wrote to the FBI: Richard Ober, FBI file 1347000-0, MuckRock, https://cdn.muckrock.com/foia_files/2016/05/04/1347 000-0_-_5541_-_Section_1_Serial__1.PDF.

93   "Tight mouthed," they called him: Ibid.

93   His academic qualifications were impeccable: Ibid.

93   obliging his colleagues to cut loose some of their paid agents: Karen Paget, *Patriotic Betrayal: The Inside Story of the CIA's Secret Campaign to Enroll American Students in the Crusade Against Communism* (New Haven, CT: Yale University Press, 2015), pp. 366–67.

94   "We had awful things in mind": Evan Thomas, *The Very Best Men* (New York: Simon and Schuster, 1996), p. 330.

94   live tax-free in North Carolina: See Bailey v. State of North Carolina; Emory v. State of North Carolina; Patton v. State of North Carolina, North Carolina Department of Revenue, www.dor.state.nc.us/practitioner/individual/directives/pd-99-1.html.

95   Published reviews went into HYDRA's maw: Report to the President by the Commission on CIA Activities Within the United States, June 1975, https://www .fordlibrarymuseum.gov/LIBRARY/exhibits/Intelligence/RockComm_Chap11 _CHAOS.pdf.

98   "the extremist anti-war movement": Briefing Papers, Special Operations Group, Counter Intelligence Staff, June 1, 1972, MuckRock, https://cdn.muckrock.com /foia_files/2016/05/16/CHAOS.pdf.

98   an FBI tap installed on the phone of Howard Zinn: Howard Zinn, FBI file 100-360217, https://vault.fbi.gov/Howard%20Zinn%20.

98   a colorful intermediary named Brian Victoria: Associated Press, "Anti-U.S. Rioting in Japan," *St. Louis Post-Dispatch*, October 22, 1968.

99   "misguided youngsters gone astray in a foreign land": CIA file 104-10064-10013, memo from Thomas Karamessines, CIA deputy director of plans, October 1, 1968, http://www.maryferrell.org/showDoc.html?docId=26357&relPageId=1&search =104-10064-10013.

99   Crewman Robert Doyon was summoned: Robert Doyon, email correspondence with the author, December 25, 2016.

100   "When you're on deck being attacked by the Commies": Bernice Foley, "Chit and Chat," *Cincinnati Enquirer*, September 8, 1968.

100   arrived on a plane from Canada: See *Organized Subversion in the U.S. Armed Forces: Hearings Before the Subcommittee to Investigate the Administration of the Internal Security Act and Other Internal Security Laws of the Committee on the Judiciary, United States Senate* (Washington, DC: U.S. Government Printing Office, 1976), p. 56.

100   a report with flow charts, footnotes, and appendices: Ibid., pp. 50–62.

100   he made a run for the Canadian border: Thomas Lee Hayes to the staff of CALCAV, July 28, 1969, Clergy and Laity Concerned Records, Swarthmore College Peace Collection, Swarthmore, PA.

101   All the papers printed her picture: "Girl Grabs U.S. Defector in Stockholm Stickup Try," *International Herald Tribune*, July 19–20, 1969.

101 It remained a secret until 1976: *Organized Subversion in the U.S. Armed Forces.*

101 he considered leaving the anti-war movement: Fukumi Shinsuke, "Dassō enjō kara beihei to no Kyoto e," *Asahi Jānaru*, May 10, 1970, pp. 38–43.

102 "I'm not going to live like a tramp!": UPI, "G.I. Deserter Comes Home from Sweden," *Chicago Tribune*, September 15, 1968.

102 It took five months for Arnett to come to trial: For the details of Arnett's trial, see "Ft. Dix Begins Deserter Trial of Viet GI," *New York Post*, February 25, 1969; Maurice Carroll, "Army Defector Who Fled to Sweden Goes on Trial at Fort Dix," *New York Times*, February 26, 1969; Frank Mazza, "Reports Tokyo Girl Got GI to Go Over the Hill," *New York Daily News*, March 4, 1969; Frank Mazza, "Army Winds Up Its Case with Film of G.I. Who Fled," *New York Daily News*, March 5, 1969; "Defector Who Left Vietnam for Sweden Guilty of Desertion," *New York Times*, March 6, 1969.

103 On the steps of the court: "G.I. Who Deserted from Vietnam Gets 4 Years; Court-Martial Votes Term After Hearing Psychiatrist; Defendant, Stunned, Appeals 'to the People' for Backing," *New York Times*, March 7, 1969.

103 "We are all in agreement about the degree of punishment": Robert L. Rummel et al. to Richard Nixon, March 14, 1969. Richard Nixon Presidential Library and Museum, Yorba Linda, CA.

7: THE SPLIT

105 "I'm a big, bad marine": Whitmore, *Memphis Nam Sweden*, p. 180.

107 that "every free man has a legal right and moral duty: Rebecca Skarbeck, "A History of Resist," http://illiad.trincoll.edu/watk/manuscripts/reshistory.htm.

110 *Look* magazine made it the focus of a lavish illustrated article: Christopher S. Wren, "Deserter in Stockholm," *Look*, October 15, 1968.

110 The Italian film producer Carlo Ponti came talent scouting: Richard Fernandez to Susan Sontag, July 14, 1969, Clergy and Laity Concerned Records, Swarthmore College Peace Collection, Swarthmore, PA.

110 Vitarelle drowned in a boating accident: "Deserter Dies in Swedish Boat Mishap," *Amarillo (TX) Globe-Times*, July 17, 1969; Daniel Lang, "Out of It," *New Yorker*, May 25, 1970.

110 "The plot is about agents who try to infiltrate the ADC: UPI, "U.S. Deserters in Sweden Are Discontented," *Los Angeles Times*, November 10, 1968.

112 He procured a 16 mm print and kept it in his office like a piece of evidence: Information from Michael P. Richard, a sociologist for whom Svahnström screened the film.

112 "A climactic sequence": Howard Thompson, "'Deserter U.S.A.' Tells of Soldiers in Sweden," *New York Times*, November 25, 1969.

113 The film premiered in Sweden on April 14, 1969: AP, "American GIs, Draft Resisters in Film," *Cincinnati Enquirer*, April 18, 1969.

113 a small knot of protestors got to their feet: UPI, Ian Westergren, "Deserters Glorified in Film," *Palm Beach Post-Times*, May 11, 1969.

114 the human evidence of the Social Democrats' opposition: See Scott, *Swedish Social Democracy and the Vietnam War*, pp. 17–22.

114 "Now the initial fascination of desertion has worn off": See John Ashley, "The Deserter," *Washington Post*, February 3, 1969.

115 Jerry Dass, a troubled former Green Beret: "Statslös USA-desertör" [Stateless USA deserter], *Dagens Nyheter*, March 23, 1969.

115 Kempe also gave the ADC the use of forty-four acres of farmland: Hayes, *American Deserters in Sweden*, pp. 165–66.

115   "The work on the farm": "ADC-Farmen," *Second Front Review*, no. 7, 1969.
117   volunteer tutors into deprived neighborhoods of Baltimore: Gene Oishi, "Quiet Side of Social Revolution: Tutors Project Makes the Grade," *Baltimore Sun*, January 30 1967.
117   Jean-Paul Sartre was there: "La 'résistance américaine' en France," *Le Monde*, April 13, 1968.
118   "The French government and its police": Warren Hamerman and Alfred Schmidt, "Les déserteurs américains en France," *Esprit*, November 11, 1968.
118   The exception was George Carrano: UPI, "Nine Servicemen and Evader Given Asylum," *Syracuse Post-Standard*, August 3, 1968.
118   "SUPPORT WARREN HAMERMAN!": "Politisk asyl åt vietnamsvägrare i Sverige!!! STÖD WARREN HAMERMAN!" [Political asylum for Vietnam refuseniks in Sweden!!! SUPPORT WARREN HAMERMAN!], flyer, Jim Walch Papers, vol. 5, 1969, Arbetarrörelsens arkiv och bibliotek [The Swedish Labor Movement's Archive and Library], Stockholm.
119   The relevant document: "Swedish Deserters," John W. Dean Collection, Richard Nixon Presidential Library and Museum, Yorba Linda, CA. This document is a summary. The full report—written on December 27, 1968, to Paul Lauter of RESIST—can be found in the Clergy and Laity Concerned Records, Swarthmore College Peace Collection, Swarthmore, PA.
121   "The ADC is a working group": Editorial, *Second Front Review*, Winter 1968.
122   "These power hungry anti-socialist beings": John McLoughlin, "Notes on Opportunism," *Second Front Review*, Winter 1968.
122   "it can continue as a paper organization": Gerald Gray, report to RESIST, December 27, 1968. Swarthmore College Peace Collection, Swarthmore, PA.

8: THE INFILTRATORS

123   On February 21, the Swedish Ministry of the Interior: Scott, *Swedish Social Democracy and the Vietnam War*, pp. 143–44.
124   "The American deserters in Sweden are a sad collection": "Vi vill berätta sanningen om desertörerna i Sverige" [We want to tell the truth about the deserters in Sweden], *Expressen*, April 15, 1969.
124   A Gothenburg judge: UPI, "G.I. Deserters Face Charge in Sweden," *Shreveport (LA) Times*, September 11, 1968.
124   Fred Pavese, a former artilleryman: William C. Mann, "Viet Deserters Have New Life, Lingering Memories," *White Plains (NY) Journal-News*, March 13, 1983.
124   In Malmö, two twenty-year-old Californians: UPI, "Sweden Admits 7 G.Is, Ousts 2," *Minneapolis Star*, September 5, 1968.
125   the Laser Arms Corporation: See John Crudele, "The Man Who Knew Too Much: Laser Arms Scam and the Mob," *New York Magazine*, March 6, 1989.
126   an SDS newspaper that accused the Standard Oil Company: "Boycott Standard Oil," *New Left Notes*, April 29, 1969.
126   an anti-war group called Clergy and Laymen Concerned About Vietnam: See Mitchell K. Hall, *Because of Their Faith: CALCAV and Religious Opposition to the Vietnam War* (New York: Columbia University Press, 1990).
126   An impressive triumvirate blessed his mission: Hayes, *American Deserters in Sweden*, p. 37.
126   *Hänt i Veckan* magazine compared him to Father Flanagan: "Själasörjaren kom" [The spiritual guide came], *Hänt i Veckan*, February 1969.

127   "I am concerned about Vietnam": Anonymous letters to CALCAV, Clergy and Laity Concerned Records, Swarthmore College Peace Collection, Swarthmore, PA.

127   "internal dissent and mistrust": Jim Walch to Thomas Lee Hayes, February 26, 1969, Clergy and Laity Concerned Records, Swarthmore College Peace Collection, Swarthmore, PA.

127   Hayes arrived in Sweden on March 21: Richard McSorley, *Peace Eyes* (Washington, DC: Center for Peace Studies, 1978), p. 43.

128   Hayes held a press conference: Report to CALCAV from T. L. Hayes and the Swedish Project, June 6, 1969, Clergy and Laity Concerned Records, Swarthmore College Peace Collection, Swarthmore, PA.

128   bought cheap at the side door of the Chinese Embassy: Deprivations recorded in Laura Furman, "Hagalund," *Southwest Review*, Spring/Summer 1994.

128   There were some bitter disappointments: Thomas Lee Hayes to Richard Fernandez, June 10, 1969; Thomas Lee Hayes to the staff of CALCAV, July 28, 1969, Clergy and Laity Concerned Records, Swarthmore College Peace Collection, Swarthmore, PA.

128   "I hope none of you have to ask why she's here": Hayes, *American Deserters in Sweden*, p. 123.

129   "Five minutes later": Ibid., p. 124.

129   "Ridiculous": Thomas Hayes to Richard Fernandez, April 18, 1968, Clergy and Laity Concerned Records, Swarthmore College Peace Collection, Swarthmore, PA.

129   Richard went home and wrote an article: Michel P. Richard, "American Deserters in Stockholm," *Interplay*, September 1970.

129   "I am having trouble forgiving myself": Michel P. Richard, email message to the author, October 15, 2015.

131   Such trials, I learned, did take place: Leif Grönbladh, *A National Swedish Methadone Program 1966–1989* (Uppsala, Sweden: University of Uppsala, 2004).

131   "We took Mandrax": Thomas Taylor, email message to the author, July 5, 2014.

131   When he arrived in Sweden in March 1968: Eva Lindgren, "USA-soldat ville inte till Vietnam igen: Han har två barn—hoppade av ändå" [USA soldier didn't want to return to Vietnam: He has five kids—went AWOL all the same], *Expressen*, March 27, 1968.

132   "lived through a mental hell": "Desertör på Gotland tog sitt liv" [Deserter in Gotland took his own life], *Fredmissionären*, November 8, 1969.

132   Deserters who had told no one back home of their whereabouts: Daniel Lang, "Out of It," *New Yorker*, May 25, 1970.

132   "If we cannot believe in our country and our merciful God": "Deserters Insults Xenia Couple," *Xenia (OH) Daily Gazette*, April 12, 1968.

132   "Anybody who can't serve their country": "War Dead Used," *Orlando Evening Star*, April 12, 1969.

132   "Michael Vale is back in town": Thomas Lee Hayes to the staff of CALCAV, July 28, 1969, Clergy and Laity Concerned Records, Swarthmore College Peace Collection, Swarthmore, PA

133   "We now know that he was on the payroll": John Takman to Thomas Lee Hayes, February 28, 1969, Clergy and Laity Concerned Records, Swarthmore College Peace Collection, Swarthmore, PA

133   The CIA was an eager subscriber: Report for the Director of Intelligence, General Staff, U.S. Army, *Abstracting Services as an Intelligence Tool for Assessing Soviet Chemical Research*, 1949, https://www.cia.gov/library/readingroom/docs/DOC_0000268326.pdf.

136   a substantial report on Mike and Bill's organization: American Deserters Com-
       mittee, FBI record 100-454113, https://archive.org/stream/AmericanDeserter-
       sCommittee/American%20Deserters%20Committee%20Pt.%2003#page/n29
       /mode/2up.

136   "classified confidential to protect a source of continuing value": Ibid.

136   one uncensored surveillance report: SÄPO record, "888-Speciella kommittéer—
       Desertörskommitteén," private source.

136   A much longer file contained information about the ADC: American Deserters,
       etc., SÄPO record, October 25, 1968.

137   Gunnar's career in espionage came to a sudden end: Gunnar Ekberg, De skall ju
       ändå dö: Tio år i svensk underrättelsetjänst [They would have died anyway: ten
       years in the Swedish intelligence service], Stockholm: Fischer, 2009).

138   "permanent staff of spies": Peter Bratt and Jan Guillou, "Sveriges Spionage"
       [Sweden's espionage], Folket i Bild/Kulturfront, March 3, 1973, http://web.
       fib.se/visa_info.asp?PostId=277&Avdelning=050&Sidrubrik=nyheter&e
       =e005.

140   a project called GLADIO: Daniele Ganser, NATO's Secret Armies: Operation
       GLADIO and Terrorism in Western Europe (New York: Frank Cass, 2005).

141   "if the preparations ever leaked to the Russians": William E. Colby, Honorable
       Men: My Life in the CIA (New York: Simon and Schuster, 1978), p. 83.

141   "Public knowledge that the CIA was building stay-behind nets": Ibid.

141   Pavese's 2003 post to a website about insects: "Cockroaches," What's That Bug?,
       May 28, 2003, https://www.whatsthatbug.com/2003/05/28/cockroaches-3/.

142   "Having the opportunity to live without confinement": Mamaroneck High
       School Class of 1966 Reunion Yearbook (1986).

9: OUT OF LOVE

143   Sir Arthur Conan Doyle's short story: Sir Arthur Conan Doyle, "The Final Prob-
       lem," in The Memoirs of Sherlock Holmes (Oxford: Oxford University Press,
       1993), p. 252.

143   Nicholas Meyer's Conan Doyle pastiche: Nicholas Meyer, The Seven-per-cent
       Solution: Being a Reprint from the Reminiscences of John H. Watson, M.D.
       (New York: Dutton, 1974), p. 21.

144   The C-SPAN video library: See www.c-span.org/person/?cliffordgaddy.

145   Cliff's book: Fiona Hill and Cliff Gaddy, Mr. Putin: Operative in the Kremlin
       (Washington, DC: Brookings Institution Press, 2013; revised 2015).

145   His father—also Dr. Clifford Garland Gaddy: Gary D. Gaddy, "Ten or So
       Things That I Learned from My Dad," Chapel Hill (NC) Herald, January 8,
       2010; Clifford G. Gaddy, Triple Coronary Bypass: A Cardiologist Tells About
       His and How to Prevent Yours (Macon, GA: Mercer University Press, 1994),
       pp. 1–3.

145   champion of Babe Ruth baseball: "They Lost Only One While Winning Four-
       teen," Danville (VA) Bee, October 3, 1960.

145   the Danville branch of the Order of DeMolay: "Town Topics," Danville (VA)
       Bee, September 29, 1960.

145   president of his school's chapter of the National Honor Society: "Gaddy
       Awarded National Merit," Danville (VA) Bee, April 27, 1964; "Local Boy Wins
       in Quarterfinals of Radio Quiz," Danville (VA) Bee, March 30, 1964.

146   his father's alma mater: Gaddy, Triple Coronary Bypass, p. 103.

146   staging Old South week: Anthony S. Parent, "Weathering Wake: The African
       American Experience," Founders' Day Convocation Address, Wake Forest Uni-
       versity, February 26, 2009, http://news.wfu.edu/2009/02/26/university

-celebrates-founders'-day/; "No Racism Meant," *Old Gold and Black* (November 21, 1967), pp. 4–5.

146   Cliff volunteered for the army: "Deserter, WFU Grad, Courageous, Says Dad," *Winston-Salem Journal*, July 19, 1969.

146   not acknowledged by the government until 1975: James Bamford, *The Puzzle Palace: Inside the National Security Agency, America's Most Secret Intelligence Organization* (New York: Viking Press, 2001).

146   the army had failed to assign him to a language school: "Gaddy Desertion Laid to Army Promise," *Danville (VA) Bee*, July 19, 1969.

146   "My only excuse": Associated Press, "Deserters Letter to Paper Explains Reasons for Action," *San Antonio Express*, August 7, 1969.

147   "Every apparent fact or story": Hill and Gaddy, *Mr. Putin* (rev. ed., 2015), pp. 7, 9.

147   Dr. Gaddy told the papers: "Deserter, WFU Grad, Courageous, Says Dad."

147   a flight from Boston to Stockholm: Ibid.

148   "What would happen if you went home now?": "Bill rymde till Sverige" [Bill fled to Sweden], *Dagens Nyheter*, November 2, 1969.

148   Beacon Press: Thomas Lee Hayes to Richard Fernandez, Clergy and Laity Concerned Records, Swarthmore College Peace Collection, Swarthmore, PA.

149   Seymour Hersh published the first account: Seymour M. Hersh, "Lieutenant Accused of Murdering 109 Civilians," *St. Louis Post-Dispatch*, November 13, 1969.

149   "We were told to make use of electrical radio equipment": Mark Lane, *Conversations with Americans* (New York: Simon and Schuster, 1970), pp. 27–28.

149   *Dagens Nyheter* observed Chuck at a press conference: "Song My var ingen enstaka händelse" [Song My was not an isolated event], *Dagens Nyheter*, December 8, 1969. "Song My" is an alternative name for My Lai.

149   Thomas Lee Hayes heard the same story: Hayes, *American Deserters in Sweden*, p. 93.

150   "Some of the horror tales in this book are undoubtedly true": Neil Sheehan, "Conversations with Americans," *New York Times*, December 27, 1970; "Desertörvittnen ej trovärdiga om Vietnamvåld" [Deserter witness not credible on Vietnam violence], *Dagens Nyheter*, December 28, 1970.

150   refusing to print a second edition: Robert Stein, "'What Am I Bid for Lyndon Johnson?' Or How the Literary Auction Works," *New York Magazine*, August 30, 1971, p. 48; Mark Lane, *Citizen Lane: Defending Our Rights in the Courts, the Capitol, and the Streets* (Chicago: Chicago Review Press, 2012), pp. 218–21.

150   Chuck gave his side of the story: Chuck Onan, email message to the author, August 9, 2017.

151   "The former route to Sweden has been interrupted": Adrian Maas to Hans Göran Franck, June 5, 1970, Jim Walch Papers, Arbetarrörelsens arkiv och bibliotek [The Swedish Labor Movement's Archive and Library], Stockholm.

151   the Alternative Stomach: *Internal Haemorrhage: Organ for American War Resisters in Sweden*, Jim Walch Papers, Arbetarrörelsens arkiv och bibliotek [The Swedish Labor Movement's Archive and Library], Stockholm.

151   a lengthy report on the problems of American imperialism: Gerry Condon to Thomas Lee Hayes, April 15, 1971, Clergy and Laity Concerned Records, Swarthmore College Peace Collection, Swarthmore, PA.

151   "I thought that I'd heard all about the bad scene down there": "The Malmö Report," unpublished typescript, Clergy and Laity Concerned Records, Swarthmore College Peace Collection, Swarthmore, PA.

151   attempted to rob a bank, and got five years: "USA-desertör greps för rån i

Köpenhamn" [U.S. deserter arrested for robbery in Copenhagen], *Dagens Nyheter*, March 25, 1970.

151   a song by a Swedish folk band: Gläns över sjö & strand [Brilliance over sea and sand], "John Babcock," on their album *Här schaktas utan pardon* [Excavating without pardon] (1971).

152   Cliff translated scholarly articles: Iu. Kapelinskii, "The Future Prospects of Soviet-American Economic Relations," *Soviet Law and Government* (January 1974), pp. 46–72; M. Burlatskii, "Systems Analysis of World Politics and the Planning of Peace," *International Journal of Politics* (Winter 1973–74), pp. 13–29; M. Vrono, "Schizophrenia in Childhood and Adolescence: Clinical Features and Course," *International Journal of Mental Health* (Fall/Winter 1973–74), pp. 7–116; D. N. Isaev, "Schizophrenia in Relation to Other Mental Disorders of Childhood," *International Journal of Mental Health* (Spring 1974), pp. 47–56.

152   He translated the essays of Yevgeny Preobrazhensky: See Donald Filtzer, *E. A. Preobrazhensky and the Theory of Expanded Reproduction in the USSR During the Period of Primitive Socialist Accumulation* (PhD diss., Glasgow University, 1976), p. 13.

152   So did Bill Jones: Gerry Condon to Richard Fernandez, November 8, 1970, Clergy and Laity Concerned Records, Swarthmore College Peace Collection, Swarthmore, PA.

153   "An organization remains politically relevant": Cliff Gaddy et al., "Dissolution Statement of the American Deserters Committee" (1970), Special Collections, Shields Library, University of California, Davis.

153   "written, of course, by none other than our old friend Michael Vale": Gerry Condon to Richard Fernandez, November 8, 1970, Clergy and Laity Concerned Records, Swarthmore College Peace Collection, Swarthmore, PA.

153   dousing himself in kerosene: Associated Press, "Deserter Burns Self," *Greenville (SC) News*, August 10, 1970; "Celebrating Desertion," Dawn.com, November 12, 2009, https://www.dawn.com/news/833213.

153   forcible repatriation to the States: Associated Press, "Deserter Hunts Help," *Orlando Sentinel*, November 21, 1970.

154   an ADC member was charged: Steven Wentworth to Richard Fernandez, December 9, 1970, Clergy and Laity Concerned Records, Swarthmore College Peace Collection, Swarthmore, PA.

154   "It's kind of tough to get out of jail this morning": UPI, "American Deserter Expelled by Sweden," *Greenville (SC) News*, November 26, 1970.

154   "We are absolutely blown out of our fucking minds": Richard Fernandez to Thomas Lee Hayes, December 10, 1970, Clergy and Laity Concerned Records, Swarthmore College Peace Collection, Swarthmore, PA.

154   "Palme wants only 'nice,' politically conscious deserters": Max Watts to "Martin," December 6, 1970, Brünn-Harris-Watts Papers, Internationaal Instituut voor Sociale Geschiedenis [International Institute of Social History], Amsterdam.

154   "the situation is getting much tighter": Gerry Condon to Thomas Lee Hayes, undated, Clergy and Laity Concerned Records, Swarthmore College Peace Collection, Swarthmore, PA.

157   the amplified voice of Jane Fonda: "Jane Fonda Speaks to Anti-War Rally," *Eureka (CA) Times Standard*, August 25, 1972.

158   "It's a drag": "Deserter of 5 Years Weds in SF," *San Mateo (CA) Times*, August 25, 1972.

158   A decade ago he adopted the pseudonym Will Hart: See Will Hart, *Alien Civilizations: Scientific Proof of Their Existence* (Privately published: Createspace Publishing Platform, 2004).

159   had identified Harry Rositzke of Operation Chaos: Don Schmitt, "William
       Moore: UFO Opportunist or Agent of Disinformation?" Open Minds TV,
       July 23, 2014, http://www.openminds.tv/william-moore-ufo-opportunist-agent
       -disinformation/29056.
159   "infuses every engagement with both credibility and content": See Dr. Rita Lou-
       ise, business website, http://soulhealer.com.
159   he described a visit he'd made to Mexico: "True Origins of Aliens," Just Energy
       Radio, July 18, 2015, https://www.youtube.com/watch?v=N3QmU9Y9eJo.
159   MHYIELD was sniffing around the offices of the ADC in Stockholm: See CIA file
       104-10071-10026, http://www.maryferrell.org/showDoc.html?docId=27605&
       search=MHYIELD#relPageId=1&tab=page.
159   Mike Bransome, a deserter whose colorful past: Michael Bransome, *Pardon Me*,
       http://pardonmeblog.blogspot.co.uk.
160   In May 1971, a deserter was convicted: Associated Press, "Army Deserter Com
       plains of Treatment in Stockholm," *Kansas City Times*, June 19, 1971.
160   Pennington ordered the pilot to fly to the United States: "Jag hade kniven å stru-
       pen i 45 minuter" [I had a knife held to my throat for 45 minutes], *Aftonbladet*,
       May 18, 1971.
160   "It is a hidden fact": Associated Press, "Army Deserter Complains of Treatment in
       Sweden."
161   an uproar in a room at the Rex Hotel in Malmö: Ulf Matson, "Så levde USA-
       dråparna i Sverige: Flickvänner gick på gatan för att försörja desertörer" [Thus
       lived the USA killers in Sweden: Girlfriends walked out onto the street in order to
       support the deserters], *Aftonbladet*, January 12, 1973.
162   "degree in 'pimpology' in Copenhagen": Vernon Boggs, "Black American
       Deserters in Sweden: From Desertion to Drugs to Despair" (master's thesis, City
       University of New York, 1973).
162   a secret report that toted up their crimes: Ibid.
162   On January 27, America's war in Vietnam came to an end: "Vietnam Accord Is
       Reached; Cease-Fire Begins Saturday; P.O.W.'s to Be Free in 60 Days," *New York
       Times*, January 23, 1973.

10: THE NEXT STEP

163   On May 24, 1970, a meeting was convened at the Club Voltaire: American
       Deserters Committee, FBI record 100-454113, https://archive.org/stream
       /AmericanDesertersCommittee/American%20Deserters%20Committee%20Pt
       .%2003#page/n29/mode/2up.
164   "We would appreciate being advised": Ibid.
164   "On almost every base": "Two Alternatives," *Next Step*, July 4, 1970.
164   "sycophancy" and "dull palaver": "More on EM Councils," *Next Step*, August 20,
       1970.
164   a white GI had thrown a glass of milk: "Mannheim—Riot Ripe!" *Next Step*,
       August 3, 1970.
165   "Let me say this as straight as I can": Letters page, *American War Resister in
       Sweden*, June 15, 1972.
165   "One of the biggest fears of the Pentagon": Editorial, *Next Step*, March 24, 1971.
166   a story about Nixon's psychotherapist Dr. Arnold A. Hutschnecker: "What's
       Nixon Up To?" *Next Step*, July 4, 1970.
168   "He was pretty unbalanced": Today William Engdahl comments on geopolitical
       matters, usually with a conspiracist tone. In January 2014, he suggested that terror-
       ist bombings in Russia were the work of Israeli intelligence (http://www.veteransto

day.com/2014/01/24/is-netanyahu-getting-back-at-putin-with-volgograd-bombings
/). In 2014 he told Russia Today that ISIS was a "false flag operation" by the CIA
and Israeli intelligence (https://www.youtube.com/watch?v=j5OYeBQdrFE). In
November 2015 he told the fringe political website the Corbett Report that he had
seen evidence that the Paris attacks of that month were "engineered to whip up
hysteria" (https://www.youtube.com/watch?v=ukHpYWkgfyo).

168   William Engdahl was a Minneapolis-born Princeton graduate: "About F. William
F Engdahl," William Engdahl personal website, http://www.williamengdahl.com
/about.php/.

168   His family background: For Walfrid, see Henry Bengston, *On the Left in America: Memoirs of the Scandinavian-American Labor Movement* (Carbondale:
Southern Illinois University Press, 1999), p. 192; for John Louis, see Harriet Sil-
verman, *J. Louis Engdahl: Revolutionary Working Class Leader* (New York:
Workers Library, 1935).

170   On March 6, 1970, three members were killed in New York City: Arthur M.
Eckstein, *Bad Moon Rising: How the Weather Underground Beat the FBI and
Lost the Revolution* (New Haven, CT: Yale University Press, 2016), p. 12.

170   The actor Dustin Hoffman: Ibid., p. 97.

172   "The British Empire": Lyndon LaRouche, Friday Night Webcast, May 23, 2014,
LaRouchePAC, http://archive.larouchepac.com/node/30865.

172   "Death to the fascist insect": Patricia Campbell Hearst, *Every Secret Thing* (Garden City, NY: Doubleday, 1982), p. 66.

11: BEYOND PSYCHOANALYSIS

175   in a 1996 episode of *The Simpsons*: *The Simpsons*, "Treehouse of Horror VII,"
Fox Broadcasting Company, October 27, 1996.

175   "In only a few decades in the late twentieth century": See Hylozoic Hedgehog
[pseud.], *Smiling Man from a Dead Planet: The Mystery of Lyndon LaRouche*,
LaRouche   Planet,   2009,   http://laroucheplanet.info/pmwiki/pmwiki.php?n
=Library.UnityNow15. "Hylozoic Hedgehog" is the nom de guerre of a former
NCLC member who joined the LaRouche organization in 1971 and quit in
1979 in disgust over its ties to the Far Right.

176   "We believe Lyndon H. LaRouche is guilty": Ibid.

176   The family's response: Lyndon H. LaRouche Jr., *The Power of Reason: 1988: An
Autobiography* (Washington, DC: Executive Intelligence Review, 1987).

176   He spent the rest of the war in Burma and India: Dennis Tourish and Tim Wohl-
forth, *On the Edge: Political Cults Right and Left* (Armonk, NY: M. E. Sharpe,
2000), pp. 75–76.

177   "He was a loner": Clara Fraser, "LaRouche: Sex Maniac and Demagogue," in
Revolution, She Wrote (Seattle: Red Letter Press, 1998), pp. 231–36.

178   as a meeting place for the Soviet spy ring: Walter and Miriam Schneir, *Invitation
to an Inquest* (Garden City, NY: Doubleday, 1965), p. 304.

179   the National Caucus of Labor Committees: See Hylozoic Hedgehog [pseud.],
*How It All Began: The Origins and History of the National Caucus of Labor
Committees in New York and Philadelphia (1966–1971)*, LaRouche Planet,
2012, http://laroucheplanet.info/pmwiki/pmwiki.php?n=Library.HIAB.

179   "The revolutionary intelligentsia": Lyndon LaRouche, "Statement of Founding
Principles of the National Caucus of Labor Committees," January 1971,
LaRouche   Planet,   http://laroucheplanet.info/pmwiki/pmwiki.php?n=Library.
FoundingPrinciplesNCLC.

181   "This group has been brought together": Charles M. Young, "Mind Control,
Political Violence & Sexual Warfare: Inside the NCLC," *Crawdaddy*, June 1976.

181   The training camp was disbanded: Jewish Telegraphic Agency, "Special Report on the Anti-Semitism of the U.S. Labor Party," December 4, 1979.

182   "We must dispose of this stinking corpse": Lyn Marcus, "Operation Mop-Up: The Class Struggle Is for Keeps," *New Solidarity*, April 16, 1973.

182   "Chairs were overturned": "Labor Committees Goons Attack the YWLL," *Militant*, April 27, 1973.

182   a conference of the Young Socialist Alliance in Detroit: Mike Kelley, "Young Socialist Alliance in Detroit Repulses NCLC Attack," *Militant*, May 18, 1973.

182   "a new, virtually unnoticed, unreported revolutionary action network": Victor Reisel, "A New Leftist Movement in Industry," *Kokomo (FL) Tribune*, September 18, 1973, p. 5.

182   "a cult of demoralized psychotics": Letters to the editor, *Workers Vanguard*, December 7, 1973.

183   "Over the period since September 1972": "Beyond Psychoanalysis," *Campaigner*, September/October 1973.

183   *ego stripping:* "A True History of Lyn Marcus and the Labor Committees," International Workers Party, 1975, LaRouche Planet, http://laroucheplanet.info /pmwiki/pmwiki.php?n=Library.ATrueHistoryOfLynMarcus.

184   "In Germany I am *Der Abscheulicher*": Lyn Marcus, "The Politics of Male 'Impotence,'" National Caucus of Labor Committees internal memo, August 16, 1973, LaRouche Planet, http://laroucheplanet.info/pmwiki/pmwiki.php?n=Library. MaleImpotence.

184   "According to Marcus": Letter from Christine Berl and Henry Weinfeld to Phyllis Dillon, April 2, 1974, National Caucus of Labor Committees records, Manuscripts and Archives Division, New York Public Library.

186   "There is a strong possibility that the government": Quoted in Hedgehog, *Smiling Man from a Dead Planet*, http://laroucheplanet.info/pmwiki/pmwiki.php?n =Library.UnityNow3.

187   "the successful seizure of world power within the decade": Marcus, "Politics of Male 'Impotence.'"

187   making secret trips to East Berlin: "East Germans Brainwash American to Spy on ICLC," *New Solidarity*, August 10, 1973.

188   "He wished to be interrogated, and stuck to it": LaRouche, *The Power of Reason: 1988*, p. 140.

12: THE BRAINWASHERS

191   "you are an empty, stinking hulk": Lyndon LaRouche to Carol White, August 25, 1972, National Caucus of Labor Committees records, Manuscripts and Archives Division, New York Public Library.

191   the Angry Brigade: Gordon Carr, *The Angry Brigade: A History of Britain's First Urban Guerrilla Group* (Oakland, CA: PM Press, 2003).

192   voice on the end of the line was Greg Rose: Greg Rose later turned FBI informant on the NCLC. See Gregory F. Rose, "The Swarmy Life and Times of the NCLC," *National Review*, March 30, 1979.

197   "There are sounds of weeping and vomiting on the tape": Paul Montgomery, "How a Radical Left Group Moved Toward Savagery," *New York Times*, January 20, 1974.

198   "Lyn, we've done it": Christopher White, "On the Track of My Assassins," *Campaigner*, February/March 1974.

199   "an actual battlefield report": Nikos Syvriotis, "'Strategy' Conference a Battlefield," *New Solidarity*, January 11, 1974.

202   "In cases directly known to us": Bob Dillon, Phyllis Dillon, et al., Memorandum

to the National Executive of the National Caucus of Labor Committees, January 2, 1974, National Caucus of Labor Committees records, Manuscripts and Archives Division, New York Public Library.

202   "We," said the reply, "are the only people in the world": Janice Chaitkin to Phyllis Dillon, January 10, 1974, National Caucus of Labor Committees records, Manuscripts and Archives Division, New York Public Library.

203   identified as a setup from the start: White, "On the Track of My Assassins."

205   went on a Manhattan radio station: *Gordon Hammett Show*, WNBC, January 18, 1974. See FCC Reports, 2nd ser., vol. 46, April 12, 1974–May 31, 1974, p. 501, https://digital.library.unt.edu/ark:/67531/metadc306590/m1/533/?q=%22l abor%20committees%22.

205   they produced a handbill: "Brainwashing Cure Leads to Psychosis Breakthrough," NCLC handbill, January 5, 1974, https://www.cia.gov/library/readingroom/docs /CIA-RDP88-01315R000300590051-2.pdf.

205   "A decision to co-opt Warren Hamerman": Lyndon LaRouche, "Morning Briefing," October 7, 1974, private collection.

205   "two insurgent government agencies": "Injunction Against CIA & NYC Police for Insurrection Against U.S. Government," NCLC handbill, National Caucus of Labor Committees records, Manuscripts and Archives Division, New York Public Library.

206   LaRouche's concluding speech that night: Lyn Marcus, "Undercover CIA-Police Plot to Take Over U.S.," *New Solidarity Extra*, January 3, 1974.

208   "to discredit the organization": Ibid.

13: THE ZOMBIE ARMY

209   "He talked virtually nonstop about his life and his theories": Montgomery, "How a Radical Left Group Moved Toward Savagery."

209   "Marcus has initiated a test for total allegiance": Jim McGourty [pseud.], "Concerning CIA Agent Vale's Recent Activities," unpublished typescript.

210   "a self-perpetuating mental zombie": White, "On the Track of My Assassins."

211   "in the event of our disappearance": Letter from Christine Berl and Henry Weinfeld to Phyllis Dillon, April 2, 1974.

211   In an internal bulletin: Lyn Marcus, "Why Christine Berl Could Be Turned into a Zombie," NCLC internal memo, New York, April 1, 1974.

211   laying out the rules of the parallel universe: Lyn Marcus, "The Present Internal Situation," NCLC internal bulletin, March 25, 1974, Lyndon LaRouche Watch, http://www.lyndonlarouche.org/larouche-internal.pdf.

211   "permitted us to recruit fantastically": Ibid., p. 2.

211   "We are faced with the fearful infinity": Ibid., p. 7.

212   *"Unless the Labor Committees are able to deploy"*: Ibid., p. 5.

213   "on how Rockefeller caused or is causing the food crisis": Young, "Mind Control, Political Violence, & Sexual Warfare."

214   "There is no agency in the world": Marcus, "Present Internal Situation."

215   "events lost in the fog of time": Warren Hamerman, email to the author, August 27, 2017.

215   "offensive counterthrusts": Warren Hamerman, "What Are the Labor Committees and the Labor Parties?" in *How the Labor Party Is Organized to Win* (New York: US Labor Party, 1976).

215   In 1974 he headed an NCLC investigation: Jean Gahururu, "Winning the Peace for an African Renaissance," *Executive Intelligence Review*, June 1, 2001, p. 51.

216   head his campaign to put American AIDS sufferers into quarantine camps:

David L. Kirp, "LaRouche Turns to AIDS Politics," *New York Times*, September 11, 1986.

216   "He was a classic bureaucrat": Hylozoic Hedgehog [pseud.], email message to the author, April 25, 2015.

216   Vale was a CIA agent: "How Britain Runs the Radical Left," *Executive Intelligence Review*, January 16, 1979.

216   the Tavistock Institute: Lyndon LaRouche, "Notes Concerning the Role of Labor Parties in Immediate Strategic Crisis," U.S. Labor Party/EAP internal document, August 24, 1977.

216   "NATO's Schwarze Kapelle": "Japan's Red Army Reactivated in CIA Terror Blitz," New Solidarity International Press Service, September 23, 1976.

216   "hit and run 'probing' operations": Warren Hamerman, "Why the Labor Committee Can't Be Taken Over by Agents," *New Solidarity*, December 1, 1975.

217   "Vale was deployed by British intelligence": Lyndon LaRouche, "British Intelligence Deploys New 'Left'-profiled Assassination Capability," New Solidarity International Press Service, May 10, 1979.

217   "has by now been determined to be one of the key operatives": McGourty [pseud.], "Concerning CIA Agent Vale's Recent Activities."

217   "brainwashed gangs of zombies": Lyn Marcus, "Rockefeller's Fascism with a Democratic Face," *Campaigner*, November/December 1974.

218   "I strongly do not recommend": Jay M. Caplan to Jim McGourty [pseud.], November 5, 1975.

218   "Selling favors to Rockefeller": "Christina Nelson Campaign Poster," *Executive Intelligence Review*, November 3, 1974.

219   "The check really helped us live like human beings": Christina Nelson to Jim's brother, November 16, 1974.

219   "a key operative for Scandinavia and the Federal Republic": LaRouche, "British Intelligence Deploys New 'Left'-profiled Assassination Capability."

220   "now working for a network which transports psychotics": McGourty [pseud.], "Concerning CIA Agent Vale's Recent Activities."

221   "enhanced excitability, motor disinhibition": Vrono, "Schizophrenia in Childhood."

221   firearms training and "Beyond Psychoanalysis" sessions: Quoted in Håkan Hermansson, *Mullvadar i socialistisk förklädnad: en rapport om ELC i Sverige* [Moles in Socialist disguises: A report on the ELC in Sweden] (Stockholm: Socialdemokraterna, 1975), p. 19.

222   "considerable collections of money": Ibid.

222   "laboratory for depression": "Labor Committee Ruins Woodcock's IMF Game Plan," New Solidarity International Press Service, July 8, 1974.

222   "the most appropriate choice for the Rockefeller forces": "Economic Collapse Destroys Myth of 'Swedish Way,' " *Executive Intelligence Review*, April 26, 1976.

222   "model for social fascist society": "The Swedish Way: Rockefeller's Northern Paradise," New Solidarity International Press Service, June 29, 1974.

222   They also implied that Israel had lied: Ibid.

222   Henry Kissinger ordered them banned from the White House: Cable, U.S. Department of State to U.S. Embassy Rome, March 4, 1975, https://wikileaks.org/plusd/cables/1975STATE048175_b.html.

222   "Fascist pressure exerted by the CIA": Cable, U.S. Embassy Bonn to U.S. Embassy London, Paris, Stockholm, et al., February 11, 1976.

222   Cliff Gaddy was named as Stockholm bureau chief: Cliff's first credit as Stockholm bureau chief appears in *Executive Intelligence Review*, September 26, 1978.

222   In 1974 the Stockholm organization had only fifteen members: Lars Åberg, Elisabeth Grundström, Harald Hamrin, "ELC," *Dagens Nyheter*, October 24, 1975.

223   "the CIA's international terrorist network": "Tavistock Terror Plays in Sweden," New Solidarity International Press Service, May 24, 1974.

223   "these doctors quickly reveal their own insanity": "ELC Confronts U.N. Sponsored Psychologists on Behavior Modification," New Solidarity International Press Service, June 29, 1974, pp. 8–9.

223   a few words in a Swedish newspaper editorial: "Palme Planning a 'Total Defense'?" New Solidarity International Press Service, December 19, 1974.

223   "expect to answer to these actions with their lives": European Labor Party flyer, 1975, quoted in Hermansson, *Mullvadar i socialistisk förklädnad*, p. 16.

223   "I have not been to a single meeting": "Så här saboterar ELC möten" [How the ELC sabotages meetings], *Aftonbladet*, October 13, 1975.

223   "hold your own meetings instead of coming to disrupt ours!": Ibid.

224   "They appear at public party gatherings and conferences": Hermansson, *Mullvadar i socialistisk förklädnad*, p. 9.

224   Hermansson was harassed in his office in Malmö: "Arbetet-man hotad after avslöjandet av EAP" [*Arbetet* writer threatened after EAP revelations], *Arbetet*, January 28, 1982.

224   "Agent Spång" of Langley: William Engdahl, "CIA-terror mot EAP: Agenter mobiliseras I Italien och Sverige" [CIA terror against EAP: Agents mobilized in Italy and Sweden], *Ny Solidaritet*, January 20, 1976.

224   a story comparing the European Labor Committees to the Children of God: "Politikens guds barn" [The children of God of politics], *Aftonbladet*, October 13, 1975.

224   threw a foil-wrapped hunk of liver at a Catholic archbishop: Rembert G. Weakland, *A Pilgrim in a Pilgrim Church: Memoirs of a Catholic Archbishop* (Grand Rapids, MI: William B. Eerdmans, 2009), p. 301.

224   abducting dogs for sexual gratification: Memo, FBI Boston office, April 4, 1975, LaRouche Planet, http://laroucheplanet.info/pmwiki/images/Fbidogsex.JPG.

224   FEED JANE FONDA TO THE WHALES: *The LaRouche Network* (Washington, DC: Heritage Foundation, 1984), p. 2; Albin Krebs, "Charges Against Peter Fonda Dropped," *New York Times*, October 28, 1981.

225   a cartoon of Chancellor Willy Brandt in Nazi uniform: Included in *Campaigner*, June 1976.

225   Brandt sued for libel and won: "Nazi Justice in W. Germany: ELP Leader Fined Heavily for Spreading Facts About Brandt," *Executive Intelligence Review*, November 29, 1976.

225   A favorite stunt was a three-person operation: Henry Bäck, *EAP—ulv i fårakläder?* [EAP—wolves in sheep's clothing?] (Stockholm: Privately published, 1983), p. 26.

225   "Take, for example, the person who describes the NCLC": Ed Spannaus, "Beyond Schacht: The Destruction of the Cognitive Powers of Labor," *Campaigner*, March 1975, p. 45.

227   "Cher Ami": Stanislaus Tomkiewicz to Mark Burdman, July 26, 1978, in author's possession.

227   In 1980 he had taken a position at its German headquarters in Wiesbaden: See Mary Burdman, "In Tribute to Mark Burdman by His Wife," *Executive Intelligence Review*, July 30, 2004, pp. 7–9.

227   an essay asserting that the British prime minister Benjamin Disraeli: Mark Burdman, "Why Israel Fights Britain's Wars of Extermination," *Executive Intelligence Review*, June 29, 1982, pp. 36–39.

227   Burdman had died in July 2004: Burdman, "In Tribute to Mark Burdman by His Wife."

14: OPERATION DESTRUCTION

228 "The most optimistic view of AD 1990": Lyn Marcus, "Rockefeller's Fascism with a Democratic Face," *Campaigner*, November/December 1974, p. 42.
229 He left the CIA in 1970: Paul Lewis, "Harry Rositzke, 91, Linguist and American Spymaster," *New York Times*, November 8, 2002.
229 Military intelligence spying on civilians: See Chtistopher Pyle, *Army Surveillance of Civilians: A Documentary Analysis* (Washington, DC: Senate Subcommittee on Constitutional Rights, 1972).
229 The FBI sending its agents provocateurs: See Betty Medsger, *The Burglary: The Discovery of J. Edgar Hoover's Secret FBI* (New York: Knopf, 2014).
229 The Watergate burglaries: See Tim Weiner, *Legacy of Ashes: A History of the CIA* (New York: Doubleday, 2008), pp. 370–72.
229 heard evidence on MKULTRA: Report to the President by the Commission on CIA Activities Within the United States, June 1975. See also Dominic Streatfeild, *Brainwash: The Secret History of Mind Control* (London: Hodder and Stoughton, 2006), pp. 67–71.
230 "They form a society of their own": Harry Rositzke, *The CIA's Secret Operations: Espionage, Counterespionage, and Covert Action* (Boulder, CO: Westview Press, 1977), p. xvii.
230 "mentioned Dick Ober's unit": See Scott C. Monje, *The Central Intelligence Agency: A Documentary History* (Santa Barbara, CA: Greenwood, 2008), p. 114.
230 Hersh's story ran in the *New York Times*: Seymour Hersh, "Huge C.I.A. Operation Reported in U.S. Against Antiwar Forces, Other Dissidents in Nixon Years," *New York Times*, December 22, 1974.
231 Operation Destruction: Information from Frank Rafalko.
232 His report revealed the operational name of: Report to the President by the Commission on CIA Activities Within the United States, June 1975.
232 "Beginning in January 1974 with the attempted assassination": "The Making of Rockefeller's International Terror Campaign," Special Report, New Solidarity International Press Service, January 2, 1976, p. B1.
232 an *Executive Intelligence Review* article: John Sigerson, "British Revive Operation Chaos," *Executive Intelligence Review*, September 5, 1978.
233 "an extensive operation of the sort catalogued by spooks": LaRouche, *The Power of Reason: 1988*, p. 141.
233 "I have made no public statements": Richard Ober to Nelson Rockefeller, June 18, 1975, CIA-RDP84-00780R006700040041-2, http://www.cia.gov.
233 "it was a breach of the code": Angus Mackenzie, *Secrets: The CIA's War at Home* (Berkeley: University of California Press, 1999), p. 20.
234 a thick file compiled in the 1950s by the FBI: Richard Ober, FBI file, MuckRock, https://www.muckrock.com/foi/united-states-of-america-10/richard-ober-24564/.
234 Richard Ober's father was an agent: Ober details from FBI file and Scottie Fitzgerald Smith's foreword to *As Ever, Scott Fitz—: Letters Between F. Scott Fitzgerald and His Literary Agent Harold Ober, 1919–1940*, ed. Matthew J. Bruccoli (New York: Lippincott, 1972).
235 "Well, we sure don't much like having you here": Ibid., p. xii.
236 "I don't like prying into their private lives": Ibid., p. xiii.
236 The bureau put these details on file: Richard Ober, FBI file, MuckRock, https://www.muckrock.com/foi/united-states-of-america-10/richard-ober-24564/.
237 "a nincompoop who went way beyond his charter": Rafalko, *MH/CHAOS*, p. 15.
237 "Autocratic": Ibid.
237 "Truly evil": Paget, *Patriotic Betrayal*, p. 391.
237 "They didn't fire him": Hersh, "Huge C.I.A. Operation Reported in U.S. Against Antiwar Forces, Other Dissidents in Nixon Years."

237   "I am not prepared to discuss further": Memorandum, Henry Kissinger to Donald Rumsfeld, December 23, 1974, https://www.cia.gov/library/readingroom /docs/LOC-HAK-424-4-3-3.pdf.

237   A brief obituary in the *Washington Post*: "Richard Ober," *Washington Post*, September 12, 2001.

238   "I looked at him and said": Phyllis C. Richman, "Let Them Eat Sweetbreads," *Washington Post*, September 17, 1989.

238   In October 1973, an American novel was published: Harry Rositzke, *Left On! The Glorious Bourgeois Cultural Revolution* (New York: Quadrangle, 1973).

239   "The practice of criticism and self-criticism": Ibid., p. 17.

239   "I envy the young, because I am old": Ibid., pp. 111–12.

239   "Sit-ins, love-ins, think-ins": Ibid., p. 57.

15: THE BELIEVERS

242   "Call It Tonkin Gulf Syndrome": Lyndon LaRouche, "LaRouche to Wall Street: 'It's Your Crap; You Eat It,' " *Ny Solidaritet*, July 23, 2014.

242   "but at least they accept that a horse is a horse": Oskar Bengtsson, "De andra partierna-Europeiska Arbetarpartiet (EAP)" [The other parties: European Workers Party (EAP)], *Contra*, no. 5 (1975): p. 4.

242   "The EAP is in all likelihood": *Hotet från vänster. Säkerhetstjänsternas övervakning av kommunister, anarkister m.m. 1965–2002* [Threat from the Left. The security services surveillance of communists, anarchists, and others. 1965–2002], (Stockholm: Justitiedepartementet, 2002), p. 267, http://www.regeringen.se/rattsdokument /statens-offentliga-utredningar/2002/01/sou-200291.

243   "How could any worker": "European Labor Party Campaigns for 20 June Elections, Fields Candidates in Sweden and West Germany," New Solidarity International Press Service, June 1, 1976.

243   the party received 108 votes: "De blanka rösterna ökade stort," *Dagens Nyheter*, September 29, 1976; *Hotet från vänster*, p. 282.

243   "Don't throw your vote away!": "Rösta på EAP till kommunfullmäktige!" [Vote EAP to the council!], *Ny Solidaritet Valextra*, August 31, 1979.

243   That year, the party's total rose to 158: "EAP," *Dagens Nyheter*, October 20, 1979.

243   A few disparaging mentions of Chuck's name: "Of 'Atrocity' and Fakery," *Indianapolis Star*, January 9, 1971; John Lofton, "Between Two, Warren Report More Credible Than Mark Lane," *Yuma (AZ) Daily Sun*, June 6, 1975.

245   "Donald Duck" has outpolled the European Workers Party: "Kalle Ankas parti större än EAP" [Donald Duck party bigger than EAP], *Dagens Nyheter*, September 5, 1985.

245   "must be financed externally": Hermansson, *Mullvadar i socialistisk förklädnad*, p. 18

245   some of the NCLC's resources came from fraud: "LaRouche Receives 15-Year Sentence," *New York Times*, January 28, 1989.

246   even his followers barely registered his declaration: "What We Need in 2016: Alexander Hamilton's Principles, LaRouche's Four Laws," LaRouchePAC, https://larouchepac.com/20161017/what-we-need-2016-alexander-hamiltons -principles-larouches-four-laws.

246   the U.S. Labor Party, launched in 1973: *National Party Conventions, 1831–1976* (Washington, DC: Congressional Quarterly, 1979), p. 197.

247   a paper bag containing $95,000 in cash: Les Brown, "NBC Ordered to Sell Time to Labor Party," *New York Times*, November 2, 1976.

247   "Parroting such code words as 'trust,' 'love' and 'unity'": "Is Jimmy Carter Brainwashed? Democrat Linked to Institute Terrorists," New Solidarity International Press Service, July 6, 1976.

247   he was awarded the Bronze Star: Peter Bourne, *Men, Stress, and Vietnam* (New York: Little, Brown, 1970).

247   In 1972 he persuaded his friend Jimmy Carter: Peter Bourne, "Jimmy Carter," Petergbourne.co.uk, http://www.petergbourne.co.uk/articles7.html.

247   "But there was no psychological manipulation": Peter Bourne, email message to the author, February 27, 2016.

248   he borrowed Peter's name for his hero: Kathleen Ryan O'Connor, "Bourne in Oxford," *GTC Magazine*, 2009, http://petergbourne.co.uk/Bourne-in-Oxford .pdf.

248   he thought Michael Vale and Bill Jones had been spooks from the start: Mats Widgren, Skype interview with the author, September 30, 2016.

248   "an agency of North American origin": *Aktuellt*, Sveriges Radio AB, TV2, Sweden, October 22, 1975.

248   "I cannot deny that it is an American intelligence organization": Ibid.

248   "That it is now expanded to Europe": Håkan Hermansson and Lars Wenander, *Uppdrag: Olof Palme: Hatet, Jakten, Kampanjerna* [Mission: Olof Palme: the hate, the hunt, the schemes] (Stockholm: Tiden, 1987), p. 116.

248   Few in the Swedish media took issue: "USA-styrt spionage mot Palme" [US controlled Espionage against Palme], *Aftonbladet*, October 13, 1975; "ELC finansieras av CIA" [ELC financed by CIA], *Aftonbladet*, October 14, 1975; "Anklagas för CIA-stöd" [Accused of CIA support], *Norrtelje Tidning*, September 14, 1977.

248   Håkan Hermansson's 1975 pamphlet: Hermansson, *Mullvadar i socialistisk förklädnad*.

249   "that the CIA, through its refusal to comment": W. E. Colby to Ben Bradlee, February 18, 1974, CIA document RDP88-01314R000300380046-2, http://www .cia.gov.

249   a substantial dossier on the Labor Committees: Memo, CIA file RDP88-01315R000300590044-0; "Stop Rockefeller's Nazi Doctors," CIA file RDP88-01315R000300590040-4; Telegram to the Office of the President, CIA file RDP88-01315R000300590053-0, http://www.cia.gov.

249   maintained by Michael Schneeberger: Memorandum on Lyndon LaRouche, September 19, 1977, within security file on Mitchell Livingston Werbell, CIA file 1993.08.05.15:16:44:840028, http://www.maryferrell.org/showDoc.html?docId =104117&search=schneeberger#relPageId=1&tab=page.

249   "We were concerned": Michael Schneeberger, email message to the author, July 4, 2015.

250   the CIA conceded that there was no Russian money in his purse: Memorandum on European Labor Committee, CIA file 0001078242, January 4, 1976, http:// www.cia.gov.

250   just over 50 percent of the popular vote: "1976 US Presidential Election Results," David Leip's US Election Atlas, http://uselectionatlas.org/RESULTS/national.php ?year=1976&minper=0&f=0&off=0&elect=0.

250   Lyndon LaRouche had scraped 0.05 percent: Ibid.

250   Turner had commanded a destroyer: Jimmy Carter, "Director of Central Intelligence Nomination of Stansfield Turner," February 7, 1977, American Presidency Project, http://www.presidency.ucsb.edu/ws/?pid=7644.

251   "Undercover case officers or agents": Stansfield Turner, *Secrecy and Democracy: The CIA in Transition* (Boston: Houghton Mifflin, 1985), p. 210.

251   "I'm not suggesting that he was advocating": United States v. Roy Frankhouser,

testimony of Charles Tate, November 3, 1987, LaRouche Planet, http://www
.laroucheplanet.info/pmwiki/pmwiki.php?n=Money.Tate3.

252   "a fascist group in its classical concept": Private papers of Stieg Larsson, *Expo* magazine, Stockholm.

252   Executive Order 11967: Jimmy Carter, "Executive Order 11967—Executive Order Relating to Proclamation of Pardon," January 21, 1977, American Presidency Project, http://www.presidency.ucsb.edu/ws/?pid=7366.

252   a court-martial and prison sentence were still possible: Myra MacPherson, *Long Time Passing: Vietnam and the Haunted Generation* (Bloomington: Indiana University Press, 1984), p. 350.

253   so-called coat hanger brigade: http://www.lyndonlarouche.org/larouche-abortion2 .htm.

253   An FBI setup: Bill McAllister, "Ogden Hopes to Be Spoiler in Va. Race," *Washington Post*, August 16, 1977.

253   "a dangerous international terrorist": Rick Hampson, "Labor Party Candidate Adds Color to State Race," *Danville (VA) Bee*, July 21, 1977.

253   "the freak show of Virginia politics": Ibid.

253   "Whig coalition": "Mrs. Gaddy Supports Alan Ogden," *Danville (VA) Register*, August 23, 1977.

253   "It was only through President Carter's intervention": "Criticizes Paper, Ogden, Gaddy," letter to the editor, *Danville (VA) Register*, August 27, 1977.

254   Ogden secured only 0.8 percent of the vote: Our Campaigns, http://www.ourcam paigns.com/RaceDetail.html?RaceID=26401.

254   Fraud at the polls: "1977 Labour Party Results Point to Election Fraud," *Executive Intelligence Review*, November 15, 1977.

254   "the real America": "Vad är 'det verkliga Amerika'" [What is "the real America"], *Ny Solidaritet*, September 9, 1977.

254   a German journalist who had reported from Beijing: James M. Markham, "LaRouche Fringe Stirs in Germany," *New York Times*, June 30, 1986.

254   a literal slow boat to China: Hedgehog [pseud.], *How It All Began*, http://laroucheplanet.info/pmwiki/pmwiki.php?n=Library.HIABChapter5Swarthmore.

254   Edward von Rothkirch was a chancer: Hedgehog [pseud.], *Smiling Man from a Dead Planet*, http://laroucheplanet.info/pmwiki/pmwiki.php?n=Library.PalimpsestWorld.

254   Roy Frankhouser was a grand dragon of the Ku Klux Klan: Ibid.

254   Instead he went to a *Star Trek* convention: Matthew L. Wald, "Larouche Taken in by Aide, Trial Told," *New York Times*, December 10, 1987.

254   a figure code-named "the Major": Information from Molly Kronberg.

255   LaRouche instructed his acolytes to hand over the cash: Information from Molly Kronberg.

255   LaRouche met with representatives of the Reagan transition team: Dennis King, *Lyndon LaRouche and the New American Fascism* (New York: Doubleday, 1989), p. 127.

255   He also had coffee with Admiral Bobby Ray Inman: John Mintz, "Some Officials Find Intelligence Network 'Useful,'" *Washington Post*, January 15, 1985.

255   a modest consultative role in the development of the Strategic Defense Initiative: Lyndon LaRouche, "I Remember Ronald Reagan," *Executive Intelligence Review*, June 18, 2004.

255   an NCLC intelligence specialist met with a contact from the Soviet mission: See King, *Lyndon LaRouche and the New American Fascism*, pp. 61–81.

255   move his headquarters from New York to Leesburg: John Mintz, "Loudoun Newcomer Lives on Heavily Guarded Estate," *Washington Post*, January 13, 1985.

255   an estate that had once been the home of the ballet dancer Rudolf Nureyev: "Private Properties," *Wall Street Journal*, April 24, 1998.

256   Björn Ulvaeus and Frida Lyngstad of ABBA: Stieg Larsson, "ELP/ELC General Information," private papers of Stieg Larsson, *Expo* magazine, Stockholm.

256   Cliff spoke in favor of extraterrestrial lasers: Clifford Gaddy, "The Question of Beam Weapons and the Present Strategic Crisis," in *Beam Weapons: The Strategic Implications for Western Europe* (Washington, DC: EIR Special Report, 1983), pp. 7–8.

256   Kerstin delivered a tirade against the peace movement: Kerstin Tegin-Gaddy, "How to Counter Appeasement and the So-Called Peace Movement," *Beam Weapons*, pp. 18–20.

256   urged NATO to open a front beyond the earth: Michael Liebig, "Why the New Strategic Doctrine Based on Beam Weapons Must Replace NATO's 'Flexible Response,'" *Beam Weapons*, pp. 21–25.

256   The LaRouchians declared that the demonstrators were controlled by Moscow: introduction, ibid., pp. 7–8; "EIR Oslo Conference Upsets Appeasers," *Beam Weapons*, p. 50.

257   "Clacking busybodies in this Soviet jellyfish front": Matthew L. Wald, "Small Town in Virginia Tense Host to LaRouche," *New York Times*, April 11, 1986.

257   popularizing and weaponizing a minor rock group called the Beatles: Konstandinos Kalimgtis, David Goldman, Jeffrey Steinberg, et al., *Dope Inc.: Britain's Opium War Against the U.S.* (New York: New Benjamin Franklin House, 1978).

257   "Once caught in the environment defined by Russell": Ibid., p. 376.

258   the view that she had a jeweled hand in the 9/11 attacks: "It Was Your Bloody Hand that Unleashed 9/11, Queen Elizabeth!," April 21, 2017, LaRouchePAC, https://larouchepac.com/20160421/it-was-your-bloody-hand-unleashed-911 -queen-elizabeth.

258   likes to pull on a gray wig and tiara: "Live Rally from HSBC in Manhattan," March 2, 2015, LaRouchePAC, https://www.youtube.com/watch?v=whzq W6VXt2U.

258   "sleep with young boys at the Carlyle Hotel?": April Witt, "No Joke," *Washington Post*, October 24, 2004.

259   The judge dismissed the case: "Nancy Kissinger Freed in Airport Row," *Philadelphia Daily News*, June 10, 1982.

259   "Nancy Kissinger made one mistake in etiquette": Bob Greene, "Let's Give Nancy One More Round," *Detroit Free Press*, March 14, 1982.

259   a Kissinger joke book full of obscene cartoons: *Some of the Latest and Bawdiest Jokes About Henry A. Kissinger* (New York: Arcana Press, n.d.)

259   They planted stories in the overseas press: See M. T. Upharsin, "Kissinger Watch," *Executive Intelligence Review*, December 15, 1989; Umberto Pascali, "'Operation Gladio' Reveals That Kissinger Ordered Moro Murder," *Executive Intelligence Review*, November 23, 1990.

259   "His heathen sexual inclinations": Lyndon LaRouche, "Henry Kissinger: The Politics of Faggotry," International Caucus of Labor Committees press release, August 3, 1982.

259   "I wouldn't want Kissinger dead": "Cadre School Question and Answer with Lyndon H. LaRouche Jr.," *Morning Briefing*, December 8, 1992, LaRouche Planet, http://laroucheplanet.info/pmwiki/pmwiki.php?n=Library.LoveEnemy1.

259   "Lyndon LaRouche Theatre": *Saturday Night Live*, NBC, April 19, 1986.

259   "Kissinger must die": King, *Lyndon LaRouche and the New American Fascism*, p. 153.

260   "ultimately was just sublimated": Ibid.

260   a dartboard bearing an image of Palme's face: "Sommarnöje med Olof Palme" [Summer entertainment with Olof Palme], *Contra* 10, no. 4 (1984).
260   "Sweden's population is led by a madman": William Engdahl, "Palme— Djävulens djävul" [Palme—the devil's devil], *Ny Solidaritet,* June 11, 1975.
260   "Behind the Democratic mask": Hermansson, *Mullvadar i socialistisk förklädnad,* p. 5.
260   "Palme was one step below Satan": Former member "xlcr4life," email message to the author, March 2017.
261   GENTLEMEN: ARE YOU AND OLOF PALME SO ENTIRELY INSANE: Lyndon H. LaRouche Jr., "Open Telex to *Aftonbladet*," New Solidarity International Press Service, October 17, 1975.
261   Victor Gunnarsson, a braggartly fantasist of the Far Right: Steve Lohr, "Swedish Suspect Was Once in Rightist Group," *New York Times,* March 19, 1986.
261   Alf Enerström, a wealthy doctor: *Granskningskommissionens betänkande i anledning av Brottsutredningen efter mordet på statsminister Olof Palme* [The review commission's report on the investigation following the murder of Prime Minister Olof Palme], Swedish State Report, SOU 1999:88, p. 549.
261   he coughed up around $150,000: Ibid.
261   Kerstin stood beside Enerström: "Hjärntvätt och fanatism bara 'lögner i massmedia'" [Brainwashing and fanaticism nothing but "lies in the mass media"], *Hallandsposten,* September 12, 1984.
261   "Freedom of speech in Stockholm community radio": "Närradions 'Palme-fascisms'" [Local radio's "Palme fascists"], *Aftonbladet,* November 22, 1986.
262   asserting that Palme was part of a heroin-smuggling syndicate: Willaim Engdahl, "Olof Palme and the Malmo International," *Executive Intelligence Review,* May 4, 1982.
262   a secretive and powerful network known as the Black Guelph: Lyndon LaRouche, "Olof Palme and the Neo-Nazi International," *Executive Intelligence Review,* June 8, 1982.
262   "They are presently the single wealthiest political force": Ibid.
262   "foul-smelling excretion from a dead world": EAP handbill, quoted in Hermansson, *Mullvadar i socialistisk förklädnad,* p. 15.
262   In May 1979, the EAP circulated a letter: "List mot Palme" [A list against Palme], *Aftonbladet,* May 17, 1979.
262   on the front page of the main Swedish evening newspaper: "'Revolten' mot Palme var en bluff" [The revolt against Palme was a hoax], *Dagens Nyheter,* May 18, 1979; "'Facklig revolt' var politisk kupp Sabotörer förfalskade namnlista" ["Union revolt" was political coup, saboteurs forged names on petition], *Dagens Nyheter,* May 18, 1979.
262   "has been after me for several years": "Sweden: Swan Song for Socialists," *Executive Intelligence Review,* May 29, 1979.
263   declaring how wounded its members felt: Kerstin Tegin to Sven Romanus, November 22, 1978, Social Democratic Party Press Office, Arbetarrörelsens arkiv och bibliotek [The Swedish Labor Movement's Archive and Library], Stockholm.
263   their use of distinctly English idioms: For instance, "toppen av isberget," a blunt translation of the English "tip of the iceberg," appears in a report sent by the EAP to the Swedish justice ministry, November 22, 1978.
263   when her party was accused of extremism or electoral misconduct: "EAP anklagas för medlemsfusk" [EAP accused of member fraud], *Svenska Dagbladet,* April 6, 1985; "Förnekar medlemsfusk" [Denies member fraud], *Nya Wermlands-Tidningen,* April 6, 1985.
263   the Channel TV-2 program *Magasinet*: Larsolof Giertta, "Varning för EAP—ett

antidemokratiskt parti" [Warnings for EAP—An antidemocratic party], *Stockholms Tidningen*, April 6, 1982, p. 36; "Gör program om EAP: TV-man hotad till livet," *Arbetet*, January 27, 1982.

263   "Okay, Olof Palme": *Magasinet,* TV-2, April 14, 1982.

263   "The general response everywhere is the same": European Labor Committees, internal memo, January 1982, private papers of Stieg Larsson, *Expo* magazine, Stockholm.

264   a smoke screen to make Sweden a safe haven for terrorists and gangsters: Engdahl, "Olof Palme and the Malmo International."

264   "a front organization using unwitting Vietnam War opponents: Lyndon H. LaRouche Jr., "How a Socialist Quarterly Drifts Toward Fascism," *Campaigner,* April 1981.

265   That bubble burst on the night of February 28, 1986: Jan Bondeson, *Blood on the Snow* (Ithaca, NY: Cornell University Press, 2005), is the best English-language account of the assassination.

265   An anonymous caller supplied the name: *Brottsutredningen efter mordet på statsminister Olof Palme* [Criminal investigation after the murder of Prime Minister Olof Palme] (Stockholm: Justitiedepartementet, 1999), p. 514.

16: THE ASSASSINS

266   he had seen someone who looked like Kerstin Tegin-Gaddy: *Brottsutredningen efter mordet på statsminister Olof Palme*, p. 514.

266   urged the detectives to put the EAP in the frame: Ibid., p. 512.

266   SÄPO had kept their names and addresses on file since 1975: *Hotet från vänster*, p. 280.

266   a *New Solidarity* contributor: *Brottsutredningen efter mordet på statsminister Olof Palme*, p. 514. This was Ulf Sandmark, still a leading member of EAP today.

266   They contacted a member named John Hardwick: Ibid., p. 515.

267   Victor Gunnarsson, a volatile eccentric: For Gunnarsson's story see Bondeson, *Blood on the Snow*, pp. 60–75.

267   "If you say what you think in Sweden today": Ibid., p. 62.

267   a cabdriver who claimed that the suspect had jumped into his taxi: Ibid., pp. 68, 74.

267   Detective Wingren had coached his witness: Ibid., pp. 68–69.

268   the police recalled him several times to take part in lineups: Ibid., p. 67.

268   "When there is no certifiably real and solid information": Hill and Gaddy, *Mr. Putin* (2013 ed.), p. 7.

269   "That was his profession in the KGB": "Mr. Vladimar Putin: Operative in the Kremlin," Brookings Institution, https://www.brookings.edu/events/mr-vladimir-putin-operative-in-the-kremlin.

269   The Kappa Alphas were given to marching around in Confederate uniforms: Parent, "Weathering Wake"; "No Racism Meant," pp. 4–5.

270   "He said, belief is not a belief": Lawrence Meyer, "Exiles' Families Say Ford Proposal Not True Amnesty," *Washington Post*, September 17, 1974. Cliff's words are an adaptation of a quote from Albert Camus.

270   "I recall Cliff mentioning on a number of occasions": Bruce G. Blair, email message to the author, April 29, 2017.

271   a report cowritten with a small group of NCLC researchers: Criton Zoakas et al., *Global Showdown: The Imperial Russian War Plan for 1988* (Washington, DC: Executive Intelligence Review, 1985).

271   when Melania Trump sued him: Dan Morse, "Melania Trump Reaches Settle-

ment in Libel Lawsuit Against Maryland Blogger," *Washington Post*, February 7, 2017.

271   "very dangerous" and a "principled adversary": Zoakas et al., *Global Showdown*, p. 5.

271   "Soviet deployed 'sleepers' were sent into LaRouche's environment": Ibid., p. 9.

272   "These Stasi operations were run during 1972–74": Ibid., p. 9.

272   that Palme's murder was the herald of a new world: "Dags för Sverige gå med i Nato," *Ny Solidaritet*, March 6, 1986.

272   to avoid questioning by the Swedish police: "xlcr4life," former LaRouche member, email message to the author, March 2017.

272   a four-page exposé on the organization: David Gelman, "Lyndon LaRouche: Beyond the Fringe," *Newsweek*, April 7, 1986.

272   "a form of terrorism": Rogan Kersh, "A Mockery of U.S. Politics," *Old Gold and Black*, April 4, 1986.

273   "laying the blame at the doorstep of the ELP": William Engdahl, Göran Haglund, and William Jones, *A Classical KGB Disinformation Campaign: Who Killed Olof Palme?* (Wiesbaden, West Germany: EIR Research, 1986), p. 8.

273   "a coordinated wave of lies and innuendo": Ibid., p. 59.

273   "the public activities of the ELP": Ibid., p. 32.

273   a federal investigation in Boston: David Gelman, "Lyndon LaRouche: Beyond the Fringe," *Newsweek*, April 7, 1986; John Mintz, "The Lash of LaRouche," *Washington Post*, April 7, 1986; "Washington Report Traces LaRouche Money to Leesburg," *Loudoun (VA) Times-Mirror*, July 3, 1986.

273   One million dollars skimmed from credit card accounts: Douglas Frantz, "Raid Bares LaRouche Dark World," *Chicago Tribune*, October 12, 1986.

273   They shredded documents and made plans to fly indicted members to Germany: John Mintz, "LaRouche Group Harried Probers, FBI Tells Court," *Washington Post*, October 10, 1986.

273   killing the prosecutor in charge of the case: Frantz, "Raid Bares LaRouche Dark World."

273   the FBI descended on LaRouche's 172-acre property: "Officers Raid LaRouche's Headquarters," *Baltimore Sun*, October 7, 1986.

274   "I will not submit passively to arrest": Philip Shenon, "LaRouche Warns U.S. on Any Move to Arrest Him," *New York Times*, October 8, 1986.

274   IRS officials were seen toasting one another: Bryan R. Chitwood, "Raid Leaves Officials 'Ecstatic.'" *Loudoun (VA) Times-Mirror*, October 16, 1986.

275   forty-five references to Victor Gunnarsson and the assassination of Olof Palme: Associated Press, "LaRouche Notebooks Refer to Slain Swedish Prime Minister, Sources Say," December 5, 1986, http://www.apnewsarchive.com/1986/LaRouche -Notebooks-Refer-to-Slain-Swedish-Prime-Minister-Sources-Say/id-519c7a99aeca ad8beb917e06b7f94cf3.

275   "The potential threat to America's democratic values and institutions": Irwin Suall, *The LaRouche Political Cult: Packaging Extremism* (New York: ADL, 1986), pp. 39–40.

275   the Swedish authorities had asked for his assistance: Associated Press, "LaRouche Notebooks Refer to Slain Swedish Prime Minister, Sources Say."

275   Ulf Karlsson: Bondeson, *Blood on the Snow*, p. 98.

275   Front pages ran censored photgraphs of Kerstin: "Kvinnan som polizen söker" [Woman sought by the police], *Aftonbladet*, April 23, 1987; "EAP-kvinnan I polis-förhör" [EAP woman in police interrogation], *Aftonbladet*, April 25, 2017.

275   Kerstin and Cliff had taken refuge: Ulf Nilsson, "Svenskan gömmer sig för polisen" [Swedes hiding from the police], *Aftonbladet*, April 24, 1987.

276 "The area is fenced off": Ibid.

276 "Not moved": "Hon Försvann med sin son" [She disappeared with her son], *Aftonbladet*, April 24, 1987.

276 Kerstin had moved in the opposite direction: Gun Fälth, "EAP-kvinna förhörd av polisen" [EAP woman questioned by police], *Dagens Nyheter*, April 26, 1987.

276 drove to the Tegin family home: *Brottsutredningen efter mordet på statsminister Olof Palme*, p. 515.

276 Kerstin had given birth to a son: Births column, *Dagens Nyheeter*, January 23, 1986.

276 interviewed by another Swedish detective: *Brottsutredningen efter mordet på statsminister Olof Palme*, p. 515.

276 his attempts to communicate with a Swedish naval commander: Ola Tunander, *The Secret War Against Sweden: U.S. and British Submarine Deception in the 1980s* (London: Frank Cass, 2004), p. 300.

277 "I survived the great Leesburg panty raid": "LaRouche," *Loudoun (VA) Times-Mirror*, October 16, 1986.

277 blamed everything on the Russians: Nancy Spannaus, "Reveal Soviet Role in Ordering Leesburg Raid and Jailings," *Loudon (VA) County News*, October 17, 1986.

277 They held a Halloween costume party: United States v. Roy Frankhouser, LaRouche Planet, http://laroucheplanet.info/pmwiki/downloads/TestimonyofLandeggerBardwell.pdf.

277 Dozens of NCLC members were indicted: Matthew L. Wald, "3 Larouche Aides Charged with Obstruction," *New York Times*, December 17, 1986.

277 "The purpose of this frame-up is not to send me to prison": Caryle Murphy, "LaRouche Convicted of Mail Fraud," *Washington Post*, December 17, 1988.

278 Jim Bakker, freshly jailed for similar crimes: Jim Bakker, *I Was Wrong* (Nashville: Thomas Nelson, 1996), p. 250.

278 LaRouche barely knew how to switch it on: Information from Carol White.

278 "a political dirty operation": Leslie Maitland Werner, "LaRouche Assets Are Seized in U.S. Bid to Collect Fines," *New York Times*, April 22, 1987.

278 during surgery to remove some anal polyps: John Sigerson, "Bush Is Informed of Responsibility If LaRouche Is Killed in Prison," *Executive Intelligence Review*, September 29, 1989.

278 putting AIDS patients into quarantine camps: "Eyewitness Account of the AIDS Crisis in Europe," *Executive Intelligence Review*, April 4, 1986.

278 He made a panic-mongering tour of Europe: "Feedback," *New Scientist,* December 5, 1985; Thomas Boghardt, "Operation INFEKTION: Soviet Bloc Intelligence and Its AIDS Disinformation Campaign," *Studies in Intelligence*, December 2009.

278 overtures toward right-wing Catholic organizations: Marla Minnicino, "NCLC Conference: Toward a New Moral Renaissance," *Executive Intelligence Review*, June 9, 1989.

279 "traced those efforts through the Ruskin circle at Oxford University": John Sigerson, "Philosophical Association Heralds 'Decade of LaRouche and Leibniz,'" *Executive Intelligence Review*, September 14, 1980.

279 "Anyone's list of great leaders of our last two centuries": Warren Hamerman, "The 'Beethoven Principle' and the LaRouche Movement," *Executive Intelligence Review*, September 14, 1990.

279 "stay-behind agents" of "Buckley family-style Carlist Gnosticism": Lyndon LaRouche, "How Bertrand Russell Became an Evil Man," *Fidelio*, Fall 1994, https://www.schillerinstitute.org/fid_91-96/943a_russell_lhl.html.

279 "Sunday activity": Tony Papert, internal memo, International Caucus of Labor

Committees, November 1, 2000, LaRouche Planet, http://www.laroucheplanet.info
./pmwiki/pmwiki.php?n=Library.NOCATHOLICSALLOWED.

280   "spreading slime-mold of tiny pro-Carlism-polluted schools": William J. Wertz,
"Catholic Schools Plot Exposed: Who Is Snuffing Your Neighbor's Kittens?,"
Executive Intelligence Review, April 19, 2002.

280   a master's thesis on the German playwright and poet Friedrich Schiller: Kerstin
Tegin-Gaddy, "Goethe's Egmont and Schiller's Stage Adaptation: Structure,
Characters, Language, and Music" (master's thesis, Duke University Press, 1991).

280   setting up an institute in Schiller's honor: See Helga Zepp-LaRouche, "The Story
of the Schiller Institute," *Executive Intelligence Review*, January 1, 1985.

280   working under a professor named Vladimir Treml: Certificate obtained from
National Student Clearinghouse.

280   a project funded by the Office of Net Assessment: Copies of Berkeley-Duke
Occasional Papers on the Second Economy in the USSR archived at www.dtic.mil
include cover notes indicating funding by the Office of Net Assessment.

281   Gross revenues of 300 to 1,800 million rubles: Clifford G. Gaddy, *The Size of the
Prostitution Market in the USSR*, Berkeley-Duke Occasional Papers on the Second Economy in the USSR (Durham, NC: Duke University Press, 1990).

281   Other scholars studied: Karl-Eugen Wädekin, *Private Agriculture in Socialist
Countries: Implications for the USSR* (Durham, NC: Duke University Press,
1987); Michael V. Alexeev, *Underground Market for Gasoline in the USSR*,
Berkeley-Duke Occasional Papers (Durham, NC, 1987); Kimberly C. Neuhauser,
The Market for Illegal Drugs in the Soviet Union in the Late 1980s, Berkeley-
Duke Occasional Papers (Durham, NC: Duke University Press, 1990).

281   a member of its Military-Economic Advisory Panel: David C. Engerman, *Know
Your Enemy: The Rise and Fall of America's Soviet Experts* (Oxford: Oxford
University Press, 2009), p. 252.

281   "If you come from a 'good background' ": Tessa DeCarlo, email message to the
author, July 10, 2017.

281   He was awarded his PhD in May 1991: Knight-Ridder Financial News, Michael
DuVally, "Yeltsin Holds the Key to Gorbachev's Fate," *Tallahassee Democrat*,
August 20, 1991.

281   he went to Russia to visit collective farms: See "Clifford G. Gaddy," Brookings
Institution, https://www.brookings.edu/experts/clifford-g-gaddy/.

281   an adjunct lecturer at Georgetown University: Angela Stent, director of the Center for Eurasian, Russian, and East European Studies and professor of government and foreign service at Georgetown University, email message to the author,
April 29, 2017.

281   a key contributor to "Order from Chaos": "Order from Chaos: Foreign Policy in
a Troubled World," Brookings Insitution, https://www.brookings.edu/blog/order
-from-chaos/.

281   "Cliff Gladly": Lyndon LaRouche, *Morning Briefing*, December 3, 2004, LaRouche
Planet, http://laroucheplanet.info/pmwiki/downloads/bfg1203.txt.

282   "a former LaRouche associate who has sold out himself": Jonathan Tennenbaum,
"Washington Is Heading for a New Iraq War," *Executive Intelligence Review*,
March 1, 2002.

282   the NCLC counterintelligence staffer: Michelle Steinberg, a member of LaRouche's
counterintelligence staff, turned up at a Brookings event on March 23, 2009. See
Brookings Institution conference transcript, "US-Russian Leadership for Global
Financial and Energy Security," http://www.ifs.ru/download.php?id=658. Steinberg's authorship of the notebooks is suggested by "Did FBI, NBC Try to Frame
LaRouche in Palme Death?," *Executive Intelligence Review*, July 24, 1992, and by
her attempts to use the courts to oblige the Boston branch of the FBI to release

"any and all documents pertaining to and surrounding the United States government's release of and/or disclosure of evidentiary material and any other documents turned over to the Swedish Police or other Swedish authorities." See Michelle Steinberg, Appellant, v. United States Department of Justice, Justia, http://law.justia .com/cases/federal/appellate-courts/F3/23/548/482742/.

282   "Mum, I'm frightened": See April Witt, "No Joke," *Washington Post*, October 24, 2004; Stuart Winer, "Jewish Student's Death in Germany Was a 'Set-up,' Expert Says," *Times of Israel*, May 20, 2015; Matthew Taylor, "'Suicide' Student Jeremiah Duggan May Have Been Pressured by Cult, Court Hears," *Guardian*, May 21, 2015, https://www.theguardian.com/uk-news/2015/may/21/briton-jeremiah-dug gan-may-have-been-pressured-by-cult-court-hears.

282   "electromagnetic lobotomy": Stieg Larsson, "Enerström gripen för skott mot polis," *Expo*, November 30, 2003; "Psykdömd Palmehatare mister läkarlegitimation," *Dagens Nyheter*, September 23, 2005, http://www.dn.se/nyheter/sverige /psykdomd palmehatare-mister-lakarlegitimation/.

282   a beautiful dossier compiled by a former MI6 officer: Ken Besinger, "These Reports Allege Trump Has Deep Ties to Russia," Buzzfeed, January 11, 2017, https://www .documentcloud.org/documents/3259984-Trump-Intelligence-Allegations.html.

283   the woods in Deep Gap, Watauga County: Sources for the murder of Victor Gunnarsson and the trial of L. C. Underwood, FindLaw, http://caselaw.findlaw.com/nc -court-of-appeals/1435151.html; "Former Assassination Suspect's Body Found in WNC," *Asheville (NC) Citizen-Times*, January 15, 1994; Clark Cox, "N.C. Mountain Murder Reveals Mysteries on Two Continents," *Richmond County (NC) Daily Journal and Moore County Citizen News-Record*, December 10, 1995.

283   He had been supplanted by Christer Pettersson: Bondeson, *Blood on the Snow*, pp. 112–57.

284   In 2011, his appeal was rejected: "Court Upholds Murder Conviction of L. C. Underwood," *Watauga Democrat* (Boone, NC), January 19, 2011, http://www .wataugademocrat.com/news/court-upholds-murder-conviction-of-l-c-under wood/article_707f4c42-2616-5096-9d17-73d39c2f4dbd.html.

290   "Far to the right": "Hatet mördade Palme" [The hate killed Palme], *Aftonbladet*, November 9, 1995.

17: THE END OF THE WORLD

292   "The British Isles has been the British Isles": LaRouchePAC webcast, September 19, 2014, LaRouchePAC, https://archive.larouchepac.com/node/31786.

293   "You don't define the behavior of mankind based on given facts": LaRouchePAC Policy Committee, May 11, 2015, LaRouchePAC, https://larouchepac.com/2015 0511/lpac-policy-committee-may-11-2015.

293   "Schwarzenegger is a sex maniac": LPAC Manhattan Project: Town Hall Event with Lyndon LaRouche, February 6, 2016, LaRouchePAC, https://larouchepac. com/20160206/lpac-manhattan-project-town-hall-event-lyndon-larouche -february-6-2016.

293   "Well it's very simple!": LPAC Policy Committee, November 30, 2015, LaRouchePAC, https://larouchepac.com/20151130/lpac-policy-committee-novem ber-30-2015.

294   "If you get Royal Family out of the picture": "Fireside Chat with Lyndon LaRouche," March 3, 2016, LaRouchePAC, https://larouchepac.com/20160229 /fireside-chat-lyndon-larouche-march-3-2016.

295   accusing his old friend of being part of the latest CIA plot: "Varning! CIA-agent sedd i Danmark!" [Warning! CIA agent seen in Denmark], *Ny Solidaritet*, August 1, 1975.

295 "at a time when our programmatic influence": Bill Jones, "CIA-agenten Vale har aldrig varit ELC-medlem" [The CIA agent Vale has never been an ELC member], *Ny Solidaritet*, November 7, 1975.

297 "Paranoid delusion": John Gray, *The Soul of the Marionette: A Short Enquiry into Human Freedom* (London: Penguin, 2015), p. 54.

300 "He got that mustache": "LaRouchePAC Talk Obama as Hitler—Sterling, VA," April 1, 2010, LaRouchePac, https://www.youtube.com/watch?v=vWj8C4EPV-U.

301 the African American Students Association at Swarthmore College: Richard Phalon, "A Socialist Caucus Denounces Gibson and His Enemies—Baraka and Imperiale," *New York Times*, September 10, 1973.

302 which, of course, he meant the British: "British Unleash 'Panama Papers,' to Escalate Regime Changes Globally, Provoke War," April 6, 2016, LaRouchePAC, https://larouchepac.com/20160406/british-unleash-panama-papers-escalate-regime-changes-globally-provoke-war.

302 "Does this strike anyone else as a very fishy story?": Clifford G. Gaddy, "Are the Russians Actually Behind the Panama Papers?" April 7, 2016, Brookings Institution, https://www.brookings.edu/blog/order-from-chaos/2016/04/07/are-the-russians-actually-behind-the-panama-papers/.

18: CLIFFHANGER

305 Terry Whitmore returned to Mississippi in 2001: "Terry Whitmore," *Memphis Commercial Appeal*, July 25, 2007.

305 breathed his last in New Jersey in 2004: U.S. Social Security Death Index, 1935–2014, Ancestry.com online database, Provo, UT.

305 his boss was a former CIA officer: Paget, *Patriotic Betrayal*, p. 4; James R. Hagerty, "Bob Kiley, ex-CIA Agent, Cleaned Up Subways and Made Them Reliable," *Wall Street Journal*, August 19, 2016.

308 "He's a festering pustule on Satan's rump!": "Don't Be a Chump for Trump," LaRouche PAC, https://larouchepac.com/20160229/ny-times-blows-whistle-killer-hillary-clinton.

308 America's best chance to defeat the British Empire: "British Frantic to Destroy Trump, Save the Empire," LaRouchePAC, February 1, 2017, https://larouchepac.com/20170201/british-frantic-destroy-trump-save-empire.

308 plotting a "color revolution": Michael Billington, Rachel Douglas, and Marcia Merry Baker, "Obama and Soros—Nazis in Ukraine 2014—U.S. in 2017?" *Executive Intelligence Review*, February 24, 2017.

309 "I sensed a note of poetry": John Sigerson, "On Composing a New Future," *Executive Intelligence Review*, March 3, 2017.

309 more evidence of British perfidy: "The Foreign Power Corrupting U.S. Politics Is Britain, Not Russia," LaRouchePAC, January 13, 2017, https://larouchepac.com/20170113/foreign-power-corrupting-us-politics-britain-not-russia.

309 Bill Jones, bowling a softball question: White House Daily Briefing, February 1, 2017, C-SPAN, https://www.c-span.org/video/?423339-1/sean-spicer-briefs-reporters-white-house&start=1644.

309 The "Senior Fellow" became a "Former Expert": "Clifford G. Gaddy," Brookings Institution, https://www.brookings.edu/experts/clifford-g-gaddy/.

309 Donald Trump's chief adviser on Russia: John Hudson, "Trump Taps Putin Critic for Senior White House Position," *Foreign Policy*, March 2, 2017; Nicholas Schmidle, "General Chaos," *New Yorker*, February 18, 2017.

309 "the Manchurian Candidate": David Remnick and Evan Osnos, "What to Make of Donald Trump's Early-Morning Wiretap Tweets," *New Yorker*, March 4, 2017.

309   The official announcement might have come sooner: Karen de Young, "Trump Adds Russia Scholar as a National Security Council Director," *Washington Post*, March 28, 2017.

310   Newspaper profiles discussed Hill's experience: Steve Robson, "Revealed: Coal Miner's Daughter from County Durham Set to Be Donald Trump's Top Adviser on Russia," *Daily Mirror*, March 4, 2017, http://www.mirror.co.uk/news/uk -news/revealed-coal-miners-daughter-county-9961725; Kyle Scott Clauss, "Fiona Hill, Trump's New Russia Expert, Went to Harvard," *Boston Magazine*, March 2, 2017, http://www.bostonmagazine.com/news/blog/2017/03/02/fiona -hill-russia-trump/.

310   A blogger in Moscow: John Helmer, "Vladimir Putin Is Safe If Donald Trump's Expert on Russia Is Fiona Hill, But Is Trump?," *Dances with Bears*, May 15, 2017, http://johnhelmer.net/vladimir-putin-is-safe-if-donald-trumps-expert-on -russia-is-fiona-hill-but-is-trump/.

310   to accuse her of being a mole for George Soros: "Roger Stone: Soros Mole Infil- trates Trump White House," June 1, 2017, Infowars.com, https://www.infowars .com/roger-stone-soros-mole-infiltrates-trump-white-house/.

310   "Disgusting": "Strobe Talbott: The Full Transcript," June 5, 2017, Politico.com, http://www.politico.com/magazine/story/2017/06/05/strobe-talbott-brookings -foreign-policy-interview-politico-215226.

ACKNOWLEDGMENTS

This book would not exist without the generous cooperation of my principal interviewees. Michele Lloyd, Jim McGourty, Christina Nelson, Chuck Onan, Mark Shapiro, Michael Vale, and Chris and Carol White told their stories, gave their time, and answered hundreds of questions about their experiences. I hope I have done them justice.

Many other people provided valuable information, some anonymously, some on the record. Rob Argento, Barry Fockler, Steve Kinnaman, Lon W. McDaniel, Don McDonough, David Minugh, Bill Schiller, Vincent Strollo, Thomas Taylor, and George Wood shared their experiences of desertion. The deserters and their milieu was described to me by George Carrano, Robert Doyon, Dee Drake, Karen Fabec, Maggie Gambell, Eric Hamerman, Margareta Herrmann, Patton Lindsley Hunter, Dan Israel, Ray Jones IV, Shelley Marshall, Jan-Erik Nyberg, Michel P. Richard, Richard Rucker, Harold and Rebecca Sadin, Olle Sjögren, Mats Widgren, and Izzy Young.

Bo Burlingham, Larry Cox, Ed Dubinsky, Don Filtzer, Norm Fruchter, Gerald Gray, Clancy Sigal, Tony Whelan, and Mike Zagarell were my guides to the culture of 1960s and '70s radicalism. Gunnar Ekberg, Frank Rafalko, Michael Schneeberger, and Richard Starnes discussed counterintelligence matters. Michael E. Miller helped me communicate with Lamont Claxton Underwood. William Rambo gave me a portrait of Victor Gunnarsson. Valuable information and assistance was also provided by Edward Bromberg, Gilli Bush-Bailey, Roger Choate, Sarah Churchwell, Jonathan Clements, Walter Donohue, Margaret Harman, Mike Higgins, Zachary Leader, John Quigley, Mel Rothenberg, Carl-Gustaf Scott, Bob Sharlet, David Smith, Miriam Spectre of the Anti-Defamation League, Jan Stocklassa, Hillel Ticktin, Janice Tidswell, Larry Turk, and Susan Weissman.

Many former followers of Lyndon LaRouche helped me to navigate the labyrinthine history of his many organizations. I am grateful to Nicholas Benton, Tessa DeCarlo, Rachel Douglas, Torbjörn Jelerup, Dennis King, Yves Messer, Sky Shields, and Nick Syvriotis. Peter Bourne, Eugene Galanter, and Lennart Levi shared their experiences of LaRouchian harassment. The pseudonymous author Hylozoic Hedgehog gave lavish help and saved me from dozens of errors. His books *Smiling Man from a Dead Planet* (2009) and *How It All Began* (2012) are essential reading for anyone who wants to understand how political groups can mutate into cults. They can be found on his website, http://www.laroucheplanet .info—a warning to the curious, which has doubtless stopped many from wasting their lives in the service of Lyndon LaRouche. I hope there is still time for current members I encountered—Margaret Greenspan, Bill Jones, Margaret Scialdone, Renee Sigerson, Dennis Speed—to spend their final years beyond its barren territory.

Molly Kronberg was a warm and generous witness. Her late husband, Ken, ran the printing company that produced the LaRouche organization's literature. On the morning of April 11, 2007, Ken Kronberg opened the briefing document emailed each morning to every member of the organization, in which its leader attacked Kronberg's printing business as a symptom of the failure of the generation of members who joined in the 1960s and '70s. "The Boomers will be scared into becoming human," it declared. "Unless they want to commit suicide." An hour or so after reading those words, Ken parked his car on a highway overpass on Route 28 and jumped to his death. Molly saw it as a gesture of defiance: "the bravest political act of his life." I would like to pay tribute to her, and to those who share her pain—particularly Erica and Hugo Duggan, whose son, Jeremiah, died in mysterious circumstances after attending LaRouche meetings in Germany in 2003. You can learn more about Ken at http://www.kennethkronberg.com. The campaign to discover the truth about Jeremiah's death can be followed at http://justiceforjeremiah.yolasite.com.

Peter Walsh provided three years of exemplary research assistance, scouring Swedish archives on my behalf. Additional research was provided by Madeline Coffey and Scott Russell. I also benefited from the wisdom of Johan Erlandsson, author of *Desertörerna* [The deserters] (2016). My thanks is also due to the staff of the Arbetarrörelsens arkiv och bibliotek, Stockholm; the British Library, the Danville Public Library, Virginia; the International Institute of Social History, Amsterdam; the Library of Congress; the National Library of Stockholm; the New York Public Library; the Richard Nixon Presidential Library and Museum; Swarthmore College Library; Alexander Correctional Institute, North Carolina; the Thomas Balch Library, Leesburg, Virginia; and the Modern Records Centre at the University of Warwick. The manuscript was read by Samira Ahmed, Mark Gatiss, Simon Guerrier, David Sweet, Nicola Sweet, Laura Thomas, and Phil Tinline, who know how highly I value their advice and opinions.

Simon Trewin, Jay Mandel, and their colleagues at William Morris Entertainment gave this book the best start I could have hoped for. During its progress into print, Luke Brown, Chris O'Connell, Bill Drennan, Fiona Lowenstein, Michael Cantwell, and Felicity McMahon offered indispensable advice on the text. It was a pleasure to be edited by Paul Baggaley and Paul Golob—particularly Paul Golob, who worked on the text with tireless patience and good humor. His influence improved the book immeasurably. As for any errors that remain, the buck stops with me.

And to Nicola, Gracie, and Connie Sweet, I am grateful for everything, as ever.